GMPLS

Architecture and Applications

The Morgan Kaufmann Series in Networking

Series Editor, David Clark, M.I.T.

Smart Phone and Next-Generation Mobile Computing
Pei Zheng and Lionel Ni

GMPLS: Architecture and Applications
Adrian Farrel and Igor Bryskin

Network Security: A Practical Approach
Jan L. Harrington

Content Networking: Architecture, Protocols, and Practice
Markus Hofmann and Leland R. Beaumont

Network Algorithmics: An Interdisciplinary Approach to Designing Fast Networked Devices
George Varghese

Network Recovery: Protection and Restoration of Optical, SONET-SDH, IP, and MPLS
Jean-Philippe Vasseur, Mario Pickavet, and Piet Demeester

Routing, Flow, and Capacity Design in Communication and Computer Networks
Michal Pióro and Deepankar Medhi

Wireless Sensor Networks: An Information Processing Approach
Feng Zhao and Leonidas Guibas

Communication Networking: An Analytical Approach
Anurag Kumar, D. Manjunath, and Joy Kuri

The Internet and Its Protocols: A Comparative Approach
Adrian Farrel

Modern Cable Television Technology: Video, Voice, and Data Communications, 2e
Walter Ciciora, James Farmer, David Large, and Michael Adams

Bluetooth Application Programming with the Java APIs
C Bala Kumar, Paul J. Kline, and Timothy J. Thompson

Policy-Based Network Management: Solutions for the Next Generation
John Strassner

Computer Networks: A Systems Approach, 3e
Larry L. Peterson and Bruce S. Davie

Network Architecture, Analysis, and Design, 2e
James D. McCabe

MPLS Network Management: MIBs, Tools, and Techniques
Thomas D. Nadeau

Developing IP-Based Services: Solutions for Service Providers and Vendors
Monique Morrow and Kateel Vijayananda

Telecommunications Law in the Internet Age
Sharon K. Black

Optical Networks: A Practical Perspective, 2e
Rajiv Ramaswami and Kumar N. Sivarajan

Internet QoS: Architectures and Mechanisms
Zheng Wang

TCP/IP Sockets in Java: Practical Guide for Programmers
Michael J. Donahoo and Kenneth L. Calvert

TCP/IP Sockets in C: Practical Guide for Programmers
Kenneth L. Calvert and Michael J. Donahoo

Multicast Communication: Protocols, Programming, and Applications
Ralph Wittmann and Martina Zitterbart

MPLS: Technology and Applications
Bruce Davie and Yakov Rekhter

High-Performance Communication Networks, 2e
Jean Walrand and Pravin Varaiya

Internetworking Multimedia
Jon Crowcroft, Mark Handley, and Ian Wakeman

Understanding Networked Applications: A First Course
David G. Messerschmitt

Integrated Management of Networked Systems: Concepts, Architectures, and their Operational Application
Heinz-Gerd Hegering, Sebastian Abeck, and Bernhard Neumair

Virtual Private Networks: Making the Right Connection
Dennis Fowler

Networked Applications: A Guide to the New Computing Infrastructure
David G. Messerschmitt

Wide Area Network Design: Concepts and Tools for Optimization
Robert S. Cahn

For further information on these books and for a list of forthcoming titles, please visit our Web site at http://www.mkp.com.

GMPLS

Architecture and Applications

Adrian Farrel
Igor Bryskin

ELSEVIER

AMSTERDAM • BOSTON • HEIDELBERG • LONDON
NEW YORK • OXFORD • PARIS • SAN DIEGO
SAN FRANCISCO • SINGAPORE • SYDNEY • TOKYO

Morgan Kaufmann Publishers is an imprint of Elsevier

MORGAN KAUFMANN PUBLISHERS

Publishing Director	Michael Forster
Senior Editor	Rick Adams
Acquisitions Editor	Rick Adams
Assistant Editor	Rachel Roumeliotis
Publishing Services Manager	Simon Crump
Senior Production Manager	Paul Gottehrer
Cover Designer	Ross Carron
Cover Image	Getty Images
Composition	Cepha Imaging PVT LTD
Copyeditor	Terri Morris
Proofreader	Pam Andrada
Indexer	Broccoli Information Management
Interior printer	Maple-Vail Book Manufacturing Group, New York
Cover printer	Phoenix Color Corp., Maryland

Morgan Kaufmann Publishers is an imprint of Elsevier.
500 Sansome Street, Suite 400, San Francisco, CA 94111

This book is printed on acid-free paper.

Library of Congress Cataloging-in-Publication Data
Application submitted

ISBN 13: 978-0-12-088422-3
ISBN 10: 0-12-088422-4

For information on all Morgan Kaufmann publications,
visit our web site at www.mkp.com or www.books.elsevier.com

Printed in the United States of America
05 06 07 08 09 5 4 3 2 1

Dedication

For my parents, June and John
— AF

To my wife Olga and my mother Eugenia
— IB

About the Authors

Adrian Farrel is co-chair of the IETF's Common Control and Measurement Plane (CCAMP) Working Group, which is responsible for the development of the GMPLS family of protocols. He also chairs the Layer One VPN Working Group, and the Path Computation Element (PCE) Working Group, which is applying remote path computation techniques to MPLS and GMPLS networks.

Building on his 20 years' experience designing and developing portable communications software, Adrian runs a successful consultancy company, Old Dog Consulting, providing advice on implementation, deployment, and standardization of Internet Protocol-based solutions, especially in the arena of MPLS and GMPLS. Before this he was MPLS Architect and Development Manager at software house Data Connection, Ltd., and Director of Protocol Development for Movaz Networks, Inc., where he gained firsthand experience of building high-function GMPLS systems.

Alongside his activity within the IETF, where he has co-authored and contributed to numerous Internet-Drafts and RFCs on MPLS, GMPLS, and related technologies, he is active in many industry forums. A regular attendee at ITU-T meetings that discuss the optical control plane, Adrian was also a founding board member of the MPLS Forum, and has contributed to and chaired many technical committees and review panels. He has also co-edited a special edition of the IEEE Communications Magazine on GMPLS. He is the author of *The Internet and Its Protocols: A Comparative Approach* (Morgan Kaufmann, 2004), which explains many of the IP-based protocols, including those that make up MPLS and GMPLS.

Adrian is based in North Wales, and lives the good life with his wife Catherine and dog Bracken.

Igor Bryskin has 25 years' experience architecting and developing computer communications products. As CTO of Inverness Systems, he was responsible for ATM software developments including PNNI. When Inverness were acquired by Virata, Igor, in the role of Chief Architect of IP Software, was responsible for the high-level and detailed architecture of the company's IP routing, MPLS, and GMPLS offerings.

Igor is currently Chief Protocol Architect at Movaz Networks, Inc., where he develops and applies protocol extensions for advanced optical switches that benefit from a GMPLS control plane.

Igor is very active within the IETF's CCAMP, MPLS, and PCE Working Groups, where he is a member of several Design Teams responsible for the development of Point-to-Multipoint MPLS and GMPLS, various extensions to GMPLS to enable protection services, and the protocols necessary to realize the Path Computation Element architecture in traffic engineering networks.

Contents

Preface

In recent years there has been an explosion in the amount of traffic carried by the Internet. In the mid-1990s it looked as though the growth curve might be exponential, and this, combined with a significant boom in the telecommunications sector around the turn of the century, encouraged everyone to believe that there would be a huge increase in demand for bandwidth in core networks. The companies that would be most able to benefit from this growing customer requirement would be those that could provision new services rapidly, and react dynamically to changes within the network.

Multiprotocol Label Switching (MPLS) began to be standardized within the Internet Engineering Task Force (IETF) and offered new and interesting ways to manage the distribution of data packets within the Internet. The concept of establishing *tunnels* from one side of the network to another made traffic engineering a realistic prospect and allowed an operator to configure a web of virtual connections through his network. These tunnels could be used to carry traffic between the end points as though down a private line.

But these MPLS technologies were all based on packet, frame, or cell switching technologies. The fundamental unit of data was a data packet (usually an IP datagram), and this posed scaling problems for the switches and routers, since they had to examine every packet to determine how to forward it. Yet within the core of the network, the transport system was built from time division multiplexing (TDM) devices that switched data streams rather than individual packets. And a new family of devices was growing in popularity that could switch the entire contents of a fiber, or even split out individual wavelengths from a fiber and switch them separately. It became apparent that these core transport devices were performing in a similar way to the end-to-end switching functions in an MPLS network, but simply operated on a different switchable quantity (TDM timeslots, wavelengths, or entire fibers, rather than packets). Perhaps the basics of MPLS control protocols could be applied within transport networks to make them more reactive, easier to control, and more receptive to the requirements of advanced service provisioning. And so Generalized MPLS (GMPLS) was born.

However, the growth in the Internet did not reach the scale of some predictions. There is continued pressure on the infrastructure of the Internet to sustain increased data traffic, and now interactive voice and video traffic, but the more modest growth prospects do not warrant huge leaps forward in technology. At the same time, Service Providers have been going through a very difficult period: they have felt the need to cut back significantly. The first reaction, to reduce capital expenditure, could only be maintained for so long; after a while it became necessary to resume the purchase of equipment to meet customer needs and to continue to grow their networks. It became important, therefore, to buy new switches and routers that provided value for money and would enable the network operators to offer new value-added services for which their companies could charge the customers. Equally significant, however, was the Service Providers' drive to cut operational expenditure, and the most significant component in this sector is salaries.

The combination of these factors means that there is still a great benefit in an automated, intelligent control plane to allow operators to configure and manage transport networks more rapidly and with less effort. There is, therefore, an opening for GMPLS after all, and as the recovery in the telecommunications sector begins to build, Service Providers will be looking to buy equipment that offers them the flexibility to provide advanced services through centralized management and automated provisioning.

Although there are several excellent books on the topic of MPLS, GMPLS has been largely neglected. There are some interesting works that touch on the subject by approaching it through descriptions of TDM or optical networking, but nothing that concentrates on GMPLS as an architecture and a set of protocols.

The aim of this book is to provide a complete picture of GMPLS, from the protocols that are used by GMPLS devices, to the advanced services and functions that a GMPLS-enabled network can support.

GMPLS is not just about protocols (the existing MPLS protocols are reused with relatively small extensions), and it is not about any particular technology (it can be applied to many, including TDM, lambda switching, and pre-existing MPLS devices). GMPLS is all about the general software architecture of a network element, and network applications on top of the protocols. The reader is presented with a description of the GMPLS architecture, the purpose of each of the key protocols that are used to provision and manage services on GMPLS networks, and applications that make these services robust and versatile.

Audience

This book is targeted at industry professionals who already have some background knowledge of networking protocols. They might have a general overview, experience in another networking sector, or a good understanding of the material in some of the chapters. The reader is looking for a thorough grounding in the details of one or more of the GMPLS aspects covered in the book and could be expected to retain the book as a reference.

The reader is expected to be familiar with IP and have a passing knowledge of the concepts MPLS and routing, although the book will provide a brief overview of MPLS.

Software architects, designers and programmers, hardware developers, and system testers will find in this book a broad description of the purpose of GMPLS, together with full details of the protocols and how they work. They will gain an understanding of the building blocks necessary to construct a GMPLS-enabled device, and will see how advanced functions can be provided using the key components of GMPLS.

Operators of transport networks will increasingly find that the equipment from which their networks are built can be controlled through GMPLS. This book will give them a clear understanding of the benefits of an *intelligent* control plane, and will show them how they can offer flexible, dynamic, and sophisticated services using the functions and features of the GMPLS protocols.

Although this book is not specifically targeted at an academic audience, it will provide a student with a lot of important information about the way GMPLS works, the advanced and complex features it can deliver, and the motivation for the design both of GMPLS devices and networks, and of the protocols themselves.

Organization of this Book

The major components of this book are interdependent. In order to fully understand how to support some of the advanced applications of GMPLS it is necessary both to understand the protocols in some detail and to have a fundamental grasp of the GMPLS system architecture. At the same time, however, the description of the protocols and architecture requires a clear understanding of the motivation, and this is driven by the applications.

In order to present the necessary material in a coherent way, this book is broken into 15 chapters. The chapters are ordered so as to group together the material on the topics of background knowledge, GMPLS protocols, GMPLS applications, the architecture of GMPLS systems, and the ways of managing GMPLS devices and networks.

Each chapter begins with a brief introduction that sets out the topics that will be covered and explains why the material is important. The chapters all end with suggestions for *Further Reading*, pointing the reader to books and other materials that provide additional information on the subject. The chapters are as follows.

Chapter 1 recaps the basics of Multiprotocol Label Switching (MPLS) technology. Specifically, it discusses label switching concepts, and introduces the concept of MPLS signaling protocols. This provides an important foundation for the concepts of Generalized MPLS (GMPLS) introduced later in the book.

Chapter 2 summarizes the transport network types (optical, TDM, etc.), and explains popular network topologies (ring, mesh, mixed, etc.). It goes on to describe how the software of a transport network element (TNE) can be broken into three major planes – the data plane, the control plane, and the management plane – and provides a general overview of each of the planes.

Chapter 3 describes the evolution of the MPLS control plane that is applicable to packet switched networks, into the GMPLS control plane that is suitable for circuit switched networks. The chapter also discusses the commercial reasoning for GMPLS.

Chapter 4 provides detailed coverage of GMPLS signaling concepts. It explains the role of signaling within a GMPLS network, and defines the signaling protocol that is used to exchange messages within the control plane in order to establish Label Switched Paths (LSPs) within the data plane.

Chapter 5 covers the GMPLS routing sub-system. Basic concepts, addressing, and routing protocols are introduced. Advanced discussion of what traffic engineering means in a GMPLS network and how paths are computed are deferred to Chapters 8 and 9.

Chapter 6 describes how links are managed in the GMPLS system, and explores the peculiarities of link management in different types of transport networks, with a special accent on Wavelength Division Multiplexing (WDM) networks. The Link Management Protocol (LMP) and its extensions for control and management within WDM systems (LMP-WDM) are introduced. The chapter also explains how link management affects traffic engineering in GMPLS.

Chapter 7 covers the important topic of service recovery through protection and restoration. GMPLS enables the placement of primary and recovery paths of multiple services in such a way that the services can be protected with minimal use of network resources. The chapter discusses the different recovery schemes that are used for link recovery, as well as for end-to-end path recovery, and segment recovery. The chapter concludes with an analysis of the consequences of control plane failures, and the challenges of managing so-called control plane partitioned LSPs.

Chapter 8 provides detailed coverage of one of the basic GMPLS applications—traffic engineering. It discusses such aspects as TE link advertisement, TE link bundling, and TE link synchronizing. Finally, it outlines the ultimate goal of traffic engineering as control of the path computation output to satisfy the requirements of GMPLS service setup and recovery, while taking into account all preferences expressed by the GMPLS management plane.

Chapter 9 discusses aspects of path computation—an application that takes as input the management plane requirements for a particular GMPLS service or group of services, and selects one or more paths on the TE graph built by the traffic engineering component that would guarantee non-blocking setup of efficient and resilient services. Path computation modes and popular algorithms are covered.

Chapter 10 continues the theme of path computation to examine the requirements of constraint-based path computation. It describes why the path computation algorithms discussed in the previous chapter are not sufficient to handle arbitrary constraints requested by the user, and what can be done to derive suitable algorithms.

Chapter 11 introduces one of the applications of GMPLS—Point-to-Multipoint GMPLS. It relies very heavily on the concepts, principles, solutions, and techniques described in the previous chapters to show how traffic engineering and path computation can be adapted to provide this important new service.

Chapter 12 gives an overview of another emerging GMPLS application: Layer One Virtual Private Networks (L1VPNs). It identifies the service as seen from the perspective of both the Service Provider and the user of the service. It describes the service components, building blocks, deployment scenarios, and the requirements for and separation of responsibilities between data, control, and management planes. The text analyzes the reference models that are needed to satisfy the requirements, and looks at how and to what extent GMPLS technology can be used to provide L1VPNs.

Chapter 13 has a focus on general GMPLS control plane architectures. Different models are explored: peer, overlay, and hybrid. It also outlines requirements to be satisfied in order to use GMPLS to control the ITU-T's Automatically Switched Optical Network (ASON).

Chapter 14 introduces provisioning systems and tools that the GMPLS control plane relies upon and interacts with.

Chapter 15 describes standard GMPLS MIB modules and puts them in the context of the existing MPLS MIB modules.

The book concludes with an extensive glossary that highlights key definitions of terms used in the book.

Conventions Used in this Book

Many of the figures in this book illustrate sample networks. These are constructed from the symbols shown in Figure 0.1. A distinction is made between IP routers and MPLS Label Switching Routers (LSRs), and GMPLS LSRs. A further distinction is made between packet switching LSRs and optical switches. General networks (whether IP routers, packet switches, or GMPLS-capable switches) are typically represented as "clouds." Network management stations are usually shown as personal computers with monitors, while larger application servers are represented as tower systems.

Protocol exchanges are shown diagrammatically using vertical lines to represent network nodes and horizontal lines to represent messages, with the message name written immediately above it. Time flows down the diagram so that in Figure 0.2 (which illustrates the events and exchange of messages required to set up and tear down a GMPLS LSP), the first event is a Path message sent by LSR A to LSR B.

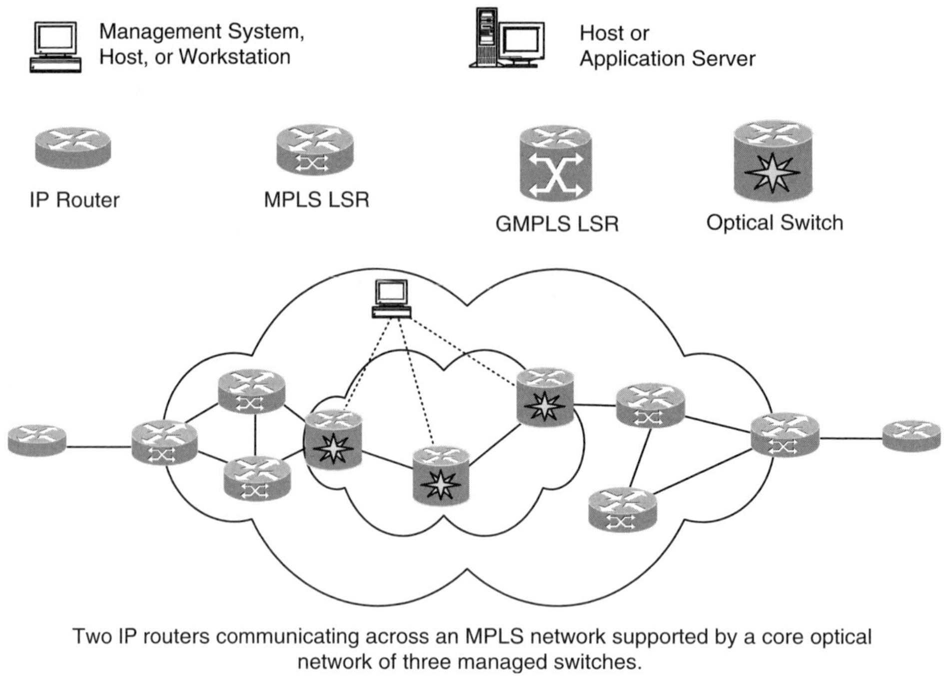

Figure 0.1 Some of the symbols used in the figures in this book.

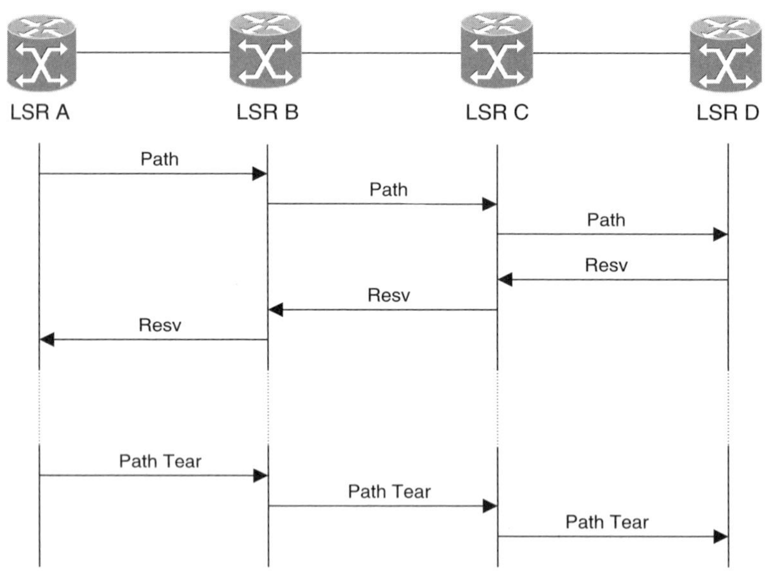

Figure 0.2 Normal LSP setup and teardown using RSVP-TE.

Dotted vertical lines are used to illustrate the passing of time, such as when waiting for a timer to expire, or waiting for application instructions.

About the IETF

The Internet Engineering Task Force (IETF) is the principal standards-making body for the Internet and in relation to the Internet Protocol (IP). Since the GMPLS family of protocols is based on IP (using IP addressing and routing, and using IP as the fundamental message transport), GMPLS belongs within the IETF. The IETF is an affiliation of individuals who work together to produce the best technical solutions in a timely manner. Membership doesn't exist as such, and everyone is free to participate in the discussions of new standards and problems with existing ones.

Most of the work of the IETF is carried out within working groups, each chartered to address a reasonably small set of problems. The GMPLS protocols themselves are the product of the Common Control and Measurement Plane (CCAMP) working group of the IETF. CCAMP is chartered to *coordinate the work within the IETF defining a common control plane and a separate common measurement plane for physical path and core tunneling technologies of Internet and telecom service providers (ISPs and SPs)*.

GMPLS standards are developed through a process of drafting. Internet-Drafts may be the work of groups of individuals or of a working group, and are published and re-published until they are acceptable. They are then put to "last call" to allow everyone to express any last-minute objections. If all is well and the draft is approved by the Internet Engineering Steering Group (IESG), it is published as a Request For Comment (RFC), the first step towards being ratified as a standard.

The CCAMP working group has a web site at http://www.ietf.org/html.charters/ccamp-charter.html, from where links exist to each of the GMPLS RFCs and Internet-Drafts.

A Note on Gender

The English language is sadly lacking a gender-nonspecific third person pronoun that may be legitimately applied to any person. Thus, within this book, where it is necessary to refer to an individual (such as a network operator or the designer of a switching device) in the third person, we have chosen to use the word *he*. This is done for consistency rather than to cause offense.

Acknowledgments

We would like to thank the staff at Elsevier for their assistance in the production of this book. Special mentions are due to Karyn Johnson and Mona Buehler, who saw the book through its birth and its adolescence respectively, but who had moved on to other jobs before publication. Our thanks to Rachel Roumeliotis for stepping in so ably to complete the project, to Paul Gottehrer for his patient work through the copyedit and proofreading process, and to Rick Adams for his constant supervision.

We are also particularly grateful to our reviewers who have given so much of their time to provide useful and detailed feedback on our style and the accuracy of the text. Without the efforts of Jean-Philippe Vasseur, Lyndon Ong, and Deborah Brungard this book would not be nearly as polished.

Adrian would like to thank his wife Catherine for her understanding of many things, not the least of which were late nights at the keyboard and mood swings caused by writer's block. Catherine was also a great help during copy-edit and proofreading, where she caught countless errors.

CHAPTER 1

Multiprotocol Label Switching

Although this book is about Generalized Multiprotocol Label Switching (GMPLS), it is useful to spend this first chapter describing the concepts of Multiprotocol Label Switching (MPLS). Those readers who are already familiar with MPLS may wish to skip this chapter.

MPLS is a data forwarding technology for use in packet networks that was developed by the Internet Engineering Task Force (IETF) building on several technologies invented by different companies. It relies on labeling each packet with a short, unique identifier (or label) that each router can use to determine the next hop for the data packet. It turns out (see Chapter 3) that the same conceptual process used to determine how to forward MPLS packets can also be used in non-packet technologies. At the same time, many of the protocols used to install the forwarding rules at MPLS routers are easily extended to provide data forwarding control in non-packet networks. Thus, the fundamentals of MPLS are an important foundation for Generalized MPLS and are a cornerstone for this book.

1.1 Some History

MPLS has its roots in several IP packet switching technologies under development in the early and mid 1990s. In 1996 the IETF started to pull the threads together, and in 1997 the MPLS Working Group was formed to standardize protocols and approaches for MPLS.

IP packet switching is the process of forwarding data packets within the network, based on some tag or identifier associated with each packet. In some senses, traditional IP routing is a form of packet switching — each packet carries a destination IP address that can be used to determine the next hop in the path toward the destination by performing a look-up in the routing table. However, IP routing has (or had) concerns about speed and scalability, and these led to investigations of other ways to switch the data packets. Added to these issues was the desire to facilitate additional services such as traffic aggregation and traffic engineering.

Since the advent of MPLS, various hardware approaches to IP routing have been developed. Some of these enhance the speed and scalability of IP routing and thus dilute the motivations for packet switching described above, but the drive for and value of MPLS remain.

1.2 Label Switching

Label switching relies on associating a small, fixed-format label with each data packet so that it can be forwarded in the network. This means that each packet, frame, or cell must carry some identifier that tells network nodes how to forward it. At each hop across the network the packet is forwarded based on the value of the incoming label and dispatched onward with a new label value. The label is swapped and the data is switched based on the label value, which gives rise to two terms: *label swapping* and *label switching*.

In an MPLS network, packets are labeled by the insertion of an additional piece of information called the *shim header*. It is found between the network headers and the IP header as shown in Figure 1.1.

The MPLS shim header carries a 20-bit label which is used to determine the path that the packet must follow. Each network node (called a *Label Switching Router*; LSR) maintains a look-up table (the *Label Forwarding Information Base*; LFIB) to allow it to determine the next hop for the data. The LFIB contains a mapping of {incoming interface, incoming label} to {outgoing interface, outgoing label}. That is, when a packet is received, the LSR determines the interface on which the packet arrived and finds the label in the shim header of the packet. It looks up these values in the LFIB and discovers the interface out of which to send the packet, and a new label value to place in the shim header. The path that an MPLS packet follows across the network is called a *Label Switched Path* (LSP). Once a packet has been labeled at the start of the LSP (the *ingress*), its path to the *egress* is well known and stable because the mappings in the LFIBs at each LSR are also well known and stable. Thus the only complexity exists at the ingress where each packet must be *classified* according to its destination and the service provided

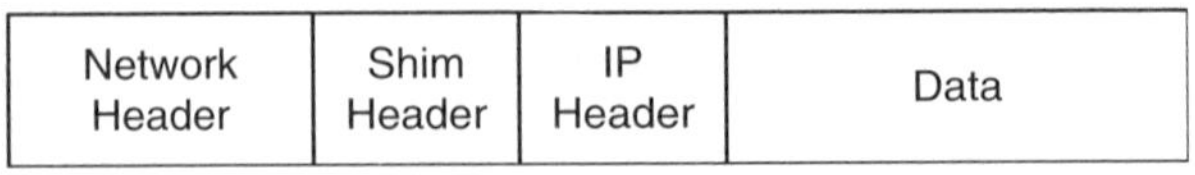

Figure 1.1 The shim header is inserted between the network protocol header and the IP header.

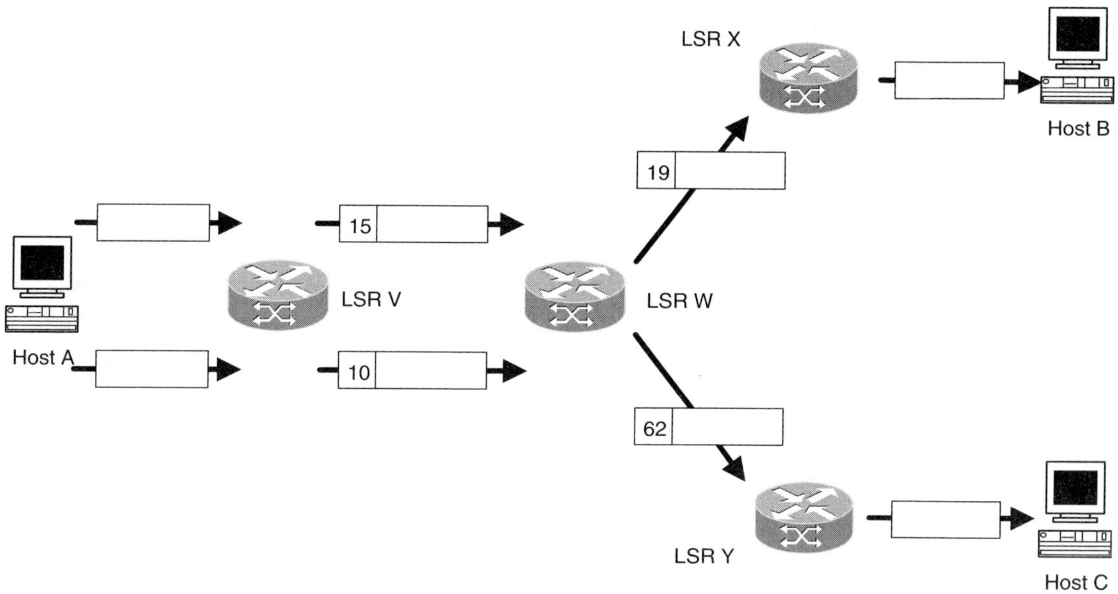

Figure 1.2 Label Switched Paths (LSPs).

(perhaps based on the application type, or the quality of service demanded) and assigned to a specific LSP.

Figure 1.2 illustrates two LSPs carrying data from IP Host A to Hosts B and C. The MPLS network is made up of four LSRs that forward the packets. Host A sends IP packets to LSR V using its routing table or a default route. LSR V is an ingress LSR and classifies the packets based on the final destination, assigns them to an LSP, and labels them by adding a shim header and setting the label value. Those packets targeted at Host B are assigned to the upper LSP and are labeled 15; those for Host C are assigned to the lower LSP and are labeled 10. Once labeled, the packets are forwarded out of the appropriate interface towards LSR W.

At LSR W each labeled packet is examined to determine the incoming interface and incoming label. These are looked up in the LFIB to determine the outgoing label and outgoing interface. The label values are swapped (incoming replaced with outgoing) and the packets are forwarded out of the designated interfaces. In the example, packets labeled 15 are forwarded out of the interface to LSR X carrying the new label 19; packets labeled 10 are forwarded out of the interface to LSR Y carrying the new label 62.

LSR X and LSR Y are egress LSRs. They also perform a look-up into their LFIBs, but the entries indicate that they should remove the shim header and forward the packet as a plain IP packet. This forwarding may be through the normal IP routing table, but can be optimized by the LFIB indicating the outgoing interface so that no routing look-up is required. Thus, in the example, if LSR V associates all packets destined for Host B with the upper LSP in the figure, and labels them with the value 15, they will be successfully forwarded through the network and delivered to Host B.

1.2.1 *Application of MPLS to Existing Switching Networks*

Some network technologies (such as ATM and Frame Relay) are already based on switching, and it is not necessary to introduce yet another mechanism. At the same time, it is useful to maintain some consistency of control through the entire network. In order to achieve this a mechanism is defined to express the MPLS label within the network layer protocol fields (the VPI/VCI or DLCI), which means that the shim header is not needed. Nevertheless, the shim header is retained for ease of conversion between network types and to encode label stacks as discussed in the next section.

In an ATM network, the whole MPLS packet is presented as an AAL5 PDU and is then segmented into ATM cells. Each cell is labeled with a VPI/VCI that is equivalent to the MPLS label (see Figure 1.3). The cells are forwarded through the ATM network and re-assembled at the end to re-form the MPLS packet.

1.2.2 *Label Stacking*

Sometimes one or more LSPs will be *tunneled* down another LSP. This provides a significant scaling benefit at the core of networks — instead of having to manage an LFIB with very many LSPs, the core LSRs only need to worry about the tunnel LSPs. This, in turn, leads to many useful application scenarios such as the construction of VPNs, or the management of bulk, flow-based LSPs as a single unit as they cross a core network. Figure 1.4 shows how LSP tunneling might be arranged. An LSP is established between LSR W and LSR Z in this figure. The LSP is used to carry other, end-to-end LSPs (such as those from P to S, Q to T,

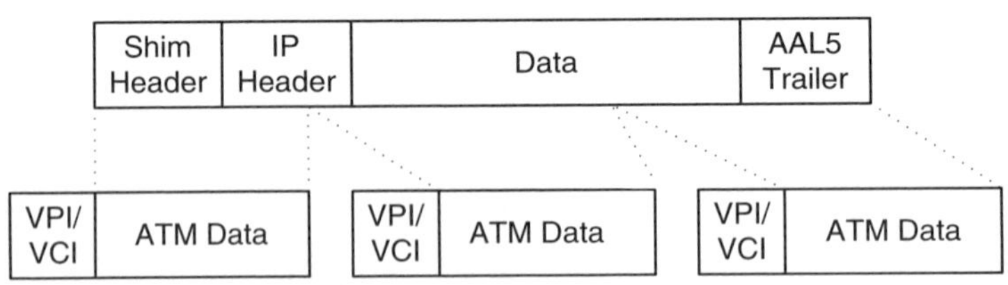

Figure 1.3 MPLS in an ATM network.

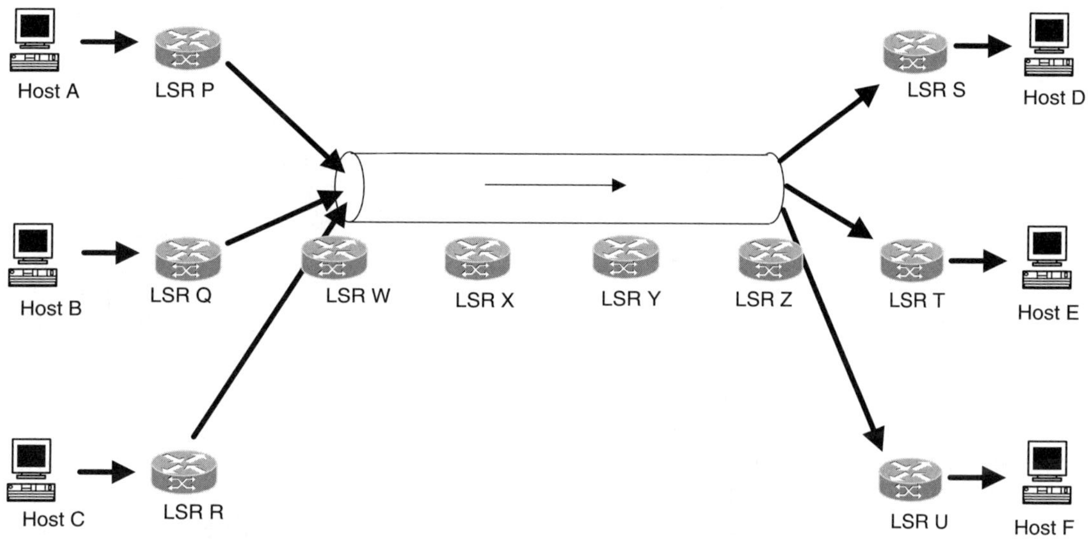

Figure 1.4 An LSP tunnel carrying multiple LSPs.

and R to U) as though they were simply stepping from one LSR to the next (i.e., from LSR W to LSR Z).

When MPLS packets are received at LSR Z in Figure 1.4, some identification is required so that LSR Z can easily determine the correct next label value and outgoing interface — it must not treat all packets the same, but must determine to which of the tunneled LSPs they belong. This is achieved using a *label stack* on each packet. When each packet enters the tunnel at LSR W, an additional label is applied to the packet. That is, the existing label is not replaced, but a further label is pushed onto the label stack. This topmost label is used to forward the packet from LSR W to LSR Z. At LSR Z, the top label is popped from the stack, revealing the label of the tunneled LSP.

A label stack is achieved simply by adding additional shim headers to the data packet as shown in Figure 1.5. The first shim header encountered represents the topmost label (the one that is actively used to forward the packet). The last shim header has a special bit set to indicate that it is the bottom of the stack.

Figure 1.6 shows how label stacks are used. LSR P takes traffic from Host A targeted at Host D and imposes a label (3). Similarly, traffic from Host C to Host F is handled at LSR R where a label (7) is imposed. At LSR W the LSP is tunneled into a new LSP and an additional label (9) is pushed onto the stack. Forwarding along the path W-X-Y-Z is as described before — the top label on the stack is swapped and the packet is forwarded (note that the labels lower down the stack are not examined or processed). At LSR Z, the label that defines the tunnel is popped from the stack, and traffic is forwarded using the next label on the stack.

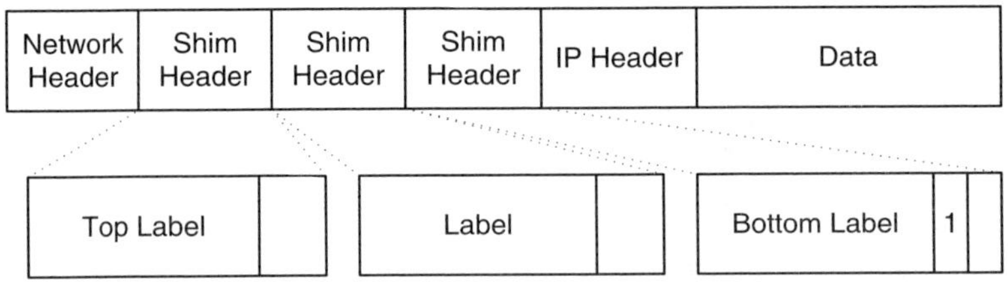

Figure 1.5 The label stack.

1.3 Signaling Protocols

How do the LFIBs get constructed on each LSR? One possibility is that network management tools are responsible for installing the entries in the LFIBs. As shown in Figure 1.7, it is possible for a centralized network management station (NMS) to send management messages to each LSR to establish the necessary label mappings. This is perfectly acceptable in a small network, but rapidly becomes a management nightmare in a large network or when trying to recover from a network failure. Signaling protocols (as shown on the right-hand side of Figure 1.7) allow a more flexible approach so that a service request is sent to the network, and the network is responsible for routing the LSP through the LSRs. The signaling protocol

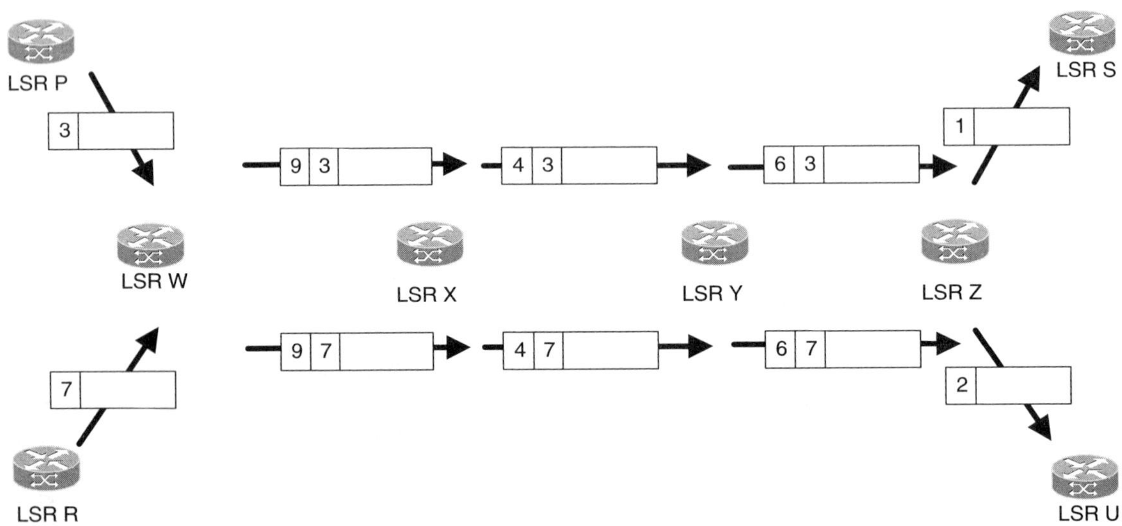

Figure 1.6 Label stacks in use.

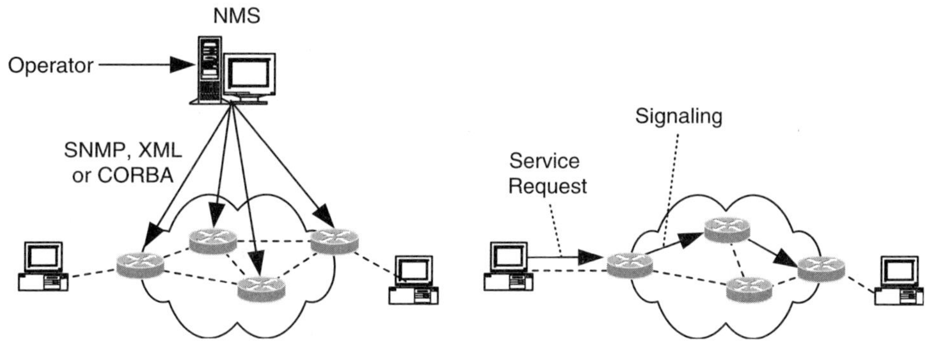

Figure 1.7 Management versus signaling control of an MPLS network.

exchanges label mapping information between the LSRs so that an LSR near the ingress (an upstream LSR) knows what label to use on a data packet that it sends toward its downstream neighbor.

The IETF has deliberately avoided mandating a single label distribution protocol for use with MPLS. This allows different protocols to be used to suit the requirements of different operating environments. Several label distribution protocols have been standardized by the IETF, but we need only concern ourselves with the one developed for traffic engineering because this technique closely models the requirements of connection oriented transport networks described in the next chapter. In this protocol (RSVP-TE) labels are allocated by the downstream LSR (with respect to the data flow) and are advertised to the upstream LSR.

1.4 Further Reading

A detailed discussion of MPLS can be found in *MPLS: Technology and Application* by Bruce Davie and Yakov Rekhter (2000), Morgan Kaufman.

The Internet and Its Protocols: A Comparative Approach by Adrian Farrel (2004), Morgan Kaufmann, provides a more detailed examination of the MPLS signaling protocols.

The MPLS Working Group has a web page that includes links to RFCs and Internet-Drafts for MPLS: www.ietf.org/html.charters/mpls-charter.html. Two key RFCs are:

RFC 3031 — Multiprotocol Label Switching Architecture
RFC 3209 — RSVP-TE: Extensions to RSVP for LSP Tunnels

CHAPTER 2

An Overview of Transport Networks

GMPLS provides a common control plane for managing a variety of different network technologies and for leveraging those technologies to enable high-function services across the network. To give some context for the chapters that follow, this chapter introduces the concept of a transport network and gives an overview of the different transport network technologies such as Time Division Multiplexing (TDM) and Wavelength Division Multiplexing (WDM).

The chapter also summarizes some of the popular network topologies (ring, mesh, mixed, etc.) and goes on to describe how the software of a Transport Network Element (TNE) can be broken into three major planes — the data plane, the control plane, and the management plane — and provides a general overview of each of the planes.

2.1 Transport

The International Telecommunications Union (ITU) defines *transport* as "the functional process of transferring information between different locations" in its Recommendation G.805 entitled Generic functional architecture of transport networks. This definition may be a little too loose for our purposes, because it would make all networks of any variety into transport networks.

A refinement of the transport concept comes within the same Recommendation, where a *transport network* is defined as "the functional resources of the network which conveys user information between locations." The key addition in this definition is the reference to the fact that the information that is transferred is *user* information. This places a clear layering structure on the network, with islands of the user network connected by one or more transport networks as shown in Figure 2.1.

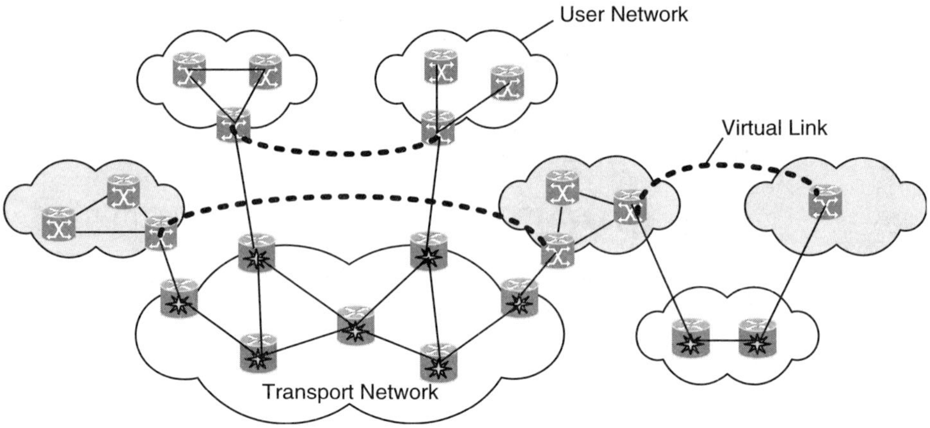

Figure 2.1 The transport network provides connectivity for islands of the user network.

Following this definition, most network technologies can provide transport, but a rule is generally applied such that there is a change of technology over the user-to-transport network boundary, and this technology change usually involves a step down the familiar networking layering hierarchy defined in the ITU's Recommendation X.200. For example, an Ethernet, Synchronous Digital Hierarchy (SDH), or WDM network might provide the transport infrastructure for an IP network. In turn, a WDM network might provide the transport connectivity for an SDH network. On the whole, IP networks are not regarded as transport networks, but MPLS is increasingly seen as a transport mechanism for IP connectivity. In this way we build up a fine-grained layering based on the transport technology. This concept will be drawn upon in later chapters.

At this point it is important to note that the term *transport* here has no correlation with the Transport Layer in the OSI seven-layer model set out in X.200. Transport protocols, such as TCP, do not provide the type of transport network service discussed here.

2.2 Transport Technologies

This section gives a very brief overview of the principles of some key transport technologies. TDM is one of the most important building blocks in deployed networks, especially for the medium to long distance transmission of voice traffic. It is gradually facing pressure from Ethernet, however, which is extending its reach and capacity from what was a very short distance technology, and from WDM, which is becoming cheaper and more available as a high-capacity transport technology. Additionally, fiber switching is touched upon as a technique that can be used to manage large volumes of data in a simple way. MPLS has already been discussed in Chapter 1 and is not revisited here.

Note that the descriptions that follow are intended to provide a very high level view and are, therefore, gross simplifications. Readers wishing to get a better understanding of these technologies are advised to look at the references listed in the *Further Reading* section at the end of this chapter.

2.2.1 *Gigabit Ethernet*

Ethernet has become a familiar technology within the Local Area Network (LAN) and is now seeing significant deployment in the Metro Area. In the LAN an Ethernet is usually deployed as a multi-access network with speeds of 10 or 100 Mbps. Until recently, the faster Gigabit Ethernet was used only as a "fat pipe" to connect Ethernet switches across relatively short distances.

In fact, the restriction on the length of a Gigabit Ethernet link (500 m) was partially a function of the desire to continue to use Ethernet in its multi-access mode, which requires an Ethernet protocol called CSMA/CD to handle the packet collisions that can arise when more than one station sends onto a multi-access link at the same time. If Gigabit Ethernet is run in half-duplex mode, and used for point-to-point connections, its reach can be extended and it can be used more widely, not just in the LAN backbone, but as a data transport technology in IP and MPLS networks.

Otherwise, Gigabit Ethernet is pretty similar to 10/100 Ethernet seen in the LAN. Various minor extensions are used to increase frame sizes while facilitating bursts of small packets as might be seen in voice networks. At the physical level, Gigabit Ethernet can operate over copper wires or optical fibers.

2.2.2 *Time Division Multiplexing*

TDM is a technique where a signal is shared among data flows by allocating each flow a well-defined and regular slice of the signal. Consider a packet technology: If two flows are to be carried down a single signal then the packets from each flow must be interspersed. This will not be an issue for applications such as file transfer, but it may be a serious problem if time-critical and time-sensitive applications share a signal with a bulk data transfer application, because that application may send bursts of large packets that will hog the transmission medium. In other words, packet multiplexing may not be able to deliver the responsiveness necessary for services such as voice transmission, even when there is sufficient aggregate bandwidth for all services.

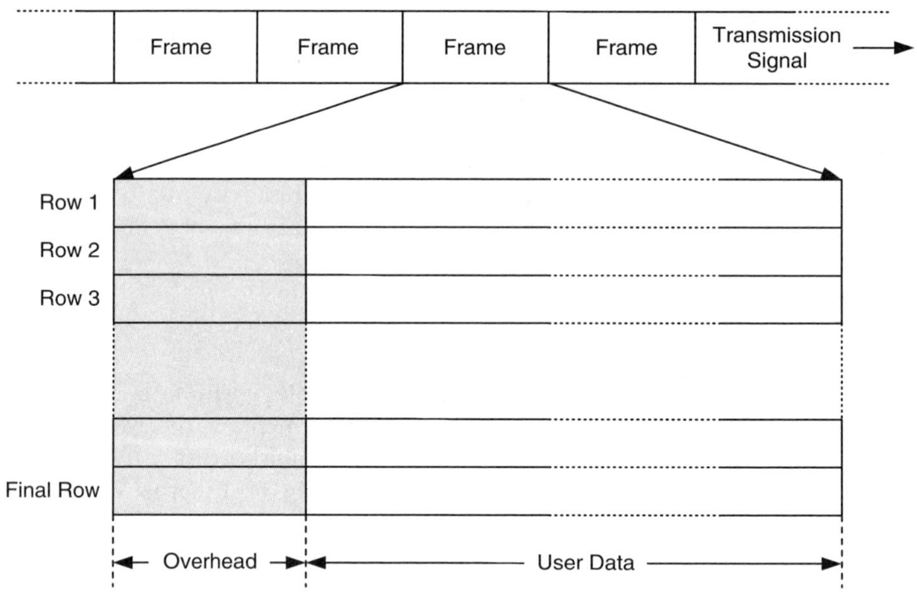

Figure 2.2 The TDM signal is broken into a sequence of frames, and each frame is composed of a series of rows.

TDM provides another way of dividing the available bandwidth so that each application gets a fair share of the resources. To achieve this, the signal is partitioned into *frames*. Each frame is a sequence of bytes transmitted on the wire or fiber, and there is a well-known number of frames per second depending on the (regular) size of each frame and the line speed. Each frame is partitioned into a number of series of bytes each of the same length; because of the way that TDM frames are usually depicted, these series of bytes are known as *rows* (see Figure 2.2). The first few bytes of each row contain control information called *transport overhead*, and the remainder of each row carries user data.

A traffic flow may be assigned one or more rows so different flows may have different fractions of the total available bandwidth. The flow treats the bytes within its rows of the frame as a continuous signal on a private medium. The TDM technology is responsible for multiplexing these signals into the frames, and for demultiplexing them from the frames at the far end of the link. In effect, each flow is allocated a regular slice of the transmission in each frame, and because there are very many frames per second (8000) there is no significant impact on a flow to this method of sharing the bandwidth. The regularity and predictability of this method of slicing up the transmission resources is known as *time slicing* and because the *timeslots* are multiplexed together to form a whole, the technology is called Time Division Multiplexing.

Figure 2.2 shows how a TDM frame is represented as a series of rows in a grid. Note that the bytes are transmitted in sequence along the rows with the last byte of row n transmitted immediately before the first byte of row $n+1$.

A TDM switch is capable of shuffling the timeslots between fibers. For example, it may take slot 1 from fiber 1 and place it on fiber 2, while taking slot 2 from fiber 1 and placing it on fiber 3. Simple TDM switches are limited to this type of switching where a timeslot's position in the frame is preserved when the slot is switched from one frame to another. In principle, a TDM switch is also capable of taking slot 3 from fiber 1 and transmitting it as slot 4 on fiber 4 (i.e., changing the position of the timeslot in the frame), but this requires some tricky synchronization and buffering of data.

There are two similar sets of standards for TDM networking. SDH is a set of framing, encoding, and processing rules developed by the ITU, whereas the Synchronous Optical Network (SONET) was developed by the American National Standards Institute (ANSI). The techniques employed by these standards are essentially the same, but the details differ significantly.

2.2.3 *Wavelength Division Multiplexing*

WDM is simply the technique of placing multiple optical signals within the same fiber. Each signal is encoded using a different optical frequency and is referenced by that frequency or the equivalent wavelength (the signals are often referred to as *lambdas* because that is the symbol used in physics to indicate wavelength). Each lambda forms a distinct optical channel that can be used to carry data independent of the data on the other channels. The data may be encoded in various ways, but a common solution is for each lambda to carry an Ethernet or a TDM signal.

In order to achieve some consistency between which wavelengths are used, the ITU has published some lists of acceptable frequencies. These lists are known as *grids* and each gives a set of uniformly spaced wavelengths suitable for a specific application. For example, in *Coarse Wavelength Division Multiplexing* (CWDM) a grid of 18 lambdas is published with a spacing of 2500 GHz (20 nm) between each lambda. For *Dense Wavelength Division Multiplexing* (DWDM), there are several grids with a typical spacing of 100, 50, or 25 GHz. The spacing of a WDM grid is a function of the WDM technology (in particular, the ability to generate, multiplex, and extract narrow-band signals) and drives the applicability of the technology.

An important issue with WDM is that the data signals can interfere with each other because they are present in the same fiber. If the tuning of one wavelength "drifts," the signal will cause distortion to other signals in the same fiber. So it is currently not possible to pack an indefinite number of optical channels into one fiber, but there is commercially available DWDM equipment that will handle over 100 channels, and the use of more than 300 channels has been demonstrated.

CWDM equipment has been cheaper to manufacture for various reasons, and has been typically used for shorter distance data transfer. The wider spacing of the lambdas means that less care has to be taken to focus the signal to the precise wavelength, but CWDM is limited to a bandwidth of 2.5 Gbps for each lambda.

DWDM requires more precision to avoid interference, but the consequence is that the signal is more focused and can handle both higher bit rates (up to 10 or even 40 Gbps) and longer distances. On the other hand, the equipment can be more expensive to manufacture.

WDM switches have three important components: They must demultiplex the separate lambda channels from the fiber, they must switch the data streams to their outgoing fibers, and they must multiplex the signals into the outgoing fibers. Two distinct types of WDM switching device exist. The first is opto-electronic (OEO) and uses filters and transceivers to receive signals and convert them to electronic bit streams; these electronic signals can then be switched through electronic components before they are regenerated as optical signals by lasers. The other type of optical switch is a photonic cross-connect or all-optical switch (PXC or OOO), which uses optical techniques to separate and switch the data (e.g., it might use a diffraction grating to separate the lambda signals before switching each lambda through an array of micro mirrors). Note that an OEO is capable of changing the lambda of a data stream on each leg of its journey, whereas the PXC can be potentially smaller and does not require the inclusion of transceivers or lasers.

Perversely, the publication of recognized lambda grids has done little to encourage the production of interoperable equipment from multiple vendors. Different vendors choose different subsets of lambdas from different grids and the likelihood of a reasonable intersection is not great.

2.2.4 *Fiber Switching*

To conclude this section it is worth pointing out that an entire fiber can be treated as an opaque data channel. That is, the user system can encode whatever data it likes into the fiber and the network will treat it as a whole. The signal may be Ethernet or TDM encoded as a single "white light" signal, it may be several CWDM channels, or it may be many DWDM channels.

A fiber switch is a device in the network that takes all data from a single fiber and replicates it onto another fiber. Because an understanding of the encoding and signal types packaged within a fiber would be important to regenerate the contents of the fiber, such fiber switches are usually optically transparent devices. That is, they do not intercept the signal and convert it to electronics before regenerating it. Instead, they switch the entire contents of the fiber using optical devices (such as micro mirrors).

2.3 Transport Network Topologies

This section examines some of the popular ways in which devices are connected together to form transport networks. It exposes the two basic building blocks (rings and point-to-point links) and shows how modern networks are constructed as meshes. Chapters 7 through 13 explain how GMPLS can be used to manage complex mesh networks and to provide sophisticated services through such meshes.

2.3.1 *Simple Rings*

Ring topology has been shown to be a very effective way of interconnecting a set of network nodes. From the token ring deployed in LANs, to ATM and TDM fiber rings, the ring has become almost ubiquitous.

One major reason for this popularity is that it decreases the amount of wiring (or fibering) and network interface cards needed to connect all of the network nodes together. This reduces the deployment cost of the network. With a simple ring like that shown in Figure 2.3, each network node can send traffic to any other node, even though all of the links are unidirectional. All that is required is that each node forwards traffic for which it is not the intended recipient.

Note that bidirectional services can be provided on a unidirectional ring such as that shown in Figure 2.3. For example, a bidirectional service between A and B

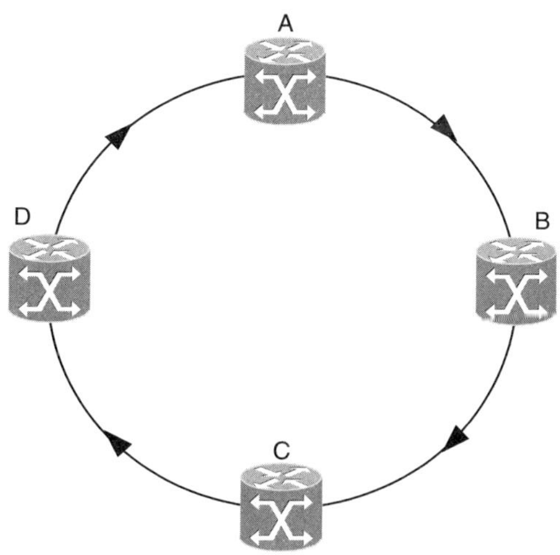

Figure 2.3 The ring is a basic unit of network connectivity.

may be provided by A sending traffic on the direct link from A to B, and by B sending traffic via C and D to reach A.

2.3.2 *Bidirectional and Protected Rings*

A ring can also be built by fibering (or wiring) connectivity both clockwise and anticlockwise as shown in Figure 2.4. This network topology makes bidirectional connectivity symmetrical so that a bidirectional service between A and C can be provided by traversing the network forward (ABC) and back again (CBA) rather than by completing the ring as would be necessary in the simple ring shown in Figure 2.3.

Bidirectional rings offer the possibility of protecting services against the failure of an individual node or a fiber cut. In Figure 2.3 a break in the link between nodes A and B makes it impossible to deliver any traffic from node A to any other node in the network, and it makes all bidirectional services impossible. But in Figure 2.4 there is always an alternative path in the event of a single network failure. Thus, if the link between A and B fails, a bidirectional service between A and B can use the paths ADCB and BCDA.

Various automated techniques exist based on the protected ring to detect network failures and switch the traffic to the alternate path. Some of these techniques operate through pre-configuration, and others use control

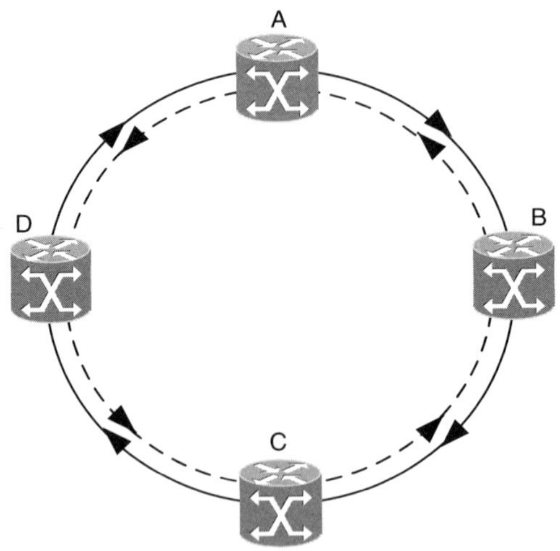

Figure 2.4 A protected or bidirectional ring is constructed simply by running a second fiber in the reverse direction.

plane techniques. Chapter 7 describes how GMPLS can be used to provide rapid and efficient service protection.

The bidirectional ring continues to offer a good price-service compromise, because it uses the lowest amount of fiber and the fewest network interface cards for the level of service. Typically the forward and reverse paths are provided by separate fibers as bidirectional optics are rare, and (again, typically) the two fibers are carried in the same fiber bundle or duct, which results in further cost savings. This clustering of the forward and reverse fibers means that it is often the case that if one fiber is cut, both will be cut, and this leads to the promotion of two protection schemes. In bidirectional or symmetrical protection, the forward and reverse paths are *fate sharing* — that is, if one path needs to switch to its protection path, then both paths are switched regardless of whether both or just one fiber was cut. For example, if the fiber from A to B is cut, but the reverse fiber from B to A remains intact, the service between A and B will switch to use the paths ADCB and BCDA. In unidirectional protection, the service between A and B would switch to ADCB but continue to use BA for the reverse path traffic. These issues are discussed further in Chapter 7.

2.3.3 *Interconnected Rings and Meshed Rings*

Ring networks, like those shown in Figures 2.3 and 2.4, can be connected together. Such a procedure allows established networks to be integrated and extended with minimal management and maintenance disruption. If all of the nodes were placed on the same large ring there would be disruption to the main ring while the nodes were added, but more important the whole ring would be vulnerable to a failure of any one link in the network. By building the network from interconnected rings, it is possible to isolate the impact of individual link failures. Thus, in Figure 2.5, a failure in the link between A and B does not impact the ability to deliver service in the two rings B, B1, B2, and D, D1, D2.

There are also considerable management benefits to constructing the network from connected rings, because each ring can become its own management domain with coordination only necessary at the points of interconnection.

Services can be provisioned within the simple rings as before so that, for example, a bidirectional service between A and B can be achieved just as described in Section 2.3.1. Each ring is self-contained in this way. But now we can also build services that span multiple rings so that traffic can be transported from B1 to D1 following the path B1, B2, B, C, D, D1. Note that this path is constructed from ring segments (B1-B2-B, B-C-D, D-D1), so there is nothing particularly clever going on except for the ability to connect traffic across rings at B and D.

In fact, a reverse path will also exist within the interconnected ring network. In our example, D1 is able to send traffic back to B1 following the path D1, D2,

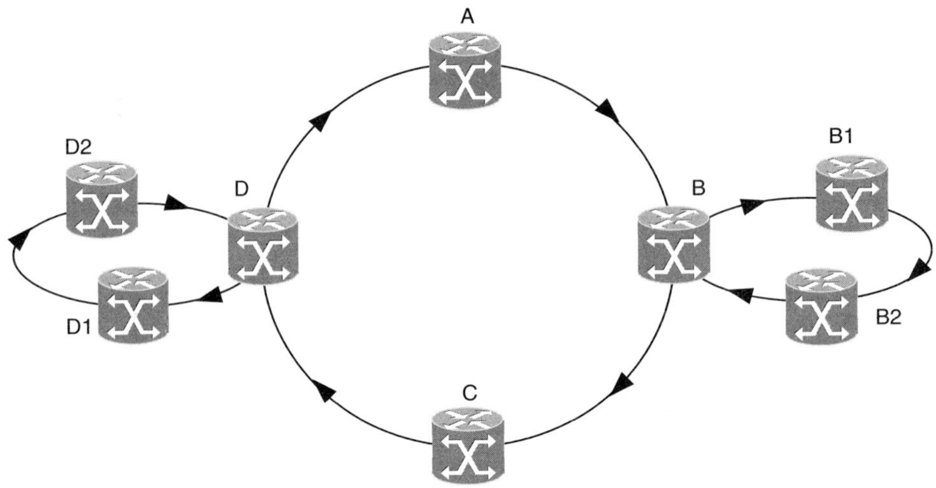

Figure 2.5 Additional rings may be subtended to the main ring to provide interconnectivity between more nodes.

D, A, B, B1. In this way, a logical ring can be overlaid on the network and the end-to-end bidirectional service can be treated in many ways as though there was just one simple ring.

Because of the way that such interconnected ring networks were typically built up, the smaller rings connected to the main ring are often referred to as *subtended rings*. This definition breaks down as more interconnections are made and more rings added. In Figure 2.6 there is a choice of paths between B1 and D1 introduced by the new rings subtended to nodes C and D1. This enables the service from B1 to D1 to be protected against a failure in any single link in the network, but requires a little more care on the part of the operator or the control plane in selecting the correct path. For example, the path B1, B2, C1, C, B2, B, C, C2, C, D, D1 may be perfectly valid, but it is unlikely that it would be considered an optimal use of network resources.

All of the rings in Figures 2.5 and 2.6 are shown as simple, unidirectional rings, but could also be constructed as bidirectional protected rings. Such a network offers huge flexibility in choice of shortest paths and protection paths, but may also include an excess of unused bandwidth.

2.3.4 *Point-to-Point Links*

At this point we need to observe that it is a simple topographical step from the ring to the point-to-point link. Consider the connections between nodes A and B

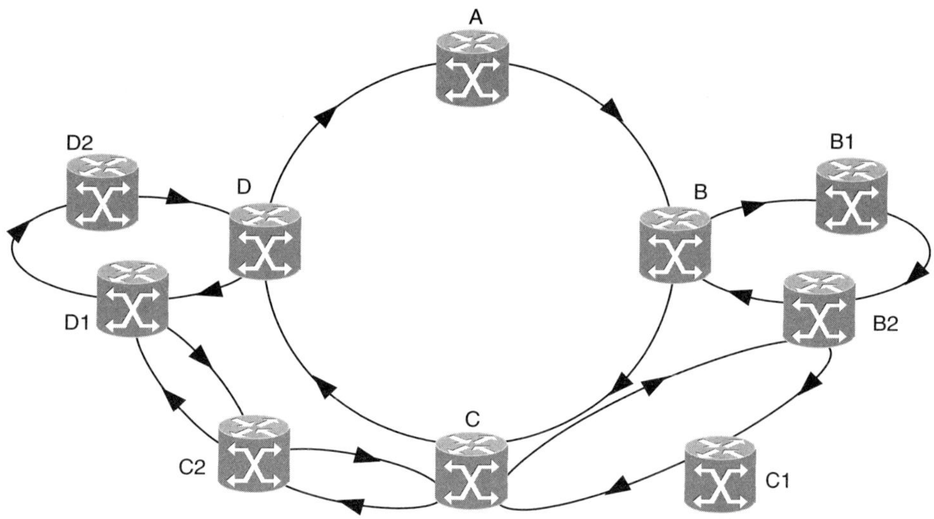

Figure 2.6 Multiple rings may be interconnected to construct a mesh of rings.

in Figure 2.7; topologically these form a simple ring. The same can be said about the links between B and C so that the whole network is built of two interconnected rings joined at node B.

Note that even in the simple network of Figure 2.7, bidirectional services can be provided between any pair of nodes. When compared with a simple ring connecting the same three nodes, the network requires more fiber runs (four against three) and more network interface cards (eight against six), a ratio that becomes more apparent as more nodes are added to the linear topology.

On the other hand, the service delivery features are somewhat different from those of a simple ring in the face of a network failure. For example, if the trunk between B and C is cut, C becomes completely isolated while A and B continue to be able to operate a bidirectional service.

There are two options to convert the linear network of Figure 2.7 to support protection. In the first (on the left-hand side of Figure 2.8) each fiber pair is protected by a second fiber pair that is ideally run in a separate duct. Thus, each

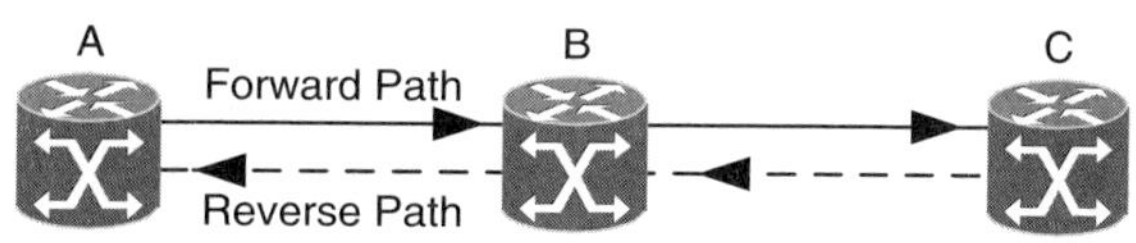

Figure 2.7 Point-to-point links can be used to provide simple connectivity.

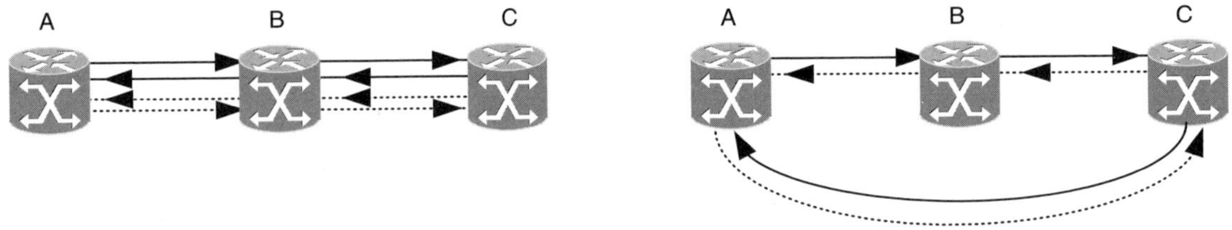

Figure 2.8 Converting a point-to-point topology to offer protection.

point-to-point link can be seen as a protected ring. In the second option (on the right-hand side of Figure 2.8) a new point-to-point link is added between A and C. This can be seen either as adding a third, two-node simple ring to the mesh of interconnected rings, or it may be viewed as converting the topology to provide a single protected ring. This second solution leads us to consider the mesh network described in the next section.

We should also note that the hardware technology for point-to-point links may be somewhat different from that used in rings. A ring may be based on selective add-drop function so that each node only initiates/terminates selective signals while forwarding all other signals around the ring. In point-to-point connectivity all signals must be terminated, because to forward them would simply result in returning them to their origins.

2.3.5 *Mesh Networks*

Figure 2.9 shows how a combination of point-to-point links and rings may be used to build a network. Point-to-point connectivity between a pair of adjacent nodes is usually provided with a bidirectional link (i.e., with a link in each direction), but that is not a requirement. Rings may also be bidirectional or unidirectional.

Although rings and point-to-point links will continue to be used for specific technologies and in legacy networks, we can expect more and more networks to be built as meshes. The flexibility that a mesh provides for the construction of sophisticated services means that it is a real winner. A Service Provider whose network is based on a mesh is able to provide value-added features such as on-demand provisioning and rapid protection without the massive over-deployment of network resources (fibers, network line cards, switches) that would be needed in simpler topologies. Chapters 5 and 7 through 13 describe how GMPLS routing and signaling protocols make it possible to manage these complex networks either automatically or with operator input, and make it simple to provide advanced services to the customer.

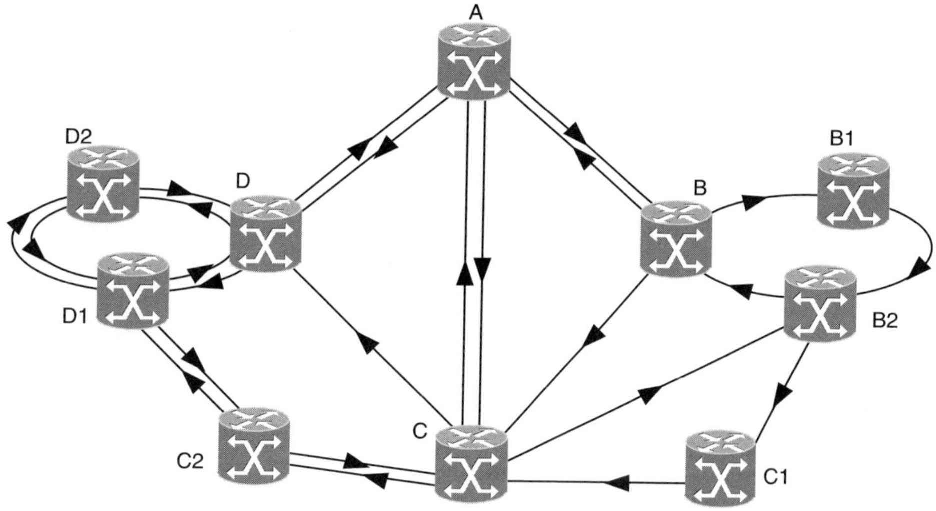

Figure 2.9 A mesh network can be built from rings and point-to-point links.

2.4 Functional Components and Planes

It is often helpful to decompose network nodes into their functional components. This makes it possible to build a more coherent architectural model, but also makes it easy to understand the roles that particular network nodes play and how they communicate. For example, one functional component might have the responsibility for managing network nodes, and another might provide the management support within a network device such as a router. These components would possibly be positioned at remote sites within the network (the Network Management Station and the router itself) and communicate with each other across the network.

When a network is seen partitioned into these functional components, messages and information move around the network between components with the same, or related, functional responsibilities. The example of communications between management components cited in the previous paragraph is one illustration. Similarly, the data-switching components of network nodes process data and distribute it among themselves. If we follow up this idea, we see that the network may be sliced into sets of functional components that communicate with each other and all of which have related responsibilities. These slices are called *planes*. Communication between planes takes place only within a network node; communications between network nodes take place only within a plane. For example, the management component on one node does not talk to the data processing component on another node.

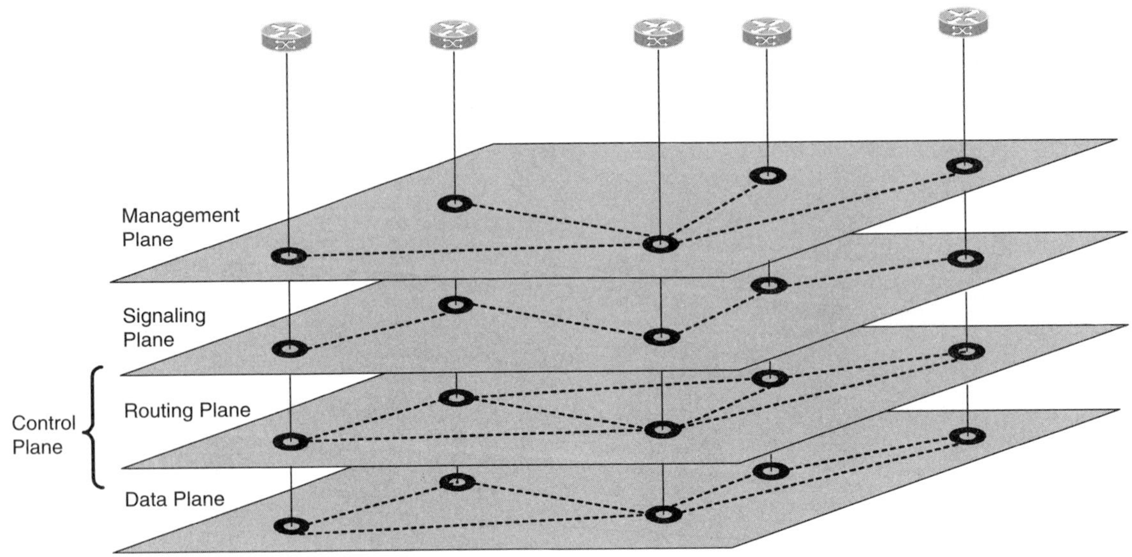

Figure 2.10 The network can be viewed based on the functional interactions between network nodes within a set of planes.

Figure 2.10 shows a simple network divided into the four planes that are usually discussed. Data is moved between devices within the *data plane*, so the connectivity in this plane is a direct representation of the physical data links in the network. The *management plane* is responsible for all management activity, such as configuration requests, statistics gathering, diagnostics, and so forth. Management is discussed in Chapters 14 and 15. The *signaling plane* and the *routing plane* are sometimes grouped together and referred to as the *control plane*. The routing protocols that dynamically distribute connectivity and reachability information, and the TE resource attributes, operate in the routing plane, whereas the signaling plane is where protocols responsible for the dynamic establishment of data plane paths exist. Grouped together as the control plane, they provide the home of all of the GMPLS protocols discussed in this book.

Just to add a little confusion, the data plane is also sometimes referred to as the *user plane* (because it carries user traffic) or the *transport plane*. Also, some people like to add another plane to their view of the network: The *application plane* facilitates communication between applications, but because application interactions tend to be end-to-end across the network, there is not a lot of value to adding this to the picture.

Figure 2.10 illustrates how a set of five network nodes may be connected together in different ways in each plane. The vertical lines represent the presence of each network node across all of the planes. The dotted lines represent the communication relationships within each plane. In the data plane, the communication paths map to the actual physical connections in the network, but in the other planes the communications use *logical connections* to form associations between the network nodes. In the example, the management relationship is shown rather simplistically with a single management controller, the routing relationship is shown as a mesh, and the signaling relationship is shown as linear. Exchanges between the planes take place along the vertical nodes, that is, at the network nodes. For example, a management request may be sent from a management station to an MPLS router through the management plane; at the router it is converted to a signaling request that is sent hop by hop through the network in the signaling plane; at each hop in the network the MPLS router programs the data plane; and the end result is a data path through the data plane on which data can be sent.

As already stated, the GMPLS protocol family operates within the control plane. Thus, most of the rest of this book is focused on the function of the control plane. However, the interactions with the data and management planes are also of fundamental importance to the way in which GMPLS works.

2.5 Further Reading

Recommendations from the ITU can be purchased from http://www.itu.int. Recommendations relevant to the discussion of transport networks are as follows:

G.805: Generic functional architecture of transport networks.

G.806: Characteristics of transport equipment — description methodology and generic functionality.

X.200: Data networks and open systems communications: open systems interconnection — model and notation.

The SONET standard for TDM is defined by ANSI in a range of standards that can be found at http://www.ansi.org. The best starting point for a general description is: T1.105: SONET.

The SDH standard for TDM is defined by the ITU in a range of Recommendations available from http://www.itu.int. A good starting point is provided by the following Recommendations.

G.872: Types and characteristics of Synchronous Digital Hierarchy (SDH) Equipment.

G.873: Characteristics of Synchronous Digital Hierarchy (SDH) Functional Blocks.

G.803: Architecture of Transport Networks Based on the Synchronous Digital Hierarchy.

CHAPTER 3

From MPLS to GMPLS

Multiprotocol Label Switching (MPLS), as described in Chapter 1, is concerned with data forwarding in packet, frame, and cell networks. Chapter 2 introduced the different transport networks that are deployed or under development. Generalized MPLS (GMPLS) is concerned with merging the two concepts so that a uniform control plane can be applied to any transport technology.

Traditionally, network elements of transport networks were provisioned via manual planning and configuration. It could take days (if not weeks) to add a new service and have it operate properly because careful network planning was required, and because network downtime might be needed to reposition other services. Removing services was also slow and painful because any mistakes could affect other services. It is obvious that the larger and more sophisticated transport networks become, the more demand there will be for dynamic provisioning using some sort of control plane and, as a consequence, for traffic engineering.

This chapter examines how GMPLS came about and how the concepts of MPLS can be applied to transport networks that use non-packet technologies. The consequent changes to the MPLS signaling and routing protocols are described in Chapters 4 and 5, whereas Chapter 6 discusses the Link Management Protocol that is added to the protocol family in order to support link discovery and verification in GMPLS networks.

3.1 The Origins of GMPLS

As interest grew in offering a control plane solution to provisioning in transport networks, one option was to develop a new set of protocols from scratch for all types of transport networks: one for WDM networks, one for TDM networks, and so forth. The obvious advantage of such an approach would be that each control plane could be designed to be very efficient for the target network. For example, a control plane designed for photonic networks could have built-in mechanisms to take care of optical impairments and wavelength continuity constraints, whereas one designed for TDM networks could take advantage of the SDH overhead bits for signaling.

The obvious disadvantage to individual, specifically tailored control planes is the enormous amount of effort needed to develop the many new sets of signaling, routing, and traffic engineering protocols and applications. Another disadvantage is the fact that services have a tendency to span networks of different types: Some segments are built from IP routers and Layer 2 switches, others from SONET/SDH switches, while the core network could interconnect optical add-drop multiplexers and cross-connects. End-to-end provisioning on such heterogeneous networks, each with its own separate control plane, would be a formidable task.

3.1.1 *Lambda Switching*

With the rapid rise in popularity of WDM networks at the end of the 1990s, vendors and Service Providers started to search for an intelligent control plane that could simplify provisioning, reduce operational expenditure, and offer the ability to provide new services. It was noticed that the basic switching operation in a WDM network was logically very similar to that in an MPLS device. That is, a switch was required to convert an input wavelength on an incoming interface to an output wavelength on an outgoing interface in an operation so similar to the MPLS mapping of {input label, incoming interface} to {output label, outgoing interface} that it made obvious sense to attempt to reuse MPLS signaling techniques. From this initial observation, Multiprotocol Lambda Switching (MPLambdaS or MPλS) was born.

The initial MPλS protocol specifications borrowed heavily from the MPLS signaling and routing protocols. They worked on the basic assumption that, although the LFIB was logically embedded in a physical switching device (such as a set of mirrors in a MEMS), the cross-connect operations in the switch were identical to those in an LFIB. The MPλS protocols needed to install mappings of {incoming lambda, incoming interface} to {outgoing lambda, outgoing interface}.

3.1.2 *Generalizing the Technology*

It wasn't long before other optical switching technologies were put forward as candidates for a similar control plane. What about fiber or port switches? Could they use techniques like MPLambdaS? How about TDM networks? Isn't a device that switches timeslots doing exactly the same type of functional operation?

Fortunately, the techniques and procedures of MPLS represented a proven technology with similar switching notions that work on heterogeneous networks and solve the traffic engineering issues that need to be addressed for all types of transport networks. So the MPLambdaS work was broadened to cover not just lambda switching, but also fiber switching, TDM, layer 2 switching, and the existing packet/frame/cell switching technologies. The concepts were truly generalized, and the work was named Generalized MPLS.

But are all of the concepts of MPLS applicable? Not completely. Some MPLS techniques were focused on establishing LSPs that matched the IP routing tables; these functions (such as that provided by the LDP signaling protocol) are not applicable to non-packet transport networks. Transport networks are more concerned with the provisioning of end-to-end connections or circuits. The MPLS protocols on which GMPLS is built were designed and implemented to apply traffic engineering to MPLS networks. Traffic engineering (described more fully in Chapter 8) is the process of placing traffic on selected, pre-computed paths within the network in order to maximize revenues from the available resources. In practical terms, this means routing traffic away from congested "hot spots," picking links that provide the desired quality of service or satisfy other application constraints, or directing data so that it utilizes underused links. But these are all packet-based, statistical concepts. Can they also apply to transport networks or should GMPLS be limited to simple control operations? Is the requirement for a rapid provisioning system that offloads some of the burden of operator function, or can we take advantage of the capabilities of the MPLS traffic engineering protocols and place intelligence within the network?

It turns out that traffic engineering has its place in a transport network. This certainly isn't every Service Provider's cup of tea. Many take the view that, although signaling and network discovery are valuable control plane tools, there is no way that they want to allow the network to make decisions about the placement of services, no matter how clever the software. Still others prefer to limit their view of GMPLS to an operator aid — a process that allows the network manager to provision services rapidly, monitor their status, and tear them down in a coordinated way. These uses of GMPLS are sufficient to make OPEX savings and get better leverage of existing equipment, but other Service Providers are enthusiastic to embrace the possibilities of a fully functional GMPLS control plane that will discover resources, advertise their availability and usage, compute paths for complex services such as path protection, and install trails to support the services.

In general, many or most of the techniques in MPLS traffic engineering are applicable to the generalized problem of the control of an arbitrary transport network. So why not just adopt the MPLS control plane and make it work on transport networks? After all, if it can handle ATM switches, why wouldn't it work, say, for digital cross-connects?

3.2 Basic GMPLS Requirements

In order to understand the way that GMPLS protocols and concepts were developed out of MPLS, it is necessary to examine some of the basic requirements of a transport network. How do the connections in a transport network differ from those in an MPLS TE packet network? The answer to this question will lead us into Chapters 4 and 5, which describe the GMPLS signaling and routing protocols.

3.2.1 *What is a Label?*

In MPLS a label is an arbitrary tag for a data packet that is used as an index into the LFIB. MPLS labels and resources are not tightly coupled. As often as not, resource management in MPLS is purely statistical, such that the available bandwidth on an interface is only logically divided up between the LSPs that use the interface. In this case the label will indicate the amount of resources statistically reserved, but does not identify any specific physical resources. Reservations represent a percentage of the available resources (for example, bandwidth), but no resources (such as buffers) are actually dedicated to supporting the flow, and the total resource reservation may actually be allowed to exceed the available bandwidth to allow for the fact that it is unlikely that all flows will be at their maximum capacity at the same time.

Where real resource reservations are used, the label on a data packet may still not identify specific physical resources. For example, network resources in MPLS may be a set of buffers used to receive data for a particular LSP from the wire and to forward it through the switch. But the resource reservation may be made from a pool of buffers that is shared between multiple LSPs — that is, no buffer is specifically allocated to one LSP, but the total number of buffers allocated for LSPs defines the size of the pool. On the other hand, an LSP may have specific resources (buffers or queues) dedicated to it, and in this case the label is more closely tied to the resources, because it identifies exactly which resources may be used for the LSP. Should an LSR decide to share resources between two LSPs, it may allocate two separate labels and map them to the same set of resources.

In transport networks the physical resources are exactly the switchable quantities. That is, in a WDM network the lambdas are switched, in a TDM network the timeslots are switched, and so forth. Thus a label that identifies a switchable data stream in GMPLS also precisely identifies a physical resource. So in a lambda switching network a label identifies a specific wavelength, in a TDM network a label identifies a specific timeslot, and in a fiber switching network a label identifies a specific port or fiber. This fact brings challenges that are not found in packet switching environments. One implication, for example, is that labels come from a disjoint set (for example, identifying the frequencies of the lambdas) rather than being arbitrary integers. Similarly, the set of valid labels is likely to be much smaller in a transport switch. Further, the interpretation of a label must be carefully understood — no longer is this an arbitrary tag, but it identifies a specific resource, and both ends of a link must have the same understanding of which resource is in use.

In GMPLS the meaning of a label is private between two adjacent LSRs, but they must have the same understanding of that meaning. TDM labels are given a special encoding so that the referenced timeslot may be deduced, but for lambda and fiber switching the meaning of the label is left as a matter for configuration or negotiation through the Link Management Protocol described in Chapter 6.

3.2.2 *Switching Types*

The switching type of a network node defines the data units that the device can manage and switch — that is, the level to which it can demultiplex the data signal from an incoming interface, switch it, and send it out of another interface. For example, MPLS routers are *packet switch capable* (*PSC*) — they can receive data on an interface (which may be an Ethernet port, a SONET port, and so forth), identify the packets in the data stream, and switch each packet separately. A photonic cross-connect is *lambda switch capable* (*LSC*) and can demultiplex individual lambdas from a single fiber before switching each lambda in a different direction. A *time division multiplex capable* (*TDM*) switch is able to recognize individual timeslots within a lambda.

Note that the grade of data signal that a switch can identify is not the same as the granularity of bandwidth that the switch can process. A lambda switch may deal in lambdas that carry 2.5, 5, or 10 Gbps signals, and if it is a photonic cross-connect it is very probably unaware of the different bandwidths. A TDM switch that can process VC-192 signals may be handling greater units of bandwidth than some lambda switches, even though it is switching a finer grade of data signal. In fact, we should really describe the switching capabilities of interfaces rather than switches, because a single network device may support a variety of interfaces with different switching capabilities, and because some devices may be capable of discriminating the signal at different levels (for example, lambda and TDM) on the same interface.

GMPLS recognizes a list of switching types that is consistent with the quantities that may be labeled (see Table 3.1). There is an obvious logic to this because it is precisely those things which can be switched that must be labeled.

3.2.3 *What is a Label Switched Path?*

Now that we have defined the switchable and labeled quantities in GMPLS, we need to decide what we mean by a Label Switched Path (LSP). In any transport network,

Table 3.1 The GMPLS switching types

Packet (switching based on MPLS shim header)
Layer 2 (switching based on layer 2 header such as ATM VPI/VCI)
Timeslot (TDM)
Lambda
Waveband (contiguous collection of lambdas)
Fiber (or port)

regardless of the switching type, we are concerned with the establishment of connections that carry data between two specific end points. This connection is sometimes called a circuit or a trail, and the end points are not necessarily the points of delivery of the service, but may be intermediate switches that need to be connected in order to help facilitate the provision of the service.

At each switch along the connection or trail, resources are *cross-connected*. That is, the switch is programmed to take traffic from an incoming resource and send it to an outgoing resource (recall that a resource may be a timeslot, lambda, and so forth, on a specific interface). Because these resources are associated directly with labels, we are able to define an LSP as a contiguous series of cross-connected resources capable of delivering traffic.

In the data plane this gives us a trail of {interface, label, cross-connect} triplets (where a label is synonymous with a resource). Note that the LSP is not a service, but supports a service by providing full or partial connectivity.

The term *label switched path* is also meaningfully applied in the control or management plane to describe the state (that is control blocks, memory, and so forth) that is used to manage the LSP within the data plane. Thus, if the data plane is programmed manually, there is a record of the LSP within the management plane, whereas if the LSP is established through the exchange of control plane signaling messages, there is LSP state in the control plane.

3.2.4 *What is Bandwidth?*

In MPLS, bandwidth — specifically bandwidth requested for an LSP — can be measured down to the finest granularity in bytes per second. The available bandwidth on a link may be divided up in any way between the LSPs that use the link. In GMPLS transport networks, because an LSP is directly related to a physical and switchable resource, the bandwidth can only be divided up according to the capabilities of the switching device — this typically forces the bandwidth division to be in large units of bytes per second. For instance, if a service over a wavelength switching network requires bandwidth of, say, 10 Kbps, then 2.5, 10, or 40 Gbps (depending on the capacity of one lambda channel) will be allocated on every link of the service path. This means that only a fraction of the allocated bandwidth will actually be used, which is clearly very wasteful.

On the other hand, in a GMPLS transport network there is no danger that a traffic flow will violate the user-network agreement and consume more than the allotted bandwidth that was allocated during service setup. This problem can easily occur in a packet network, especially if only statistical admission control is applied, but the limits of the physical resources in a transport network mean that it is absolutely impossible to over-consume bandwidth.

Various advanced techniques (such as the use of hierarchical LSPs and Forwarding Adjacencies described in Chapter 8) have been developed to help GMPLS make optimal use of bandwidth where the service needs to use only a small proportion of the available resources. This is easier in some technologies than in others because, for example, TDM readily supports the aggregation of multiple small data flows into one larger flow.

3.2.5 *Bidirectionality of Transport Connections*

MPLS LSPs are unidirectional — that is, they provide connectivity for unidirectional transfer of data within the network. Services offered by transport network Service Providers are almost always bidirectional, offering equal connectivity and data transfer capabilities in both directions. Further, there is often a requirement for the connectivity in each direction to share common links (such as fiber pairs) to provide *fate sharing*. It is possible, of course, to construct bidirectional connectivity from a pair of unidirectional LSPs that have the same end points and run in opposite directions. However, there are numerous advantages to having a single signaling exchange establish a bidirectional LSP and a single control plane state managing both directions instead of having two unidirectional LSPs. For example, from the fate sharing and recovery point of view it is advantageous that if one direction becomes inoperable, resources associated with the other direction are immediately released. Resource contention, which may happen when two bidirectional tunnels are established simultaneously from both directions under conditions of limited link label spaces — the usual case on transport networks — can be resolved in a simple way if resources for both directions are allocated simultaneously. Besides, a single bidirectional LSP requires only one control plane state on each node, and hence consumes half as much memory as two unidirectional LSPs. It can also be set up more smoothly, quickly, and with less processing because it needs only one set of control plane messages to be exchanged.

3.2.6 Separation of Control and Data Planes

In a packet switching environment, control plane messages can be delivered through the same links as the data packets. Thus, control and data channels can be considered coincident. This is not the case for transport networks. One of the reasons why transport network nodes can forward large volumes of data with such great speed is that the nodes switch entire timeslots, wavelengths, bands of wavelengths, or entire fibers without recognizing individual packets. This feature means that control plane messages cannot be delivered through the same channels as the data traffic.

In some cases one "data" channel on every link is dedicated for control traffic delivery — for example, a lambda on a WDM link, or a timeslot on a TDM link (the in-fiber-out-of-band model). In other cases, control traffic uses separate links or even separate networks (out-of-fiber-out-of-band model). It is not unusual for a control message to pass through several controllers before it reaches its destination — the controller that controls the next data switch on the LSP. There are also configurations where a separate single broadcast network interconnects all controllers so that each of them is only one hop away from any other.

The separation of control and data plane channels brings a lot of complications and challenges for the GMPLS protocols. For example, identification of data links is no longer implicit in the signaling message, but must be made explicit. Similarly, additional control plane techniques are needed to verify the connectivity and aliveness of data plane links, because the successful delivery of signaling messages can no longer be used. Further, mechanisms need to be added to the signaling protocols to allow the management of data plane failures. For example, if some controller is notified by a data plane hardware component about a failure, it should be able to send an appropriate notification to a node that is responsible for service recovery. It also should be possible to set up and shut down services in an alarm-free manner, so that no false alarms are raised.

The corollary of control and data plane separation is that failures on one or more controllers or control plane connections do not necessarily mean that there is any problem delivering data traffic. In fact, data services, albeit only partially controlled, can continue to function properly indefinitely. New features are needed in the signaling mechanisms so that the control plane can recover from failures and re-assume control of existing data services.

3.2.7 Tunneling and Hierarchies

LSP tunneling using hierarchical LSPs is an MPLS concept supported by label stacking. But label stacks are only efficacious where shim headers are used to

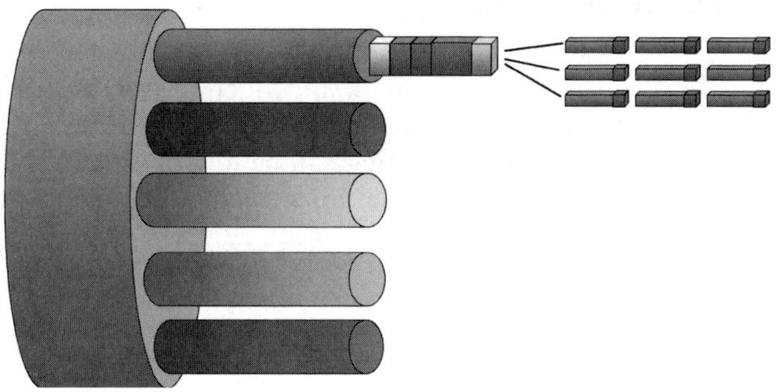

Figure 3.1 The hierarchy of switching types.

encode the labels. That is, they can only be used in packet, cell, or frame networks. In non-packet environments, where the label is implicit and directly associated with a physical resource, it is not possible to produce a label stack. Consider, for example, a lambda network: Although it is conceptually possible to encapsulate the signal from one lambda LSP into another lambda LSP, this encapsulation can only be done on a one-for-one basis, and it is impossible to determine the correct lambda to use for the encapsulated LSP when it emerges from the far end of the tunnel. There is no mechanism to encode this information with the data.

However, the concept of hierarchical LSPs does have a different meaning in GMPLS. Because we are now dealing with a variety of switching types (packet, TDM, lambda, and so forth), we can observe that there is a natural hierarchy of switching based on the granularity. LSPs may be nested according to this hierarchy just as the physical resources are nested. So, as shown in Figure 3.1, lambdas may be nested within a fiber, timeslots within a lambda, and packets within a timeslot. This form of LSP hierarchy allows for aggregation of tunnels offering more scalable traffic engineering, and more efficient use of bandwidth in core transport networks, as well as facilitating the integration of different switching types to provide end-to-end connectivity.

Various techniques are needed in GMPLS signaling and routing to make hierarchical LSPs properly useful. These include the Hierarchical LSP (H-LSP), where an LSP tunnel is presented as offering point-to-point connectivity across the network so that LSPs may be routed through the tunnel; non-adjacent signaling that allows control messages to be exchanged between the ends of a tunnel; and LSP stitching, which brings the concepts of the H-LSP into the single switching-type network. All of these techniques are discussed further in Chapter 8.

3.3 Further Reading

This chapter has provided an introduction to GMPLS and leads into the next three chapters, which describe the detailed foundations of GMPLS. Additional, more substantial reading can be found at the end of each of those chapters. At this point the only additional reading recommended is:

RFC 3945 — Generalized Multi-Protocol Label Switching (GMPLS) Architecture

CHAPTER 4

GMPLS Signaling

This chapter introduces GMPLS signaling. It explains the role of signaling within a GMPLS network and defines the signaling protocol that is used to exchange messages within the control plane in order to establish LSPs within the data plane.

This chapter provides detailed coverage of GMPLS signaling concepts and interfaces, as well as the basic signaling protocol (RSVP-TE, borrowed from MPLS), and how it was extended to satisfy the needs of GMPLS.

4.1 Introduction to Signaling

Signaling is the process of exchanging messages within the control plane to set up, maintain, modify, and terminate data paths in the data plane. In the GMPLS context, these data paths are LSPs. The collection of signaling messages and processing rules is known as the *signaling protocol.*

Signaling messages are exchanged between software components called *signaling controllers* throughout the network. Each signaling controller is responsible for managing the data plane components of one or more data switches. In GMPLS the data switches are called *Label Switching Routers (LSRs)* and it is usual for the signaling controller to be present on the LSR so that the whole forms a single unit within the network. However, the GMPLS architecture supports two divergences from this collocation: First, the signaling controller may be physically diverse from the data switch, with a management or control protocol used to communicate between the two; secondly, a single signaling controller may manage more than one data switch. These possibilities are shown in Figure 4.1.

Signaling controllers communicate with their neighboring signaling controllers through *control channels* in the control plane. A control channel is a link, which may be physical or logical, between signaling controllers responsible for data switches that are adjacent in the data plane. Signaling controllers that are linked

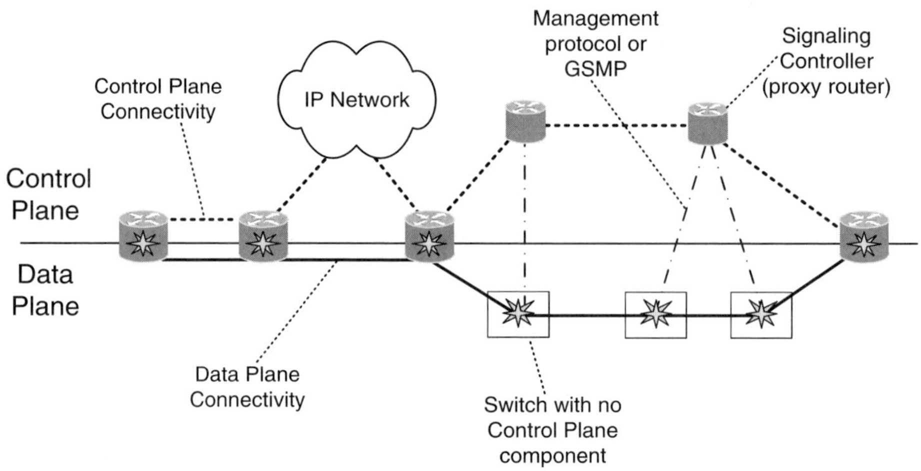

Figure 4.1 Possible configurations of signaling controllers and data switches.

by a control channel are described as adjacent (even though they might not be physically adjacent) and, once they are communicating with each other using the signaling protocol, they have established a *signaling adjacency*.

Control channels may utilize the data links between a pair of LSRs. In this case the signaling messages are mixed in with the data, and the control channel is described as *in band*. This is the case, for example, in mixed IP and MPLS networks.

In optical networks it is unusual to mix the control and data traffic, because this would require that each data switch was able to examine the data stream and extract the signaling messages to deliver them to the signaling controller. This operation is unlikely as it requires expensive equipment that would not otherwise be needed, and might be impractical in many optical devices (such as photonic cross-connects). So the control channel messages must be carried some other way. One option is to utilize the overhead bytes available in some data encodings (such as TDM) and carry the signaling messages within the same fiber as the data signal. This technique is feasible, but may not deliver sufficient bandwidth for the signaling needs and may also clash with other uses of the overhead bytes.

A preferable mechanism for *in-fiber-out-of-band* control channel support is to dedicate a specific data channel for the signaling traffic. This may be a dedicated wavelength, or a specific timeslot, and is known as the *optical supervisory channel* (*OSC*). The OSC must be terminated at each switch and all of the traffic must be delivered to the signaling controller; this is feasible because the signaling messages are not mixed in with the data.

Alternatively, the control channel connectivity may be provided by a diverse physical connection (for example, a copper Ethernet link) that runs parallel to the data link being managed. In fact, such an *out-of-fiber-out-of-band* control channel can utilize a physical connection that follows a completely different physical path from the data path, and may be routed through a completely separate network.

These different control channel mechanisms can be mixed, and offer GMPLS considerable flexibility and resilience. Two great benefits of the out-of-band control channel are that a single control channel may be used to manage more than one parallel data channel, and that the control channel can be protected against individual link failures within the control plane.

4.1.1 *Addressing*

A core requirement of signaling is that it can identify the links and nodes that are to be used by the LSP that is to be established within the data plane. This means that the data plane links and nodes must be given unique identifiers. At the same time, the signaling messages must be delivered to the correct signaling controllers within the control plane. This means that the signaling controllers must also be given identifiers, and that these must be routable within the control plane.

Because the GMPLS protocols were developed by the IETF, their focus is on the use of IP addresses. These are used as identifiers within the control and data planes. The separation of data and control channels described in the previous section indicates that there should be a separation in the addressing used within the data and control planes. This is both feasible and desirable.

Within the control plane, the purpose of addressing is to ensure that signaling messages can be successfully delivered to the correct signaling controller. This is easily achieved using the normal IP addressing and routing mechanisms that are well understood. The control plane, then, is an IP network.

The control plane in MPLS was *in-band*, meaning that the control (that is, signaling) traffic was mixed with the data. In this mode of operation, it is easy for the control plane to indicate which data link it is referring to — the link used by the control message *is* the link over which data traffic will be sent. However, with the separation of control and data planes in GMPLS networks, such an assumption is no longer valid, and transport links and nodes must be given their own identifiers. Because GMPLS is rooted in the Internet, the protocols assume that IP addresses will be used as identifiers in the data plane. But it must be clearly understood that the address space used within the data plane is distinct from that used in the control plane — the two may overlap or be disjoint. In fact, the addresses used in the data plane are really just unique identifiers and nothing can be deduced or assumed from the values that are assigned — subnetting rules are often used for data plane identifiers (for example, to identify the two ends of a data plane link), but these are a convenience, not a requirement.

All of this means that a signaling message must carry two sets of addressing information. The first concerns the delivery of the message within the control plane (where is it from? where is it going?), and the second defines the route of the LSP within the data plane (which links and nodes should it traverse?).

Further discussion of addressing within a GMPLS network can be found in Chapter 5.

4.2 Basic GMPLS Signaling

The previous section discussed the basic principles and units of signaling in GMPLS. It should be observed that there were originally two signaling protocols specified for GMPLS networks — RSVP-TE and CR-LDP (Constraint-based Routed Label Distribution Protocol). Work on the latter has been halted by the IETF because it is generally recognized that only a single signaling protocol is necessary (see RFC 3468 for more details).

The remainder of this chapter, therefore, concentrates only on the messages and features of RSVP-TE. However, in recognition of the fact that GMPLS is bigger than the signaling protocol that happens to be in use (and that other protocols, such as extensions to ATM's PNNI, might also be suitable as GMPLS signaling protocols), this section, and the remainder of the book, makes heavy use of abstract signaling messages.

4.2.1 *Sessions, Tunnels, and LSPs*

In RSVP, a *session* is the grouping of traffic flows to a particular destination. The session is identified by an IP address (IPv4 or IPv6) of the destination and a port identifier at which to deliver the data at the destination. The important feature of a session is that all traffic flows that share the session can share resources within the network. Thus, it makes sense to allow multiple sources to initiate traffic flows that form part of the same session where it is meaningful to the application — for example, in voice conferencing.

RSVP-TE introduced the concept of an *MPLS Tunnel*. An MPLS tunnel, like a road tunnel, has an entrance and an exit: Except in disastrous cases, the entrance to the tunnel defines the exit, and insertion of data into the tunnel guarantees its delivery to the exit point. In traffic engineering, the tunnel provides a basic building block, because applications are interested only in the delivery of data from here to there, and can leave it to the network to determine how to support the tunnel with the resources that are available. RSVP-TE identifies the MPLS tunnel by reusing the concept of the session: Each tunnel is known by its destination and a 16-bit Tunnel Identifier (replacing the port ID), which distinguishes multiple tunnels that run to the same destination. Additionally, it is recognized that tunnels may want to allow resource sharing with traffic flows from many sources, or may want to keep the flows separate. This is achieved by introducing a third identifier, called the Extended Tunnel Identifier, which can be set to a unique value by a source — the source usually uses one of its IP addresses for this purpose.

The three elements that identify the session are combined within a single RSVP-TE protocol object, the Session object, and the inclusion of this object on an RSVP-TE message indicates to which session it applies.

In GMPLS the focus is on delivering an end-to-end service, which may be considered as a tunnel. But a session is not enough to deliver the data: We need LSPs to transfer the data. Each service is supported by one or more LSPs. LSPs themselves have the properties of tunnels (that is, by labeling the data and sending it out of a specific interface on the source node, we have selected an LSP, and consequently the destination) and are sometimes referred to as *LSP Tunnels*. In order to avoid confusion in this book, we shall retain the term "tunnel" to apply to a service, and simply use "LSP" to indicate an LSP. Because of the tunnel-like properties of an LSP, the data source is known as the *ingress* and the destination is called the *egress*.

A service may actually be supported by more than one LSP. This can be done for load sharing, bandwidth aggregation, protection, and so forth, as described in the later chapters of this book. Such LSPs are usually described as *parallel*, not because they are strictly parallel within the network, but because they connect the same source and destination pair in support of a single service.

Each LSP is identified as part of a session by the use of the Session object, and in GMPLS the concept of a session is reduced to a signaling construct that allows LSPs from the same session to share resources — a fact that is useful for make-before-break modification of LSPs as described in Section 4.3.8. The LSPs that support an individual service may be part of the same session or may belong to different sessions. The LSP must also be identified in its own right within the session. To do this, RSVP-TE (LSPs do not exist in RSVP) uses an IP address of the sender (IPv4 or IPv6) and a 16-bit LSP ID that is unique within the context of the sender address. Note that the use of a sender address means that we are dealing with point-to-point LSPs because they are constrained by the destination address of the session and the source address of the LSP — point-to-multipoint tunnels and LSPs are discussed in Chapter 11.

The elements that are used to identify an LSP within the context of a session are collected together in the Sender-Template object. Inclusion of the Sender-Template object in an RSVP-TE message restricts the meaning of the message to the specific LSP.

GMPLS inherits the Session and Sender-Template objects from RSVP-TE without any change. Thus, the identification of sessions and LSPs within GMPLS is unchanged from MPLS-TE.

Recall (from Chapter 3) that an LSP is a concept in both the control and data planes. In the data plane an LSP is a strict forwarding path defined by mappings of {incoming interface, incoming label} to {outgoing interface, outgoing label}. The data plane LSP may be established through signaling or through management action (configuration of the switch), or may even be a physically invariable path established through fibering or wiring. Within the control plane, an LSP is really the state established by the signaling protocol for the management of the data plane LSP; that is, the data plane LSP is established and maintained by the control plane messages. Nevertheless, it is a useful shorthand to refer to the control plane state that maintains the data plane LSP as "the LSP."

4.2.2 *LSP Routes*

An LSP is a path through the network formed of cross-connected labels (resources) on a series of data plane links. The route that the LSP uses can be selected in three ways depending on the requirements of the application that is establishing the LSP, and the capabilities of the network. The computation of routes for LSPs is heavily dependent on the information distributed by the routing protocols as described in the next chapter.

- The route can be left completely open for the network to select. In this case, the application (or operator) that requests the LSP simply specifies the destination, and the route is selected on a hop-by-hop basis as the signaling messages are routed across the network. At each LSR the best data plane next hop toward the destination is chosen, and the messages are forwarded accordingly. Note that this technique does not use the routing table (this is not IP routing), but utilizes the Traffic Engineering Database (TED) that contains information specific to the data plane.
- The route of the LSP may be completely specified by the application or operator. If the operator knows the state of the network and wishes to place an LSP along a specific path using certain resources, he can supply an *explicit path* to the control plane (which may check the validity of the supplied path). The signaling messages will attempt to install the LSP along this route.
- Alternatively, the operator or application may leave the selection of the route to the control plane, but request that an end-to-end path be computed that satisfies a set of constraints. *Constraint-based path computation* (such as CSPF) is discussed at length in Chapter 10, and forms a crucial part of a GMPLS system. In essence, the control plane selects a route for an LSP through the network, taking account of a set of requirements such as bandwidth, service type, and specific links and LSRs that should be included on the path (that is, a partial route). The control plane is supplied with these constraints and

performs the computation. Note that there is only a small semantic difference between a path that is computed off-line and supplied to the control plane, and a path that is computed by the control plane on demand. However, the later a path computation is performed, the more chance there is of it being based on up-to-date information.

Because the control plane may be supplied with an explicit path or with a list of LSRs to include on the path, there has to be a way to distinguish between a sequence of hops that must be traversed without intervening LSRs (*strict hops*), and a series of LSRs that must be traversed in the specified order, but which can have intervening hops if the computation generates them (*loose hops*). This is achieved by flagging each hop in the explicit path as either strict or loose.

The route of an LSP is part of the information that must be signaled when the LSP is established. The route is encoded in the Explicit Route object (ERO) as a series of hop sub-objects. Each sub-object encodes an IP address of an LSR or an interface, and can be marked as loose or strict. Note that the addresses used are data plane addresses. That is, the separation of control plane and data plane addressing is maintained.

Note that an ERO that specifies links could include incoming or outgoing interfaces at each hop. That is, the sub-object of an ERO could specify the address of the interface through which the data should arrive at an LSR, or the address of the interface out of which the data should be sent from the LSR. Both techniques are useful: the former because it identifies from within the ERO which data link is used for the incoming data; the latter because it saves an LSR from having to work out which data link to use to reach the next LSR along the route of the LSP. In practice there is no consistent approach to the use of interface addresses in EROs. Some implementations use only outgoing interfaces, some use only incoming interfaces, some use interface addresses and LSR identifiers, and some use incoming and outgoing addresses. Nothing can be assumed.

The ERO may also contain non-specific hops. These may be expressed as IP prefixes (allowing the choice of a range of addresses), or Autonomous System (AS) numbers (letting the route find its way through a distinct domain). Such non-specific hops may be marked loose or strict according to whether they must be reached directly or may be arrived at indirectly from the previous hop, and multiple nodes within the non-specific hop may be used before the next hop is used regardless of whether the next hop is strict or loose.

In practice, the network tends to be divided into *computation domains*. If the operator or application does not supply a full explicit path to the destination, then the first LSR in the computation domain will compute a full path to the end of the domain (which might be the egress of the LSP). This means that it is highly unusual to see LSPs signaled with no explicit route, and where loose hops are used it is usually to identify a sequence of computation domains (perhaps by specifying the address of the entry point into each domain).

Given the way that the route of an LSP may be only partially specified, it is useful to have the control plane record and report the actual route of the LSP. This can also be checked against the route that was requested, to ensure that the path is satisfactory. GMPLS uses the Recorded Route object (RRO) to capture this information and report it on signaling messages. The data plane addresses of the interfaces and LSRs traversed by the LSP are encoded in the RRO just as they would be for an ERO (except that the loose hop flag is not used in an RRO), and this feature may be used to convert a partial route into a strict explicit route simply by taking the RRO and using it as an ERO.

Route recording is under the control of the ingress LSR. If it wants to know the route of an LSP it adds an RRO to the signaling messages that it sends, and all other LSRs along the LSP are obliged to add their information to the object so that when it is returned to the ingress on other messages it describes the full route of the LSP.

4.2.3 *Labels and Resources*

The essence of LSP setup using a control plane is the exchange of labels. An LSR must know how to label the data when it sends it toward its downstream neighbor for that LSR to know on which LSP the data is flowing. The label distribution mode for GMPLS unidirectional LSPs is *downstream on demand.* That is, the upstream LSR signals that it wishes to establish an LSP to the destination specified in the Session object, and the downstream LSR responds by saying which label should be used to carry the data if the LSP is successfully established.

In non-packet networks, labels are directly associated with resources, as discussed in Chapter 3. This means that when a label is assigned, it is not simply an arbitrary tag that identifies the LSP in the data plane, but it is also a physical resource in the hardware, such as a timeslot, a wavelength, or a whole fiber. It is important, therefore, that the control plane should communicate what sort of LSP is required, what resources should be allocated, and therefore what type of label to use.

In GMPLS, the label is requested using the Generalized Label Request object. This allows the ingress to specify three parameters to the LSP.

- The LSP Encoding Type indicates the way data will be packaged within the LSP. Values include Packet, Ethernet, SONET/SDH, Digital Wrapper, and Lambda.
- The Generalized PID (G-PID) identifies the use to which the LSP will be put — that is, the payload. In general, the G-PID is of use only to the egress LSR and allows it to know whether it can successfully terminate the LSP;

in other words, whether it will be able to process the signal that it receives. The G-PID is based on the standard Ethertypes, but the set of acceptable values is extended considerably to handle non-packet payloads such as all of the different SONET and SDH encodings.

- The Switching Type governs the type of label that is allocated. The field indicates what type of switching should be performed on the LSP when the data is received by the downstream LSR. This information can often be deduced from the link that carries the LSP, because many devices can only handle one switching type, but it is important for more sophisticated LSRs that can perform different switching on a signal received on one of their interfaces. Values for this field are the same as the basic GMPLS switching types: Packet-Switch Capable (PSC), Layer-2 Switch Capable (L2SC), Time-Division-Multiplex Capable (TDM), Lambda-Switch Capable (LSC), or Fiber-Switch Capable (FSC).

The downstream LSR allocates a label according to the available resources and the switching type. It needs to inform the upstream LSR of this label choice, and it does so by sending the selected label back in a Generalized Label object. This object is simply an unformatted sequence of bits that encodes the label, and no label type is sent with the label because it is assumed that the context of the Generalized Label Request will identify the use to which the label is to be put. Most labels (packet, lambda, fiber) are encoded simply within a 32-bit field; the packet label uses the low-order 20 bits, and other labels are specific to the local context, usually giving a number that identifies the port or wavelength to use. But consider that two interoperating switches may not use the same identifiers for wavelengths, and certainly will assign different port numbers for the fibers that attach them. For this reason a specific rule is stated that lambda and fiber labels are given in the context of the downstream (that is, advertising) LSR. The upstream LSR must map these labels to identify the real resources to use, either through configuration or through information discovered by the Link Management Protocol described in Chapter 6.

TDM labels are slightly different because the hardware needs to agree on a range of parameters in order to correctly encode the signal. Five separate fields (identified by the letters S, U, K, L, and M) are packed into 32 bits of generalized label to indicate the SONET or SDH hierarchy of the switched component of the TDM signal.

In fact, the Generalized Label object is entirely arbitrary, and is defined as a length and an unformatted string. Its content is a local matter between neighboring LSPs and must be deduced from the context. This allows implementations to place any useful switching information within the Generalized Label object so long as they explain its interpretation to their neighbors. It also allows for multiple labels to be negotiated and assigned to a single LSP so that, for example, multiplexing or virtual concatenation in TDM can be expressed by the presence of more than one TDM label within the Generalized Label object, and the data for the LSP can be split between the specified timeslots. The same technique can be applied to G.709 encapsulation.

SONET/SDH aficionados will observe that the information in a Generalized Label is not enough to allow the correct interpretation of a TDM label and consequent encoding of a TDM signal. Similarly, for other LSPs, we need to know what data rate to use and how much physical resource to reserve to support the LSP. This remaining information comes from a knowledge of the traffic parameters requested when the LSP is set up. This is an important part of the description of the LSP because it defines the service that is to be supported.

RSVP-TE already includes a Sender-TSpec object that is used to encode the desired traffic parameters for a packet-based LSP. This concept is extended in GMPLS to include encodings for non-packet LSPs. The basic content remains unchanged for GMPLS packet LSPs; that is, the object may encode an IntServ traffic descriptor that may simply describe the bandwidth requirements, or may detail other Quality of Service parameters. In theory, traffic parameters are requested when an LSP is requested (using the Sender-TSpec object that represents a description of the planned traffic flow) and are confirmed when the LSP setup is confirmed (using a FlowSpec object representing a commitment to resource reservation that will support the traffic flow). In practice, most LSPs are requested just with a statement of the bandwidth, and this will not be varied when the LSP is established. This extends nicely to non-packet technologies where, in most cases, bandwidth is the only TSpec parameter that makes any sense. However, as observed above, for TDM LSPs the label needs additional context from the traffic parameters to give it meaning. The SONET/SDH traffic parameters are discussed along with the TDM label format in a dedicated RFC (RFC 3946) and include a type for the elementary signal (for example, STS-1), a request for contiguous concatenation, a count of contiguous concatenated components, a count of virtually concatenated components, a unit multiplier so that the LSP can be made up of multiple identical signals as described by the remainder of the traffic parameters, a type of transparency requested, and a profile type to describe additional capabilities such as monitoring that are required for the LSP.

4.3 LSP Establishment and Maintenance

The previous sections described the basic building blocks for GMPLS signaling. We can now look at how these are put together in order to set up, maintain, and tear down LSPs.

4.3.1 Basic Messages

GMPLS signaling is built on the messages defined for RSVP-TE, which are, themselves, derived from the RSVP specification. It is helpful to consider GMPLS signaling in terms of abstract messages and then to look at how these abstract messages map to RSVP-TE messages — this allows GMPLS as an architecture and a series of procedures to be fully open to the implementation of other signaling protocols even though RSVP-TE is currently the protocol of choice.

LSP establishment is initiated by the ingress LSR, which is located at the upstream end of the LSP. The LSP is requested using an *LSP Setup* message, and confirmed from the downstream LSR using an *LSP Accept* message. An LSP establishment may be confirmed using an *LSP Confirm* message. Errors may be discovered and propagated either downstream or upstream using *LSP Downstream Error* or *LSP Upstream Error* messages. An LSP may be released (torn down) either in the upstream direction or toward the downstream LSRs using *LSP Upstream Release* or *LSP Downstream Release* messages initiated by any LSR along the path of the LSP. Finally, information about the data plane status of an LSP may be propagated using an *LSP Notify* message. Table 4.1 shows how these abstract messages can be mapped to RSVP-TE protocol messages.

4.3.2 RSVP-TE Messages and Objects

GMPLS RSVP-TE signaling messages are carried in IP datagrams sent between signaling controllers. This is a feature inherited from the original RSVP specification, but much of the motivation for this feature has changed. In RSVP it was desirable that the resource reservations followed the flow of the traffic in the network, and to achieve this, the RSVP messages were encapsulated

Table 4.1 GMPLS Abstract messages mapped to RSVP-TE Protocol messages

Abstract message	RSVP-TE Protocol message	Reference section
LSP Setup	Path	4.3.3
LSP Accept	Resv	4.3.3
LSP Confirm	ResvConfirm	4.3.3, 4.4
LSP Upstream error	PathErr	4.3.6
LSP Downstream error	ResvErr	4.3.6
LSP Downstream release	PathTear	4.3.7
LSP Upstream release	PathErr	4.3.6, 4.3.7
LSP Notify	Notify	4.3.6

in IP datagrams that were addressed to the ultimate destination of the flow. Thus if there was some change in the network, the signaling messages (as the data traffic) would be re-routed automatically. In a GMPLS network, however, the aim is to have the data traffic follow the resource reservations. That is, the control plane messages follow a well-defined path between signaling controllers and establish more stable paths within the data plane. GMPLS signaling messages, therefore, are encapsulated within IP datagrams that are addressed to the next signaling controller.

Note that the use of IP as a transport mechanism (without any transport protocol) means that the signaling protocol, must be responsible for coping with the unreliable nature of IP data delivery.

Each GMPLS RSVP-TE message is constructed according to a common template. The message (within the IP datagram) starts with a message header. This header is common to all of the signaling messages, and identifies the message type and the length of the message. The common message header also includes a checksum to detect any corruption to the message, because no transport protocol is used to provide this feature.

After the common message header, the signaling messages are built from a series of *objects*. Each object is encoded in a standard way as a length-type-variable (LTV) triplet. Parsing messages is made particularly easy by this method of construction. Each object is used to encode a specific set of information (for example, the parameters related to the route of the LSP being managed, or the parameters that describe the traffic and bandwidth for the LSP), and the nature of the information is indicated by the type field in the object. Each object may be constructed of a series of *sub-objects* providing a unit of information, and these sub-objects are usually encoded as TLV (type-length-variable) constructs. Figure 4.2 shows how a GMPLS RSVP-TE message is built within an IP datagram.

For each signaling message there is a set of mandatory objects without which the message is not valid. There is also a set of objects that may be optionally included according to the function and features that are being signaled.

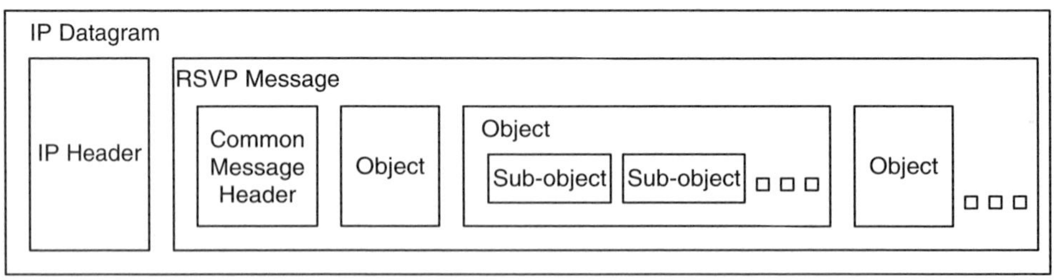

Figure 4.2 A GMPLS RSVP-TE message is carried in an IP datagram and is constructed from a common header and a series of objects.

The inclusion rules for objects are defined in the RFCs that specify the base and extension protocols. In all cases, there is a recommended ordering of objects within a message, but this is accompanied by the caveat that, although all implementations should build messages with the objects in the stated order, each should be prepared to receive a message with the objects in any order (where that would not create ambiguity).

4.3.3 *LSP Establishment*

LSP establishment is initiated by the ingress LSR sending an LSP Setup message to the next hop in the path of the LSP. It determines this by looking at the explicit route for the LSP or by computing the next hop toward the destination. The LSP Setup request carries the identifier of the parent session (Session object) and the identifier of the LSP (Sender-Template), as well as the parameters that describe the requested LSP (Label Request, Sender-TSpec, and Explicit Route objects).

The LSP does not exist until it has been accepted by the downstream LSR, which sends an LSP Accept message to supply the label that must be used to identify the traffic (Label object) and to confirm the resource reservation (FlowSpec object). A possible message exchange would be for each downstream LSR to receive an LSP Setup and respond immediately with an LSP Accept while forwarding the LSP Setup further downstream. This procedure would lead the ingress to believe that the LSP was fully established before the request had reached the egress, and it also would not allow for the LSRs further downstream to fail the LSP setup or vary the parameters. The mechanism used, therefore, is as shown at the top of Figure 4.3: The LSP Setup is forwarded downstream hop by hop until it reaches the egress. At each LSR the traffic parameters are checked to make sure that the LSP can be supported, and the next hop is determined. When the LSP Setup reaches the egress, it is converted to an LSP Accept that is returned, hop by hop, to the ingress. At each LSR the label advertised from downstream is bound to the label for the upstream interface (that is, the associated resources are cross-connected in the data plane), and the label for the upstream interface is advertised upstream to the next LSR. When the LSP Accept is received by the ingress and it has cross-connected its resources, it is ready to start transmitting data.

It is a matter of some debate whether resources (and labels, because labels are representations of resources) are reserved when handling the LSP Setup or the LSP Accept. Obviously, the label and resources for the downstream interface are not known until they are advertised by the downstream LSR in the Label object on the LSP Accept message, but an LSR could pick an upstream label and reserve it to avoid conflict with future LSP Setup messages. This issue is discussed further in Section 4.4.

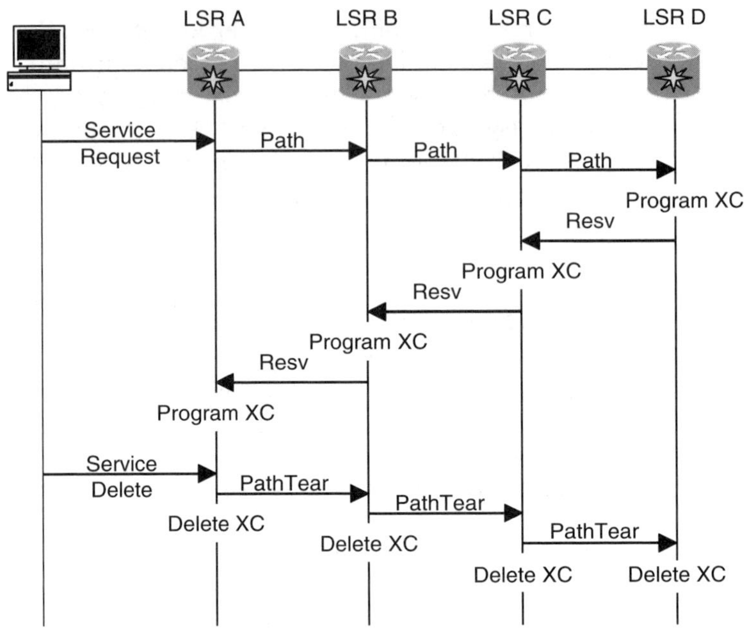

Figure 4.3 Message exchange for LSP establishment and teardown.

RSVP-TE also defines the ResvConfirm message that can be requested by the egress (by the inclusion of the ResvConf object in the Resv message). This message allows the egress to know whether the LSP was successfully established. GMPLS systems very rarely use the LSP Confirm message because of several small factors that combine to make it needless.

- There is an explicit teardown procedure that is usually used if an LSP fails to set up.
- Message exchanges are reliable (see Section 4.3.4).
- In non-packet LSPs a signal will be initiated (for example, a laser will be turned on) when the LSP is established, regardless of when data transmission starts.

4.3.4 *Reliable Message Delivery*

An important feature of GMPLS message exchanges is that the transfer of messages between adjacent LSRs is "reliable"; that is, a message will be transmitted and retransmitted until it is acknowledged. Any failure will not go undetected, but will be reported to the protocol component.

Reliable message delivery can be achieved in a variety of ways. For example, CR-LDP uses a reliable transport (TCP) to ensure delivery. GMPLS RSVP-TE, however, does not use a transport protocol, but runs directly over IP; this means that it must be responsible for its own reliable delivery. It achieves this by allocating a separate identifier to each message and encoding it in a Message-ID object. A message sender retransmits the message (usually on a reasonably rapid timer, of the order of 10 ms, but often with an exponential decay) until it receives an acknowledgement from its neighbor or gives up. The acknowledgement may be in the form of a Message-ID-Ack object carried on any protocol message being sent in the reverse direction, but if no such message is ready to be sent, the neighbor may send an RSVP-TE Ack message specifically to carry the Message-ID-Ack.

As we will see in the next section, reliable delivery is a significant feature of how LSPs are maintained in GMPLS. It also means that LSP establishment is not the trial and error process that it was in RSVP-TE, but is much closer to a hard state protocol.

4.3.5 *LSP Maintenance*

Once an LSP has been established we want it to remain in place until the service (the GMPLS tunnel) is no longer required. At the same time, if there is some sort of failure within the network, we want the control plane to notice and tidy up.

The original specification of RSVP is infamous for the way it handles these requirements as they relate to packet flows. RSVP knows that the packets are forwarded according to the shortest path first (SPF) routes derived by the IP routing protocols, so if there is a problem in the network it knows that the routing protocols will "heal" the network and find another route to the destination. Therefore, RSVP specifies that the Path messages should be periodically retransmitted (*refreshed*) and that they should follow the same routes toward the destination as are used for the data. In this way, if there is a change in the network, the Path messages will adapt to these changes, new Resv messages will be returned, and resources will be reserved on the new routes. This phenomenon, however, leaves the problem of the resources reserved on the old routes — these resources need to be released so that they are available for use by other traffic flows. An explicit release message could be used, but there may be no connectivity (the network may have become broken), and such an explicit release runs the risk of getting confused with reservations that are still required on parts of the path where the old and new routes are coincident.

To get around this problem, RSVP notes that if the upstream router is retransmitting Path messages, a downstream router can assume that the resources are no longer required if it does not see a retransmitted Path message within a reasonable period of time (usually set to around three times the retransmission interval to allow for some loss of messages and some jittering of the retransmission timer). Similarly, RSVP specifies that the Resv message should be retransmitted so that it can detect faults and changes in the same way, and can clean up as required.

This makes RSVP a *soft state* protocol and leads to some concerns about scalability. If each Path and Resv message must be retransmitted every 30 seconds then each router will generate two messages and receive and process two messages for each flow every 30 seconds. If a router sees 10,000 flows, it must generate around 650 messages every second, and also receive and process the same number of messages every second. And all of this is in steady state.

In order to address these scaling concerns, various extensions for *Refresh Reduction* were specified in RFC 2961. In essence these protocol extensions help to reduce the processing necessary on receipt of a refresh message by providing a shorthand way to identify the refreshed message and know that nothing has changed (the Message ID described in the previous section is used), and by allowing a list of Message IDs to be refreshed within a new message, the Summary Refresh (SRefresh) message.

RSVP-TE, and thus GMPLS, signaling inherits all of this baggage; in effect, GMPLS signaling is a soft state protocol. But if GMPLS is used with an explicit route where the path of an LSP will not vary even if the network changes, a lot of this functionality is superfluous. This is even more obvious if GMPLS is used for circuit switching in a transport network where we really do not want dynamic and fluid changes to the route of the LSPs. We might even want the LSP to remain within the data plane even if there is a complete failure of the control plane (see Chapter 7).

There are several observations about GMPLS signaling that help to reduce the dependence on message refreshing.

- Increased refresh time. Given the stable nature both of transport networks and the traffic engineered LSPs that are provisioned by the GMPLS signaling protocol, it is acceptable to increase the refresh period for the Path and Resv messages. Clearly, any increase reduces the processing load on the LSRs. Refresh periods of ten minutes are often mentioned as perfectly acceptable, and this may be viewed as overly cautious since, given the other observations that follow, refreshing is only actually required to clean up after errors where the control plane has become discontinuous.
- Separation of control and data plane. As has already been described, GMPLS facilitates the separation of control and data planes so that signaling messages may be routed through a separate control network. This has the important consequence that no inference can be made about the state of the data plane from failures in the control plane. So, if a control plane link goes down, the control plane messages can be re-routed to reach the neighboring LSR by another route, but this has no implications for the path which the data takes.

That is, a change in the path along which a Path message is delivered has no bearing upon the route that the data will take.

- Explicit teardown is more extensive in GMPLS. The LSP Upstream Release is added to the LSP Downstream Release that existed in RSVP-TE (see Section 4.3.7) so that LSPs can be torn down by either the downstream or the upstream LSR. Additionally, rules for modifying LSPs (see Section 4.3.8) mean that if an LSP needs to be redirected onto another path, this can be achieved by allocating the resources on the new route before the data is switched to the new path. Thus there is explicit control of the change in route, and the process does not rely on refresh messages.
- Reliable message delivery. Reliable message delivery closes two holes in the signaling procedures that previously required regular refresh messages, both caused by the risk of message loss because the RSVP-TE protocol messages are carried directly over IP. First, during LSP establishment it is possible that a Path or Resv message could get lost; this would mean that the LSP would neither be set up nor fail — it would be left in limbo. In this case, the refresh process ensures that a new message is sent after the refresh interval has expired and, unless the network is in a very poor state, this allows the LSP setup to continue. Secondly, during LSP teardown it is possible that a PathTear message could be lost. This hole was closed by letting the downstream LSR use the absence of Path refresh messages to deduce the need to release the LSP. In both cases, reliable message delivery as described in Section 4.3.4 ensures that messages have a far greater chance of delivery. If a Path or Resv is not delivered despite the retransmission attempts, the LSP setup is deliberately aborted. If an LSP Up/Downstream Release message is lost, GMPLS can still recover and clean up the old LSP since Path or Resv refresh messages will not be received. Although this tidy-up process will be slow (larger refresh periods), this is not an issue because it is a rare case and is associated with reclaiming network resources and not provisioning new services.
- Smaller numbers of LSPs. GMPLS networks typically have far fewer LSPs than there are micro-flows in an IP network. A large optical switch might have the capacity to terminate 80 lambdas on a single fiber and might have 20 ports requiring it to maintain 1600 LSPs if it is fully populated and saturated with traffic. In reality, optical switches see far less traffic than this whether in GMPLS or manually provisioned networks, and even packet LSRs do not see many thousands of TE LSPs. The consequence is that scalability is less of an issue and the impact of refresh processing is less pronounced. It should be noted, however, that assumptions about protocol operation that are based on network size are invariably overtaken by events — the Internet is now far larger than anyone ever imagined it would be.
- Continued use of refresh reduction. The refresh reduction procedures described earlier in this section remain available in GMPLS systems. However, it should

be noted that although many LSRs support this function, at the time of writing it has not been necessary to enable it in a deployed GMPLS network because of the other features listed above.

4.3.6 *Error Cases*

Errors may be reported as from upstream or from downstream using *LSP Downstream Error* or *LSP Upstream Error* messages, that is the RSVP-TE ResvErr or PathErr messages. The LSP Downstream Error message is not used significantly in GMPLS, but it has some value during LSP establishment if an LSR cannot satisfy the reservation request carried on an LSP Accept (Resv) message. For example, it may be that the label supplied by the downstream LSR is not acceptable to the upstream LSR, perhaps because the associated resource has failed or is in use for some other purpose. In this case, the upstream LSR may respond with an RSVP-TE ResvErr indicating that the label cannot be used.

The LSP Upstream Error message is more widely used. It has a role in LSP establishment failure when the LSP requested in an LSP Request (Path) message cannot be satisfied. For example, it may be impossible to route the LSP according to the explicit route supplied, or there may not be sufficient resources available to satisfy the request. The LSP Upstream Error message is sent in response to the LSP Request and can supply sufficient information to allow the LSP to be re-routed to avoid the problem.

The LSP Upstream Error message is also used to report failures or problems with LSPs that have already been established. For example, if there is a data plane fault this may be reported in the control plane through an LSP Upstream Error message — note that data plane faults tend to be easily detected at downstream LSRs, but are harder to discover at upstream LSRs. The Link Management Protocol (see Chapter 6) can be used to help isolate the fault — that is, determine where on the data path it arose — but the signaling protocol is the correct mechanism to propagate the error through the control plane.

Both types of error message (upstream and downstream) carry information to help the receiver determine and localize the error. An Error Code classifies the error, for example as a routing error, an admission control error, or as a policy error. An Error Value qualifies the Error Code to provide greater information about the problem. Additionally, the error message contains an IP address of the reporting LSR, and may use TLVs to indicate the specific link on which the problem arose.

The way that Error messages are handled is the subject of debate among implementers and there is no clear resolution of the correct behavior. According to the original specification of RSVP, error messages sent from downstream to upstream are not supposed to remove control plane state. This was particularly possible because of the soft state nature of the protocol — if the flow was re-routed as a result of the error, the protocol would clear up automatically. On the other hand, the error reported might be sufficiently innocuous that no change was required.

In the specification of RSVP-TE for MPLS traffic engineering no change was made to this assumption, but implementations made some compromises and assumptions. This applied particularly to certain Error Codes, which were assumed to remove the LSP from both the data and control planes.

GMPLS implementations tend to adhere to the original premise of the RSVP specification. That is, the LSP Upstream Error message is propagated upstream, hop by hop toward the ingress. During LSP setup, any LSR may rectify the problem and issue a new LSP Setup message (for example, modifying the route of the LSP). When the error message reaches the ingress it may modify the LSP Setup, retry the old request, or clean up by issuing an LSP Downstream Release message (see the next section). Thus, an error that is reported by the control plane in GMPLS does not disturb the LSP in the data plane until the ingress makes that decision — this feature is important in the circuit-based networks that GMPLS tends to control because data connectivity must be preserved as far as possible.

Similarly, an LSP Downstream Error message does not remove the LSP, except that during LSP establishment it will gradually unpick the LSP toward the egress if no individual LSR is able to rectify the problem. When the LSP Downstream Error message reaches the egress, it will send out an LSP Upstream Error message to the ingress.

Because error propagation as described above involves hop-by-hop message exchange, GMPLS also includes a mechanism designed to allow problems to be reported direct to a network entity that can take immediate recovery action. This entity may be the ingress or egress of the LSP, but it might also be some intermediate repair point, or even a management entity not on the path of the LSP. This mechanism uses the LSP Notify message and provides a high function mechanism for rapid repair of active LSPs, and for the management of other protection services described in later chapters.

When an LSP Setup message is sent through the network, it may include a Notify-Request object that contains the IP address of the LSR or network entity to which LSP Notify messages should be sent. Any LSR may insert a Notify-Request object into an LSP Setup message that does not already contain one, or may update the address in the object so that it becomes the recipient of any LSP Notify messages sent from downstream. Similarly, an LSP Accept message may include a Notify-Request object to ask that errors are reported direct from upstream LSRs. Further, Notify-Request objects may be nested in a stack so that there are nested domains of reporting (see the description of segment protection in Chapter 7).

There is an obvious scaling issue when a link that carries many LSPs fails. Such a situation might cause the generation of a large number of LSP Notify messages that could either swamp the local control plane or simply delay the delivery of the error report. GMPLS handles this by allowing a single LSP Notify message to report multiple instances of the same error (different LSPs) by the inclusion of the Session and LSP identifiers for each LSP.

4.3.7 *LSP Teardown*

The usual mechanism for LSP teardown is for the ingress that originally requested the LSP to send an LSP Downstream Release message. As this progresses through the network the LSP is removed from the data plane and all control plane state is discarded. There is no response to this message and, in fact, no response could be handled since all control plane state has been deleted (see Figure 4.3).

The Downstream Release (PathTear) is the only mechanism provided in RSVP and RSVP-TE, but GMPLS also introduces the LSP Upstream Release to allow an egress LSR to cause the LSP to be torn down. This message is achieved using the RSVP-TE PathErr with a new flag that indicates "Path state removed" — that is, the flag indicates that, unlike normal processing of the PathErr message, the LSP has been discarded by the sending LSR.

This simple mechanism also allows a transit LSR to tear the LSP down. It sends both an LSP Downstream Release and an LSP Upstream Release to cause the downstream and upstream components of the LSP to be removed.

4.3.8 *LSP Modification*

The ability to modify an existing LSP is an important feature. It may be that the requested service changes, for example because the user or application requires more or less bandwidth, or because the required quality of service parameters change. Alternatively, changes within the network may mean that the LSP is re-routed within the network.

This second point is very significant within a traffic engineered network, because LSPs should be placed in order to make optimal use of the available network resources and to most easily provide the contracted services. At the same time, planned outages in network resources (for example, for maintenance) may require that LSPs be moved away from one link and onto another link.

Thus it is desirable to be able to modify existing LSPs and these changes must be made with the smallest possible impact to traffic. It is not acceptable, for example, to tear down the existing LSP and to re-provision it with different parameters, because such an operation would cause major disruption to the data. Instead, one of two modification processes may be applied.

The first process is called *in-place modification*. It relies on simply changing the parameters to the LSP Setup message and sending it out along the path of the existing LSP. This type of message is recognized as not being a Refresh precisely because the parameters have changed, and also because the Message ID (if in use) is changed. Only a very limited set of LSP parameters can be changed using in-place modification. For example, the route of the LSP cannot be changed because that would simply not be "in place" — it would result in disruption to the data path as new connectivity was established on the new route. Similarly, in some technologies it is not even possible to modify the bandwidth allocated for an LSP using in-place modification because the bandwidth is so closely tied to physical resources — a change in bandwidth would mean moving the LSP to other resources, which would disrupt the traffic. However, in-place modification does have uses for modifying the control plane state and function. For example, the request to record the route of the LSP may be turned on or off, and the technique is useful for changing the administrative state of the LSP (see Section 4.5).

An important consideration for the use of in-place modification is whether the modification could fail, and what would happen if the modification request failed. Any failure would require the modification request to be unpicked, which would at best be confusing.

The alternative to in-place modification is called *make-before-break*. In essence, the make-before-break procedure replaces one instance of an LSP with another instance by establishing the second instance (make), switching the data to the new instance, and then tearing down the old instance (break). In this case the traffic suffers only the smallest of hits as it is switched between two equally functional LSPs — in packet networks this can be achieved with no impact to the traffic, whereas in optical networks the hit is usually between 2 and 5 ms.

Make-before-break is a fine process if the route of the new LSP is entirely diverse from that of the old LSP. But what happens if the two LSPs need to share one or more links within the network? In this case there is an element of over-provisioning implicit in the process, and this may cause significant problems in some scenarios (for example, when the resources are simply not available to support both LSPs at once). The solution is to ensure that the LSRs can recognize that the two LSPs are closely related, and to allow them to "share" resources. This is perfectly safe because we know that only one of the LSPs will actually be carrying traffic at any time.

To achieve successful make-before-break we ensure that the two LSPs have very similar identities. The whole of the Session object is the same for both LSPs, and the Sender Template differs only in the actual LSP ID itself. This means that both LSPs are identified as supporting the same tunnel. Then, to permit resource sharing, the LSPs are flagged as having *Shared Explicit* style through the use of the Style object in the LSP Setup messages. This allows LSPs from the same Session to share resources.

And what does resource sharing actually mean? In a packet network that uses statistical admission control it means either that the link is allowed to be oversubscribed, or that one instance of the bandwidth allocation is not counted. In packet networks that use real resource allocation, sharing means that the same buffers are made available for both LSPs. In all packet networks, following the instructions of the RSVP-TE specification, the two LSPs (the old and the new) do not share labels even when they share a link — this is considered important because it means that there is no problem resolving the old and new cross-connects in the label forwarding hardware.

However, in non-packet networks the label directly represents the resource. Thus it is impossible to share resources without sharing labels as well, and the GMPLS signaling protocol must behave slightly differently. In practice, this involves using the physical technology utilized for $1+1$ protection (see Chapter 7) so that split and merge points can exist along the path of the LSPs with data transmitted along both paths at the location of a split point, and the best signal chosen at any merge point.

4.3.9 *Bidirectional LSPs*

In most transport networks connectivity is required to be bidirectional (this differs from MPLS networks where connectivity is established to support IP-like data flows that may be unbalanced or may take different routes through the network). One might hope to use the same labeled resource (timeslot or lambda) in each direction, but this is not always possible because of the interaction with unidirectional LSPs and with failed physical resources. So labels must be carefully managed during LSP establishment.

To complicate the procedure, it is the upstream LSR that is responsible for allocating the label to be used by data on the reverse path (mirroring how the forward path is handled). The label must be carried on the LSP Setup message so that the downstream LSR may learn which label to use. GMPLS uses the presence of this label in an Upstream Label object on an LSP Request message to indicate both that a bidirectional LSP is required and which label should be used on the reverse data path.

4.4 Fine Control of Label Allocation

Normally GMPLS signaling establishes an LSP with the label to use on each link assigned by the LSR at the downstream end of the link, and signaled to the upstream LSR using the Label object on the LSP Accept message, as described in previous sections. However, in some situations, the upstream LSR may wish to constrain the choice of label. For example, the upstream LSR may know that only certain transceivers are operational, or may be limited in which resources it can switch from the downstream interface to its upstream interface.

To restrict the downstream LSR's choice of label for the LSP, the upstream LSR may supply a set of acceptable labels in a Label Set object carried on the LSP Request message — the downstream LSR must select from this set or fail to establish the LSP.

The upstream LSR may also want to suggest a preferred label on the Path message, so that it can pipeline the programming of its cross-connection while signaling to the downstream LSR. This is particularly useful for devices that take time to program (for example, a MEMS device may take a few tens of milliseconds to reposition its mirrors and then let them stabilize), since if each device is only programmed when the LSP Accept message is propagated, the LSP setup time may be as long as

$$2 * (n - 1) * T_m + n * T_x$$

where there are n LSRs, T_m is the time to propagate a message between two LSRs, and T_x is the time to program a cross-connect.

Pipelining on the forward path (that is, when the LSP Setup message is processed) involves the upstream LSR selecting a label, forwarding the LSP Setup message, and then starting to program the switch in the background. Note that pipelining cannot be used on the reverse path (that is, when processing the LSP Accept message) because it is a requirement that by the time the LSP Accept reaches the ingress LSR all resources are in place. This point is explained further in the section below.

If pipelining is used to program the devices as the LSP Setup message is processed, the time may reduce to

$$2 * (n - 1) * T_m + T_x$$

Control of the label by the upstream LSR to enable pipelining could be achieved by supplying a Label Set with just a single element, but then the downstream LSR has no flexibility. Instead, a Suggested Label object is used on the LSP Setup message to recommend which label the downstream LSR should use. The downstream LSR is free to select a different label, in which case the benefit of pipelining is lost, but no harm is done.

If the source of the LSP (the ingress) wishes to exert control over the label to be used on a specific hop in the LSP's route, it may do so by adding information to the explicit route that is signaled in the LSP Setup message. In *explicit label control*, each strict hop in the Explicit Route Object may be followed by sub-objects that indicate the labels to use in the forward and reverse directions for the LSP on that hop. The LSR at the upstream end of the hop removes the sub-objects from the Explicit Route object and converts them into a Label Set object with only one member (the downstream LSR is given no flexibility to select a different label) and an Upstream Label object, respectively.

In fact, explicit label control could also be applied to loose hops, but the meaning is slightly less obvious. Would it mean that the same label had to be used on every step along the path of the LSP where the loose hop is expanded, or would it mean only that the specified label must be used on the last hop to the address specified as the loose hop? Several implementations do allow the use of labels within the ERO for loose hops, but only where the loose hop is a hop to an explicit LSR or link (that is, not when the loose hop is an Autonomous System or a prefix), and in this case, the meaning is interpreted as applying control over the label used on the final hop of the loose path to that LSR or link.

The explicit label control feature is particularly useful at the LSP's egress when the next hop or outgoing port can be controlled through signaling by the ingress LSR. The outgoing port may indicate a customer facing port, or may be used to connect a signaled LSP to a manually configured permanent LSP to create a *soft permanent LSP*.

If an LSR is supplied with a label that it does not like or cannot use (either in a Label object on an LSP Accept message, or in an Upstream Label object on an LSP Setup message), it must respond with an error message (LSP Downstream Error or LSP Upstream Error, respectively) to reject the LSP establishment. The LSR that sent the message may select another label and try again, but this could be a painful and ultimately futile procedure. To ease matters, the LSR that wishes to reject the chosen label may supply a list of labels that would have been acceptable in an Acceptable Label Set object included on the error message.

Two last questions arise: When should the resources actually be allocated, and when is it safe to start transmitting data? The first question has been touched on in the above discussion of pipelining. Although the definition of RSVP-TE assumes that resources are not allocated until the LSP Accept message is seen (because until then in RSVP we do not know exactly how much resource to reserve, and in RSVP-TE we do not know which label to reserve), GMPLS can clearly benefit from reserving resources while processing the LSP Setup message.

To safely start transmitting data it is clear that all of the resources must be reserved and the cross-connects must be in place. This is important because we cannot have unterminated lasers active through MEMS devices that are still positioning their mirrors — this might impact other services, and might be a safety hazard to human operators. For the forward direction data flow the process is simple: The ingress LSR does not start transmitting data until it has received an LSP Accept message and programmed its own switch. This just requires that each

LSR must make sure that it has completed programming its own resources before it sends the LSP Accept message upstream.

For the reverse direction data flow on a bidirectional LSP the egress must determine when it is safe to start transmitting. This could be done by requesting a confirmation of the LSP Accept using a three-way handshake, but the LSP Confirm message that exists in RSVP as the ResvConfirm for this purpose is not reliably delivered and is rarely used in GMPLS. Instead, it is assumed that by the time an LSP Setup message has been received by the egress LSR and it has programmed its resources, it is safe for the egress to start transmitting. This means that each LSR must make sure that it has completed programming its own reverse path resources before it sends the LSP Setup message further downstream. Note that to some extent, this removes any benefit of pipelining as described previously.

4.5 Other Signaling Objects

A key requirement of GMPLS signaling protocols is that they should be easily extensible and future-proof. The way that RSVP-TE messages are constructed from objects makes this very easy and the object identifiers are divided up into three groups: those that must cause an error response if they are not supported, those that must be silently dropped if they are not supported, and those that must be forwarded unmodified if they are not supported. This makes the protocol very easy to extend so that new function can be added and carried transparently across islands of legacy LSRs. GMPLS includes several new objects that add features to the previous version of RSVP-TE and new objects are proposed all the time so that new functions can be added to signaling.

An important additional object in GMPLS facilitates alarm-free LSP establishment and teardown. In optical equipment an alarm is usually raised if a receiver (for example, a transceiver) is activated but is not receiving light or an appropriate signal. This is an important mechanism for discovering faults in the network, but is only valid if the alarm is genuine. During LSP establishment and teardown receivers may be active but legitimately not receiving a signal. For example, when a transit LSR processes an LSP Accept message it selects a label for its upstream link and programs the resources — this might include activating a receiver on the upstream interface, but the ingress LSR is not yet transmitting data so an alarm would immediately be raised.

To combat these bogus alarms, GMPLS defines the Administrative Status object to allow the ingress to control the status of an LSP. The object includes a flag to control the alarm status for the LSP, and the ingress can indicate on the initial LSP Setup message that all alarms should be disabled. Once the ingress has received the LSP Accept message and has started to send data, it can change the flag to indicate that alarms should now be turned on. The new flag setting is sent out in the Administrative Status object of a new LSP Setup message using the procedures of in-place modification as described in Section 4.3.8.

4.6 Multiple Domains

Establishing LSPs across domain boundaries provides a special challenge for the control plane and particularly for the signaling protocol. A domain in the GMPLS context is considered to be any collection of network elements within a common sphere of address management or path computational responsibility. So, for example, a domain may be defined by the administrative boundaries within the network where those boundaries may lie between Service Providers or between sub-divisions of a Service Provider's network. Examples of such domains include Autonomous Systems and IGP areas. But recall that there is a separation between the control plane and the data plane so that any division of either the control plane or the data plane can create a domain.

In practice, there are two important features that determine the relevance of a domain boundary:

1. Can the signaling message be routed to the next signaling controller?
2. Is it possible to compute the next hop towards the destination within the data plane?

Thus it is most convenient to define a domain as a zone of routing and computational capability; a domain boundary is the point beyond which a signaling controller cannot see well enough to be able to reliably route a control message or compute the path of an LSP.

Signaling offers a core feature to help handle domains: the explicit path loose hop (see Section 4.2.2). Using loose hops, the ingress LSR may indicate a set of abstract nodes along the desired path (for example, the domains, or the domain border nodes, and the destination) but not specify the intervening hops. The details of the path are filled in when possible, usually at a domain border node.

Three additional tools enhance the ability to signal across multiple domains in GMPLS. The first allows an ingress to specify exclusions from a path. This is useful because, when only a loose hop is used in the explicit path, the ingress has no other way to restrict which links and nodes are included within the path. If, for example, the ingress knows that a particular link is unreliable, or is aware of the path of another LSP that supports the same service, it may wish to inform the downstream LSRs that will expand the loose hop of the links and nodes to avoid. This is done by the inclusion of a new message object, the Exclude Route object, which provides a global list of links and nodes to exclude; or by the inclusion of special exclusion sub-objects within the Explicit Route object.

The second utility adds support for crankback routing within GMPLS signaling. Crankback routing is not new, and has been used in PNNI and TDM networks. It facilitates "trial-and-error" progression of signaling messages across a multi-domain network. When an LSP setup request is blocked because of the unavailability of suitable resources on a path toward the destination, an error report (LSP Upstream Error) is returned with a description of the problem. A new path computation may be attempted excluding the blocking links, nodes, or domains. Note that the use of crankback routing within a single domain approximates to random-walk routing and is not recommended, and the same can be said of a path that crosses many domains.

Hierarchical (nested) and stitched LSPs provide the third building block for support of inter-domain LSPs. These technologies are described in detail in Chapter 8.

Another solution to the computation of the path of an inter-domain LSP is provided by the Path Computation Element (PCE) described in Chapter 9.

4.7 Further Reading

Further details of the messages, protocol objects, and field values for RSVP, RSVP-TE, and GMPLS signaling can be found in:

The Internet and Its Protocols: A Comparative Approach by Adrian Farrel (2004), Morgan Kaufmann.

RFC 2205 — Resource ReSerVation Protocol (RSVP): Version 1 Functional Specification

RFC 2961 — RSVP Refresh Overhead Reduction Extensions

RFC 3209 — RSVP-TE: Extensions to RSVP for LSP Tunnels

RFC 3468 — The Multiprotocol Label Switching (MPLS) Working Group decision on MPLS signaling protocols

RFC 3471 — Generalized Multi-Protocol Label Switching (GMPLS) Signaling Functional Description

RFC 3473 — Generalized Multi-Protocol Label Switching (GMPLS) Signaling Resource ReSerVation Protocol-Traffic Engineering (RSVP-TE) Extensions

RFC 3946 — Generalized Multi-Protocol Label Switching Extensions for SONET and SDH Control

draft-ietf-ccamp-rsvp-te-exclude-route Exclude Routes — Extension to RSVP-TE

draft-ietf-ccamp-crankback Crankback Signaling Extensions for MPLS and GMPLS Signaling

CHAPTER 5

GMPLS Routing

The process known as "routing" in GMPLS is really not routing at all, but the distribution of information that will be used as the basis of the path computation that determines how LSPs will be placed within the network. This chapter introduces the concepts of GMPLS routing, focusing on the protocols used and the information distributed. Advanced discussion of what traffic engineering means in a GMPLS network and how paths are computed is deferred to Chapters 8 and 9.

GMPLS routing information distribution is based on extensions to IP routing protocols. Note that traffic engineering information distribution is currently limited to within an IP routing area — because there are two IP routing protocols that interoperate in a scalable way within an area (OSPF and IS-IS), both of these protocols were extended by the IETF. This chapter introduces the extensions to the protocols in an abstract way before describing how the individual protocols were extended.

5.1 Routing in IP and Traffic Engineered Networks

In an IP network, routing is the process of determining the next hop for an IP packet on the shortest path toward its destination. This decision is made by each router in turn as the packet progresses through the network and is based on information in the routing table that is either manually configured or built by routing protocols.

The chief routing protocols used within an area (OSPF and IS-IS) are link state protocols. Each router is responsible for distributing information about itself and its interfaces (that is, the local ends of its links). This information principally consists of the state of the link (active) and the cost of forwarding data through the router's interface onto the link. The information is distributed by the routing protocol to all routers in the area and each uses an algorithm to determine the *open shortest path* toward a destination, where "open" means that the links (interfaces) used are active and able to carry traffic, and "shortest" means least cost — that is, the sum of the costs of all the links to the destination is minimized.

Each router in an IP network is actually only concerned with the next hop on the open shortest path because it knows that the next router will apply the same determination to the same link state information, deduce the same shortest path, and forward the packet to the next router.

Traffic engineering, however, is a different paradigm. Traffic engineering (TE), as explained in Chapter 3, is the process of placing traffic on selected, pre-computed paths within the network. The aim is to route traffic away from congested "hot spots," and to pick links that provide the desired quality of service or satisfy other application constraints. IP routing does not achieve this; in fact, IP routing tends to converge traffic onto common "core" links in the network, and attempts to moderate this behavior by dynamically changing the cost of network links are neither practicable nor particularly successful.

As explained in Chapter 4, once the path of an LSP is known, the signaling protocols can be used to ensure that the LSP is installed on precisely that path. But the path must first be computed, and this requires access to the link state information distributed by the routing protocols. However, the link state information is not sufficient for traffic engineering purposes because it only tells us about the state of links (up or down) and their relative costs. For traffic engineering we need more information, not least the availability of unused bandwidth on the links. First and foremost, we need to discover traffic engineering links (TE links) as abstractions representing network resources along with their attributes such as available bandwidth.

5.2 Basic Traffic Engineering Data

To compute a path through a traffic engineered network, we need to know which links exist, what bandwidth they have available, and what the costs of using the links are. (Note that the cost of using the TE link may be set to a different value from the cost for forwarding IP packets over the link. The two are kept separate to allow mixed TE and non-TE behavior.) From this, we can compute a path that uses only links that have sufficient bandwidth, but which is otherwise the shortest or cheapest path to the destination. This is just one, albeit popular, criterion for path computation and it is called *constraint-based shortest path first* (*CSPF*); however, there are many other alternative techniques — for instance, one could compute a path that goes over links with sufficient bandwidth and guarantees minimum end-to-end delay and delay variation. We can apply sophisticated algorithms based on predicted network demand, we can select mutually independent paths to support protection or load sharing, and we can apply additional constraints such as the avoidance of certain links and routers that we do not trust (as they may be prone to failure).

Network resources available for traffic engineering path computation are modeled in (G)MPLS as *TE links*. Not every data link in the network is necessarily a TE link, and the concept of a TE link may be extended to cover "bundles" of links between the same pair of routers, and even to encompass LSPs. These advanced concepts are covered in Chapter 8.

TE links are actually advertised as link ends. That is, the routers at each end of a TE link are responsible for advertising the capabilities of the TE link as they perceive it. A TE link is not complete and available for use until both of its ends have been advertised and correlated. In the case of point-to-multipoint traffic engineering (see Chapter 11), a TE link may have more than two ends.

The database of all TE links and the associated information is known as the *Traffic Engineering Database* (*TED*). It is this database that is processed by the path computation algorithm to compute a traffic engineered path. In fact, most path computation algorithms operate on a *TE network graph* built using information from the TED.

The full set of traffic engineering information that is available and distributed by the routing protocols (see Section 5.3) is shown in Table 5.1.

5.3 GMPLS Routing Information

GMPLS networks are complex traffic engineering networks and are not necessarily packet-based. To establish an LSP across a transport network successfully it is not sufficient to know the available bandwidth on each of the links in the network as advertised as part of the basic TE data: We must also know the switching capabilities of the links at each LSR. As described in Chapter 3, each LSR may be able to switch the data arriving on a link in one or more ways depending on the LSR's abilities with regard to that link. Thus the routers must also advertise the switching capabilities for each TE link that they advertise.

Additionally, transport networks may offer the ability to protect traffic on individual TE links. That is, in the event of the failure of the physical connection (fiber, wire, and so forth) over which the traffic is flowing, another, parallel connection may be able to transfer the traffic. The switch to the protection connection can be achieved using GMPLS protocols as described in Chapter 7, but it may also be performed at the transport layer without the involvement of the GMPLS protocols, thus providing a very rapid and robust mechanism for traffic protection. The protection properties of the TE links also need to be advertised so that the information is present in the TED. This allows path computation to select paths through the network that have the desired link protection capabilities.

Table 5.1 Traffic engineering information describing the capabilities of TE links

Information	Meaning
Router address	A link-independent, reachable address of the reporting router. That is, an address of the router that will not disappear if an interface goes down, and which can be used to send control messages to the router in the control plane. This is used to associate the TE link with a specific router that is advertising the link end.
Link type	Used to distinguish between point-to-point and multi-access TE links. Currently only point-to-point TE links are defined.
Partner router (known as Link ID)	For point-to-point links this is the Router ID of the router at the other end of the TE link.
Local interface IP address	The address of an interface on the advertising router that corresponds to this link. It is the identifier of a numbered TE link's local end.
Remote interface IP address	The address of a remote interface at the other end of the TE link. It is the identifier of a numbered TE link's remote end. Note that this provides for correlation of advertisements by adjacent routers, but also implies a degree of coordinated configuration.
Traffic engineering metric	A metric for use in traffic engineering path computation. This metric may be different from the standard link metric used for normal routing. This allows different weights to be assigned for normal and TE traffic.
Maximum link bandwidth	The link capacity. That is, the maximum amount of bandwidth that can be used by traffic on this link in this direction (from the router originating the information). It is possible that not all of this bandwidth can be used for traffic engineering (see below).
Maximum reservable bandwidth	The largest amount of bandwidth that may be reserved on this link in this direction. This value may be greater than the maximum bandwidth if over-subscription is supported, or smaller if some bandwidth is always held back such as for non-TE best-effort traffic, or as preserved protection capacity.
Unreserved bandwidth by priority	A series of eight amounts of bandwidth that are currently available for reservation at each of the priority levels zero through seven. This construct allows for preemptable bandwidth, and segmentation of the available bandwidth by priority.
Administrative group	The administrative groups or resource colors to which this link belongs. Allows additional constraints to be applied to path computation so that links of particular qualities can be selected or excluded. The definition of administrative group is a local, network-private task.

The bandwidth parameters advertised for packet-based traffic engineering still apply in GMPLS, but because of the switching characteristics of transport links, and because of the way bandwidth is partitioned according to physical resources, it is also necessary to signal the maximum and minimum bandwidth that may be allocated to any LSP on the link. Consider, for example, a WDM link that has 15 lambdas. Each lambda might be able to support a 2.5-Gbps service, but simply advertising that the link had 37.5 Gbps available might lead to an attempt to route a 10-Gbps LSP down the link. Conversely, for layer 2 and TDM TE links it may be advantageous to control the lower size limit of a bandwidth allocation so that the link is not swamped with many, very small LSPs, and so a minimum LSP bandwidth figure is also advertised.

Lastly, because GMPLS supports protection and restoration of services by the establishment of protection LSPs (see Chapter 7) it is important to understand which TE links in the network might be at risk from the same failures. For example, all fibers that run through the same duct are at risk from the same man operating a backhoe. For risk-diverse protection paths to be computed, the TED needs to know which links share a risk. This can be achieved by having LSRs advertise the *shared risk link groups* (*SRLGs*) to which each link belongs.

All of this information builds on the TE information described in the previous section. Chapter 8 describes additional GMPLS information that might be useful to further enhance the ability of path computation algorithms to compute paths through GMPLS networks. This information includes limited ability to cross-connect signals between pairs of interfaces, the availability of specific labels (for example, lambdas) on links, and optical impairments.

5.4 Overview of IP Routing Protocols

As has already been stated, the traffic engineering and additional GMPLS information used to build the TED is distributed by the IP routing protocols OSPF or IS-IS. Both of these are link state routing protocols, which means that each router is responsible for advertising information about the state of all the links it terminates. Further, each router must redistribute all information that it receives from any other router. In this way, all routers receive information about all links in the network and can build exactly the same table of available links and routes.

So that the routing protocol can operate, each router must establish connectivity with each of its neighbors. A *routing adjacency* is a routing protocol conversation between a pair of routers, and governs the exchange of link state information. The routing protocols "discover" their neighbors and establish adjacencies by sending Hello messages, and they continue to send these messages periodically to ascertain that the links and their neighbors are in good health.

Because, in IP and MPLS packet networks, the control channel over which the routing protocol messages are exchanged is coincident with the data channel over which data is sent, the existence of a healthy routing adjacency can be used as evidence of a healthy data channel.

It is worth noting that not all physically adjacent routers necessarily establish routing adjacencies. Specifically, if several routers are connected to each other via a multi-access network, they establish adjacencies only with the elected Designated Router and Backup Designated Router. This creates a hub-and-spoke adjacency structure, which is beneficial from the scalability point of view.

When a router starts up (or when a new link becomes available) it must use the routing protocol to distribute information to all of its neighbors about all of the links that it terminates. It sends out these advertisements as soon as it can, and, if there is a change in the status of any of its links, it sends out an updated advertisement. This process is carefully rate-limited to avoid destabilizing the network, either through an excess of control messages or through rapid fluctuations in network state. Further, the router periodically refreshes the advertisements of the state of all its links so that the protocol is resilient to lost messages and so that the other routers in the network can use timeouts to purge their routing tables of old or incorrect information. Since these refreshes are relatively infrequent, routers may also "withdraw" link advertisements to ensure rapid removal of link state from the routing tables on other routers.

The last step in the routing protocol is that a router must also redistribute all the advertisements it receives from its neighbors. In a well-connected network this may mean that there is some excessive distribution of link state information, but the process ensures that all information about all links in the network reaches all routers. This process is called *flooding* and has the advantage that it ensures reliable distribution of information, and the disadvantage that it requires the involvement of every router in the domain — even those that do not understand or wish to use the advertised information.

5.4.1 *Operation of Routing Protocols in GMPLS Networks*

The GMPLS routing protocol extensions leverage the function of the IP routing protocols just described. The requirement is that traffic engineering and GMPLS information about every TE link is distributed to every LSR in the network, and the protocols are pretty good at doing that. But it does not follow that every router that participates in the routing protocol needs to understand the TE and GMPLS information — only those that are actually responsible for advertising the information and those that compile a TED actually need to actively process the data. Nevertheless, all routers must still forward all the information. This function is achieved by making the TE and GMPLS information *opaque*. That is, it is passed between routers with an indication that says, "This is not routing information for your immediate use in routing IP packets. It is application information that you are being requested to flood. Please deliver it to the application and pass it along to your neighbors." In our case, the "application" is GMPLS TE.

Recall (from Chapter 3) that GMPLS networks support a separate control and data plane. We can no longer make any assumptions that the control channel through which the routing protocol messages are exchanged is coincident with the data channel (that is, the TE link) about which it is advertising information. Thus, the TE links that are advertised correspond to the data channels that can be used for the computation of the paths of LSPs, but the control channels along which routing adjacencies are formed do not play any part in the transfer of data, and are not present in the TED.

There is no contradiction with this separation of TE links and routing adjacencies, because the routing protocol is being used to distribute the TE information and is not actually being used as a routing protocol that determines the paths. In fact, there is a secondary separation of control and data planes that should be considered — just as the signaling controller introduced in Chapter 4 may be physically diverse from the data plane switch, so the *routing controller* (the control plane component responsible for advertising routing information about the TE links that terminate on a data plane switch) may be physically separated from the switch in the data plane. Further, a single routing controller may be responsible for advertising on behalf of more than one data switch. Of course, in these cases, some communications channel (perhaps running a management protocol) is needed to coordinate between the switch in the data plane and the routing controller in the control plane.

The separation of control and data planes supports the separation of address spaces. The addresses that identify the links and switches in the data plane may come from a different (that is, independent) space from those used by the routing controllers when they communicate in the control plane. These spaces may even overlap, and although this can cause significant confusion for the operator, it does not impact the operation of the control plane, path computation, or LSP signaling in any way, because the TE information signaled by the routing protocol is kept separate from the routing information used to route control plane messages.

There is, however, one important relationship between the TE information and the control plane information. Once the explicit route of an LSP has been computed (using the TE information), it must be signaled through the control plane as described in the previous chapter. The explicit route is given to the signaling controller as a series of TE link end-point addresses, or the addresses of the data switches. All of these addresses are data plane addresses, but the signaling message must be delivered within the control plane: It must find its way in turn to each of the signaling controllers that are responsible for the data switches along the LSP. To do this, there must be a relationship in the TED that allows the control plane to map from the TE links and switches to the routing controller that advertised their existence. In GMPLS this is accomplished by mandating that the Router Address, which is the ID of a data plane switch, must be a routable address in the control plane (see Table 5.1).

5.5 Protocol-Specific Extensions

This section gives the briefest of overviews of how the traffic engineering and GMPLS information is carried by the existing routing protocols. Further details of the operation of OSPF-TE and ISIS-TE can be found in Chapters 8 and 9, and readers wishing to see the bits and bytes are referred to the references in the *Further Reading* section at the end of this chapter.

5.5.1 *OSPF*

As already described, the TE and GMPLS information needs to be exchanged between routers "opaquely" so that routers do not process it as part of their IP routing, but will hand it off to the TED and pass it on to other routers. OSPF already posses the *opaque Link State Advertisement* (*LSA*) for exactly this purpose. The LSA is the basic unit of information exchange within OSPF, and each possesses a type indicator to show its purpose. One such indicator is opaque, which lets routers know that the information is not part of IP routing.

Within the opaque LSA there are further type indicators to identify the type of information. New values are defined to encompass the TE and GMPLS link information that has already been described.

Note that OSPF opaque LSAs have *flooding scope*. This means that each opaque LSA is labeled to say whether it should be sent to every router in the Autonomous System, limited to every router in the routing area, or kept within the local network. All TE and GMPLS opaque LSAs are sent to every router in the routing area (see Section 5.6.2 for a discussion of inter-domain traffic engineering).

5.5.2 *IS-IS*

The basic unit of information transfer in IS-IS is a routing information TLV. Each TLV is encoded as a type indicator, a length, and a value. Multiple TLVs may be collected together into Link State Protocol Data Units (LSPs, but not Label

Switched Paths) for distribution between routers, but the important unit of information remains the TLV.

TE and GMPLS information distribution in IS-IS is achieved using new TLVs defined for the purpose, and these carry exactly the same information as in OSPF; that is, all of the information described in Sections 5.2 and 5.3. For this information to be grouped together and handled as one unit, these new TLVs are defined to include sub-TLVs, each encoding one smaller piece of information — these sub-TLVs are an innovation for the IS-IS protocol.

5.6 Advanced Features

This section briefly introduces two advanced features associated with GMPLS routing: graceful shutdown of TE links, and inter-domain routing (which is discussed in greater detail in Chapter 8).

5.6.1 *Graceful Shutdown*

The link state routing protocol function gives a routing controller the ability to introduce a new TE link, or to withdraw a TE link from service. It does the latter, for example, when it becomes aware that a fiber has failed or that an interface card has been pulled. This information is important to the signaling function because it means not only that no new LSP should be computed to use the failed TE link, but that all existing LSPs that use the link are broken.

But it is also useful to define a half-way state between active and failed. In this state all existing LSPs can continue to function normally, but no new LSP should be attempted. This state can actually be achieved quite simply using the parameters described in Sections 5.2 and 5.3. All that a routing controller needs to do to prevent new LSPs being signaled is to advertise that there is no more available bandwidth on the link (that is, that the maximum bandwidth that may be allocated to a new LSP is zero).

There is concern that this process does not quite prevent all new LSPs. Suppose a "best effort" LSP was requested with zero reserved bandwidth: Wouldn't it be possible to compute a path that used TE links for which all of the bandwidth had been withdrawn as described above? This is certainly the case, although it really only applies to packet switched links, because requesting a zero bandwidth timeslot or lambda is meaningless. One suggested option to handle this case is to use the GMPLS routing parameter that defines the minimum LSP bandwidth that may be allocated on the TE link — if this is set to some non-zero figure then a TE link with zero available bandwidth will not be available for any LSP. An alternative that is being discussed in the IETF's CCAMP working group is to extend the GMPLS routing information by presenting a new flag that says "active, but no new LSPs allowed."

This half-way state is particularly useful for graceful shutdown of a data plane resource. For example, it may be necessary to take an interface card out of service so that it can be replaced. If the card is simply pulled it will cause data hits to all traffic carried through the card, and if the services are not protected this hit may be very significant. However, if we simply notify the services so that they can re-route their LSPs, there is a risk that, as the bandwidth becomes available, new LSPs will be computed to use the TE link. Hence the recommended sequence of events is as follows.

- Withdraw all available bandwidth on the TE link so that no new LSPs will be computed to use it.
- Notify all services that use the TE link that they must modify their LSPs to use different paths through the network.
- As each LSP is removed from the link, free up the resources, but continue to advertise that no bandwidth is available.
- Once all LSPs have been removed the TE link can be shut down and the card removed.

Obviously this process requires a small signaling extension to notify the services that the TE link is going out of service, but this is very easily achieved using new error codes for existing signaling messages.

5.6.2 *Inter-Domain Traffic Engineering*

So far, this chapter has only discussed the operation of GMPLS routing within a single routing area. In general, traffic engineering information distribution is strictly limited to within one routing area because of the large amount of data involved and because of the potential for this information to change very rapidly. If TE information was to be distributed across the whole Internet there would be a very great risk that the routing protocols would simply not be able to keep up. In fact, we would immediately lose all of the scaling benefits achieved by separating the network into routing areas, and, of course, we would lose all of the management and secrecy attributes associated with separate Autonomous Systems.

In its work on GMPLS traffic engineering, the IETF has recognized that there is a fundamental unit of network applicable to path computation. It is the collection of network nodes that have full visibility of the TE links that interconnect them, such that any could compute a path to any of the others. This collection is termed a *path computation domain*. Such a domain may map to a routing area or to an Autonomous System.

The question becomes: How do I establish a traffic engineered GMPLS LSP from one domain to, or across, another? In order to achieve this I would ideally have full visibility of all of the TE information between the source and destination, but to do so would violate the definition of the path computation domain. There are, in fact, three possible configurations to be solved. As shown in Figure 5.1, it is possible that one domain may be wholly contained in another, that there may be a linear series of domains, or that there may be a choice of domains.

There is one problem consistent with each of these configurations: When a signaling request reaches a domain boundary, a path must be computed across the domain to the other side (or to the egress). This is a simple problem because at the domain boundary there is full visibility within the domain (all TE information has been distributed within the domain by the routing protocol) and so the computation can be made.

There are other problems that are more tricky. First, should the LSP be routed through the nested domain or around it? Secondly, which of the domain

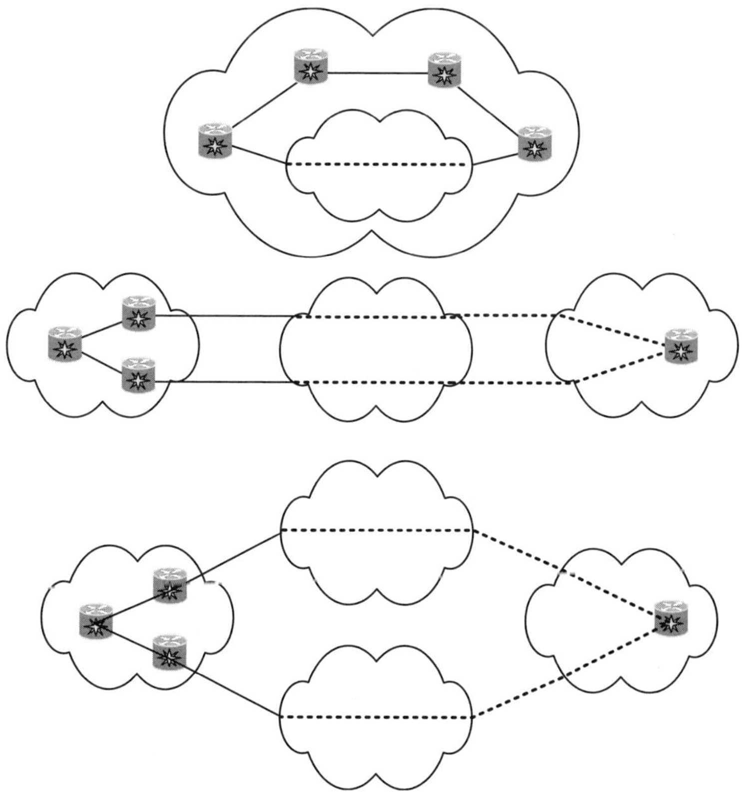

Figure 5.1 Inter-domain path computation configurations.

interconnection points should be used to achieve the best end-to-end path? And in the third case, which domains should be used to provide the path of the LSP? None of these questions can be answered simply because the correct answer requires knowledge of the TE link state and GMPLS information from outside the domain of the node that is computing the path.

Various suggestions have been made to summarize TE and GMPLS information so that it can be "leaked" from one domain to another. The idea is that this summarization would be a considerable reduction compared with the full TE information and would, therefore, perhaps be acceptable without compromising the function or the routing protocols. Two approaches have been suggested. One summarizes a domain as a *virtual node* presenting all of its external TE links and defining limited cross-connection abilities between these external TE links across the summarized domain. The other approach summarizes the domain as a set of edge-to-edge TE links.

Neither suggestion is, as yet, well developed, although some work has been suggested to add TE extensions to the inter-AS routing protocol, BGP. Instead, work is focusing on the Path Computation Element (PCE) that provides a proxy path computation server. To compute a path that leaves a domain, a request may be sent to the external PCE, and it may have wider visibility or may cooperate with PCEs from other domains in order to determine the best path.

The whole issue of multi-domain path computation and the way that PCE works is discussed at greater length in Chapters 8 and 9.

5.7 Further Reading

Further details of the messages, protocol objects, and field values for the traffic engineering and GMPLS extensions to OSPF and IS-IS can be found in *The Internet and Its Protocols: A Comparative Approach* by Adrian Farrel (2004), Morgan Kaufmann.

IETF RFCs and Internet-Drafts on this subject are as follows:

RFC 3630 — Traffic Engineering (TE) Extensions to OSPF Version 2
RFC 3784 — IS-IS Extensions for Traffic Engineering
RFC 3945 — Generalized Multi-Protocol Label Switching (GMPLS) Architecture
RFC 4202 — Routing Extensions in Support of Generalized Multi-Protocol Label Switching
RFC 4203 — OSPF Extensions in Support of Generalized MPLS
RFC 4205 — IS-IS Extensions in Support of Generalized MPLS
draft-ietf-ccamp-inter-domain-framework A Framework for Inter-Domain MPLS Traffic Engineering

CHAPTER 6

Link Management

GMPLS network nodes may be connected together by many data channels or links. Each channel may be a fiber, but there may be many channels within a single link — for example, separate lambdas within a WDM fiber. A pair of nodes that are connected in the data plane and that run GMPLS control plane protocols need to be able to identify and refer to each data channel in an unambiguous way that their neighbor can clearly understand. Because there is usually no one-to-one correspondence between data channels and the paths that are used for control plane communication, it is necessary for the data channels to be specifically identified at each node.

It is certainly possible to configure this information at each LSR, but as the number of data channels increases, this becomes a tremendous management overhead prone to error and completely inflexible to fibering changes within the network. The problem is handled by the Link Management Protocol (LMP) that helps switches discover the capabilities and identifiers of links that connect them. The protocol also determines the operational status of links and helps the LSRs to detect and isolate faults in optical networks where some switches do not utilize electronic components on the data path (all-optical switches are often called OOOs, or photonic cross-connects, PXCs).

This chapter describes how links are managed in a GMPLS system, and explores the peculiarities of link management in different types of transport networks with a special accent on WDM networks. The Link Management Protocol (LMP) and its extensions for control and management within WDM systems (LMP-WDM) are introduced. This chapter also explains how link management affects traffic engineering in GMPLS.

6.1 Links, Control Channels, and Data Channels

A channel is defined as an independent connection between a pair of network nodes. Control channels carry signaling, routing, and other control messages.

Data channels carry data. With an in-band packet network such as Ethernet, there is usually a single channel between a pair of nodes that carries both control and data messages. An out-of-band signaling network has a distinct control channel such as a reserved wavelength in a fiber, a reserved timeslot, or perhaps an Ethernet link that runs parallel to the fiber. The control channel could even run through a distinct IP network and pass through many routers before reaching the next hop on the data path. If there are multiple parallel fibers providing links between two nodes, each may be identified as a data channel, but it is not necessary to have more than one control channel.

6.2 The Link Management Protocol

The Link Management Protocol (LMP) is a point-to-point application protocol that is run over UDP using port 701. This means that the LMP messages are scoped just to the single exchange between GMPLS devices that are adjacent in the data plane, and that the protocol must take responsibility for recovering from control plane errors because UDP is an unreliable transport protocol.

LMP requires that the addresses of control channels are configured at each node. In order to maintain an LMP adjacency, it is necessary to have at least one active control channel between the two nodes. It is acceptable to have more than one control channel to provide a degree of robustness. In LMP the Node ID is usually taken from the IGP that is running in the network. In any case it should be globally unique, and must be sufficiently unambiguous to allow any one node to distinguish its peers. The Control Channel ID (CCID) is required to be unique on any one node.

The protocol has several distinct functional units.

- Control Channel Management starts with Initialization, during which the LMP neighbors exchange messages to bring the control channel into use and to establish their identities and capabilities. Once the control channel is active, Control Channel Maintenance is achieved through the regular exchange of Hello messages.
- The Link Discovery process in LMP helps an LSR determine the existence, connectivity, and nature of the data links to and from its neighbor. Initially one node knows its local identifiers for the data links that it believes connect to the adjacent node, but it does not know the state of these links nor the identifiers used by the other node to refer to them — the sequence of messages exchanged during link discovery resolves all of its questions.
- Link Capabilities Exchange may be used as an additional step after Link Discovery so that the LSRs can tell each other about the specific features of

the data links. This optional phase may not be necessary if it is well known that only one type of link is supported, but it can also be very useful to build traffic engineering links out of multiple parallel physical links through the process of summarization. That is, it helps the TE system to identify the remote IDs of components of a TE link, and to verify the operational health of each component link so that the TE topology can be independent from IGP adjacencies.

- Link Verification can be conducted at any time to check the status and connectivity of the data links between two LMP peers. This may be carried out on a timer just to check that everything is functioning correctly, or it may require specific operator intervention, perhaps after a failure. The link verification processes are identical to the link discovery procedures.
- Fault Isolation is one of the most important features of LMP. It is particularly important in networks where switches normally operate in transparent mode, meaning that they do not examine the data signal. Devices such as photonic cross-connects may not normally notice if there is a disruption to the signal, and LMP helps to isolate and report faults that may occur. The process is initiated by a downstream node that detects a problem on a data link, perhaps when it notices loss of light, signal degradation, or a framing problem.
- Although Authentication is not a formal part of the LMP specification, it is important to note that procedures do exist to allow LMP peers to verify that they are communicating with each other and that their messages have not been tampered with. This may be particularly important because the LMP messages may be routed through an IP network.

6.2.1 LMP Messages

LMP messages are constructed from a common message header that identifies the message type and length, followed by a series of message objects. Each object is identified by a Class indicating the type of the object and a Class Type that determines the use to which the object is put. The object carries a length field indicating the size of the whole object, and the rest of the object is given over to data that is formatted according to the Class and Class Type. An object may contain sub-objects using the same encoding rules.

Because LMP is carried by the UDP transport protocol, it must take measures to ensure that messages are reliably delivered. The various functional units are therefore defined with protocol exchanges that include positive acknowledgements and use message identifiers to correlate the requests and responses. The message identifiers are not assumed to have any specific order, and it is the responsibility of the message sender to ensure that the message identifiers used allow it to unambiguously resolve the responses.

Reliable message delivery is attempted by the sender running a retransmission timer for all messages it sends. If the acknowledgement message is not received in a relatively short time the sender can retransmit the message. If the message fails to be acknowledged after several retransmissions, there is probably a problem with the control channel — hopefully the control channel maintenance process will already have discovered the fault.

6.2.2 *Control Channel Management*

An LMP control channel comes into service when one end sends a Config message. The Config message identifies the local end of the control channel (with a CCID) and carries negotiable parameters to apply to the use of LMP between the two nodes. The receiver of a Config message replies with a ConfigAck message to accept the parameters and supply its own identifiers. The ConfigAck message includes the node, control channel, and message identifiers from the received Config message so that there is no ambiguity. If the receiver of the Config message wishes to negotiate the configuration, it sends a ConfigNack message (including its preferred configuration parameters) and the initiator either gives up or modifies and re-sends its Config message.

The Config/ConfigAck exchange defines one LMP peer as the initiator and one as the responder. In the event that both peers send a Config message at the same time, the one with the numerically greater local node ID is designated as the initiator and does not respond to the received Config message.

Multiple control channels may be active at the same time between a pair of LMP peers. They simply perform the same initialization steps on each control channel. The benefit is that, should a control channel fail, LMP processing can be immediately transferred to another control channel. In practice, however, implementations rarely maintain multiple control channels simultaneously. They rely on the fact that it is relatively fast to establish a new control channel by exchanging Config messages, or the understanding that UDP datagrams may be routed by various means to deliver the LMP messages for a single control channel.

Control channels are kept alive by the regular exchange of Hello messages. The Hello Interval is one of the parameters negotiated on the Config exchange, and both peers are required to send a new Hello message every time the timer interval expires. The Hello messages are not a request/response pair. If either peer fails to receive a Hello message within the Hello Dead Interval (also negotiated on the Config exchange) it declares the control channel dead, stops sending its Hello messages, and may start to establish a new control channel or to listen for protocol messages on some other existing control channel.

Figure 6.1 shows two control channels between LSRs A and B. The first control channel (CCID 1) is activated by LSR A — this is the primary control

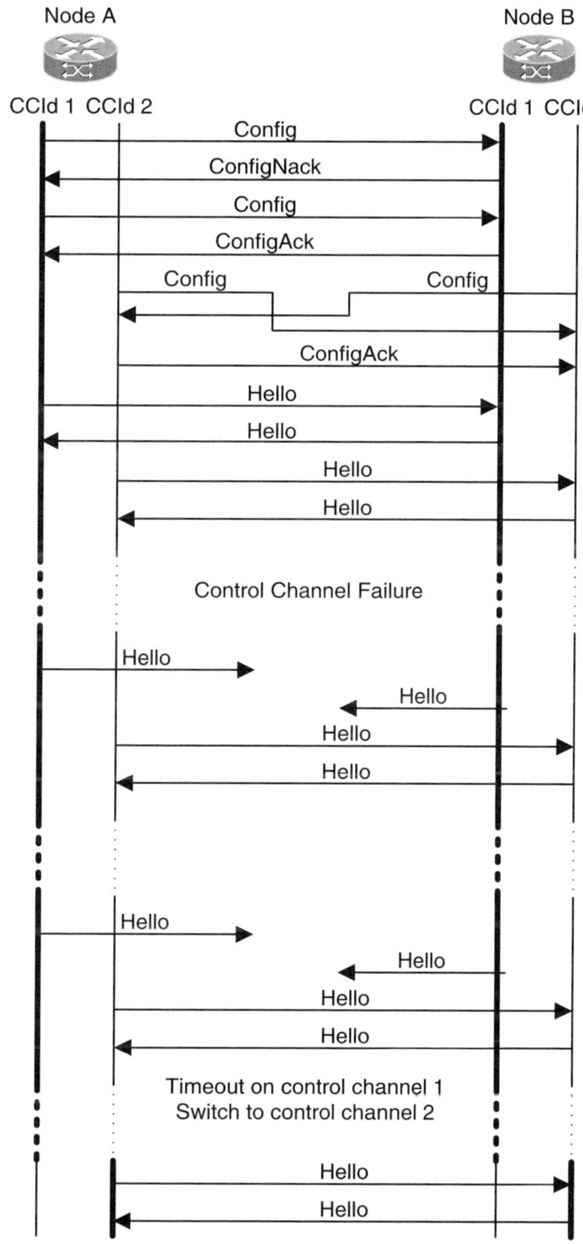

Figure 6.1 Dual control channel establishment in LMP showing configuration negotiation, simultaneous Config messages, and control channel failure.

channel shown by a solid vertical line in the figure. LSR B rejects the parameters using a ConfigNack, and LSR A issues a new Config message that is accepted by LSR B.

The second control channel is activated by both LSRs at the same time — this is the backup control channel used in case of a failure of the primary control channel, and is shown in Figure 6.1 by a thin vertical line. Because LSR B has a larger node ID than LSR A, it becomes the initiator and LSR A responds with a ConfigAck. Both LSRs immediately begin exchanging Hello messages on both control channels.

After a while the Hello messages on the control channel with CCID 1 do not get through, but the messages on the other control channel are fine. When the Hello Dead Interval expires, the LSRs switch over to the other control channel by designating it as the primary. They both stop sending Hello messages on the failed control channel and must resort to a new Config exchange if they want to re-activate it.

6.2.3 *Link Discovery and Verification*

Link Discovery and Link Verification are identical processes that lead to the discovery of the connectivity of data links between a pair of nodes and the determination of their statuses. Initially one node knows its local identifiers for the data links that it believes connect to the adjacent node, but it does not know the state of these links nor the identifiers used by the other node to refer to them. It needs this information if it is to successfully signal connections such as LSPs using the links. In GMPLS, LSRs use the interface ID mappings determined by LMP link verification to signal exactly which link is to carry an LSP, and clearly an LSR that receives a signaling message needs to have the same understanding of the link identifier as the LSR that sent the message. The information is also needed by the traffic engineering components to synchronize the advertisements of both ends of the TE links in order to correctly install edges between vertices on the network representation graph (see Chapters 8 and 9).

The link verification process is bounded by the exchange of BeginVerify/ BeginVerifyAck and EndVerify/EndVerifyAck messages. The node that wishes to verify the links sends BeginVerify and the partner node responds with a positive acknowledgement or a BeginVerifyNack if it is unable or unwilling to comply. When the verification process is complete, the initiator sends an EndVerify message and this is acknowledged by the responder. As with Config messages, these messages carry message IDs to match responses to their requests. Additionally, a verify ID is used on the BeginVerifyAck message and on the EndVerify exchange to disambiguate multiple simultaneous link verifications.

The link verification process may be applied to all links between a pair of nodes or may be limited to a single link specified by using a non-zero local link ID. If the remote ID of the link is known to the sender it may also be supplied. If the verification is for a single link, the response contains the other node's identifier of the link.

The BeginVerify message carries objects to describe the verification procedure that will be applied. The principal issue is the transport verification mechanism to be used. This is important because transport verification requires some interference with the data signal to identify which data channel is in use.

Ideally, LMP would send a packet down the data channel being verified and the receiver would spot the packet, enabling it to both verify that the data channel is active and to match the source link ID to its own link ID. The LMP Test message can be used in this way provided that the source has the ability to insert Test messages into the data channel and the destination has the ability to detect them. Although this is clearly the case for packet media, it is often not the case in optical and TDM switches, so other methods of indicating the data channels are used. In TDM, the overhead bytes are used, whereas in optical networks there are proposals to signal simply by turning lasers on and off — a process that is clearly disruptive of traffic! For these non-packet cases, the Test message is sent over the control channel and the selected transport verification mechanism is applied to the data channels. The initiator of the verification process may offer several verification mechanisms and the responder must select just one that will actually be used.

The link verification process and message exchange is captured for the initiator in the pseudocode in Figure 6.2, and for the responder in Figure 6.3.

6.2.4 *Link Capabilities*

Once nodes have established data channel connectivity using the link verification procedures it may be useful for them to exchange information about the capabilities of the data channels. This is particularly important where the data channels between a pair of nodes have different qualities. The Link Property Summarization exchange can also be used to verify the integrity of the link configuration if link identifiers are configured rather than discovered using Link Verification.

Link Summarization consists of the exchange of LinkSummary and LinkSummaryAck/Nack messages. Each LinkSummary message may report on multiple data channels that belong to a single link. The Ack message simply agrees to the distributed parameters, whereas the Nack message includes an error code to indicate the failure reason and may list the data channels that are being failed if the failure does not apply to all the data channels in the original LinkSummary message.

```
START
  send BeginVerify
  IF receive BeginVerifyNack
    end procedure
  ELSE receive BeginVerifyAck
    DO for each link
      DO while retrying link
        send Test message
        IF Test NOT carried in payload
          modify transport characteristics
          (for example, change the overhead bytes)
        ENDIF
        sleep waiting for Test response
        IF Test response received
          IF response is TestStatusSuccess
            set configuration for link
          ELSE response is TestStatusFailure
            set link as unusable
          ENDIF
          send TestStatusAck
          BREAK out of the retry loop
        ENDIF
      ENDDO
      IF Test NOT carried in payload
        restore transport characteristics
      ENDIF
    ENDDO
    send EndVerify
    receive EndVerifyAck
  ENDIF
END
```

Figure 6.2 Pseudocode to describe the verification procedure at the initiator.

The attributes of a data channel that may be exchanged (in addition to the link IDs) include whether the link is a port as opposed to a component link, whether the data link is currently allocated for user traffic, and whether the data link is currently in a failed state and not suitable for user traffic. Further sub-objects in the LinkSummary message describe the switching types and encoding types that the link supports the minimum and maximum reservable bandwidths, and a wavelength ID.

6.2.5 *Fault Isolation*

Fault isolation is an important optional feature of LMP. It is particularly useful because some optical switches are "transparent," meaning that they switch and propagate light signals without examining them. They may switch data by fiber,

```
START
  receive BeginVerify
  IF verify process is NOT acceptable
    send BeginVerifyNack
    end procedure
  ELSE
    send BeginVerifyAck
    start dead timer
  ENDIF
  DO forever
    IF receive a Test message
      IF Test is in payload
        send TestStatusSuccess message
      ELSE
        start to test the transport
      ENDIF
    ENDIF
    IF transport pattern detected
      send TestStatusSuccess message
      stop testing the transport
    ENDIF
    IF dead timer expires
      IF currently testing the transport
        stop testing the transport
      ENDIF
    send TestStatusFailure message
    ENDIF
    IF TestStatusAck message received
      IF currently testing the transport
        stop testing the transport
      ENDIF
      restart the dead timer
    ENDIF
    IF EndVerify message received
      IF currently testing the transport
        stop testing the transport
      ENDIF
      stop the dead timer
      send EndVerifyAck
      BREAK out of permanent loop
    ENDIF
  ENDDO
END
```

Figure 6.3 Pseudocode to describe the verification procedure at the responder.

wavelength, or timeslot without inspecting the signal itself. Consequently, if the signal fails because of some fault upstream, the optical switches may simply not notice.

The worst case of this behavior would result in the failure going undetected until the signal reached the egress node where it was due to be converted back to an electrical signal to be forwarded into a packet switched network. To repair connections by means such as re-routing traffic to backup paths it is necessary to localize the fault; otherwise the repair may be inefficient or might continue to utilize the failed link. The problem is compounded by the fact that when a transparent device decides to examine a signal it might only be able to do so destructively; that is, by completely disrupting the downstream signal.

LMP provides a mechanism to isolate and report faults. The process is initiated by a downstream node that detects a problem on a data link. This node sends a ChannelStatus message upstream using the control channel and immediately receives an acknowledgement. The upstream node receiving a ChannelStatus message that reports a failure knows that it is safe to destructively examine the data signal and checks to see whether it is receiving a satisfactory signal from its upstream neighbor. If it is receiving a good signal, the fault has been isolated and the upstream node returns a ChannelStatus message to say that the link is fine. If the upstream node is not receiving a good signal, it sends a ChannelStatus message both upstream and downstream to its neighbors to report the problem. Note that it is possible for the upstream node to have already spotted the fault when it receives the ChannelStatus message from its downstream neighbor.

Nodes may request channel status information at any time using the ChannelStatusRequest and ChannelStatusResponse exchange. This may be particularly useful when a router or switch is initialized when it is desirable to find out the status of all the links. Figure 6.4 shows a simple example where the data channel failure is detected downstream from the actual failure and is isolated using LMP.

6.2.6 *Authentication*

Confidentiality is not considered a requirement of LMP, but it is necessary to authenticate message senders to protect against spoofing that might disrupt data services. This is especially important where the control channel passes through an arbitrary IP cloud on its way between two nodes that are adjacent in the data plane. The LMP specification suggests that LMP security is in the domain of the IP and UDP transport mechanisms and recommends the use of IPSec.

6.2.7 *Implications for Traffic Engineering and Link Bundling*

Between a pair of adjacent switches there may be a large number of physical links (such as optical fibers). It makes a lot of sense to bundle these links so that the

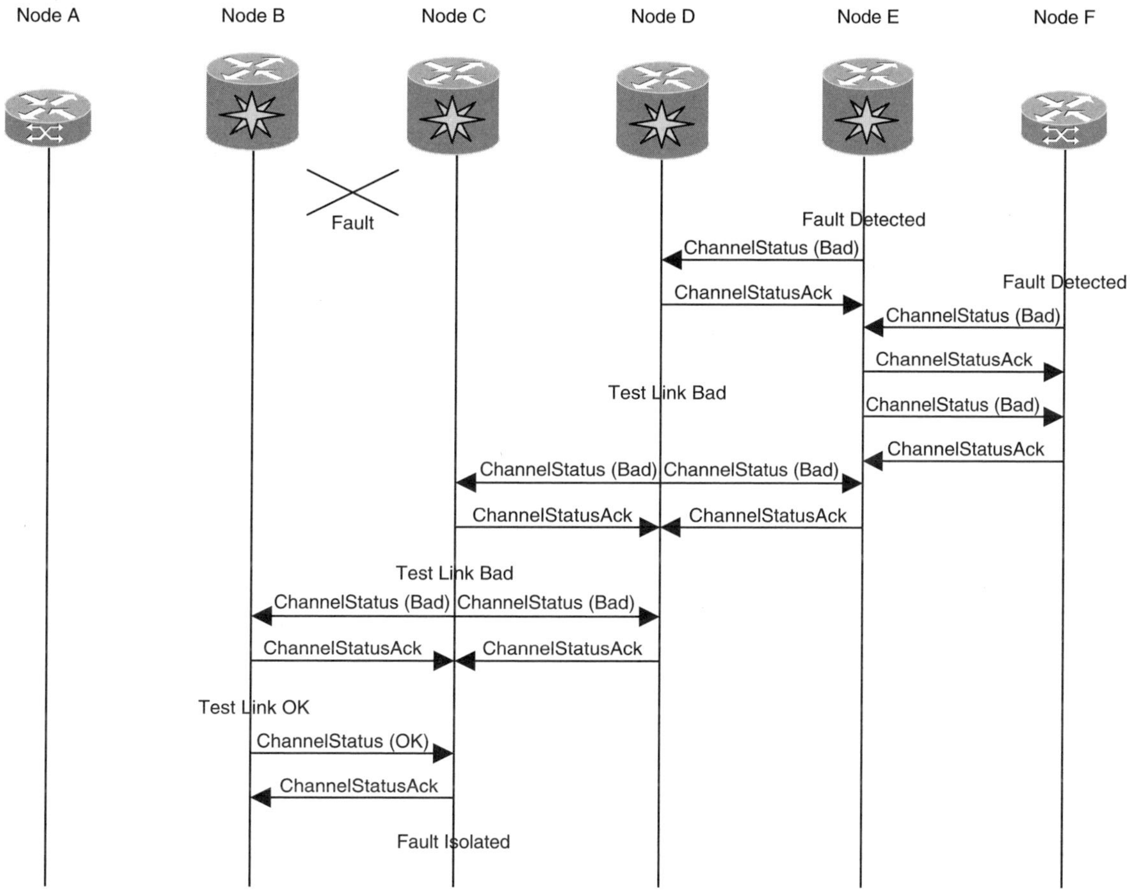

Figure 6.4 LMP message exchange for fault isolation and reporting.

routing protocol is not over-burdened, and to manage the resulting TE Link as a single entity.

However, even if individual links or fibers are not identified through the routing protocol they still need to be indicated by the signaling protocol so that both peers understand which data link is to be used to carry a specific data flow. GMPLS uses the link ID for this purpose, but there is still a need for the nodes to agree on the identifiers assigned to each link so that they can communicate unambiguously. This agreement can be achieved through configuration, but LMP allows for a protocol-based exchange of link identifiers. In fact, LMP contains procedures for exchanging link identifiers, for verifying the connectivity of links, and for exchanging link properties so they can be grouped into a single TE link.

6.3 Device-Level Resource Discovery

Many hardware companies specialize in the manufacture of Add-Drop Multiplexors (ADMs) or Optical Switches (OXCs) and do not necessarily integrate both functions into their products. Even when they do, they see architectural or commercial benefits to separating the components. The separation normally applied collects the ADM together with any line amplifiers as a single component called the Optical Line System (OLS).

In such a distributed model there are optical links between the ADM and the OXC that need to be configured, verified, and monitored. Doing this will enable the OXC to correctly understand the resources that are available to it and will help it isolate faults. Many of the features necessary for this function are already provided by LMP, so it is natural to extend the protocol for use between the OXC and OLS. This extended protocol is called LMP-WDM, is shown in Figure 6.5, and is discussed in the next section.

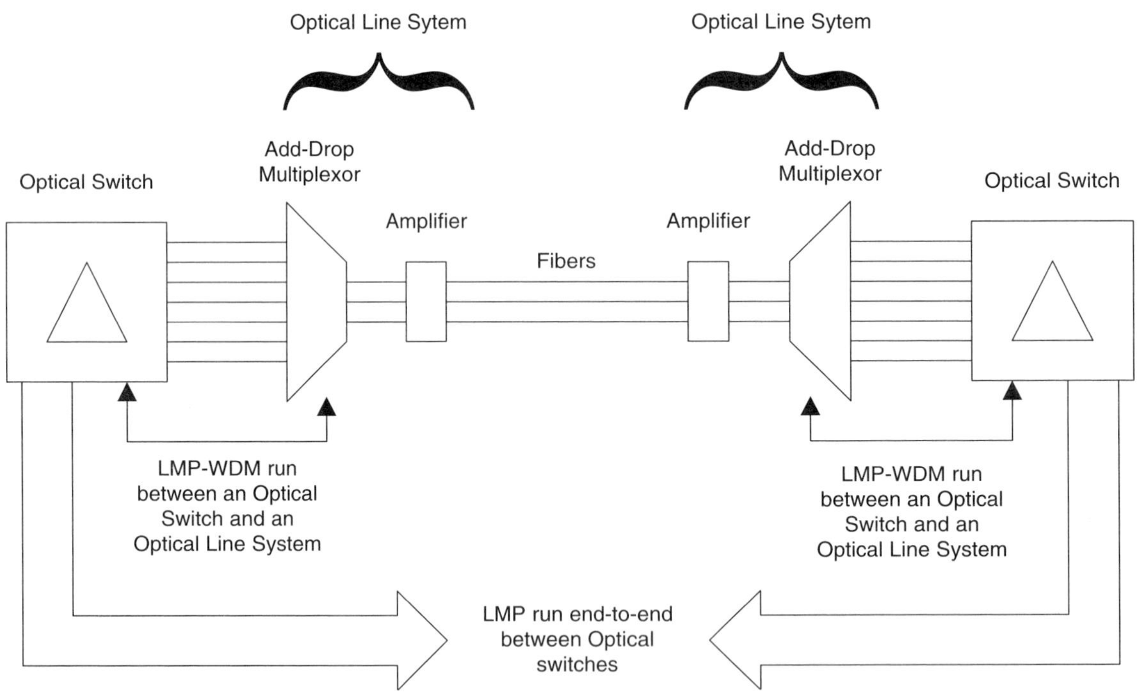

Figure 6.5 LMP-WDM runs between an optical switch and an optical line system.

6.3.1 *LMP-WDM*

LMP-WDM is an extension to the LMP for use within Wave Division Multiplexing (WDM) switches. That is, it is a version of LMP that is run between the components of a switch rather than across a network.

The use of LMP-WDM assumes that some form of control channel exists between the OXC and the OLS. This may be a dedicated lambda, an Ethernet link, or a backplane. In order to distinguish between control channels set up between OXCs and those between an OXC and an OLS, a new object is introduced on the Config message where it is used in addition to the existing objects if the control channel is used for LMP-WDM.

No changes to the messages are required for link verification, but it should be noted that the links tested during LMP-WDM link verification are components (segments) of the links that would be tested in LMP link verification between a pair of OXCs. Therefore it is important not to run the two link verification procedures at the same time.

Several additions may usefully be made to the link summarization process to report the characteristics of the optical links between the OXC and the OLS. The Link Summary message contains a series of objects to describe the link, and each object contains a sequence of sub-objects describing the link in detail. LMP-WDM defines new sub-objects specifically for OXC/OLS link properties, including the following.

- A list of shared risk link groups (SRLGs) to which the link belongs
- A bit error rate (BER) estimate
- A list of the GMPLS protection types supported by the link
- The span length of the fiber between the OXC and OLS in meters
- An administrative color for the link

Fault management is also inherited from LMP.

Currently LMP-WDM is not widely used. The rapid progress in the development of all-optical components has slowed down considerably in the last few years and LMP-WDM remains somewhat unproven.

6.4 Further Reading

A more detailed description of LMP and LMP-WDM can be found in *The Internet and Its Protocols: A Comparative Approach* by Adrian Farrel (2004), Morgan Kaufmann.

The protocols are defined in an RFC and an Internet-Draft that is soon to become an RFC.

RFC 4204 —	Link Management Protocol
draft-ietf-ccamp-lmp-wdm	Link Management Protocol (LMP) for Dense Wavelength Division Multiplexing (DWDM) Optical Line Systems

CHAPTER 7

GMPLS and Service Recovery

Transport network resources do fail. Fibers get cut, and cross-connects, amplifiers, DWDM devices, network controllers, and control channels go out of service unexpectedly. Considering the huge amounts of data carried over transport networks, a single such failure, even for a short period of time, can cause a lot of damage to users of services that happen to traverse the point of failure. Users do not generally tolerate losses of data or connectivity. Usually there is a very stringent requirement on the time within which a service must be recovered after its interruption. The only way for transport Service Providers to meet this requirement is to over-provision their networks so that, at any point in time, active services could be diverted from any potential point of failure onto some other network resources. But even this is not sufficient. There should also be an intelligence that can rapidly detect and localize failures as well as switch the services away from them. Likewise, there should be an intelligence capable of computing diverse primary and recovery paths, so that a single failure will not affect them both. Finally, there should be an intelligence that can place primary and recovery paths of multiple services in such a way that the same network resources could protect multiple services and could be used for so-called extra-traffic services while there are no failures in the network, thereby considerably lessening the cost of over-provisioning without providing a significantly reduced ability to protect against failures.

In this chapter we will discuss how GMPLS enables such intelligence. We will start with identifying failures that may happen in transport networks. We will describe responsibilities of different network elements in detecting and correlating them and sending failure notifications to the elements that are provisioned to perform recovery actions. We will discuss different recovery schemes that are used for link recovery, as well as those used for end-to-end path and segment recovery. At the end of the chapter we will analyze the consequences of control plane failures and the challenges of managing so-called control plane partitioned LSPs.

7.1 Failures in Transport Networks

There are numerous ways to classify failures within transport networks. Depending on the type of failed network element, the failures can be broken into two groups: control plane failures and data plane failures. The failures of the latter group (for example, fiber cuts, cross-connect failures) directly affect services using the failed elements, whereas the failures of the former group (for example, controller, control channel failures) make services unmanageable or only partially manageable.

Further, depending on the type of a failed component, the failure can be classified as a hardware (electronic or optical component defect), software (bug), or configuration (operator mistake) failure. Additionally, Service Providers distinguish failures caused by internal events (that is, some network imperfection), and by external events (for example, electricity breakdown, flood, digging accident, etc.).

Many failures can be prevented: Fiber-optic cables can be placed deeper in the ground within armored casings, hardware and software components can be tested more thoroughly, personnel can be better trained, high-quality security systems can be installed to protect against hacker attacks. However, it is well understood and widely accepted that failures cannot be completely eliminated. Therefore, transport networks must handle failures in such a way that they cause minimal disruption (if any) for affected services. In other words, networks must be able to survive any single failure or multiple simultaneous failures.

This is a very challenging task. First of all, networks are required to have enough resources to accommodate user traffic under conditions of one or more failures. Equally important is that there must be an intelligence that could support rapid failure detection and localization and that could switch the affected services onto alternative paths, so that user traffic is not affected to an extent beyond the level that was agreed upon between users and Service Providers.

The next section provides some definitions that are necessary to quantify the network survivability.

7.2 Network Survivability Definitions

Let us make the following definitions.

- The *availability* of a network element is the probability that the element can deliver some specified Quality of Service (QoS) at some point of time.
- The *failure* of a network element is the moment when the element stops delivering the specified QoS.
- The *repair* of a network element is the moment when the element regains its ability to deliver the specified QoS.

- A *fault* (also known as an *outage*) is the period of time when a network element is not functional — that is, the period of time between a failure and subsequent repair.

Note that not every defect in a network element can be categorized as a failure. Some defects degrade the quality or level of services using the affected element, but do not fully disrupt them, which leaves their QoS parameters within an acceptable (agreed upon) range. Some defects do not have a notable impact on existing services, but might prevent further services from being established. In this chapter we will only consider those defects that fully disrupt services — that is, stop delivering the specified QoS — as failures.

Network element availability can be calculated according to the formula:

$$A = 1 - Tmr/Tmbf$$

where

A	is the network element's availability,
Tmr	is the element's mean time to repair,
$Tmbf$	is the element's mean time between failures.

For hardware elements the mean time to repair may typically be quite large because it will involve the dispatch of a service engineer (a truck-roll). Nevertheless, the mean time to repair is normally a considerable order of magnitude less than the mean time between failures. Any other state of affairs would require the service engineer to camp out on site with the equipment. For software components the mean time between failures is often considered to be quite short: Although a lot of effort is put into testing, software does not have a good reputation for reliability and stability. However, software repair is generally achieved simply by reloading the software so that the mean time to repair is very small. Thus, it is usually the case that $Tmr \ll Tmbf$, and so A is some number very close to 1.

Suppose a network is built of n network elements. The network availability can be computed as the compound:

$$AN = A1 * A2 * \ldots * An$$

where AN is the network availability and $A1, A2, \ldots, An$ are the availabilities of each of the network constituents. Note that this formula is correct only if one assumes complete independence of failures of all network elements.

It is also worth mentioning that because $Tmr \ll Tmbf$ for each element, the probability of two or more simultaneous failures is often considered negligible, and many recovery schemes are provisioned for a single failure scenario.

7.3 Service Recovery Cycle

One can distinguish the following stages of a service recovery process.

- Fault detection
- Fault hold-off
- Fault localization
- Fault correlation
- Fault notification
- Recovery operation
- Traffic recovery

The five first stages are collectively called *fault management*. Fault detection is the only stage that cannot be accomplished without interaction with the data plane — all other stages can be realized by either the control plane or the data plane independently or by cooperation between the two planes.

When a fault occurs, the nodes adjacent to the failed link or node do not detect the fault instantly. It takes some time for the hardware dedicated to fault detection (for example, components monitoring signal overhead bytes, power level, and so forth) to identify the failed component, define the exact fault state, and notify the entity responsible for fault management (for example, the GMPLS control plane). The *fault detection time* may depend heavily on the data plane technology (for example, TDM or WDM), how intrusive each node is in the processing of signals (for example, whether electronic components are used for timing synchronization, signal regeneration, or signal monitoring), and whether the signal is normally expected to be continuous or only present when data is being transferred.

The fault management entity does not usually react to the fault notification right away. First, it moves the service into the *fault hold-off* state. This is necessary because a lower network layer may have a recovery scheme of its own, and it is highly undesirable to have multiple layers simultaneously trying to recover from the same fault, as that might actually lead to service disruption and would certainly result in inefficient use of network resources. It is also possible that the fault will self-heal very rapidly (or has even been misreported) and that the service will resume without any need for intervention. Hence, generally speaking, there is a need for some hold-off time to give a chance for other layer(s) to attempt to recover. If after the hold-off time the fault indication is still not removed, the service recovery is moved into the next — *fault localization* — stage. Note that in most cases the fault managing entity is collocated with a fault detecting entity; however, this is not always the case. When the two entities are physically separated an additional stage of the service recovery cycle — *fault report* is required.

Multiple nodes may detect the same failure. For example, after a fiber cut, all downstream nodes are likely to detect a loss of signal (LOS), and all nodes downstream as far as the next point of regeneration will report a loss of light (LOL). The fault managing entity needs to understand where on the network the failure actually occurred through a process of *fault localization* in order to define proper recovery scope. For services that have only end-to-end protection fault localization is not urgent and can be performed after the traffic is switched onto a recovery path (that is, after the recovery cycle is completed). On the other hand, if the recovery action will involve switching only a segment of the path to a recovery path, it is clearly important to determine where the failure is located. If the failure happened on the protected segment, local recovery is sufficient, but if the failure happened outside the protected segment, some upstream entity (perhaps the service head end) must be notified in order to take the necessary recovery action. Thus, failure localization is important. We will discuss end-to-end path and segment protection later in this chapter.

In some transport technologies (for example, SONET/SDH networks) failure localization is supported by the data plane. In others (for example, Optical Transport Networks) some other out-of-band means are needed, and the GMPLS control plane (more specifically LMP, see Chapter 6) provides such function. It is worth noting that there is no absolute need for an additional failure localization procedure in the control plane, even in the case of segment protection because all nodes that detect the failure can report it to a *deciding entity* (that is, an entity that controls the recovery procedures), which can perform the localization by examining the Traffic Engineering Database and/or analyzing the paths of the impacted services. However, specific failure localization procedures built into the control plane mean that faults can be localized more rapidly, services recovered more quickly, and recovery actions can be more precisely tuned to the specific failure.

With or without the failure localization stage, at least one of the failure-detecting nodes must play the role of reporting entity — sending the fault notification to the deciding entity. The dispatch of fault notifications may be delayed until the *fault correlation* stage is completed. To understand why this stage is desirable, keep in mind that a single failure may cause multiple fault indications. For instance, a fiber cut triggers fault indications for all services going through the affected link. It is possible (and very likely) that the same node performs the role of deciding entity for many or all of these services. For this case the GMPLS signaling protocol allows for the aggregation of fault indications and for sending the related notifications within a single message. Fault notifications must be delivered reliably (with possible re-transmission), and so, from the scalability point of view, such aggregation is a considerable improvement compared to delivering fault notifications for each service individually. Thus, during the fault correlation stage the fault-reporting node waits a certain amount of time to gather all fault indications, and groups them together according to the fault notification destination address.

During the *fault notification* stage a fault notification message arrives at the deciding entity from a fault-reporting node. The message can be delivered either via the data plane (for example, using the SDH overhead RDI signal) or via the control plane (for example, the GMPLS RSVP Notify message). In any case it is crucial that the message is delivered in a reliable manner. Note that when the control plane transports a fault notification message, the message does not necessarily follow the control plane path used to establish the service — the general flexibility of the network is used to deliver the message over the shortest available path.

On receipt of a fault notification message the deciding entity either relays it to another deciding entity or starts the *recovery operation* stage. Most of the remainder of this chapter is dedicated to an analysis of recovery operations. Depending on the type of recovery scheme provisioned for the service, the recovery operation on the deciding entity may range from doing nothing (for unprotected services, or for unidirectional 1 + 1 protection) to computing and setting up an alternative path and switching the traffic onto it (full re-routing).

Service recovery cycle is not completed by the recovery operation stage. It takes some non-negligible time for the traffic to settle down on the alternative path. This happens during the *traffic recovery* stage.

The overall service recovery time T can be computed as:

$$T = Td + Th + Tl + Tc + Tn + Tr + Tt$$

where

Td — fault detection time,
Th — hold-off time,
Tl — fault localization time,
Tc — fault correlation time,
Tn — fault notification time,
Tr — recovery operation time,
Tt — traffic recovery time.

Some services have very stringent requirements on the service recovery time (notoriously, 50 ms is often stated as an absolute maximum recovery time for voice traffic). In principle there are two fundamentally different approaches to meet these requirements.

In the first approach the traffic is permanently bridged (that is, cross-connected) onto two alternative paths and selected by the receiver from the path that has the better quality signal — this is called a 1 + 1 protection scheme. When a failure happens on one path, the receiver simply selects data from the healthy channel. The advantages of this approach are simplicity, best possible service recovery time, and independence from the recovery domain (see the definition in Section 7.7.1) size. The obvious disadvantage is that it is very expensive: One needs to allocate twice the network resources compared to the same unprotected service, and specialist equipment may be needed both to generate the signal on more than one path, and to monitor and select the received signals at the merge point (although the latter function can be controlled through the use of fault notifications).

The second approach is to use other protection schemes that are more efficient from the resource utilization point of view (for example, 1:N protection) and to provision multiple small, sometimes overlapping, protection domains, so that it is guaranteed that, no matter where on the protected path a failure occurs, the relevant deciding entity will always be near (one or two hops away from) the point of failure. Fast recovery is achieved in this case by minimizing the two most significant components of service recovery time — Tn and Tr — the fault notification, and recovery operation times. This approach is called *local repair*. Fast re-route and path segment recovery that will be discussed later in this chapter are two examples of the local repair.

7.4 Service Recovery Classes

Depending on the way alternative service paths are provisioned, service recovery can be broken into two classes: service protection and service restoration. Because most of the control plane aspects — path computation and selection, advertising, signaling, and so forth — are identical for both classes, the common term *service recovery* is used most of the time. Only when there is a need to highlight peculiarities of one of the two classes are the terms *protection* or *restoration* used instead.

In the early days of GMPLS, when the work on service recovery had just begun, there was a very clear distinction between service protection and service restoration. The former was defined as a class of service recovery where one or more alternative paths were fully established (that is, computed and signaled, with resources reserved, selected, and committed on all links, cross-connects programmed and prepared to switch traffic on all nodes) *before* a failure was detected. Service restoration was defined as a class of service recovery where no control plane actions related to the provisioning of alternative path(s) occurred until after failure had been reported to the deciding entity. In other words, in the case of service restoration, only when the deciding entity receives a fault notification is it supposed to trigger an alternative path setup starting from the path computation function.

The definition of service protection remains unchanged. However, it turned out that there could be many other ways to provision alternative paths that were definitely not under the umbrella of service protection, and did not quite fit into the definition of service restoration. For example, one or more alternative paths could be computed in advance, so that the process of service restoration could be started from the point of path selection rather than requiring the path computation phase. This scheme potentially yields a better recovery time compared to one of full restoration, but at the cost of a possibility that at the moment of service restoration the pre-computed paths will not be available because they were not provisioned and, therefore, their resources could have been taken by other services. Furthermore, one or more of the pre-computed paths could be pre-selected and pre-signaled, so that only activation is required after failure detection and indication.

Thus, the definition of service restoration was changed. The difference between service protection and restoration is now much subtler. Essentially, a service recovery scheme that does not require any *provisioning* signaling for the alternative path after the failure indication is classified as service protection. Everything else is service restoration. Note that some service protection schemes (most, in fact) require some synchronization between nodes initiating and terminating the protecting path and, therefore, some switchover signaling, but this is not classified as signaling for the purpose of provisioning.

Both service recovery classes have their pros and cons. The obvious advantage of service protection is the significantly better recovery times. The important advantages of service restoration are efficiency and flexibility in the use of network resources. To understand this, keep in mind that in the service protection model it is not known in advance which of the nodes or links on a protected path will fail. Therefore, the protected and protecting paths must be provisioned to be as diverse as possible, so that a single failure will not take both paths out of service simultaneously. Two diverse paths use more network resources than the one (shortest) path needed by an unprotected service. In the service restoration model the alternative path does not have to be fully diverse from the primary path. The only requirement is for it to be disjoint from the links or nodes that actually failed. In fact, the alternative path will be likely to reuse those resources unaffected by the failure of the primary path. This is the first reason why service restoration is more efficient than service protection. The other reason is that, until the failure happens, the resources that will be required to support the alternative path can be used by any other services in the network in any way. Note that while it is true that some service protection schemes allow for the reuse of resources required to support the protecting paths in order to carry extra-traffic services, the possibilities for this reuse are limited. It is possible, for instance, to reuse the entire protecting path in a service protection scheme for a single extra traffic service, but it is not possible to reuse it partially for multiple services as in case of service restoration.

Service protection does not provide for recovery from unexpected failures. For instance, many protection schemes are designed on the assumption that there will not be simultaneous failures on a protected path. Such schemes protect against a single failure of any link or node on the path; however, they may not provide the ability to recover from simultaneous failures of two or more links, even when feasible alternative paths exist. Furthermore, it is not expected that both protecting and protected paths will fail simultaneously. There are situations, however, where a single failure takes both the protecting and the protected paths out of service. For instance, the two paths could be provisioned to be not completely diverse either willingly (fully diverse paths are too expensive), or unwillingly (the information about physical layout of the fibers was not available at the time of path computation). Again, service protection provides no recovery from such situations. On the other hand, service restoration (especially full re-routing) has no problem recovering from unexpected failures, provided, of course, that a suitable alternative path is available.

As was mentioned earlier, service restoration has several flavors. These flavors also have their relative pros and cons, but, as a general rule, more pre-planning yields a better recovery time but is more rigid and less efficient.

7.5 Recovery Levels and Scopes

Depending on the object of protection — TE link or service path — one can identify two different levels of recovery.

1. Link level recovery (also referred to as span recovery)
2. Path level recovery

In the context of this book we define a *span* as an abstraction associated with network resources that are necessary to deliver user traffic between a pair of nodes that are adjacent in the data plane. From the traffic engineering perspective, a span can be represented (and advertised) as a separate TE link. Alternatively, several spans interconnecting the same pair of nodes can be collectively represented as a single (bundled) TE link. See more details on TE link advertising in Chapter 8.

In the case of span recovery, all services traversing a particular span are protected against any failure detected on the span. Specifically, when the span fails, *all* span-protected services are switched simultaneously onto some other parallel span (that is, a span interconnecting the same pair of nodes as the failed one). It is worth emphasizing that not all protected services are recovered through this operation — only those that are provisioned to be span-protected. In the span recovery model the deciding entities are located on the span's ends, and the recovery operation is triggered either by local failure detection or by a failure notification message received from the opposite end of the span. We will discuss span recovery in Section 7.6.

In the path level recovery model *each* protected service is recovered from a failure independently. It means that if some failure affects multiple services, the failure is indicated separately for each of them, and, generally speaking, multiple fault notification messages are sent to different deciding entities located on different nodes, which trigger independent recovery operations. One can distinguish different scopes of path level recovery, depending on which part of the path a particular recovery scheme is provisioned to protect. The scopes are:

- End-to-end recovery
- Local recovery

In the case of end-to-end recovery, an alternative path, starting and ending on the same pair of nodes as the protected path, provides recovery from a failure of any link or node on the protected path. In the case of the service *protection*, the alternative path is usually required to be fully disjoint from the protected path. This is because, at the time that the alternative path is provisioned, it is not known exactly where the failure will happen; hence care must be taken to avoid the situation where a single failure makes both protected and protecting paths unusable. In the case of service *restoration*, an alternative path needs to be disjoint from the protected path only at the point of failure. In the end-to-end path recovery model the deciding entities — called the point of local repair (PLR) and merge node (MN), see definitions in Section 7.7.1 — are always located on the ends of the protected path. We will discuss end-to-end path recovery in Section 7.7.2.

Two methods of local recovery will be discussed in this chapter: fast re-route (FRR), and path segment recovery.

In the FRR model each resource of a protected path — link or node — is separately protected by an individual backup tunnel. The important feature of this model is that the point at which the paths diverge (the PLR) for each protection domain is guaranteed to be located within one data plane hop of any point of failure. The backup tunnels also merge with the protected path very close to the resource they protect. The point at which the paths re-merge (the MN) is immediately downstream, being either the next hop (in case of an NHOP tunnel) or the next-next hop (in case of an NNHOP tunnel). The close proximity of the PLR and MN to the point of failure makes the FRR recovery time the same as, or better than, in the span protection model, while retaining the granularity of path level recovery.

The FRR model makes use of two types of backup tunnel: *facility bypass tunnels*, and *detour tunnels*. The former protects all paths that traverse the protected resource (that is, only one facility bypass tunnel per resource is needed). The latter protects each path individually (that is, one detour tunnel is required per resource per path).

A major problem with FRR is its poor applicability for non-packet switched networks. Facility bypass tunnels cannot be applied even conceptually because they require the notion of a label stack, and there is no such thing within a single switching capability in circuit-switched networks. In theory the FRR detour model could be used for local protection of transport network services. However, making it feasible requires a certain level of network density, which is not the case in currently deployed transport networks built of ring interconnections. Furthermore, an LSP protected in this way requires a lot of protection resources for the detours, which can neither be used in failure-free conditions to support extra traffic nor be shared with other LSPs, because resource sharing and over-subscription have very restricted applicability in non-packet environments. This fact makes FRR even less attractive and less likely to be deployed in transport networks, especially considering the cost of transport network resources. FRR will be discussed further in Section 7.7.5, more for the purpose of providing a complete picture of existing recovery mechanisms than in the context of transport networks.

The path segment recovery model is similar to the end-to-end path recovery model. The difference is that in the case of path segment recovery the alternative path protects some segment (or sub-network connection, to use the ITU-T term) of a protected path rather than the entire path. One may see end-to-end path recovery as a special case of path segment recovery with a single recovery domain covering the whole path. In general, though, multiple concatenated, overlapping, and/or nested recovery domains are provisioned for a segment protected path, each of them separately protecting a path segment from failures, and each possibly doing so in a different way. In the case of path segment recovery, the deciding entities (the relevant PLR and MN) are likely to be closer to the point of failure, so the overall recovery time of a segment protected path is likely to be better than that of an end-to-end protected path. On the other hand, unlike FRR, the path segment recovery model is not limited to protecting one resource at a time, and thus it works well on both dense and sparse topologies. Even more importantly, it requires many fewer protection resources, which, with careful network planning, could be shared between several protected paths and could also be used for carrying extra traffic if there are no failures in the network. Hence the model is very applicable for transport networks. We will discuss segment recovery in detail in Section 7.7.3.

It is important to note that the flexibility provided by the GMPLS control plane is such that all of the recovery models mentioned above are completely independent and can be provisioned for the same service in any combination. For instance, it is possible to require end-to-end recovery in addition to span protection for a path (recall that in MPLS/GMPLS a path onto which a service is mapped is called a Label Switched Path or LSP). Likewise, it is possible for packet switched LSPs to combine the FRR technique with path segment recovery to get the optimal trade-off between recovery time, resource utilization efficiency, and level of control of the backup LSP topology.

7.6 Span Recovery

In the context of this chapter, the term *recovery* usually means both protection and restoration. However, at the time this book was written, link-level (span) restoration was neither standardized nor deployed. Therefore, in this section the terms *span recovery* and *span protection* are used interchangeably.

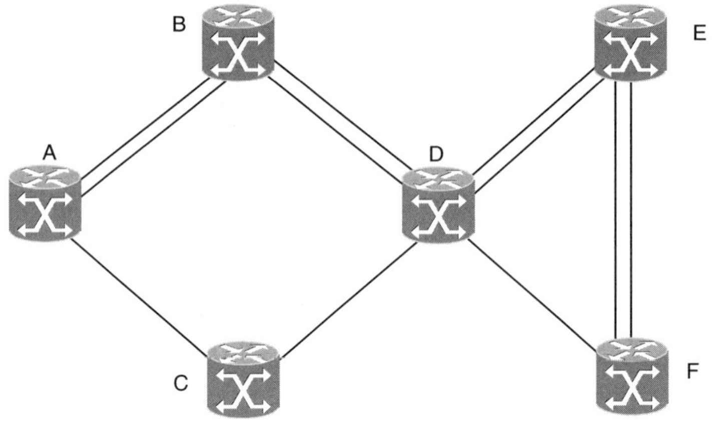

Figure 7.1 Span protection.

A service that takes path A-B-D-E-F in the network depicted in Figure 7.1 can be provisioned as span protected. This is because each pair of adjacent nodes along the path is interconnected with two parallel links, so that one of them can protect the other. The following schemes of span protection are defined.

- Dedicated unidirectional 1 + 1
- Dedicated bidirectional 1 + 1
- Dedicated 1:1 with extra traffic
- Shared M:N
- Enhanced

Each span protection scheme requires a consistent view of the association of protected and protecting spans for every link. The GMPLS Link Management Protocol (LMP) and/or local configuration should satisfy this requirement.

7.6.1 *Dedicated Unidirectional 1 + 1 Span Protection*

In this scheme a TE link contains at least two parallel spans, and for every working span there is a dedicated protecting span. All traffic traversing the link is permanently bridged onto both spans on one side of the link, and is selected from one of the spans on the other side (usually from one that has a better quality signal). When the selection function detects a failure, it autonomously starts receiving data from the other span. Similarly, when the failure is restored, the failure-detecting node may switch back (also autonomously) to receiving data from the restored span. Note that in this model there could be periods of time when traffic in one direction is received from one span, while in the opposite direction it is received from the other.

From the Traffic Engineering point of view the combination of protected and protecting spans is advertised as a single TE link. The Link Protection Type attribute is specified as "Dedicated 1 + 1," and the Interface Switching Capability (ISC) Descriptor attribute is defined only by the protected span. The bandwidth parameters of the protecting span are not advertised.

If an LSP is required to take advantage of 1 + 1 span protection, its path must be computed with the constraint of the Link Protection Type attribute to be no worse than (that is, numerically greater or equal to) Dedicated 1 + 1. Furthermore, the LSP should be signaled with the Dedicated 1 + 1 link protection flag set in the GMPLS Protection object so that each hop knows that it must utilize 1 + 1 span protection. As was pointed out earlier, no signaling happens after a span failure is detected — in 1 + 1 protection, the failure-detecting node simply starts receiving data from the protecting span.

Dedicated unidirectional 1 + 1 span protection guarantees the best possible recovery time for all LSPs protected in this way. However, the scheme is also the most expensive: It requires double the resources for protection purposes.

7.6.2 *Dedicated Bidirectional 1 + 1 Span Protection*

This scheme is very similar to the previous one. The only difference is that when one of the nodes terminating a link detects a link failure, *both* nodes switch to receive data from the protecting span. Likewise, when the failure is restored and reversion mode operation is locally configured, both nodes switch back to receiving data from the restored span. This is in contrast with the unidirectional 1 + 1 span protection model (see the previous section), where only the failure-detecting node switches to receive data from the other span during protection switchover and reversion switchback operations. In both schemes both nodes never stop bridging data onto both spans.

It is worth noting that whether the protection is unidirectional or bidirectional is a local matter for a particular link. There are no differences in link advertisement for unidirectional and bidirectional 1 + 1 span-protected links. Likewise, there are no differences in path computation and signaling of LSPs willing to take advantage of link protection of either type.

The required switchover synchronization is performed according to the following rules.

- When one of the link-terminating nodes detects the link failure, it switches to receive data from the protecting span and sends a Switchover Request to the node at the opposite end of the link (the message is sent only if the sending node has not already received a Switchover Request from the other end; otherwise, Switchover Response is sent instead).

- When one of the link-terminating nodes receives a Switchover Request, it switches to receive data from the protecting span (if it has not already done this due to a locally detected failure) and sends a Switchover Response.

Similarly, when the failure is restored and the reversion mode is configured, switchback synchronization is performed according to the following rules.

- When one of the link terminating nodes that has previously detected link failure (or acted on a Switchover Request) realizes that the failure is restored, it switches back to receive data from the restored span and sends a Switchback Request to the node at the opposite end of the link (again, the message is sent only if the node has not itself received a Switchback Request from the other end; otherwise, a Switchback Response is sent instead).
- When one of the link-terminating nodes receives a Switchback Request, it switches to receive data from the protected span (again, if it has not already done this yet because of locally detected failure restoration) and sends a Switchback Response.

Special care must be taken to handle span *flapping* — the situation where the span failure indication/restoration sequence happens many times in quick succession. The switchback procedure is not usually started immediately on the failure restoration event. Rather, it is triggered on the expiration of the so-called Wait-to-Restore Timer (WRT) started by the failure restoration event and cancelled by a new failure indication event. This mechanism guarantees that switchback happens only after the restored span has been functional for some time.

There is a need for signaling to synchronize the switchover and switchback — Switchover/Switchback Request/Response messages. This signaling can be provided by the GMPLS Control Plane (via LMP or GMPLS RSVP Notify messages), or by the data plane (for example, SONET/SDH APS signaling).

7.6.3 *Dedicated 1:1 Span Protection with Extra Traffic*

Under this scheme, there is a dedicated protecting span for every working (protected) span. Traffic is always sent over only one of the spans. This is in contrast with the 1 + 1 span protection schemes where traffic is always bridged onto both spans. Normally (that is, before link failure is detected), the data is sent over and received from the protected span in both directions, while the protecting span is either idle or carries some extra traffic. Note that the ability to handle extra traffic requires support of resource preemption by the control plane. The GMPLS control plane provides such support.

When a failure is detected on the protected span, the span-protected LSPs are moved onto the protecting span: Both link-terminating nodes switch to send and receive their traffic over the protecting span. In case of resource contention, the resources allocated for any extra traffic LSPs are preempted by the span-protected LSPs causing the interruption of the extra traffic. When a failure of the protected span is restored and the reversion mode is locally configured, the span-protected LSPs are switched back onto the protected span, thus releasing the protecting span, so that it can start carrying extra traffic again.

During the protection switchover procedure, special care should be taken to avoid misconnection — the situation where traffic is sent to an unintended receiver. Under 1:1 span protection a misconnection may occur; for instance, when a node switches to receive normal traffic over to the protecting span before the node on the other end of the link stops sending extra traffic over the protecting span.

A 1:1 span-protected link is advertised to the TE network domain as a single TE link. The Link Protection Type attribute is specified as "Dedicated 1:1" and the ISC Descriptor attribute is built as a combination of the attributes of the protected and protecting spans according to the following rules.

- For priorities higher (that is, numerically lower) than the priority configured for extra traffic LSPs, the advertised attribute matches the attribute of the protected span. Thus, bandwidth parameters of the protecting span are not advertised.
- For priorities lower than or equal to those of the extra traffic LSPs, the advertised unreserved bandwidth is computed as the sum of the unreserved bandwidth of both protecting and protected spans, and the Maximal LSP Bandwidth value is set equal to the greater of MaxLSPBandWork and MaxLSPBandProtect, where MaxLSPBandWork is the Maximal LSP Bandwidth available on the protected span, and MaxLSPBandProtect is the Maximal LSP Bandwidth available on the protecting span.

In this way, every TE domain controller can always tell which resources are available on the link for normal and extra traffic.

If there is the need to establish a 1:1 span-protected LSP, its path must be computed with the constraint of the Link Protection Type attribute to be no worse than (numerically greater or equal to) Dedicated 1:1. Furthermore, the LSP should be signaled with the Dedicated 1:1 link protection flag set in the GMPLS Protection object.

When one of the link-terminating nodes detects a failure on the protected span, it initiates protection switchover, which is performed according to the following rules.

- The failure-detecting node immediately stops using the protecting span for sending/receiving data of those extra traffic LSPs whose resources need to be preempted by the span-protected LSPs. Head ends of such extra traffic LSPs are notified about resource preemption (via GMPLS RSVP Notify or PathErr messages). If a Switchover Request from the opposite side of the link has not been received yet, such a request is sent to the node at the remote end of the link; otherwise, a Switchover Response is sent.
- On receipt of a Switchover Request the receiving node immediately stops using the protecting span for sending/receiving data of the extra traffic LSPs that are about to be preempted. It also stops using the protected span and starts using the protecting span for sending/receiving traffic of the span-protected LSPs. After that, a Switchover Response is sent to the opposite side of the link.
- On receipt of a Switchover Response the receiving node stops using the protected span and starts using the protecting span for sending/receiving traffic of the span-protected LSPs.

When the failure is restored and the reversion mode is configured, switchback synchronization is performed, but only after the WRT interval has passed without further failures. Under the dedicated 1:1 with extra traffic span-protection scheme, the switchback procedure is carried out according to the following rules.

- When one of the link-terminating nodes that has previously detected a link failure realizes that the failure is restored and the restored span is failure-free for some (WRT) time, it starts sending data on and selecting data from the span-protected LSPs on both the protecting and protected spans. After that it sends a Switchback Request to the node at the opposite end of the link.
- On receipt of a Switchback Request the receiving node stops using the protecting span and starts using the restored protected span for sending/receiving data of the span-protected LSPs. It also sends a Switchback Response to the opposite end of the link.
- On receipt of a Switchback Response the receiving node stops sending/selecting data onto/from the protecting span.

Note that these switchback procedures involve a short period of time where the sending node that originates the procedure bridges the traffic onto both spans (as in 1 + 1 protection). This is necessary to ensure that the switchback procedure does not cause significant disruption to the traffic flow. Once the switchback procedures are completed, the released resources become available again for extra traffic LSPs.

As in the case of the bidirectional dedicated 1 + 1 span protection model, the switchover/switchback synchronization signaling can be provided either by the GMPLS Control Plane (via LMP or GMPLS RSVP Notify messages) or by the data plane (for example, SONET/SDH APS signaling).

Dedicated 1:1 span protection with extra traffic is more complex than 1 + 1 span protection schemes and yields worse recovery times. However, it is more efficient from the bandwidth utilization point of view because it allows the use of protection bandwidth for extra traffic in the steady state.

7.6.4 *Shared M:N Span Protection*

In the case of shared M:N (M < N) span protection there are two sets of spans interconnecting a pair of adjacent nodes. The first set contains N (working) spans that carry normal traffic and are protected by the second set of M (protecting) spans. The spans from the second set do not carry normal traffic but may carry extra (preemptable) traffic. M and N are configurable values (for example 1:5, meaning 1 protecting span protects 5 working spans). The fact that M < N makes this scheme even more efficient than the dedicated 1:1 span protection — the same number of protecting spans protects more working spans — but it is clearly more vulnerable to multiple simultaneous failures.

When a failure affects one or more working spans, both span-terminating nodes switch onto one or more protecting spans. Because the amount of protection resources is less than the amount of protected resources (M < N), it is possible that not all span-protected LSPs can be recovered. Which LSPs are actually recovered is a matter of local policies (for instance, those that have higher holding priorities). When the failure is restored, the traffic affected by the failure may be switched back onto the restored working span(s), releasing the protecting span(s) back to the protecting pool, and thus making it/them available for extra traffic again.

In contrast to all previously described span protection schemes, where link-terminating nodes play the same role in the switchover and switchback procedures, this scheme is not symmetrical. This is because, generally speaking, it is not known prior to the detection of a failure which of the protecting spans will be switched onto when a particular working span fails. Therefore, it is necessary that one of the nodes (playing the *master* role) is responsible for the allocation of a protecting span and for letting the other node (playing the *slave* role) know about its choice. Which of the nodes plays which role is either configured, based on the results of some neighbor discovery procedures (for example, via LMP), or algorithmically determined. In the latter case, for instance, the node with the larger node ID could be determined as the master, with the other node as the slave.

Both sets of spans are advertised to the TE network domain as a single TE link. The Link Protection Type attribute is specified as "Shared M:N" and the ISC

Descriptor attribute is built as a combination of the attributes of the protected and protecting spans according to the following rules.

- For priorities higher (that is, numerically lower) than the priority configured for the extra traffic, the advertised attribute is compiled as the union of the ISC Descriptors of *only* the working spans. The procedures are described in an Internet-Draft that documents link bundling.
- For priorities lower than or equal to the priority of the extra traffic, the advertised attribute is compiled as the union of the ISC Descriptors of *all* spans (both working and protecting).

If there is a need to establish an M:N shared span-protected LSP, its path must be computed with the constraint of the Link Protection Type attribute to be no worse than (numerically greater or equal to) Shared M:N. Furthermore, the LSP should be signaled with the Shared M:N link protection flag set in the GMPLS Protection object.

When the master node detects a failure on one of the working spans it initiates the protection switchover procedure, which is performed according to the following rules.

- The master node allocates a protection span from the pool of available protecting spans. It immediately stops using the allocated span for sending/receiving data of those extra traffic LSPs whose resources need to be preempted by the span protected LSPs. Head ends of such extra traffic LSPs are notified about the preemption (via GMPLS RSVP Notify or PathErr messages). After that, the master node sends a Switchover Request to the slave. The message contains the IDs of the failed (working) and selected (protecting) spans.
- On receipt of a Switchover Request the slave immediately stops using the specified protecting span for sending/receiving data of the extra traffic LSPs that are about to be preempted. It also stops using the specified (failed) working span and starts using the protecting span for sending/receiving traffic of the span-protected LSPs. The slave also sends a Switchover Response back to the master. The message contains the IDs of working and protecting spans.
- On receipt of a Switchover Response the master completes the switchover procedure. Specifically, it stops using the failed working span and starts using the protecting span for sending/receiving traffic of the span-protected LSPs.

When the slave node detects a failure on one of the working spans, it sends a fault indication message specifying, among other things, the ID of the failed span. On receipt of the message the master node performs the exact same actions (described above) as if it had detected the failure itself.

As was mentioned before, the master may discover that not all span-protected LSPs can be recovered via shared M:N span protection. Those that cannot be recovered (usually, ones provisioned with lower holding priority values) are individually notified with a failure indication event, which is likely to trigger some path level recovery scheme.

When the master node detects that a previously indicated span failure is restored, it may (depending on whether the reversion mode is locally configured or not) start switchback synchronization.

- The master node starts the WRT. If during the life of the WRT it neither detects a failure of the restored span nor receives a fault indication message from the slave regarding the restored span, it starts sending and selecting data for the span-protected LSPs onto/from both protecting and restored spans. It also sends a Switchback Request to the slave. The message includes the IDs of the restored and protecting spans.
- On receipt of a Switchback Request the slave stops using the protecting span and starts using the working span for sending/receiving data for the span-protected LSPs. It also sends a Switchback Response to the master.
- On receipt of a Switchback Response the master stops sending/selecting data onto/from the protecting span and releases the span back to the pool, thus making it available again for protecting the working spans and for carrying extra traffic.

When the slave node discovers that a failure that it previously indicated to the master node has been restored, it sends a fault restoration message specifying the IDs of the restored and protecting spans. On receipt of the message the master performs the same actions (described above) as if it had detected the failure restoration itself.

The necessary fault notification and switchover/switchback synchronization signaling can be provided either by the GMPLS Control Plane (via LMP or GMPLS RSVP Notify messages) or by the data plane (for example, SONET/SDH RDI/APS signaling).

7.6.5 *Enhanced Span Protection*

Enhanced span protection is defined as any protection scheme that provides better (more reliable) span protection than dedicated 1 + 1 span protection. A good example of enhanced span protection is the four-fiber SONET BLSR ring, which is discussed later in this section.

Every TE link that participates in such a span protection scheme is advertised with the Link Protection Type attribute set to the "Enhanced" value.

Path computation for an LSP that needs to use enhanced span protection should be constrained to selecting TE links advertising the Enhanced link protection type. The LSP should be signaled with the Enhanced link protection bit set in the GMPLS Protection object.

Four-Fiber SONET BLSR Rings

The SONET BLSR ring (Figure 7.2) is a popular way to interconnect SONET digital cross-connects. Each node on the ring is connected to each of its neighbors by two pairs of fibers. In the steady state, one pair of fibers carries traffic in both directions (in the diagram on the left of Figure 7.2, the working fiber pair constitutes the outer ring), whereas the other fiber pair is reserved for protection purposes. In the event of a failure, the fault-detecting nodes (nodes B and C in our example) loop the traffic back onto the protecting fiber pair.

Suppose there is a bidirectional service provisioned between nodes A and D. Before the failure, the service was using the path A-B-C-D with reverse path traffic using D-C-B-A. In both cases, the outer fiber ring is used. After the failure the service path is A-B-A-F-E-D-C-D with reverse path traffic using D-C-D-E-F-A-B-A. Where the same traffic appears to flow in both directions between a pair of nodes (such as between C and D in this example) it is using both rings. Thus, no matter which link or node on the ring fails, the traffic of all services going over the ring is rapidly recovered, provided that there is no more than one fault per ring at any moment. Readers interested in self-healing rings are

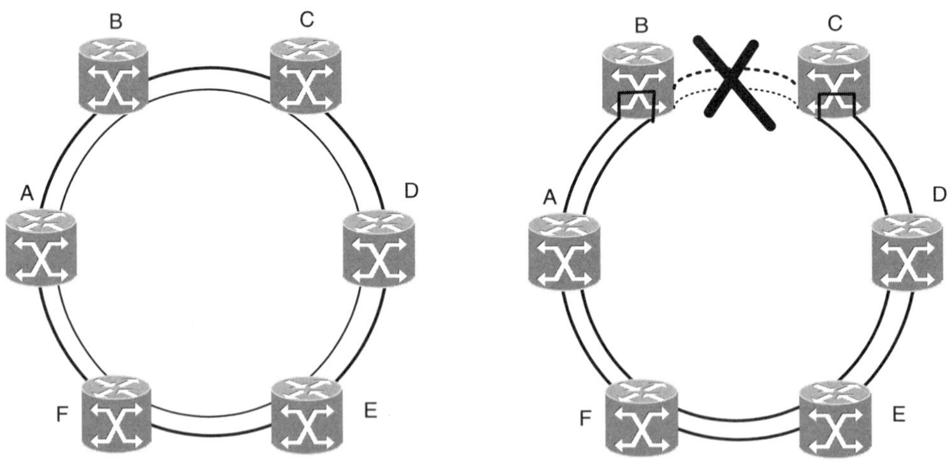

Figure 7.2 Four-fiber SONET BLSR.

referred to the references in the *Further Reading* section at the end of this chapter.

Note that, from a GMPLS point of view, we are still talking about a single span. That is, the BLSR ring provides support for a single hop in the GMPLS network. Thus the paths A-B-C-D and A-B-A-F-E-D-C-D in this example provide a single TE link between A and D which are GMPLS nodes. The nodes B, C, E, and F are part of the lower-layer transport system that provides connectivity for the GMPLS network.

7.7 Path Recovery

In this section we will discuss service recovery on the path level — that is, recovery of entire LSPs (end-to-end recovery) or individual segments of LSPs (segment recovery and fast re-route). We will start by introducing the notion of the *path recovery domain,* because it is important for all types of path level recovery. After that we will discuss in detail end-to-end path recovery, segment recovery, and the fast re-route technique.

7.7.1 *Path Recovery Domain*

Consider the fragment of a network depicted in Figure 7.3. Assume that a working LSP of some protected service goes through nodes A-B-C-D-E. A path recovery domain for the service could be defined as a part of the network where some scheme is provisioned to recover the service from failures of a segment of one of the service's LSPs (normally a working LSP, but protecting LSPs can also be protected). In the end-to-end path recovery model, the recovery domain covers the entire protected LSP. In case of path segment recovery, the protected LSP spans multiple recovery domains, which, generally speaking, may overlap, nest one within another, and so forth. It is reasonable to think of end-to-end path recovery as a special case of path segment recovery, where the protected segment is the entire LSP.

Figure 7.3 shows a recovery domain. It provides recovery from any fault that might happen on the segment A-B-C-D-E. The LSP going through nodes A-G-F-E is called a recovery LSP. This is the LSP that carries traffic for the service after a failure on the protected segment has been detected.

The timing of when a recovery LSP is established relative to the moment of failure detection distinguishes the notions of path protection and path restoration. If the recovery LSP is fully pre-established — no provisioning signaling is necessary

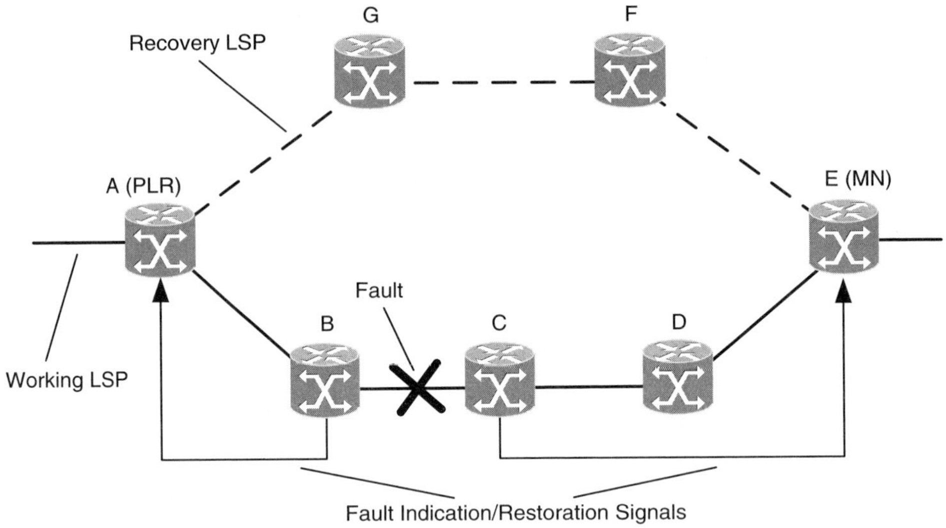

Figure 7.3 Path recovery domain.

after the detection of a failure — then the recovery domain provides *path protection*. In all other cases:

- Recovery path was not pre-computed; or
- Recovery path was pre-computed but not pre-selected; or
- Recovery path was pre-computed and pre-selected but not pre-signaled; or
- Recovery path was pre-signaled, resources were pre-allocated but not pre-selected; or
- Recovery path was pre-signaled and resources were pre-allocated and pre-selected but not activated.

These are all different types of *path restoration*.

The node originating the recovery LSP (node A) is the PLR, and the node terminating the recovery LSP (node E) is the MN. Both nodes have special but similar roles as deciding entities in the path recovery cycle. In the data plane they are responsible for bridging traffic onto protected or protecting LSPs. They are also responsible for selecting incoming data from one of the LSPs. In the control plane they are expected to receive fault indication/restoration signals, and trigger and coordinate the switchover/switchback processes. Additionally, the PLR is, on many occasions, responsible for path computation/selection/re-optimization of the restoration LSP.

7.7.2 End-to-End Path Recovery

Each LSP can have an end-to-end path recovery scheme of one of the following types provisioned for it.

- Unidirectional 1 + 1 protection
- Bidirectional 1 + 1 protection
- 1:N protection with extra traffic
- Pre-planned re-routing without extra traffic
- Full re-routing
- Unprotected

The type of required end-to-end path recovery is signaled using the LSP flags in the GMPLS Protection object. There is another section of the Protection object — LSP status — that is important in the context of end-to-end path recovery. It is used to distinguish a protected LSP from the associated protecting LSP, an LSP that is fully established from one that needs some further activation signaling before it can carry traffic, and an LSP that actually carries traffic from one that is idle.

An end-to-end path protected LSP has a single PLR (its head end) and a single MN (tail end).

Unidirectional 1 + 1 Protection

In this scheme a protected LSP head end computes two link-, node-, or SRLG-disjoint paths — one for the protected LSP (for example, A-G-F-E in Figure 7.4) and another for the protecting LSP (for example, A-B-C-D-E). The protecting LSP is fully established at the same time as the protected LSP. In the data plane both head and tail ends (nodes A and E, respectively) bridge outgoing traffic onto both LSPs and select incoming traffic from one of the two (for example, from the one that provides a better quality signal). When a failure is detected anywhere on the protected LSP, selectors on one or both ends autonomously switch to receive traffic from the fault-free channel. Neither fault notification nor synchronization of any sort is required. Because the protecting LSP is permanently used for carrying traffic, its resources cannot be shared with LSPs that protect other LSPs. Neither can it be used to carry extra traffic. Thus, the scheme is not efficient, although it is simple and guarantees the best possible service recovery time.

The notion of the *Shared Risk Link Group* (*SRLG*) will be defined and discussed in detail in Chapters 8 and 10. For now it is sufficient to know that sometimes TE links cannot be considered independent in the sense that a single

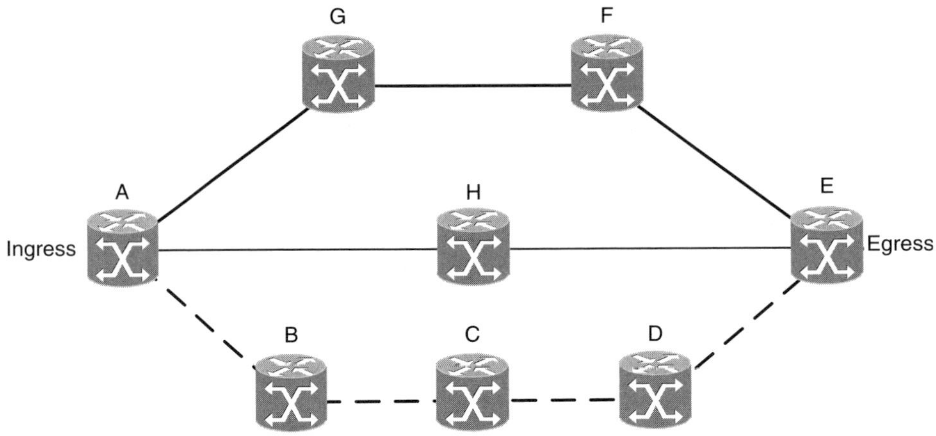

Figure 7.4 End-to-end 1 + 1 protection.

failure may affect two or more links at the same time. For example, multiple fibers may be carried within a single conduit: If the conduit is cut it would make all these fibers (and hence the associated TE links) unusable. Such TE links are said to belong to a particular SRLG. Part of TE link advertisement supplies a list of SRLGs to which the link belongs. This makes it possible for any path computing entity in the network to select protected and protecting paths in such a way that the paths have non-overlapping unions of SRLGs of the links that constitute the paths. Such paths are referred to as *SRLG-disjoint*.

Bidirectional 1 + 1 Protection

This protection scheme works like the previous one with one exception: The selectors on both ends always select data from the same channel. This means that after fault detection the selectors switch to receive data from the second channel even if the fault affected only one direction of the protected channel. This synchronization requires signaling, which is performed according to the following rules.

- A node on the protected LSP detects a failure and reliably sends a Fault Indication Signal (FIS) to the PLR and MN, identifying the point of failure.
- When the PLR receives either an FIS or Switchover Request, or locally detects the failure, it immediately stops receiving data from the channel that was affected by the failure, and starts receiving data from the alternative channel. After that, it sends a Switchover Request to the MN, unless by that time it has

already received such a request from the MN. In the latter case the PLR sends a Switchover Response to the MN.

- Likewise, when the MN receives either an FIS or Switchover Request, or locally detects the failure, it immediately switches to receiving data from the alternative channel. It also sends a Switchover Request to the PLR, if by that time such a request has not yet been received. In the latter case a Switchover Response is sent instead.

GMPLS provides a convenient mechanism — the GMPLS RSVP Notify message — for fault notification and switchover synchronization signaling. Note that the messages do not need to follow either the working or protected LSP; they can take advantage of the general flexibility of the control plane network. However, it is imperative that the messages are delivered reliably. Fortunately, the GMPLS signaling protocol has a mechanism that guarantees reliable message delivery.

1:N Protection With Extra Traffic

In this model an end-to-end protecting LSP is signaled over a path that is link-, node-, or SRLG-disjoint from several protected LSPs. Suppose we have a couple of services carrying normal traffic over paths A-B-C-D-E and A-G-F-E (Figure 7.5), which require protection. The LSP, protecting both of them, can be provisioned over the path A-H-E, which is disjoint from the paths taken by both protected LSPs. Note that the protected LSPs are also mutually disjoint to avoid possible contention between them for the shared protection resources (something that might

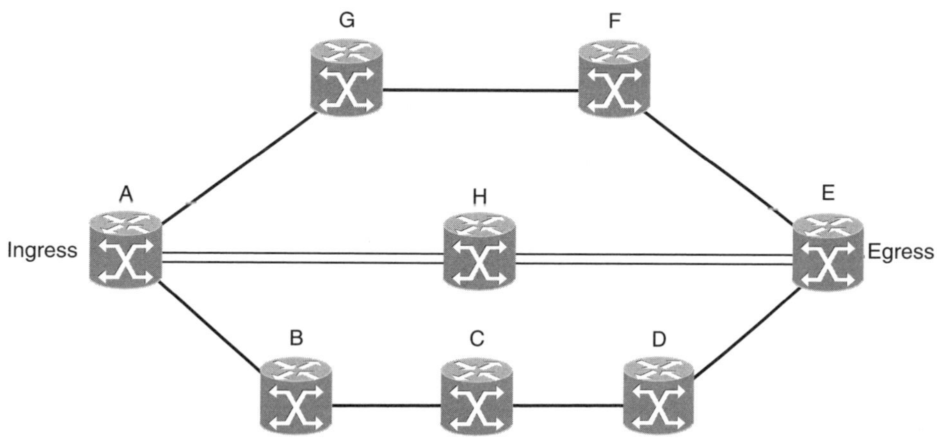

Figure 7.5 End-to-end 1:N protection with extra traffic.

happen if the protected LSPs shared a link and it was that link that failed). As in the schemes described earlier, the protecting LSP is fully pre-established; however, normal traffic is not bridged onto it in the steady state because that would result in a mix of traffic from both protected LSPs. This means that the protecting LSP could be used to carry extra traffic. To make the mapping of extra traffic services onto the shared 1:N protecting LSPs possible, it is necessary that the advertising of the TE links taken by the LSPs should count resources allocated for the LSPs as unreserved on priorities lower than or equal to the priority of the extra traffic.

When a failure occurs on one of the protected LSPs, both of its ends switch sending and receiving traffic onto/from the protecting LSP, if necessary preempting its resources from carrying extra traffic. As in all other cases, when resource preemption is involved, special care must be taken to avoid misconnections. In this particular model, a misconnection may happen if the selector on one of the ends switches to receiving data from the protecting channel before the opposite end stops sending extra traffic. Such misconnection, even if lasts for a very short period of time, can cause serious damage to the service user, and is considered as a confidentiality breach.

It is possible that more than one protected LSP will attempt to claim resources of the protecting LSP. This could be triggered even by a single failure if the protected LSPs were not sufficiently disjoint. It may also happen because of multiple simultaneous failures (for example, if links GF and CD fail). If such a situation arises, only one of the protected LSPs (the one with the highest provisioned holding priority, or simply the one that makes the request first) will actually be recovered. The other affected LSPs must try some different recovery scheme(s). For instance, they could be fully re-routed (as described later in this section).

The fault notification and switchover synchronization signaling has the following sequence.

- A node on one of the protected LSPs detects a failure and sends an FIS to both ends of the LSP (that is, to the PLR and MN).
- When the PLR receives an FIS or locally detects the failure, it immediately stops using the protecting LSP for sending/receiving extra traffic. If by that time it has also received a Switchover Request from the MN, it switches to transfer normal traffic from the LSP affected by the failure to the protecting LSP, and also sends a Switchover Response to the MN. Otherwise, the PLR sends a Switchover Request to the MN.
- When the MN receives an FIS or locally detects the failure, it immediately stops using the protecting LSP for sending/receiving extra traffic. If by that time it has also received a Switchover Request from the PLR, it switches normal traffic from the protected LSP to the protecting LSP and sends a Switchover Response to the PLR. Otherwise, it sends a Switchover Request to the PLR.

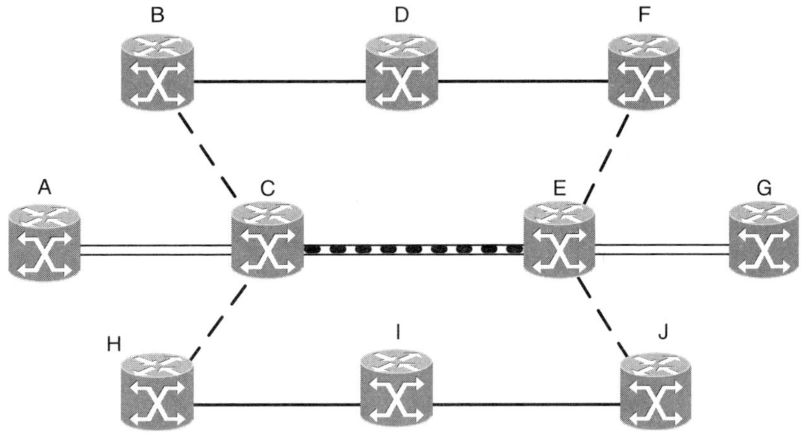

Figure 7.6 Pre-planned re-routing.

- When either the PLR or MN receives a Switchover Response, the receiving node switches to sending/receiving normal traffic using the protecting LSP, if this has not been done yet.

As in the case of bidirectional 1 + 1 protection, the fault notification and switchover synchronization (GMPLS RSVP Notify) messages need not follow the path of either of the LSPs.

The protection scheme described here is more complex than the earlier schemes. It also yields a worse recovery time due to the fact that normal traffic starts to be carried over the protecting LSP only after failure detection. However, for the same reason, the scheme is more efficient, because the protection resources are provided at a favorable ratio and can be used in steady state for carrying extra traffic. It is important to keep in mind that this reuse of the protection resources is limited only to extra traffic services that happen to coincide with the full path of the protecting LSP by passing through the ingress and egress of the protection LSP (usually, this is restricted to extra traffic services that originate and terminate on the same nodes as the protected/protecting LSPs). It is not possible, for example, to partially share resources of the protecting LSP with other protecting LSPs as in the case of the pre-planned re-routing model (see Figure 7.6 above).

Pre-Planned Re-Routing Without Extra Traffic

This scheme assumes that a protecting LSP is pre-signaled to be disjoint from a protected LSP or from several mutually disjoint protected LSPs. In contrast with all of the path protection schemes described earlier, the resources on the links of the protecting LSP are allocated but are *not* bound into cross-connects. Thus, the protecting LSP cannot be used to carry extra traffic. More than that, after failure detection the protecting LSP must be activated (that is, signaled to bind the cross-connects) before the normal traffic can be switched onto it. Hence the scheme yields worse recovery times compared to the 1:N path protection model with extra traffic. The legitimate question is, what is this scheme good for?

The scheme is useful because all resources pre-planned for use by each of the protecting LSP links can also be pre-planned for use to protect some other protected LSPs, not necessarily originated/terminated on the same nodes. This enables far wider protection at the cost of fewer protection resources, provided that all LSPs protected in this way are unlikely to fail simultaneously. More than that, the fact that resources are pre-planned for the protecting LSP does not mean that they cannot be fully activated for some other LSPs carrying extra traffic (which makes the name of this scheme confusing!). The distinction is that the protecting LSP cannot carry extra traffic, but the protection resources can be assigned to some other preemptable LSP that *does* carry extra traffic.

Thus, the model provides the most flexible way of sharing protection resources, where *arbitrary* segments of protecting and extra traffic LSPs are shared. In other words the sharing is partial and is not limited to end-to-end sharing as in the case of the 1:N protection model with extra traffic.

Consider the segment of a network depicted in Figure 7.6. Suppose that there are two end-to-end protected LSPs established — B-D-F and H-I-J. The first one is protected by an LSP going through B-C-E-F, and the second by an LSP going through H-C-E-J. Assuming that the protected LSPs cannot fail simultaneously, resources on link CE can be shared between the two protecting LSPs. Furthermore, suppose there is a preemptable extra traffic LSP going through A-C-E-G. In the steady state the same resources on link CE that are pre-planned for the protection of both protected LSPs can also be allocated and fully activated for the extra traffic LSP.

This recovery scheme falls under the definition of path restoration rather than path protection because some provisioning signaling is needed after fault detection (to activate the resources of the protecting LSP that is about to start carrying normal traffic). With careful placing of protected LSPs and pre-planning of protecting LSPs it is possible to achieve *full mesh restoration*, where a relatively small amount of resources, allocated for protection purposes, covers a relatively large amount of resources carrying normal traffic. Additionally, the pre-planned protection resources are available for carrying extra traffic. For path computing entities to take advantage of such resource sharing, each TE link should advertise the shared protection resources as unreserved on priorities equal to or lower than the extra traffic priority. And, of course, the control plane must support resource preemption, so that normal traffic can bump out extra traffic when a protected LSP fails.

The fact that the protecting LSP resources must be allocated but not activated during LSP setup is signaled using the LSP Status section of the GMPLS Protection object (the LSP is signaled as "Secondary," not as "Primary" as in all other recovery schemes). The resource activation signaling can be piggy-backed on the Switchover Request. In this case the message should be delivered hop by hop along the protecting LSP from the PLR to the MN, so that controllers along the path have a chance to stop using the resources for extra traffic and bind them into the LSP cross-connects. It is also important to bear in mind that the scheme's switchover paradigm is asymmetrical, meaning that FISs should be delivered to the master (the role normally assumed by the PLR, but sometimes by the MN), which controls the switchover procedures as follows.

- The master unbinds the resources of the protecting LSP from the cross-connect to which they are currently bound and stops using them for sending/receiving extra traffic. It also sends a notification to the head end of the extra traffic LSP about the resource preemption. Then it activates the resources by binding them into the protecting LSP cross-connect and, after that, sends a Switchover Request (GMPLS RSVP Notify message) along the protecting LSP to the next controller.
- Every controller along the Switchover Request path (including the slave) performs the same operations as the master, although some optimizations may be made to reduce the number of preemption notifications sent. Additionally, the slave immediately starts to send/receive traffic for the LSP affected by the failure using the protecting LSP, and sends a Switchover Reply direct to the master.
- On receipt of a Switchover Reply the master starts sending and receiving the normal traffic over the protecting LSP.

Full Re-Routing

This path restoration scheme assumes no pre-provisioning of a recovery LSP before the actual failure of the LSP that carries normal (that is, subject for recovery) traffic. Consider the network shown in Figure 7.7.

Assume that there is an unprotected LSP going through nodes A, B, D, and E and carrying normal traffic. At some point in time a failure is detected on the link BD. The end-to-end full re-routing scheme works as follows.

- A failure-detecting node (node B and/or node D) sends an FIS message to the LSP's head end (node A).
- The head end computes an alternative path or selects a pre-computed alternative path. The alternative path must be divergent from the point of failure (say, path A-C-D-E).

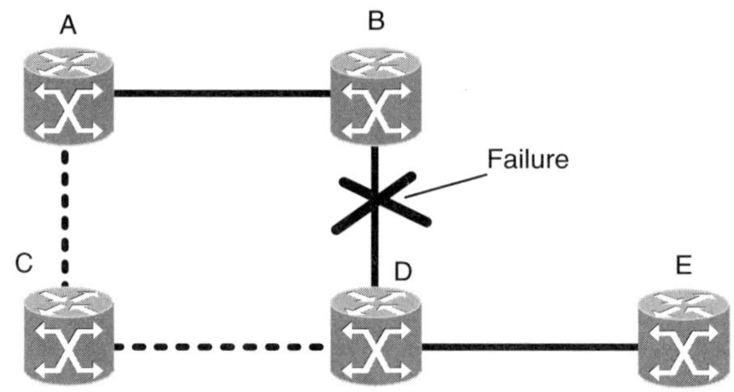

Figure 7.7 Full re-routing.

- The head end re-routes the LSP onto the new path, using the make-before-break procedure to take share resources already reserved on any parts of the path that are common.
- If the re-route fails for any reason, a new attempt is made to compute or select an alternative path divergent from the point of original failure and the point at which the re-route failed.

This procedure repeats itself until the LSP is successfully re-routed, or the head end fails to determine an alternative path divergent from all points of failure.

Compared to all of the recovery schemes described previously, this scheme yields the worst service recovery time. This is because of the extra time required for path computation and the establishment through signaling of the recovery path after the service head end receives the FIS. Note that establishment of the recovery LSP might fail several times before it is eventually set up and can be used for normal traffic delivery, which makes things even worse.

However, the full re-routing model also has some great qualities. First, it is the most efficient scheme from the resource utilization point of view. This is because it does not claim resources for recovery purposes until an actual failure occurs; hence the resources are fully available for other services (not limited to extra traffic services). Also, if full re-routing is provisioned for the service, it is likely that the re-routed LSP will take the shortest path which may be congruent with the original LSP for most of its path, whereas a protected LSP must take a fully diverse path which is usually longer (and so requires more network resources).

Secondly, the scheme can handle all failures, including unexpected and multiple simultaneous failures, provided that a feasible, fault-free path still exists in the network. On the other hand, all protection schemes recover only from failures that they are provisioned to protect against, and do not "like" any surprises. For example, it is normally assumed that a working LSP and its protecting LSPs cannot fail at the same time. But if they do (perhaps because they take paths that are not sufficiently disjoint), the service will not be recovered. Likewise, if several failures happen at the same time in a network where the full mesh restoration scheme was pre-provisioned on the assumption that no more than one failure could happen, only some of the services will be able to recover, while the rest (the lower priority ones) will not. There is no such problem with the full re-routing approach.

Thirdly, the scheme can recover services on topologies where path protection simply is not feasible. This is because, when a protection scheme is provisioned, it is not known *a priori* exactly where a failure will occur. Therefore, path protection requires at least two maximally disjoint paths to avoid the situation where a single failure breaks both working and protecting LSPs. In the full re-routing case, however, by the time a recovery path is selected it is already known which elements of the LSP have failed. Thus, the recovery path does not have to be fully disjoint from the original path: The only requirement is that it must avoid the point(s) of failure. In our example (Figure 7.7), a service going from node A to node E cannot be fully protected in principle, because two fully disjoint paths between the service source and destination cannot be found, but, as we see, it can be re-routed.

Considering the qualities of the full re-routing approach, it makes good sense to provision a hybrid recovery scheme, so that a segment and/or end-to-end protection scheme(s) could be engaged, with the full re-routing scheme available as a last resort if all of the protection schemes fail to recover the service.

Reversion

After protection switchover happens, normal traffic is delivered over the protecting LSP rather than over the failed working LSP. There are numerous reasons why this situation is not meant to persist. First of all, the protecting LSP is usually longer than the LSP it protects and hence is more expensive and may provide a lower quality service. More important the traffic is no longer protected and, if the protecting LSP fails, the service will be disrupted. The protection resources could also be shared between multiple services (for example, under the shared 1:N with extra traffic model), and so all other services that used to be protected are no longer protected, and the extra traffic, which used to be delivered over the protecting LSP, has been disrupted and must now be mapped onto some other LSP. Finally, the resources of the failed working LSP are locked (still allocated for the LSP) and cannot be used for any other purposes.

There are two ways that the service could be handled after its working LSP fails and protection switchover occurs. In the first approach (called the *non-revertive* mode) the service head end attempts to redirect the service LSPs onto new path(s), which may or may not use links and nodes of the previous path(s) that were not affected by the failure. Once the operation succeeds the unused resources of the previous working and protecting LSPs are released. In the case of shared protection, the protecting LSP is released to perform its steady state functions; that is, to protect other services and carry extra traffic.

Note that the non-revertive mode is not always possible — there might simply be no available or feasible alternative paths, divergent from the point of failure. In this case the second approach, the *revertive* mode, is a better choice. Reversion (also referred to as *protection switchback*) happens in the following way: The control plane simply waits until the fault conditions are removed, and then has the service head and tail ends synchronously switch to sending/receiving traffic onto/from the restored working LSP.

The reversion procedures are similar to the switchover procedures described earlier. The fault-detecting/reporting node receives an indication from the data plane that the fault conditions have been cleared, and sends a Fault Restoration Signal (FRS) message to the PLR and/or MN (service head and tail ends, respectively, in the case of end-to-end protection). These nodes use switchback synchronization signaling and re-program the data plane to move normal traffic back onto the restored LSP.

Note that despite the similarity of the reversion and switchover procedures, their goals and the conditions under which they happen are fundamentally different. Switchover occurs because one or more failures have just been detected. This means that the traffic has already been disrupted; hence it is crucial for the operation to be started and completed as fast as possible. Reversion, on the other hand, happens when the traffic is stable and properly delivered over the protecting LSP. There is no rush either to start reversion or complete it; the goal is to make the switchback as smooth as possible in order to minimize any second traffic hit. Note also that during reversion there is no extra traffic involved; hence there is no danger of misconnection. Therefore, no constraints on the sequence in which the PLR and MN re-program their data planes are imposed.

Let us consider the sequence of events that happen during reversion within, say, the shared 1:N protection scheme.

- Each node that previously detected the failure receives an indication from the data plane about the fault restoration, and sends FRS messages to the PLR and/or MN.
- On receipt of an FRS or Switchback Request, or if the fault restoration is locally detected, the PLR/MN immediately starts bridging outgoing traffic onto both working and protecting LSPs, and begins to select incoming data from the LSP with a better signal. It also sends a Switchback Request to the opposite end of the LSP unless the request has already been received. In the latter case a Switchback Response is sent instead.
- On receipt of a Switchback Response the receiving node stops using the protecting LSP for sending/receiving data. The LSP is marked as available for protection and extra traffic delivery.

Recall the discussion of "flapping" in Section 7.6.2, and how the problem is handled in the span protection model. A similar issue needs to be addressed in path-level protection schemes as well. Consider, for example, the situation where the power level of an optical signal on a particular frequency is jittering around the "Signal Degrade" threshold. In this case, the local control plane might receive multiple sequences of failure detection/failure restoration indications in quick succession, which, in turn, could repeatedly trigger switchover and switchback procedures. This is a highly undesirable situation for any service because each switchover involves a traffic hit. To avoid such a condition the failure restoration-detecting node does not generate the FRS right away. Rather, the failure restoration event starts the Wait-to-Restore Timer (WRT), which is cancelled by any further failure indication received before the timer expires, and the timer is started again upon a subsequent failure restoration event. Only if no further failure indications are received during the life of the WRT is the FRS sent to the PLR and/or MN. This mechanism guarantees that the switchback happens only after the restored resource is functional for some time and may be judged to be stable. A smart implementation does not use a permanent WRT interval. Rather it uses exponentially increasing values to mitigate the resource flapping effect even more.

Pre-Planned Failures

Routine maintenance and periodic testing are always required for network resources. This is true even if the resources are engaged in carrying live traffic. The only way to conduct such maintenance without disrupting the services mapped onto the resources is to re-route the traffic onto some other path, complete all maintenance and testing operations, and then return the traffic back to its original path. Note that this is exactly the sequence of events that happens during automatic fault protection switchover and switchback procedures, which means that the necessary control plane infrastructure is in place already. All that is needed is the introduction of some external commands (typically issued by a network operator through the NMS, EMS, or CLI) to simulate the failure indication/restoration events that are normally generated by the data plane. For example, one such command may be called "Forced Switch for Normal Traffic." It causes the unconditional switchover of the normal traffic onto the protecting LSP. A similar command, "Manual Switch for Normal Traffic," causes the same switchover, but only on the following conditions.

- No fault conditions are known to exist on the protecting LSP (that is, no failures were reported by the data plane).
- No management commands of a higher priority than the Manual Switch For Normal Traffic command are in effect blocking the execution of the command.

The examples of such commands are: "Lockout of Recovery LSP" and "Lockout of Normal Traffic." The first command locks access to the protecting LSP for any traffic (normal or extra), while the second one disallows only normal traffic.

A further command, "Manual Switch for Recovery LSP," causes switchback of the normal traffic onto the working LSP unless the latter has active fault conditions or was locked via the "Lockout of Working LSP" command.

7.7.3 *Path Segment Recovery*

In the path segment recovery model separate recovery schemes are provisioned to protect individual path segments rather than an entire path. Each of the schemes used can be of any of the types that are defined for end-to-end path recovery (see the previous section). All failures are handled just as in the case of end-to-end path recovery with two caveats.

- In the case of path segment recovery any node on a protected LSP (that is, not necessarily the LSP ends as in the case of end-to-end path recovery) may play the role of PLR and/or MN.
- A node on a protected LSP may belong to more than one (overlapping, nested) segment recovery domain and thus may use more than one pair of PLRs/MNs to trigger the recovery from a locally detected failure. This is a useful feature in situations when some PLRs/MNs fail to provide the expected recovery for some reason. This is in sharp contrast to the end-to-end path recovery model, where LSP ends are the only PLR/MN, and a failure of the control plane on either of them makes the LSP unrecoverable in many recovery schemes.

Consider the network presented in Figure 7.8. Suppose that an LSP going through nodes A-B-D-E is a path segment protected LSP: Segment A-B-D is protected by the recovery LSP A-C-D, and segment D-E is protected by the recovery LSP A-F-E. Thus, we have two recovery domains: one starting on PLR A and terminating on MN D, and the other starting on PLR D and terminating on MN E. Note that node D performs the role of MN in one domain and of PLR in the other.

The question is, why not use an end-to-end recovery LSP taking the path A-C-D-F-E instead, since this is link-disjoint from the working path? After all, it would be simpler and require fewer control plane states. But there are numerous advantages in using the segment recovery as follows.

One can see that each recovery domain used in segment recovery is smaller, compared to the end-to-end recovery domain, in the sense that for any possible failure the PLR and MN that are supposed to handle the failure are closer to each

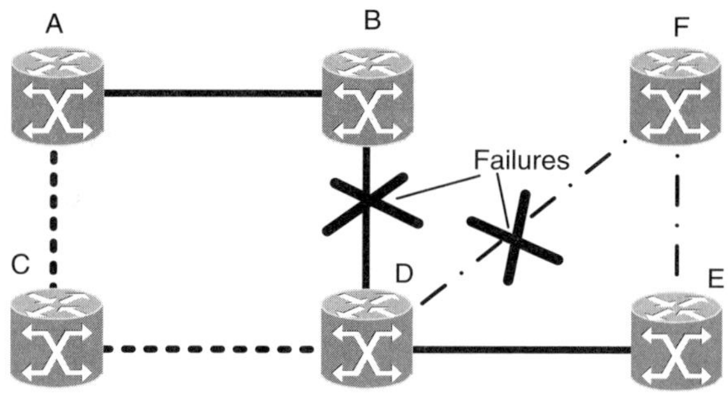

Figure 7.8 Path segment recovery.

other and also to the point of failure. This is important for any recovery scheme that requires fault notification and switchover synchronization signaling simply because there are fewer hops for a signaling message to travel. This usually results in a significant decrease in the overall recovery time.

Segment recovery may provide better protection than end-to-end recovery. In our example, end-to-end recovery could be achieved using an LSP A-C-D-F-E, which uses the same resources as were proposed for the segment protection LSPs. But suppose that two failures — one on link BD, and one on link DF — happen simultaneously, as shown in Figure 7.8. These failures would disrupt the end-to-end protected service since both the protected and recovery LSPs would be affected. The segment-protected LSP, on the other hand, would be recovered in this case as long as a fault-free segment either on the protected LSP or the associated recovery LSP exists in each domain. That is, the traffic in our example would follow the path A-G-D-E.

In some network topologies a service may take a path, for which it is only possible to protect some segment(s), but not the entire path. Consider, for example, a service delivered by the network presented in Figure 7.7 traversing nodes A-B-D-E. There is no alternative path for the service that is fully disjoint from its working path; hence end-to-end protection is not feasible. However, an LSP going through nodes A, C, and D can protect the segment A-B-D. Such protection, albeit imperfect, is still better than no protection at all.

In other cases, alternative end-to-end paths may exist, but could be difficult to compute. Consider, for example, a service traversing multiple TE domains. Computing end-to-end alternative paths in this case is a challenge, especially if the paths may go through separate Service Providers' networks. It is much simpler to compute a single path for the working LSP in a distributed way with each domain border node on the path expanding the path segment within its TE visibility. While doing so, the border nodes can, at the same time, compute paths to be used for recovery of the segments. They have no problem performing such computations because all the recovery paths are located within their TE visibility. TE visibility and computation domains are discussed further in Chapters 8 and 9.

There may be cases when it would make sense to protect a service in different ways on different network fragments. Some of the fragments may be underused, and provisioning dedicated 1+1 protection of the working LSP segments traversing them is reasonable. On the heavily used network fragments, on the other hand, allocating an extra 100% of network resources for protection purposes may prove to be too expensive, and shared protection or pre-planned re-routing could be a better choice.

It may seem that the path segment recovery method always leaves some LSP nodes unprotected as single points of failure: By definition a segment recovery domain must start and stop on some intermediate nodes, leaving them unprotected (for example, node D in Figure 7.8). Fortunately this need not be the case. Suppose that there is an additional sequence of links interconnecting nodes B and H (see Figure 7.9). The link(s) can be used for a recovery LSP specifically dedicated to protect against node D failures.

This is *overlapping segment recovery*, where a new recovery domain starts before some other recovery domain (that started somewhere upstream) is terminated. Generally speaking, GMPLS path segment recovery is very powerful as a concept. It can support numerous complex path recovery topologies, and the overlapping path segment recovery scheme is just one example (see Figure 7.10). GMPLS signaling has a remarkably simple and efficient way (via a stack of GMPLS RSVP NotifyRequest objects — see the more detailed description below) of advertising the PLRs and MNs along the path of a protected LSP, so that each node on the path has a prioritized list of relevant PLRs/MNs it can notify to trigger the LSP recovery from a failure detected by the node. For example, a node located somewhere between MN3 and MN1 (Figure 7.10c) knows that only PLR1 and MN1 can take care of locally detected failures, while all other PLRs/MNs are of no use. Likewise, a node located upstream of MN2 knows that in case of a failure it needs to notify PLR2 and MN2 first, and only if they fail to provide the recovery should it try PLR1/MN1. Note that the node would know nothing about the PLR3/MN3 pair.

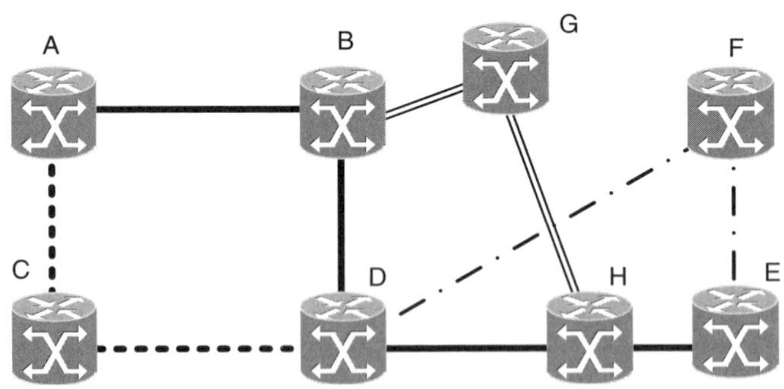

Figure 7.9 Overlapping segment recovery.

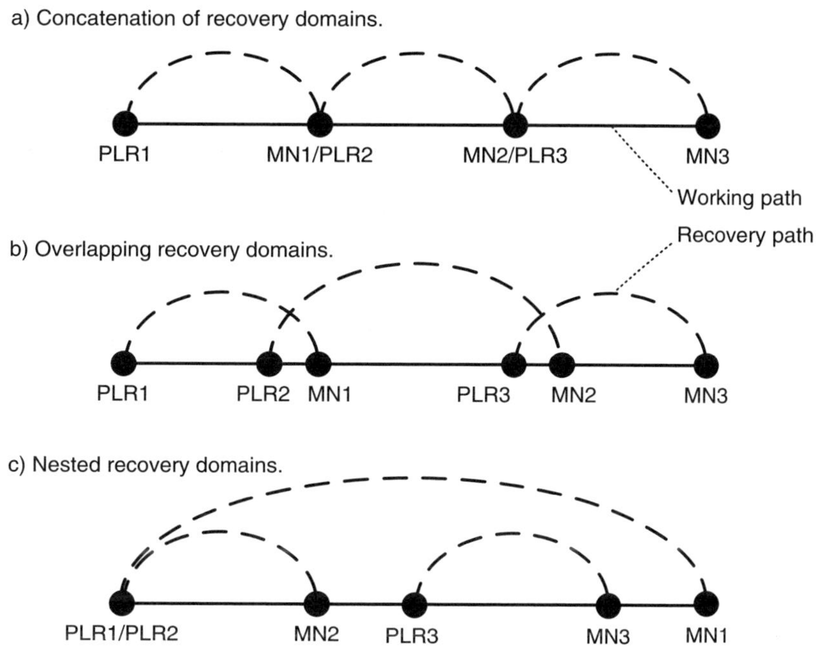

Figure 7.10 Segment recovery domains may be concatenated, overlapping, or nested.

One may wonder why anybody would need such a complex recovery scheme. The main reason for this is the ability to recover from multiple simultaneous failures. Imagine, for example, that the control plane on the PLR of a 1:1 protection domain fails. If, before it is restored, some node along the protected LSP detects a failure and sends an FIS to the PLR, the protection switchover will not happen, and service will be disrupted, possibly for a significant period of time. However, if the fault-detecting node is aware of some other PLR, it will send the FIS notification to it as soon as it realizes that the first choice PLR has failed to provide the required recovery, and so the service could still be recovered. There may also be a case where both protected and protecting LSPs fail simultaneously. When a PLR receives the FIS notification and realizes that the locally originated protecting LSP is, for some reason, not available, it may relay the FIS to some upstream PLR that starts an overlapping or nesting recovery domain. Consider the case where a node located between PL3 and MN3 (Figure 7.10c) detects a failure and sends the FIS to PL3. The latter may realize that the protecting LSP interconnecting PL3 and MN3 is also not available because of the same or an unrelated failure. In this case the PL3 simply forwards the FIS to PLR1/MN1, which will switch the traffic onto the outer protecting LSP.

The rest of this section analyzes two ways that path segment recovery for a particular service can be provisioned. The first approach assumes explicit provisioning of recovery domain types, boundaries, and possibly recovery paths using the GMPLS RSVP Secondary Explicit Route objects (SEROs). The second approach relies on the dynamic computation of recovery domains by the network. The hybrid approach — when the management controls certain recovery domains, while others are dynamically established — is also possible and sometimes very useful.

Explicit Provisioning of Segment Recovery

Recall that RSVP-TE includes a way to control the path taken by the LSP that supports a particular service. Specifically, the entire path or some parts of the path can be encoded within the Explicit Route object (ERO), and the signaling infrastructure makes sure that the LSP follows the specified path even if routing protocols would define a different one. A similar approach is taken to support segment recovery in an Internet-Draft that describes the technique: Parameters of all or some recovery domains (the identities of the PLR and MN, the type of recovery, strict or loose recovery path, and so forth) can be explicitly signaled within SEROs — one SERO per domain.

Each SERO should contain at least three sub-objects. The first sub-object is of type Protection. This type was introduced specifically for SEROs and identifies the type of recovery scheme to be provisioned within the domain, and the signaling parameters to be used while provisioning the recovery LSP in case they are different from the parameters used for signaling the protected LSP. The other two objects are of type IP. They identify the domain's PLR and MN, respectively. An SERO may optionally include any number of further sub-objects of any type as defined for EROs. They should be located within the SERO between sub-objects associated with the PLR and MN and specify (strictly or loosely) a recovery path.

Every node, while processing the protected LSP Setup message (RSVP Path), analyzes the set of SEROs within the message. If it discovers that the first IP sub-object of one of the SEROs is associated with one of the locally assigned IP addresses, it realizes that it needs to start a new recovery domain — that is, perform the PLR function. In this case, it extracts the SERO from the message and uses the information encoded within the object to trigger the setup of an appropriate protecting LSP, or stores the encoded route for the purpose of LSP restoration. Furthermore, it adds a new object to the stack of NotifyRequest objects in the LSP Setup message of the protected LSP to specify a new recipient of Notify messages by supplying a local IP address on which the PLR is willing to receive fault notifications. This makes sure that nodes within the domain learn about the PLR address.

The node where a recovery LSP converges with the protected LSP assumes the MN role. Specifically, it terminates the recovery LSP and removes the associated PLR's NotifyRequest object from the LSP Setup message. This prevents nodes located downstream from the MN from learning about the PLRs that *cannot* handle failures that they detect — that is, PLRs that control recovery domains to which the downstream nodes do not belong. The MN also adds a new NotifyRequest object to the protected LSP Accept message (RSVP Resv) to specify a local IP address. This ensures that nodes within the domain learn the identity of the MN.

These manipulations of the NotifyRequest objects guarantee that no matter how complex the topology of the recovery domains (nested, overlapped, and so forth), each node on the protected path will have a sorted list of valid PLRs (that is, a stack of NotifyRequest objects in the RSVP Path message) and MNs (a stack of NotifyRequest objects in the RSVP Resv message), which the node can alert if it detects a failure.

There is another signaling object, the Secondary Record Route Object (SRRO), which was introduced specifically for the purpose of path segment recovery signaling. Before sending the protected LSP Setup message, the MN, in addition to updating the protected LSP Record Route Object (RRO), also adds to the message the entire path taken by the locally terminated recovery LSP encoded as an SRRO. Likewise, before sending out the protected LSP Accept message, the PLR, in addition to updating the protected LSP RRO, also adds to the message the entire path taken by the locally originated recovery LSP encoded as an SRRO. Thus, both ends of the service have access to the entire topology of network resources consumed by all protected (mainly, working) and all recovery LSPs.

Let us see how explicit provisioning of path segment recovery works in an example. Suppose that we need to provision $1+1$ segment protection for the service whose working LSP traverses the nodes A, B, D, and E, as shown in Figure 7.8. In this case, the LSP Setup message for the working LSP will contain an ERO = {A-B-D-E} and two SEROs: $SERO_1$ = {A-C-D} and $SERO_2$ = {D-F-E}. Nodes A and D, while processing the message, will realize that each is instructed to set up one $1+1$ protecting LSP and they will trigger the establishment of these LSPs. Node A will also remove $SERO_1$ from the outgoing working LSP Setup message and add to the message a NotifyRequest object indicating its local IP address. Likewise, node D will remove $SERO_2$ from the outgoing working LSP Setup message and add to the stack of NotifyRequest objects another one indicating its local IP address.

When the first protecting LSP Setup message arrives at node D, the node will realize that it needs to perform MN function for the first recovery domain. Hence it will perform the following actions.

- Remove from the stack of NotifyRequest objects in the outgoing working LSP Setup message (RSVP Path) the object that indicates the originator of the terminated recovery LSP (that is, node A). This may require the modification of an LSP Setup message that was sent previously.

- Insert into the working LSP Setup message the entire path of the recovery LSP (that is, the received RRO) encoded as an SRRO.
- Add to the stack of NotifyRequest objects in the LSP Accept message (RSVP Resv) for the working LSP an object that indicates its local IP address. Again, this may require that an update of a message that was sent previously is generated.

Node E performs similar operations while terminating the second recovery LSP.

Note that node D in our example performs the MN role for the first recovery domain and the PLR role for the second one. When the second recovery LSP Accept message arrives at node D, the latter as a PLR will conduct the following actions.

- Remove from the stack of NotifyRequest objects in the outgoing working LSP Accept message (RSVP Resv) the object associated with the terminator of the second recovery LSP (that is, node E). Again, this may require the modification of an LSP Accept message that was sent previously.
- Insert into the accept message the entire path of the locally originated recovery LSP encoded as an SRRO.

Node A performs similar operations while processing the accept message of the first recovery LSP.

By the time the setup of the working LSP is complete, the service head and tail ends will know about all links onto which the service is mapped. Note that node B will be aware of only one PLR (node A), and only one MN (node D). Likewise, the only PLR that node E will know about is node D. It is also important to note that node E will not know that node A is also a PLR, which is good because node A cannot help to recover from the faults detected by node E.

Note that a node on a protected LSP may know about more than one PLR/MN pair. This would be the case if the node belongs to more than one overlapping domain and/or to a domain nested entirely within some other domain. For example, node E in Figure 7.9 will be aware of two PLRs — D and B. Thus, when the node detects a failure it will first send the fault notification to node D. However, if the notification is not acknowledged (perhaps because the control plane of node D is not functional), the fault notification will be sent to the other PLR — node B.

Dynamic Provisioning of Segment Recovery

Explicit provisioning of segment recovery is convenient, but it assumes that some entity on the service head end is capable of identifying recovery domains and producing the SEROs. This is a big assumption because the head end may not have adequate computation capabilities to do the job. Furthermore, it may not have access to all of the necessary information. This is especially true if the service needs to traverse several TE domains.

One way of solving this problem is to have a remote Path Computation Element (PCE) generate the SEROs (see Chapter 9 for more details on the remote PCE model). However, this approach has its own issues, especially in the standardization of the very complex semantics of path computation requests.

An alternative is to put the task of determining recovery domains in the network. Currently, the Internet-Draft that describes segment recovery defines the following procedures for the dynamic provisioning of segment recovery.

- The desired recovery type for all service recovery domains is provisioned in a separate section of the Protection object of the LSP Setup message for the working LSP. Thus, in contrast to recovery domains that are provisioned via SEROs, dynamic recovery domains are limited to having the same recovery type.
- Every node on the working path may assume the role of PLR. If the node decides to do so, it attempts to compute a recovery path. Different policies may be applied when computing the path. For instance, an objective could be to determine the path that most rapidly converges with the working path. Alternatively, an attempt may be made to determine the path protecting the largest segment of the working path starting from the computing node.
- If the recovery path is successfully computed, it is either stored for service restoration purposes or the setup of the protecting LSP is triggered. In the latter case the Protection object of the outgoing LSP Setup message for the working LSP contains the "Segment recovery is in place" flag set to let downstream nodes know that they should not also attempt to establish more recovery LSPs — this avoids unnecessary allocation of protection resources.
- When a node on the working LSP terminates a protecting LSP (that is, realizes that it should perform the MN role), it resets the Segment recovery in place flag in the Protection object of the outgoing LSP Setup message for the working LSP, so that the node itself or some downstream node can attempt to start a new recovery domain.

It is important to mention that the dynamic provisioning of recovery domains is different from explicit provisioning only in the area of defining boundaries of the domains and computing recovery paths. All other aspects, such as advertising of identities of PLRs/MNs via NotifyRequest Objects, collecting RROs/SRROs, and so forth, are the same. Furthermore, explicit and dynamic methods of path segment recovery provisioning are not mutually exclusive. It is quite possible for an operator to provision one or more recovery domains via strict or loose SEROs, and to let the network figure out how to protect the other segments of the working LSP for which the operator has not specified any protection LSPs. In such a case, explicit provisioning always takes precedence, and a node on the working path will not attempt to compute a dynamic recovery path if it detects a "local" SERO in the LSP Setup message (that is, an SERO with the first IP sub-object indicating a locally assigned IP address).

Let us go back to our example presented in Figure 7.8 and see how the dynamic provisioning of path segment recovery works. Suppose 1 + 1 dynamic segment protection is requested for a service going from node A to node E. Suppose also that no SEROs are specified, and the service working path is provisioned to traverse nodes A-B-D-E. Before sending out the LSP Setup message for the working LSP, the service head end (node A) notices that dynamic 1 + 1 protection is required and realizes that no protecting LSPs are under construction yet (that is, the Segment recovery in place flag is not set). Therefore, it computes a recovery path (A-C-D) and triggers the setup of the 1 + 1 protecting LSP. After that, the node sets the Segment recovery in place flag in the Protection object and sends the LSP Setup message for the working LSP downstream. The flag will prevent all other nodes on the path from originating additional segment-protecting LSPs. Note that even node D, which will eventually need to establish the second protecting LSP, will likely not do this immediately on the receipt of the working LSP Setup message. This is because by the time the LSP Setup message for the working LSP arrives at node D, the LSP Setup message for the first protecting LSP (A-C-D) may still be on its way, and hence node D cannot know that it is the MN for the first recovery domain. However, when it receives the first protecting LSP Setup message, it will realize that the first recovery domain ends and a new one is needed. Hence at the time node D receives the second of the two LSP Setup messages regardless of the order of their arrival, it will compute a new recovery path (D-F-E) and trigger the establishment of the second 1 + 1 segment-protecting LSP. As was mentioned earlier, the way nodes on the working path learn about identities of relevant PLRs/MNs, as well as how the service head and tail ends learn about the segment recovery topology, is identical to the method described for when the segment protection was provisioned via SEROs.

The procedures here for dynamic path segment recovery have some serious flaws. Notice that the service in the example is left unprotected against the failure of node D — the node that terminates one protection domain and starts another. This is not just because of the topological constraints; the same protection topology would be dynamically installed for the service in the network presented in Figure 7.9, despite the fact that an additional network segment (B-G-E) can protect against node D failures. This happens because during the establishment of the services, node B would realize by examining the Segment recovery in place flag that some upstream node (specifically node A) has started the establishment of a protecting LSP, which is not terminated on node B. Hence node B would never attempt to compute and establish an additional protecting LSP going over B-G-E. In general the scheme described here does not produce overlapping protection domains — the only way to avoid single points of failure in the path segment recovery model.

Furthermore, if the service needs to traverse multiple TE domains, it could easily be the case that a PLR will not be capable of identifying an existing recovery path due to limitations in the TE visibility. Consider, for instance, the situation when the working LSP (Figure 7.9) goes through two domains with node D as a boundary node between the two (that is, nodes B and E are in different TE domains). In this case, even if we somehow force node B to try to compute a recovery path, it will not be able to accomplish this because it does not have visibility into the neighboring TE domain. Note that node D could do the necessary path computation, because as a border node it has visibility into both TE domains. However, it needs a way to signal the resulting path to node B so that the latter can originate the protecting LSP establishment. This mechanism does not form part of the current dynamic path segment recovery method.

Finally, the dynamic segment recovery scheme gives no solution for how segment recovery resources could be shared between several services. This is because PLRs that compute dynamic recovery paths do not know anything about LSPs that do not go through themselves. In particular, they do not know which protecting LSPs are established in the network and what working LSPs they protect (a useful piece of information when deciding if resources protecting some LSP could be also used to protect other LSPs). In the model, where a node computes recovery paths protecting against its own failures and failures of its links, the computing node does not know about all LSPs on the network. However, it does know about LSPs that traverse it and that need to be segment protected, so it can keep track of the recovery paths that have been computed for their protection and use this knowledge when computing a recovery path for a new service. Obviously, a node computing a recovery path protecting against its own failures cannot originate the recovery LSP following the computed path. Hence, again, there is a need to signal the computed path to the PLR somehow.

Currently, the authors of the GMPLS segment recovery architecture (among them the author of this book) are discussing an alternative solution for dynamic path segment recovery to address the issues just described. In a nutshell, every node on the protected LSP may try to compute one or more paths protecting against the node's failure and/or the failures of its links. The computed paths are signaled along the protected path in the upstream direction in the LSP Accept message (RSVP Resv) for the working LSP, and are encoded in objects specifically introduced for this purpose — Dynamic SEROs (DSEROs). The semantics of the DSERO are identical to that of the SERO. When a node, while processing the accept message for the protected LSP, discovers that one or more of the DSEROs have a first IP sub-object that indicates a locally assigned IP address, the node may attempt to originate one or more recovery LSPs. If more

Table 7.1 DSEROs for Dynamic Segment Protection

Node	DSERO	PLR	MN
A	None		
B	A-C-D	A	D
D	B-G-E	B	E
E	D-F-E	D	E
	B-G-E	B	E

than one such DSERO is detected, the processing node may choose to set up a single recovery LSP (for example, the one covering the longest segment of the protected LSP). To see how this approach works, let us consider once again the establishment of a segment protected LSP as shown in Figure 7.9. Following the logic described in this paragraph, the LSP nodes produce the DSEROs as shown in Table 7.1.

By the time the establishment of the protected LSP is complete, three recovery LSPs (A-C-D, B-G-E, and D-F-E) are installed. Note that node D has produced a path identical to one of the paths computed by node E. Obviously in this case node D does not need to add the locally computed path to the LSP Accept message — the proper DSERO has already been inserted into the message by node E.

Path Segment Recovery Operations

In many ways, path segment recovery is very similar to end-to-end path recovery described earlier in this chapter. Generally speaking, a node of a segment protected LSP, when detecting a failure, sends an FIS message to a PLR and/or MN, which triggers the switchover synchronization procedures. Likewise, when a previously reported failure is restored and the reversion mode has been provisioned for the service, the node that detects the failure restoration sends an FRS message to the PLR and/or MN, which synchronously switch traffic back onto the restored segment.

However, there are a couple of important differences between the two models of path recovery. First, in the case of end-to-end recovery there is only one PLR and only one MN — the service head and tail ends, respectively — whereas in the case of segment recovery any transit node of the protected LSP may play PLR or MN roles, or both roles at the same time. More than that, in the case of nested recovery domains the same node may act as multiple PLRs and/or MNs for the same protected LSP.

Secondly, every node located on an end-to-end protected LSP belongs to a single recovery domain, while a node on a segment protected LSP may belong to zero, one, or several (overlapping, nested, and so forth) recovery domains. As was pointed out earlier, segment recovery signaling guarantees that by the time a segment protected LSP is established, each node on its path is aware not only about all PLRs/MNs that can help to recover from locally detected failures, but also of the order in which the PLRs/MNs should be alerted so that fault-related notifications will be sent to the closest ones first. Only if this closest pair of PLR/MNs fails to provide the expected recovery (perhaps because the control plane on, say, the PLR is out of service at the time), should the FIS message be sent to the next best (closest) PLR/MN and so forth until the fault reporting node realizes that service is recovered or it runs out of PLRs/MNs to notify. Obviously, during the reversion process, only those PLRs/MNs that previously managed the service recovery (that is, not necessarily the closest ones) should be notified about the fault restoration.

7.7.4 *Combining Segment and End-to-End Recovery*

One might get the impression that path segment and end-to-end recovery methods are alternative solutions for service recovery. They are not! It makes perfect sense to provision both end-to-end and segment recovery for the same service at the same time. In fact it is valid to see end-to-end recovery as a simple case of segment recovery, where the entire working path of a service constitutes a single segment protected within a single recovery domain. Likewise, the combination of end-to-end and segment recovery could be seen as a special case of nested segment recovery where the end-to-end recovery domain nests all other (segment recovery) domains provisioned for the service.

Consider a service going from node A to node E in the network presented in Figure 7.11. Suppose the working path is A-B-D-E. There are several options to protect the service.

Option 1: end-to-end protection using the protecting LSP A-I-H-G-E. The problem with this scheme is that the recovery time of any recovery type apart from 1 + 1 protection is unlikely to be good enough because the PLR (node A) and MN (node E) are likely to be too far away from a point of failure. Yet using 1 + 1 protection makes the service 100% more expensive because the protection resources cannot be shared with any other service.

Option 2: shared segment protection using A-C-D and D-F-E protecting LSPs. This looks better than option 1, because the protection is shared (hence less expensive) and the PLRs/MNs are closer to any point of failure (hence recovery time is better). But what if node D or any other resource not covered by the segment recovery (perhaps because of topological constraints) fails? In such a case the service could not be recovered.

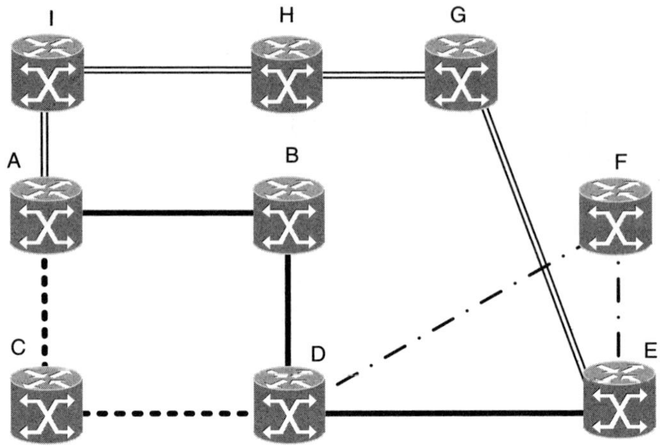

Figure 7.11 Combining end-to-end and segment recovery.

Option 3: shared end-to-end protection with shared segment protection. This option seems to work the best. When a resource covered by segment protection fails (for example, node B and/or link DE), the service will be recovered very rapidly. If node D fails the end-to-end protection will be engaged. The recovery time will not be as good, but at least the service will be recovered. Furthermore, suppose something unexpected happened. For example, links BD and AC fail at the same time, or node E detects a failure on node DE but the control plane on node D, which is supposed to manage the switchover procedures, is out of service at the moment. Again, thanks to the end-to-end protection, the service will still be recovered. The only issue here is that once we consider multiple simultaneous failures, one of them can affect the end-to-end protecting LSP as well; the service will not be recovered in this case.

Option 4: end-to-end full re-routing with shared segment protection. This combination handles multiple simultaneous failures even better. Initially, recovery uses the shared segment protection LSPs, but, no matter what goes wrong, the service head end may always take into account all failures, compute a new recovery path (provided, of course, that such a path still exists), set up the restoration LSP, and switch traffic onto it. Understandably, the recovery time would be the worst in this case, especially because of potential crankbacks and retries needed to set up the restoration LSP. But such recomputation is only invoked when the segment protection has failed to deliver the required recovery. Note also that the recovery and working paths do not need to be fully diverse. The only requirement for the recovery path is to be disjoint from all points of failure; all healthy links can be shared. This is good, because a fully disjoint end-to-end path is not always available.

7.7.5 *Fast Re-Route*

Fast Re-Route (FRR is a local recovery technique introduced in MPLS for the protection of packet switching network services. In this model every node, while processing an LSP Setup (RSVP Path) message, may realize that the LSP is requested to be FRR protected. The indication of such a requirement is the presence of an object (Fast-Re-Route), specifically introduced for this purpose, and/or the fact that certain flags in the Session-Attributes object are set.

To install the local protection, the processing node attempts to determine a recovery path protecting against a failure of either the immediate downstream link or node. In other words an attempt is made to compute an alternative path divergent from the downstream link or node in the protected LSP, and terminating on either the immediate next hop node (protecting against a failure of the link) or the next-next hop node (protecting against a failure of the next hop node) along the path of the protected LSP. The computed node learns about the identity of the next or next-next hop nodes by looking into the RRO or ERO of the protected LSP, or by examining the local Traffic Engineering Database (TED). If the recovery path is successfully determined, the computing node assumes the PLR function and originates the protecting LSP. Depending on whether the LSP protects against the failure of the next link or the next node, it is called either a Next Hop (NHOP) or Next-Next Hop (NNHOP) backup tunnel.

Obviously, an NNHOP backup tunnel also provides protection against a failure of the immediate downstream link; thus, protection-wise, it is better than an NHOP backup tunnel. However, the NNHOP backup tunnel consumes more protection resources and topologically may not be available. Hence, FRR includes a way to signal whether NHOP-type protection is sufficient, or whether NNHOP backup tunnels are required. If the protecting LSP is successfully established, its head end (that is, the PLR) signals that local protection is in place in the RRO carried in the LSP Accept message, so that the head end of the protected LSP can learn which (if any) links/nodes are left unprotected. Similarly, the PLR that has detected a failure and switched the traffic onto a local NHOP or NNHOP backup tunnel, signals the fact that local protection is engaged and that re-routing of the protected LSP may be desirable in the RRO carried in the LSP Accept message. Consider the examples presented in Figures 7.12 and 7.13.

In both examples an FRR protected LSP (A-D-E-G) is established. In the first example, each of the nodes of the protected LSP apart from the LSP tail end establishes an NHOP backup tunnel protecting the links AD, DE, and EG, respectively. In the second example, nodes A and D set up NNHOP backup tunnels protecting against failures of nodes D and E.

In the steady state, FRR protection resources are not used for service traffic delivery. The good thing about FRR (possibly the only good thing!) is that it guarantees that, no matter where a failure is detected, a suitable PLR/MN pair will

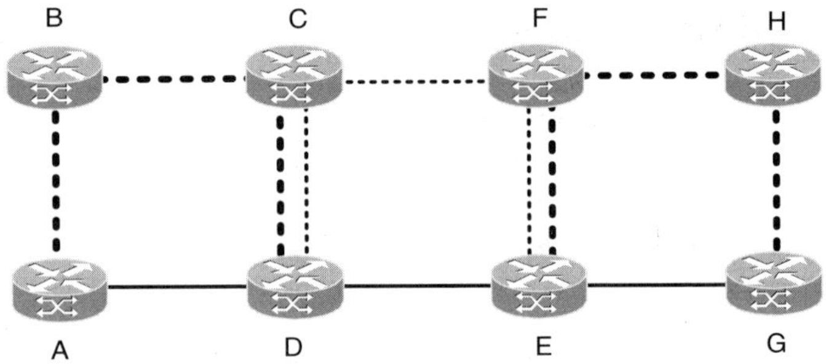

Figure 7.12 FRR protection with NHOP tunnels.

always be found within a single IP hop of the point of failure, and hence a recovery time close to that provided by $1+1$ protection can be achieved without the permanent bridging of traffic onto the working and protecting LSPs.

Depending on how a backup tunnel handles failures, it can be either a *detour tunnel* or a *facility bypass tunnel*. Detour tunnels protect each LSP individually. For instance, if N LSPs use some TE link, there would be N detour tunnels installed to protect them from the failure of the link. Resources on common links are always shared between detour tunnels protecting the same LSPs and cannot be shared with detour tunnels that protect other LSPs. This is true even when the LSPs protected by FRR are mutually disjoint and can be assumed not to fail at the same time, and arises because in the FRR model, resources are shared in a "classic" way — on the basis of a common RSVP Session object, and different LSPs have different Session objects.

A single facility bypass tunnel provides protection against the failure of a link or node for all LSPs using the link/node.

Consider, for example, the piece of network presented in Figure 7.14. Suppose there are two LSPs protected by FRR: A-C-D-G and B-C-D-H. In order to protect

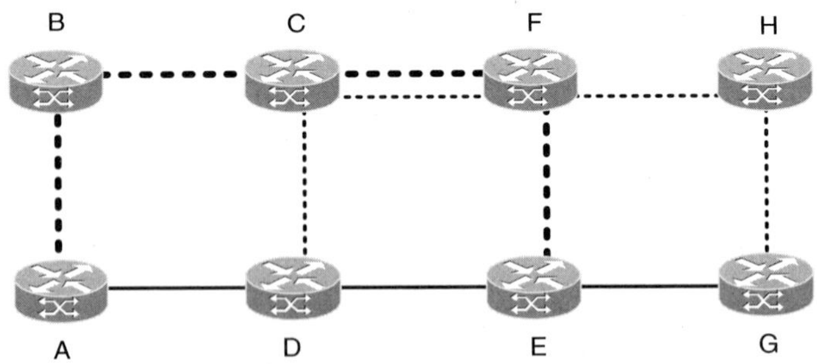

Figure 7.13 FRR protection with NNHOP tunnels.

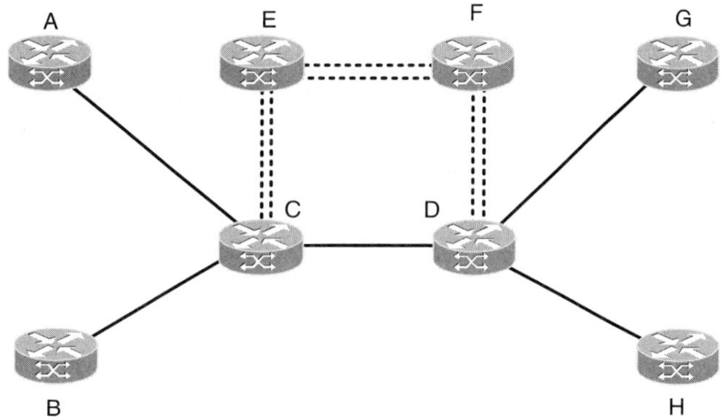

Figure 7.14 FRR protection with NHOP detours.

against failures on link CD there are two NHOP detour tunnels installed (both with path C-E-F-D).

In Figure 7.15 the protection against CD's failure is provided via a single facility bypass tunnel (C-E-F-D). MPLS has a useful construct (the label stack) that allows for multiplexing/de-multiplexing several tunnels onto/from one tunnel. Specifically, when node C detects a failure on link CD, it can start to forward data packets from both protected services over the tunnel C-E-F-D. The label stack of each outgoing packet will contain two labels. The outer one is common for all protected LSPs and is associated with the bypass tunnel itself. The inner label is LSP specific, and hence the node that terminates the bypass tunnel (node D) is capable of figuring out to which service an incoming packet that is received over the facility bypass tunnel belongs. The way node C learns about LSP specific labels understood by node D depends on the label scope. If the global (node-scope) label

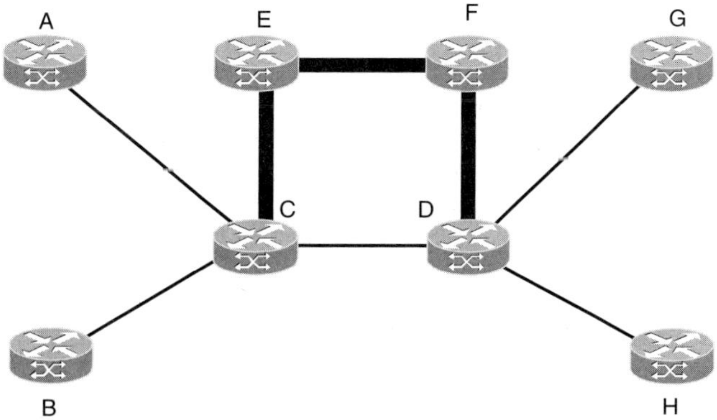

Figure 7.15 FRR protection with NHOP facility bypass tunnel.

space is in use, this knowledge usually comes through collecting the RROs of the protected LSPs. If interface-scope label spaces are in use, additional signaling is needed in order to negotiate labels for the LSPs over the bypass tunnel. This feature is particularly relevant when NNHOP FRR tunnels are in use.

A common misconception is that facility bypass tunnels provide a way to share protection resources between LSPs. They do not! Protection resources can only be shared between mutually disjoint LSPs, and by definition facility bypass tunnels only protect LSPs that *share* the same protected resource. To see this let us assume that each of the two protected LSPs requires 10 MB of bandwidth to guarantee the requested QoS. Obviously, on each link of the bypass tunnel 20 MB must be reserved to ensure that the QoS of both services will not be violated. Note that this is the same amount of protection bandwidth that would be allocated for two detour tunnels. To lessen the amount of protection resource required, the facility bypass tunnel must either only protect a subset of the affected LSPs, or must offer a lower quality service with shared resources and delivery that comes close to being only best effort.

The facility bypass tunnel approach does reduce the amount of control plane state that is required. In our example, for instance, a facility bypass tunnel requires a single control plane state per tunnel link, whereas two detour tunnels providing the equivalent protection require a control plane state per detour per link and hence twice as much control plane state per link. Reducing the amount of control plane state associated with protection is a valuable quality for packet switching networks, especially in cases when no strict bandwidth protection guarantees are required or where there are very many LSPs traversing a single link. However, it is much less important in the context of transport networks, where the overall number of LSPs (and hence the amount of control plane state) is much lower.

An FRR-style local recovery model is not appealing for transport network services for several reasons. Let us start with the facility bypass tunnel approach. It requires the use of the label stack construct, which is not necessarily applicable in transport networks (or generally speaking, any kind of circuit switching networks). You could argue that the label stack is also required for the support of Hierarchical LSPs (H-LSPs), and that we know how to support H-LSPs in transport networks using implicit label stacks. It is true that we can use a higher level H-LSP to construct a facility bypass tunnel and nest the affected protected LSPs within it. But what would we gain? Suppose the LSPs protected by FRR in Figures 7.14 and 7.15 exist in a TDM network and are used by SONET services carrying OC-12 payloads. To protect them against the failure of link CD, two OC-12 detour tunnels could be provisioned (Figure 7.14). Alternatively, a single OC-48 facility bypass tunnel could be installed (Figure 7.15), and after link failure the payload of the two affected services could be adapted into/extracted from the tunnel. In the latter case more protection resources would be allocated (one OC-48 H-LSP versus two OC-12 detours because of the different granularities of the resource allocation). Besides, the facility bypass tunnel would also require some adaptation resources for inserting/extracting the OC-12 payload into/from the OC-48 pipe. This is assuming that nodes C and D have the ability to originate/terminate higher-level H-LSPs and have the necessary adaptation resources available — not a small assumption considering that *each* node of a protected LSP may have to be a PLR and/or MN. And in exchange for all these troubles we would save one control plane state on links CE, EF, and FD!

Using the detour approach to protect transport network services makes better sense, but realistically the approach is not feasible either. First, it requires an alternative path for every link or node of a protected LSP. This is possible only in a dense mesh network topology where each node has high degree; that is, where many network arcs (links) meet at each vertex (node). This is not the case in currently deployed transport networks, which are usually built as the interconnection of rings. Secondly, each transport network detour would require the allocation of an expensive resource (for example, timeslot, wavelength channel) on every link taken by the detour. In a packet switching environment it is realistic to set up detours wherever possible (especially if bandwidth protection is not required) for the cost of only extra control plane states. This is not the case in transport networks: Resources allocations are very "real," and the allocated resources cannot be used in the steady (fault-free) state; neither can they be shared with other services. This is not good.

Note that hierarchies are not always as freely available as they are in a TDM network. For example, in a lambda switching network, the only realistic hierarchy that is available is to nest lambdas within a fiber. The use of an entire fiber to provide a facility bypass tunnel is equivalent to 1:1 span protection and is a highly resource intensive way to use the available resources.

Fortunately the path segment recovery model (described in Section 7.7.3) works very well for transport services. In fact we strongly believe that it is a much better solution for the local recovery of PSC network services as well. With the exception of facility bypass tunnels (which can be easily introduced to the segment recovery if needed) there is nothing in FRR that path segment recovery cannot provide and, at the same time, the latter has some serious advantages.

- The path segment recovery approach is not limited to protecting one resource at a time: A protected segment may contain an arbitrary number of LSP links. Hence, there is not such a stringent requirement for network topology density. Path segment recovery works equally well for mesh and ring topologies. It also provides more efficient utilization of protection resources, because, by protecting 2, 3, ..., n links rather than one link or node at a time, it is possible to achieve acceptable service recovery times while spending many fewer network resources compared to FRR with bandwidth protection guarantees.
- In FRR all protecting detours and facility bypass tunnels are dynamically computed. In segment recovery some or all recovery domains may be fully

or partially provisioned by making use of SEROs. This means that Service Providers may take complete or partial control of the layout of resources allocated for protection of services they sell. This is a very valuable quality: Service Providers appreciate predictability very much and do not like surprises.

- In FRR it may also be the case that a PLR is not in a position to determine a path for a detour or bypass tunnel it is supposed to originate. A good example is defining an NNHOP detour protecting against ABR failures: As was discussed earlier, the ABR itself is in a better position to compute such a path because it has the TE visibility into both neighboring domains. Therefore, there is a need to signal such a path back upstream to the PLR. Segment recovery has a very lightweight naturally integrated mechanism for such signaling (DSEROs), whereas FRR does not have one and has to depend on some form of remote PCE protocol.
- FRR does not provide information about the exact topology of local recovery tunnels established for a particular service. The only information available is the flags in the RRO of the LSP Accept message that declare whether local protection is available or not on particular nodes along the protected path. This is in contrast with the path segment recovery approach, where the SRROs of an accept message for a protected LSP describe all resources committed or pre-planned to protect the service. It is possible, for example, to convert SRROs into SEROs and use them in an LSP Setup message with the guarantee that the exact same local protection layout will be installed for the service the next time it is provisioned.
- FRR relies on the fact that backup paths are computed after a protected LSP is established. It is a well-known fact that because of the greedy nature of path computation algorithms it could easily be the case that a primary path yields no diverse backup paths to protect one or more resources. In the path segment recovery model primary and backup paths may be computed and provisioned simultaneously; thus, the described situation can be avoided.
- Path segment recovery is not limited to protection: An SERO can identify either a protection or a restoration domain. FRR describes only how protection tunnels can be provisioned. It is not clear how FRR can guarantee bandwidth protection and have the protection bandwidth usable in the steady state at the same time. The path segment recovery approach, on the other hand, fits nicely into the full mesh restoration model.
- FRR provides no solution for unexpected events such as the situation where a single failure affects both protected resource and protecting tunnel, or where there are multiple failures (simultaneous, or in quick succession). Segment recovery provides a way to provision complex recovery schemes (for example, nested and/or overlapped recovery domains), so that a service can withstand multiple failures.

7.8 Control Plane Recovery

Control and data planes in transport networks are separated so that control plane messages do not necessarily flow along the links they control. One of the consequences of this is that the two can fail independently. Let us consider the following cases in respect to the relationship between control and data plane failures of a particular LSP.

1. Control plane is functional on all nodes; data plane failures are detected on one or more nodes.
2. Control and data planes fail at the same time on one or more nodes.
3. No data plane failures are detected (that is, user traffic is not affected); control plane fails on one or more nodes.
4. Control and data planes fail on different nodes.

So far in this chapter we have considered only case 1. We implicitly assumed that once a failure is locally detected, the FIS message is delivered to the appropriate PLR/MN, which uses the synchronizing signaling to perform the protection switchover operation, computes and signals a new path disjoint from the point of failure, or tears down the affected LSP. These assumptions require the control plane to function on all nodes of the protected and protecting LSPs.

Case 2 might seem a difficult one, but in fact it is not. If the data plane on a node fails, traffic of a service traversing the node is affected. Hopefully, the neighboring nodes detect the failure and the traffic is switched away from the failed node. Note that the failed node itself does not need to be involved in the recovery process, so it is not very important whether the control plane on the node is healthy or not. But the shortest path for propagation of the FIS or switchover signals might be through the control plane of the failed node/link. In this case, the fact that the fault-related messages are targeted at the PLM/MN and may be delivered by any route (not just hop-by-hop along the path of the failed LSP) is particularly important.

Having said that, it is fair to point out that for the purpose of reversion after the data plane restoration the control plane on the node must be recovered as well. Anyway, this case is not any different from the case of a failure of a packet switch (for example, an IP router, or Ethernet switch), where the data and control planes are inseparable. Therefore, the rest of this chapter is dedicated to cases 3 and 4.

Case 3 is a peculiar one. From the user's perspective the service looks perfectly healthy. However, if the control plane on even a single node of the working LSP fails, the LSP (and hence the service) becomes unmanageable. Imagine, for instance, that the data plane on a node with the failed controller detects a traffic-affecting failure. Unless 1 + 1 protection is provisioned or unless the failure is more widely detectable, the service might not be recoverable, because the PLR/MN responsible for the recovery might never learn about the fault. Likewise, if the control plane fails on the PLR or MN, there would be no entity to manage the switchover process unless there are nested recovery domains. Finally, if even one controller along the path of an LSP fails, it is impossible to modify the LSP in any way, and it is even awkward to just tear the LSP down. This is because the GMPLS signaling protocols use a hop-by-hop signaling paradigm and cannot tolerate gaps in the signaling message path.

Thus, it is very important to recover from control plane failures as soon as possible, and to re-synchronize the control plane state with the data plane state even for LSPs that have no failures in the data plane. This, however, is not always easy to accomplish, and the period of time when the user traffic is delivered over an LSP with a broken control plane might not be negligible. We call such LSPs *control plane partitioned LSPs*. It is important to be capable of managing them despite the challenges of the control plane gaps. Specifically, it is important to be able to carry out the recovery operations triggered by fault notification messages. Hence case 4 should be considered as well.

In the rest of this section we will discuss failures of the control plane elements and the events that might cause them. After that, we will provide a brief analysis of different techniques for re-synchronization of the control plane states. At the end, we will describe a way in which control plane partitioned LSPs could be managed.

7.8.1 Control Plane Failures

It is convenient to represent the control plane of an intelligent transport network as a set of network controllers interconnected via control channels, where a *network controller* (or simply *controller*) is an entity realizing the control plane intelligence (for example, routing and signaling protocol speakers, path computer, traffic engineering applications), and a *control channel* is an abstraction that characterizes the network resources necessary to deliver control plane messages between adjacent controllers. An important difference between a transport and a packet switching network is that transport network control channels are conceptually separate from the TE links they manage, even if they share the same optical fibers. Likewise, transport network controllers are logically separate from the data switches they manage, even when the controllers and associated switches are collocated on the same physical devices (see more details in Chapter 8).

The control plane learns about data plane failures only through failure indication events generated by the data plane. Control plane failures, on the other hand, are detected by controllers themselves (for example, by detecting a loss of the signaling adjacency with one of its neighbors). Control and data plane failures may coincide in some cases. For example, a fiber cut may bring the *Optical Supervisory Channel* (*OSC*) out of service and may also disrupt all data channels between two adjacent nodes. However, generally speaking, control and data plane failures are separate.

A *control plane failure* is a failure of a controller or a control channel. Numerous events may cause control plane failures: configuration errors (for example, a control interface was removed, or an important protocol was not enabled), software bugs (a controller software component was upgraded to a new release that had been insufficiently tested), hardware failures (failures of a shelf processor, Ethernet card, OSC controller), and so forth.

A special case of a control plane failure is the *controlled failure* caused by a software upgrade. To take advantage of new features, bug fixes, the software on a network controller must be upgraded to a new release from time to time. There are usually some active services currently mapped to LSPs on links and data switches managed by the controller to be upgraded. Obviously, the upgrade is not a reason to interrupt the services; the upgrade must be conducted with minimal (if any) effect on the user traffic. During the upgrade, new software is downloaded onto the controller and the controller is rebooted, making the controller's behavior very similar to recovery from any other nodal fault (for example, a software crash). The controller attempts to reconnect to the network and to re-synchronize the states of the LSPs with which it was involved in provisioning during its previous "life." In a way it is simpler to handle a software update than a crash because the former is predictable and can be planned in advance. The upgrade, however, has challenges of its own. For instance, the new release may not be 100% backward-compatible with the old one, and because it is impossible to carry out the upgrade on all controllers simultaneously, there is always a chance that additional (real) control plane failures could happen when some controllers already have the new software activated and some do not.

It was mentioned earlier that control plane recovery is not just the removal of the conditions that have caused the failures. It also includes a process of the re-synchronization of control plane state for all LSPs that continue to exist in the data plane. What exactly do we mean by an LSP control plane state? It is simply a record of the LSP. It contains provisioning parameters (for example, preferred and alternative paths, bandwidth, recovery requirements) as received/sent from/to upstream/downstream neighboring controllers. It also contains information dynamically learned about the LSP (for example, the actual path taken by the LSP, alarms detected on local and remote TE links). The LSP state may also point to the states of other related or co-dependent LSPs. For instance, if a controller happens to be a PLR for the LSP, the LSP state might include a pointer to the state of the associated protecting LSP. Finally, the LSP state also contains a record of the identity and status of all local network resources allocated for the LSP, and the identity of a management entity owning the LSP (that is, the entity that triggered the LSP Setup and is responsible for its teardown). That is all very important information for the correct operation and management of the LSPs;

once it is lost it is difficult (if not impossible) to dynamically modify or even tear down the LSP, let alone to conduct protection switchover procedures. Hence it is crucially important that once the control plane failure is restored and the affected controller is restarted and reconnected to the network, the allocated resources are reclaimed and the states are restored for all LSPs (certainly for all active LSPs, and preferably also for the LSPs in setting up and tearing down state as well).

7.8.2 *Control Plane Re-Synchronization via Signaling*

The GMPLS RSVP-TE signaling protocol is very versatile. One of its remarkable features is that it allows a controller recovering from a control plane failure to take full advantage of cooperation with other controllers in the network, while re-synchronizing the states of the LSPs with which the controller was involved before the failure. Specifically, during the re-establishment of signaling adjacencies with its neighbors (via the GMPLS RSVP Hello message exchange), the recovering controller may signal its willingness to re-synchronize the states for such LSPs. For each such LSP, the neighbors signal back to the recovering controller to provide all information that has been sent to and received from the controller during its pre-failure (that is, pre-reboot) life. The information includes the LSP provisioning parameters (bandwidth, recovery requirements, and so on), primary and recovery paths (which may have been previously computed dynamically by the recovering controller), locally detected data plane alarms, and so forth. Once it has this information available, it is quite straightforward for the controller to check it against the local data plane records, re-allocate resources used by the active LSPs, recreate relevant LSP states, and release any resources whose allocation is not known to the network.

Due to the adjacent (that is, hop-by-hop) nature of RSVP-TE, the recovery synchronization procedures described here only work if both neighbors of the recovering controller are fully active. If one neighbor also has a failed control plane, the recovering controller must wait until its neighbors have recovered before it can complete the full re-synchronization of all LSPs.

7.8.3. *Control Plane Restoration Using Local Databases*

Another way to restore the "pre-failure" control plane states is by storing them into local database(s) that can survive reboots. Control plane implementations adopting this approach might save all significant state changes for every LSP, so that after reboot the controller could restore the states by simply reading them from the database(s). Such implementations have major problems for two reasons: It can never be known in advance when a failure will happen, and for each state there is always some piece of information that may be lost simply due to the timing of the failure. These two reasons make re-synchronization using a full-state database virtually impossible to test because of the tremendous number of different test cases.

A simpler and more predictable approach stores a compressed copy of every message that is sent or received by the controller in the database(s). After reboot the controller simply replays the stored messages as they were received from the network. One good thing about this approach is that a message is either available or lost, and RSVP-TE is very good at recovering from message losses. There is much less effort required to sufficiently test this technique in order to make sure it is reliable. The other good quality of this approach is that it can be easily integrated with signaled re-synchronization (see Section 7.8.2): It makes no difference whether a re-synchronization message is received from a neighbor or replayed from the database. Whenever a discrepancy between the stored and network state is detected, the network state always "wins."

The disadvantage of methods based on database re-synchronization is that they include additional processing in the normal steps of LSP management. This may include writes to non-volatile memory which are comparatively slow, and so this form of protection against control plane failure can significantly slow down the LSP setup process.

7.8.4 *Control Plane Restoration Using Data Plane State*

It could be that neither of the methods described in Sections 7.8.2 and 7.8.3 is an option for the restoration of control plane state. Consider, for example, the case where the network controllers must go through a major software upgrade, and the new software is significantly incompatible with the previous version. Usually in this case, the new software is downloaded onto the controllers, all of them are taken out of service, and after that one by one they are rebooted with the local databases removed (this is necessary because the old local databases would be unintelligible to the new version of the software).

The only way to restore the control plane states in such cases is by making use of the LSP information provided by the local data plane. A controller may query local cross-connects, line cards, and customer-facing ports, and so on, and realize that it used to manage the head end of a particular LSP. Using this information about the LSP bandwidth, data encoding type, available from the data plane state, it can start to build the LSP Setup message (RSVP Path) using the information. Note that there is no way for the controller to identify the LSP destination or the path taken by the LSP, but it does not have to. All it needs to do is to determine the outgoing link ID and the identity of the controller managing the remote end of the link. This information can be provided by LMP or can be deduced from the TE database. Having identified the next hop controller, the head end can send the LSP Setup message to the downstream neighbor, which will realize (perhaps, by looking into the Session object and detecting a special value in place of the LSP destination) that this is not an ordinary LSP Setup message. The neighbor controller verifies the information encoded within the message for consistency with the information provided by its local data plane, and identifies the next downstream controller and forwards the message to it. The process repeats itself on all controllers along the path until the LSP Setup message reaches the controller managing the LSP tail end. The latter triggers the LSP Accept message in the upstream direction. Note that the accept message contains the proper LSP destination address, so that all controllers along the path can complete the LSP control plane state restoration.

Clearly, not all details of the previous state can be restored this way. Things like relationships between LSPs may be hard to recover, although where 1 + 1 protection is in place, the data plane may be able to provide sufficient information. Full recovery of all relationships between LSPs may require additional manual intervention.

7.8.5 *Managing Control Plane Partitioned LSPs*

A node with a failed control plane stops responding to control messages received from its neighbors, and stops originating its own messages. LSPs going through the node (provisioned before the failure) may still be operational; that is, they may still be fully functional in the data plane. However, these LSPs become unmanageable even on the nodes that have not experienced control plane failures. Consider, for example, the network presented in Figure 7.16.

Suppose an LSP going through nodes A-G-F-E was dynamically provisioned before the controller on node G failed. Suppose also that the management entity on the LSP head end (node A) decides to tear down the LSP. The LSP Tear message (RSVP PathTear) will never make it past node G to nodes F and E because of the hop-by-hop nature of the RSVP protocol. Hence the control plane state will not be removed on these nodes and, more important, resources allocated for the LSP will not be released and hence will not be available for other services. A similar problem will arise if an attempt is made to re-route the LSP on an alternative path (for example, A-B-C-D-E): Even if the operation succeeds, the resources on nodes F and E will be stuck allocated for the LSP.

RSVP-TE includes a mechanism especially designed to recover from this sort of problem. The soft state mechanisms are designed to timeout an LSP state for which no state refresh message is received within an appropriate time interval. When the neighboring control plane entity has failed, this should certainly happen, and node F should be able to determine a failure and release the state.

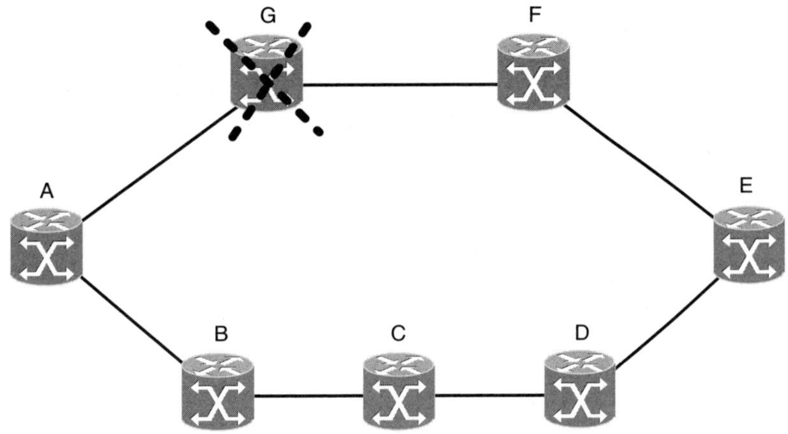

Figure 7.16 LSP with one controller in failed state.

However, in the normal course of affairs we want the data and control planes in our transport network to operate independently. That is, the failure of a control plane should not disrupt the function of the data plane — in particular, when a neighbor control plane stops responding to RSVP-TE Hello messages, no attention is paid to the lack of state refresh messages. Thus it is the very ability of the data plane to be robust in the face of control plane failures that causes us to be unable to tear down LSPs after node G's control plane has failed.

Unfortunately, it may take a non-negligible time to restore control plane failures (for example, it may be that more than a simple reboot is required — a new controller CPU card may need to be shipped). Thus, there is a need to be able to perform some minimum set of management operations on LSPs with one or more non-operational controllers (that is, control plane partitioned LSPs). The set should include:

1. The ability to perform data plane recovery operations — that is, delivery of fault notification messages to PLRs/MNs, and switchover synchronization messages between PLR and MN.
2. The ability to distribute data plane alarm information.
3. The ability to delete the LSP.
4. The ability to re-route the LSP away from the nodes with failed control planes.

Note that case 1 presents no problems, provided, of course, that the control plane on the PLR and MN is operational. This is because the fault notification and switchover synchronization signaling is realized either via data plane signaling, or by using GMPLS RSVP Notify messages which (unlike other GMPLS signaling messages) are sent directly to the intended recipients over a path that does not need to follow the LSP path. For example, if node F in Figure 7.16 locally detects a data plane failure, the FIS message can be sent to the PLR (node A) over the path F-E-D-C-B-A. Note, though, that such a path is not the shortest path in the network and its successful delivery requires either that the routing protocol's database has converged to account for the failure at node G, or that some form of explicit path is used to route the FIS.

However, if there is the need to tear down or modify an LSP, or to signal about newly detected data plane alarms, the protocol requires the use of messages (specifically, RSVP PathTear, Path, Resv) that use hop-by-hop progression through the network. Hence, for control plane partitioned LSPs, some tunneling technique may be needed to deliver the messages to nodes located beyond the points of control plane failure. In our example, for instance, if we want to tear down the LSP A-G-F-E, we need to find a way to deliver the LSP tear message (RSVP PathTear) from node A to node F.

At the time of writing, the discussions within the IETF of how to manage control plane partitioned LSPs have just begun. One of the ideas is to use a slightly modified targeted GMPLS RSVP Notify message for the purpose of non-adjacent signaling. There are some serious advantages to this approach compared to other tunneling techniques.

- There is a mechanism in place for a controller to advertise itself as a notify target (via NotifyRequest objects within RSVP Path and Resv messages). This makes it easier to identify tunnel remote ends.
- The technique is already integrated with the signaling protocol — there is no need for external infrastructure for tunnel management.
- The GMPLS RSVP Notify message is always delivered reliably — there is no need to worry about message losses.
- The GMPLS RSVP Notify message allows for grouping of signaling information related to multiple LSPs as long as they share the same notify target. This is a valuable quality for conditions when the control plane network is strained by the failures of one or more controllers.

To make the GMPLS RSVP Notify message useful for the non-adjacent signaling, the following slight modifications are required.

- Addition of the ability to encode the list of data plane alarms (both locally detected and learned from remote nodes) into the Notify message in the same way as for GMPLS RSVP Path and Resv messages.
- Introduction of the notion of unsolicited Notify messages. That is, the Notify message sent to an address that was not advertised via a NotifyRequest object, but learned by some other method such as through analysis of the Record Route Objects or through inspection of the local Traffic Engineering Database.

- Introduction of new Notify message types: Delete Request, Delete Response, Alarms, and Alarms Response. These would be in addition to the current Notify message types for FIS, FRS, Switchover Request, Switchover Response, Switchback Request, and Switchback Response.

Tearing Down Control Plane Partitioned LSPs

The procedures for tearing down a control plane partitioned LSP in the downstream direction using these proposed extensions to the Notify procedures are as follows.

- When a controller that is processing an LSP Tear message (RSVP PathTear) realizes that its immediate downstream neighbor is out of service, it does not forward the message as it would normally do (the message would be lost anyway). Rather, it sends a Delete Request Notify message to the address found in a NotifyRequest object of the previously received LSP Accept message (RSVP Resv). Additionally, it may send the same Notify request to the controller located immediately downstream from the failed neighbor. The latter is necessary to handle the case, where the LSP is control plane partitioned in several places, and/or the case where no NotifyRequest objects are found in the LSP Accept message (this might be the case where the LSP is unprotected, although the LSP destination could serve in this case).
- A recipient of a Delete Request Notify message acknowledges the receipt by sending back a Delete Response Notify message, and triggers the LSP teardown in both directions in the usual way (by sending RSVP PathTear and PathErr [with state-removal flag] messages to its immediate downstream and upstream neighbors, respectively).

Consider, for example, how the unprotected LSP A-G-F-E (Figure 7.16) is torn down from the LSP head end. Node A detects that the control plane on node G is not functioning (node G has not responded to the RSVP Hello messages for some time). Hence, instead of sending a PathTear to node G, node A sends a Delete Request Notify message direct to node F, which completes the LSP release. Node A can learn the address to which the Notify message should be sent by looking into the RRO of the LSP Accept message that it received for this LSP.

A control plane partitioned LSP is torn down in the upstream direction in a similar way.

- When a controller that is processing an upstream release for an LSP (RSVP PathErr with the state-removal flag set) detects a failure of its immediate upstream neighbor, it sends a Delete Request Notify message to an address found in a NotifyRequest object of the previously received LSP Setup message (RSVP Path). Additionally, it may send the same request to the controller located immediately upstream from the failed neighbor, or to the head end of the LSP.

- A recipient of the Delete Request Notify message acknowledges the receipt by sending back a Delete Response Notify message, and triggers the LSP teardown in both directions in the usual way by sending RSVP PathTear and PathErr (with state-removal flag) messages to its immediate downstream and upstream neighbors, respectively.

So, for example, the unprotected LSP A-G-F-E (Figure 7.16) can be torn down by the tail end (node E), sending a PathErr message with the state-removal flag set. This message is successfully processed by node F, but it determines that the control plane at node G is not operational, so it sends a Delete Request Notify message direct to node A. Node A responds to the Notify request and removes the state for the LSP.

Re-Routing Control Plane Partitioned LSPs

It may be desirable to re-route a control plane partitioned LSP away from the failed controllers. This obviously requires re-routing the LSP in the data plane as well. Provided that there is a way to tear down such an LSP, the re-routing operation presents no additional challenges. For example, the LSP A-G-F-E (Figure 7.16) can be re-routed onto path A-B-C-D-E in the usual make-before-break manner: First, a new LSP is created, and, after that, the old one is torn down in the way described above.

Distributing Alarm Information Over Control Plane Partitioned LSP

In order to track down data plane failures and to understand the operation of LSPs, it is very useful to have a consistent view of all active data plane alarms reported along the path of each LSP. This is achieved by allowing a controller to include information about locally detected alarms in the control plane messages that it passes to its upstream and downstream neighbors. The method, however, relies on the hop-by-hop signaling and so assumes that all controllers are functional. Specifically, all locally detected alarms are encoded as Alarm-Spec objects and are added to outgoing RSVP Path and Resv messages. Obviously this approach does not work on a control plane partitioned LSP because the alarms need to get propagated past the node with the faulted control plane. This problem can be addressed through the use of Alarms/Alarms Response Notify messages in the following way.

- When a controller learns about a local alarm, it would normally add the new alarm information into an outgoing RSVP Path message. However, if it detects that the control plane on its immediate downstream neighbor is out of service, it generates an Alarms Notify message, adds to the message the information about all locally detected alarms and also all alarms learned from upstream controllers, and sends the message to an address found in a NotifyRequest object of the previously received RSVP Resv message. Additionally, it may send the same message to the controller located immediately downstream from the failed neighbor.
- Similarly, the controller would normally add the new alarm information into an outgoing RSVP Resv, but if the controller realizes that the control plane on the immediate upstream controller is not functioning, it adds information about all locally detected alarms, and also all alarms learned from downstream alarms, into an Alarms Notify message, which it sends to an address found in a NotifyRequest object of a previously received RSVP Path message and/or to the controller located immediately upstream from the failed neighbor.
- When a controller receives an RSVP Path message with a non-empty list of Alarm-Spec objects that has changed from the last set received, it would normally add its own local alarms and forward the message downstream. However, if it detects that its immediate downstream neighbor is out of service, it generates an Alarms Notify message, copies in the received Alarm-Spec objects, adds Alarm-Spec objects for its own locally detected alarms, and sends the message to an address found in a NotifyRequest object of the previously received RSVP Resv message. Additionally, it may send the same message to the controller located immediately downstream from the failed neighbor.
- Similarly, when a controller receives an RSVP Resv message with a non-empty list of Alarm-Spec objects that has changed from the last set received, it would normally add its own local alarms and forward the message upstream. However, if it detects that its immediate upstream neighbor is out of service, it generates an Alarms Notify message, copies in the received Alarm Spec objects, adds Alarm-Spec objects for its own locally detected alarms, and sends the message to an address found in a NotifyRequest object of the previously received RSVP Path message. Additionally, it may send the same message to the controller located immediately downstream from the failed neighbor.
- In all cases the recipient of an Alarms Notify message acknowledges the receipt by sending back an Alarms Response message, and distributes the encoded alarm information in both directions as usual (that is, within RSVP Path and Resv messages).

Grouping of Non-Adjacent Signaling Messages

All of the previous sections have described the use of non-adjacent signaling messages (that is, different types of GMPLS RSVP Notify messages) that are delivered on a per-LSP basis. It is also possible to group together Notify messages of the same type but related to different LSPs, so long as the messages share the same notify target. Suppose there are two LSPs, A-G-F-E and A-G-F, established on the network presented in Figure 7.16. Suppose also that node A detects a failure of the control plane on node G and decides to tear down both LSPs. In this case it may send a single Delete Request Notify message to node F requesting the release of both LSPs.

7.9 Further Reading

Network Recovery: Protection and Restoration of Optical SONET-SDH, IP, and MPLS by Jean-Philippe Vasseur, Mario Pickavet, and Piet Demeester (2004), Morgan Kaufmann, provides a thorough and detailed analysis of many of the techniques for span and path protection in transport networks. In particular, it provides additional information about self-healing rings.

Further details of GMPLS protection and restoration techniques can be found in the following IETF Internet-Drafts and RFCs.

draft-ietf-ccamp-gmpls-recovery-terminology
  Recovery (Protection and Restoration) Terminology for Generalized Multi-Protocol Label Switching (GMPLS)

draft-ietf-ccamp-gmpls-recovery-functional
  Generalized Multi-Protocol Label Switching (GMPLS) Recovery Functional Specification

draft-ietf-ccamp-gmpls-recovery-analysis
  Analysis of Generalized Multi-Protocol Label Switching (GMPLS)-based Recovery Mechanisms (including Protection and Restoration)

draft-ietf-ccamp-gmpls-recovery-e2e-signaling
  RSVP-TE Extensions in support of End-to-End GMPLS-based Recovery

draft-ietf-ccamp-gmpls-segment-recovery
  GMPLS Based Segment Recovery

RFC 4201
  Link Bundling in MPLS Traffic Engineering

The definition of Notify messages and NotifyRequest objects can be found in the following RFC.

RFC 3473
  Generalized Multi-Protocol Label Switching (GMPLS) Signaling Resource ReserVation Protocol-Traffic Engineering (RSVP-TE) Extensions

The details of alarm information reporting may be found in the following Internet-Draft.

draft-ietf-ccamp-gmpls-alarm-spec
GMPLS — Communication of Alarm Information

The Fast Re-Route mechanism used in MPLS controlled packet switching networks is described in the following RFC.

RFC 4090
Fast Reroute Extensions to RSVP-TE for LSP Tunnels

CHAPTER 8

GMPLS and Traffic Engineering

Service Providers have come to realize the importance of traffic engineering techniques because they allow them to optimize utilization of network resources and bring more revenues. In fact, one of the biggest reasons for the success of MPLS as a technology is its ability to implement traffic engineering at a low cost, especially in terms of operational expenditure. Dynamic computation of optimal paths through the network, dynamic provisioning of tunnels, and proactive distribution of traffic between the tunnels are examples of how MPLS pushes the intelligence for operation of a traffic engineered network into the network itself and away from proprietary central management stations, thus allowing for the building of efficient and cost-effective multi-vendor networks. In this chapter we will discuss what traffic engineering is, how it applies to GMPLS-controlled transport networks, and how it is different from traffic engineering in packet switching networks. We will define the notions of a transport service, network controller, data switch, and control channel, as well as control interface, data interface, data link, and link attributes in the context of traffic engineering. We will go on to discuss ways that GMPLS nodes learn about other nodes and links, so that path computation elements can determine optimal paths for services with specified attributes. Finally, we will analyze the peculiarities of traffic engineering on networks that span multiple regions and administrative domains.

8.1 Evolution of Traffic Engineering

RFC 2702, *Requirements for Traffic Engineering Over MPLS*, states that traffic engineering is a technology that is concerned with performance optimization of operational networks. In general, this is a set of applications, mechanisms, tools, and scientific principles that allow for measuring, modeling, characterization, and control of packet-based user data traffic in order to achieve specific performance objectives. What are these objectives? There are two classes.

The first class is traffic-oriented and hence directly visible to end users. The performance objectives of this class include Quality of Service (QoS) enhancement of traffic streams, minimization of data loss, minimization of delay, and the provision of a certain level of throughput for high-priority traffic flows in conditions when some network links are congested.

The second class of performance objectives is resource-oriented. These objectives are important only to Service Providers and irrelevant to users of services they sell. The objectives concern optimization of resource utilization. To put it more simply, traffic engineering in this respect is a technology that can answer questions like these: Given the network resources that I have, how can I keep all my users happy? Can I sell more services without adversely affecting my current users? How can I avoid the situation where some network resources are severely overused while others are underused or not used at all? What network assets can I add, and where do I need to add them, in order to improve my network performance? How can I protect the services that I sell from network outages? To be competitive, Service Providers must find good answers to all these questions and in a timely manner.

Note that traffic engineering is most important only for well-used networks. Under-used networks that provide simple services to a few clients do not experience congestion and, therefore, do not need traffic engineering. For networks that provide constantly growing amounts of service of different types and levels of complexity, on the other hand, traffic engineering is very important because it can yield substantial savings in capital and operational expenses. Note that this draws a distinction between traffic engineering as a function and the act of computing paths through the network. The latter is also required to provide protection and recovery services. Because both traffic engineering and other path-specific services use the same features of path computation, we consider them together in this chapter.

Traffic engineering is an important function of the network control plane. Originally, it was introduced to fight congestion on overloaded links that were caused by its routing protocols (more specifically, their shortest-path-first nature).

There are two reasons why congestion can happen.

- The network is under-provisioned; that is, the amount of traffic is such that one or more network links cannot accommodate it, and there are no alternative paths that can deliver the traffic to its destination.
- Traffic is mapped onto paths that use overloaded links despite one or more alternative paths available in the network that could deliver the traffic, which, albeit more expensive, would use under-subscribed links. Congestions of this type happen because routing protocols that are used to determine the paths are oblivious of the bandwidth usage on network links. They determine paths that are shortest; ones that have the minimal sum of metrics associated with path links.

Congestion of the first type is of no concern to traffic engineering because no action in the control plane can possibly make up for the lack of physical resources in the network, but congestion of the second type can be mitigated through traffic engineering. As is pointed out in RFC 2702, traffic engineering is useful when a service path is dynamically computed, and there is more than one path available that can deliver the service traffic. Traffic engineering is all about learning what resources are available on the network, determining feasible paths, and choosing the optimal ones.

Traffic engineering has gone through an interesting evolution. The major problems it was created to address are as follows.

1. How to control paths taken by services without changing Internet routing protocols in a fundamental way.
2. How to make sure that a service path can always deliver QoS no worse than that pledged for the service in the Service Level Agreement.
3. How to guarantee that service resilience to network failures is at least no worse than committed.
4. If a better path becomes available after a service has been established, how to make the service switch to this path with minimal user traffic disruption. How to guarantee that this kind of optimization will not violate network stability.
5. How to bill services so that users will be interested in paying more for better services.

8.1.1 *Traffic Engineering Through Modifying Network Link Metrics*

One might suggest controlling traffic flows by modifying the metrics associated with network links. After all, that is what link metrics are for — to make links (and the paths composed of the links) more or less attractive depending on some operator-controlled policies. What about the traffic engineering goals for the policies?

Consider the network shown in Figure 8.1. Note that each link metric has a value of 1. Suppose that there are two services provisioned on the network: service 1 taking path AFGE and service 2 going over path HFGI. Note that both services are directed to use link FG by the Shortest Path First algorithm. Suppose also that there is some entity (human or application) that is monitoring the level of congestion on the links. When it is detected that the congestion on link FG exceeds some threshold, some logic could increase the link metric by some value (say, 2 to a value of 3). This would force service 1 to switch onto the preferable (lower cost) path ABCDE and would make link FG less congested because it will be relieved from carrying traffic for service 1. When some time later the level of congestion goes below some other threshold, the same logic could decrease the metric for link

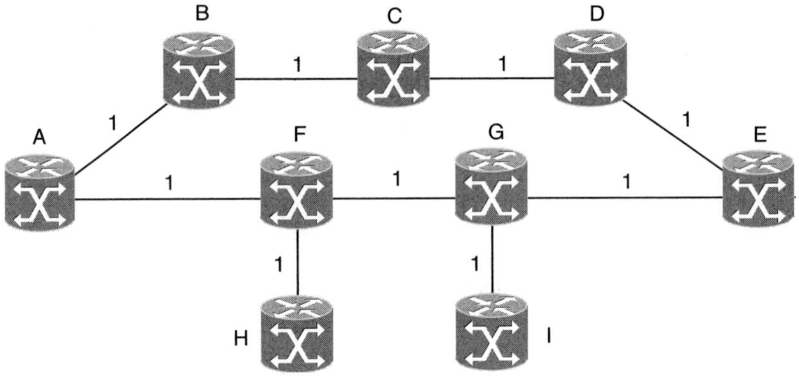

Figure 8.1 Traffic engineering through modifying link metrics and ECMP.

FG — say, by 1. The new metric assignment would keep service 1 on path ABCDE, but might attract other services to use link FG.

Unfortunately the tweaking of link metrics is not so straightforward. Neither is it harmless. In fact, it may cause much more severe problems than the ones it is trying to solve. The tricky part is to decide which metrics to modify, when, and by how much. If one performs the modification too early, traffic can be switched from slightly congested to uncongested low capacity links, immediately causing more severe congestion. If one does it too late, the traffic may experience a hit because it will take at least a few seconds before the routing tables converge and services take the intended new paths. And what if the traffic bursts that triggered the congestion come and go in quick succession? This might cause continual modification of the network metrics, which results in significant load on the routing protocols and disruption to traffic. It is quite obvious that modifications of link metrics require very careful network planning: Mistakes can be very costly, and there is no guarantee that such modifications will not affect services that are perfectly healthy and even going over paths disjoint from the links whose metrics are going to be modified.

8.1.2 *Traffic Engineering Through ECMP*

Suppose the metric of link FG in Figure 8.1 has a value of 2 instead of 1. We then have two paths from node A to node E, ABCDE and AFGE, that have equal costs (4). In such cases a routing protocol running on node A would normally pick one of the paths (say, AFGE) and create a forwarding table entry instructing node A to forward packets going to node E through link AF. However, with relatively small modifications, the routing protocol could provide next hop forwarding information for all paths that have equal costs (in our example, it would be links AF and AB) and let the data plane forwarder decide which of the paths to take for any given packet.

The most obvious and straightforward way to take advantage of several paths is simply to alternate between them in a round-robin way so that the traffic load is evenly distributed. This, however, would almost certainly break the order of data flows and might trigger higher layer IP protocols such as TCP to perform numerous unnecessary retransmissions. The smarter way to use parallel paths is to segregate flows according to packet source IP address, destination IP address, transport level ports, payload protocol type, DiffServ color, or any combination of the above and forward different flows over different paths. This is called *Equal Cost Multi-Path* (*ECMP*) forwarding.

Many existing routing protocol implementations support ECMP. It is useful because it provides an easy and safe way for load balancing; however, it is not much help. The same reasons that have made links of one path congested may cause congestion on two or three equal cost paths, and we might start losing data despite the fact that some other slightly more expensive but completely unused paths are available. Besides, if we do have congestion, how do we make sure that packets of a lower priority service are dropped before packets of a higher priority service?

8.1.3 *Traffic Engineering Through Service Type Based Routing*

The next attempt to achieve the traffic engineering goals was through separate routing of data flows that are associated with different service types. A limited number of application types that have different network service requirements can be identified. For instance, a Voice Over IP (VoIP) service imposes tight constraints on end-to-end packet delivery, delay, and delay variation, but can tolerate occasional packet drops; a file transfer service does not care much about the delay but expects minimal packet drops. The main concerns for a WEB browsing application is speed (especially in the download direction) and low cost. Once application/service types are identified, it is possible to:

- associate with each link on the network graph, not one but a set of link metrics (one per service type), and have a routing protocol build separate forwarding tables for each service type;
- have the packet forwarder on every node determine the service type associated with a packet (perhaps by looking into the DiffServ color or other bytes within the packet header or payload), and choose the appropriate forwarding table for forwarding the packet.

This method achieves two goals. First, some kind of load balancing is provided: Data flows associated with different service types are routed over different paths even if they originated on the same source and are directed to the same destination. Secondly, the data plane can be provisioned in such a way that QoS requirements for different service types are appropriately accommodated, so that data packets get respective forwarding treatment. As a result, the network is in a position to meet committed SLAs and bill its clients accordingly.

However, there are some issues with this approach. It is assumed that each router on the network applies the same forwarding policy on any given packet as the rest of the routers. But what if packet forwarding rules (which can be very complex, and cannot be dynamically provisioned or updated) on one router are different from the others? In this case the router might make forwarding decisions that are not expected by other routers, and loops can easily occur. Besides, this approach does not help if the network is used predominantly for one service type.

8.1.4 *Traffic Engineering Using Overlays*

Introducing overlay networks was a big step forward in traffic engineering. In this model (see Figure 8.2) a Service Provider core network is built of layer 2 switches (ATM or Frame Relay) that are good at providing QoS support; whereas the overlay network is composed of Service Provider edge IP routers interconnected via layer 2 virtual channels provisioned by the core network. Each pair of edge routers is usually connected by more than one channel. Extra channels are needed for load balancing, delivering different QoS, and for recovery purposes.

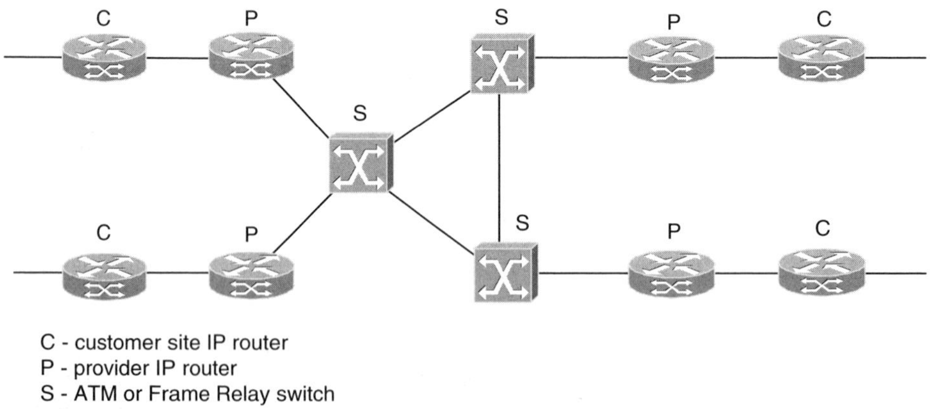

Figure 8.2 IP overlay network.

The great thing about this model is that each data flow can be routed individually, even if all of them are associated with the same service type. When a packet enters the Service Provider network, it can be classified depending on the ingress data port and/or the contents of the packet header and/or the payload. Once the packet is classified (and, thus, the associated data flow is identified), it can be placed on a virtual channel that connects the ingress and egress edge routers along the data flow path and supports the expected QoS. The user network can shape the traffic so that it will not violate the SLA contract, and the provider network can police traffic that "behaves badly," so that it will not adversely affect data flows of other users. The forwarding decision for every packet is made only once (by the ingress router and not by any core network element); hence loops could not be produced. The load balancing can be easily achieved by provisioning parallel (not necessarily equal cost) virtual channels. In the case of network failures, traffic can be switched onto pre-provisioned virtual channels that are disjoint from the channels affected by the failures.

One of the problems with the overlay model is its poor scalability: Each layer 2 virtual tunnel requires a direct routing adjacency (peering) between its ends. This results in the well-recognized n-squared problem in the control plane. The major inconvenience with overlays is the complexity required to support two control and management planes — IP and ATM/Frame Relay — and, consequently, high operational costs. It would be simpler, cheaper, and better overall to provision virtual QoS channels on heterogeneous networks using a single unified control plane.

8.1.5 *Traffic Engineering Based on MPLS*

The innovation of MPLS technology offered simple, efficient, and elegant answers to many of the questions raised by traffic engineering.

MPLS Traffic engineering protocols allow nodes to advertise not just their presence and topological connectivity, but attributes of their links as well. This makes it possible for provider network edge nodes or off-line path computation elements to compute paths with the necessary constraints; therefore, services taking the paths have a good likelihood to be successfully established and operational.

MPLS signaling protocols make it possible to set up services along dynamically computed or manually provisioned paths that could be different from those that are identified by routing protocols. If a better path becomes available for some active service, the latter can be re-routed onto the new path with little or no effect on the user traffic. In case some high priority service cannot be placed on the network because the required resources are not available, it is possible, to automatically preempt the resources from some lower priority service.

The Label Switched Paths (LSPs) produced by the MPLS signaling protocols have similar qualities to the virtual paths of the overlay model. A service mapped onto an MPLS LSP can deliver the required QoS because the necessary resource reservations were made during the LSP setup; data packets are switched based on MPLS labels without looking into packet headers or payloads.

The big advantage of the MPLS model versus the overlay model is the ability of MPLS LSPs to be dynamically provisioned in heterogeneous networks (for example, composed of IP routers, ATM switches), using a single unified control plane. It is possible to set up multiple LSPs between any pair of edge routers for the purpose of load balancing. MPLS LSPs also naturally eliminate the n-squared problem intrinsic to the overlay model of virtual tunnels because there is no need for a routing peering between the ends of an LSP.

From the service resilience point of view, MPLS networks perform much better than overlay networks. The MPLS signaling protocols have an in-built mechanism to notify an LSP ingress node, or any other node responsible for service recovery, about LSP failures. Thus, the ingress node can take service recovery actions without waiting for routing tables to converge. For example, the node can establish an LSP diverted from the failed links and switch traffic onto it away from the LSP affected by the failures. To get an even better recovery time, a service can be mapped on multiple LSPs — one working and one or more protection LSPs separately protecting one link, one node, or one segment of the working LSP — so that recovery actions can be performed on a node close to the point of failure. Once network failures are repaired, the affected services can be automatically switched back (restored) onto the original LSPs.

The MPLS node graceful restart procedures allow for a failed node to quickly synchronize its control state with its neighbors; thus LSPs going through the failed node can be managed via the control plane, and all other nodes can have the correct representation of the node resources available for other LSPs.

Probably the best part of MPLS traffic engineering for Service Providers is that the bulk of its components and mechanisms are built into MPLS protocols and standard applications. Therefore, the network can be built of devices of different types and from different vendors. As a result, multiple services can be offered on a single infrastructure.

8.2 Traffic Engineering in Transport Networks

Automatic traffic engineering is not needed on networks that are manually provisioned. It is the responsibility of the network operators and planners to direct services through parts of the network that have sufficient resources to support the services. Congestion is usually discovered at the planning stage and is handled by manually redirecting other services during a period of network maintenance, or by installing new equipment (such as additional fibers or lasers) within the network. If congestion occurs in a live network, it is the direct result of a provisioning or planning error.

When transport networks were provisioned manually, traffic engineering did not need to be a dynamic process. Network operators examined the current state of the network and placed each new circuit according to the available resources. If there was a shortage of resources, or some form of congestion, the operator might reposition existing service, or commission the installation of new equipment. This contributed to the slow speed of service provisioning.

Further, most transport networks were built on ring-based technologies which made the networks topologically quite simple, and which meant that traffic engineering could only add limited value.

As transport networks became more complex, with the interconnection of rings and the topology beginning to look more like a mesh, GMPLS was introduced to handle the dynamic provisioning of services. Traffic engineering in these networks began to look more interesting.

Because GMPLS is based on MPLS technology, it makes sense to consider employing the MPLS traffic engineering techniques in transport networks, but there are several ways in which a transport network differs from an MPLS packet-based network.

Transport Connections are Bidirectional

MPLS LSPs are unidirectional, while services offered by transport network Service Providers are almost always bidirectional. So, while MPLS services may also be bidirectional (constructed from an LSP that runs in each direction), transport services must attempt to use the same physical resources (fibers) in both directions to give a level of *fate sharing* for the forward and reverse data flows. This means that the traffic engineering algorithms used must manage the availability of resources in both directions.

Labels Identify Resources

In MPLS labels and associated resources are decoupled; there is no correlation between a label and the resources that are allocated to support the LSP that uses that label. In transport networks, however, the label is synonymous with the resource. A label indicates exactly which resource is reserved — for example, in a lambda switching network — and the label precisely identifies the WDM wavelength of the transport circuit LSP that has been established.

This means that some simple tunneling techniques that "pick up" an LSP and redirect it down a tunnel and are used for MPLS traffic engineering cannot be applied in transport networks. Also, resource sharing, which is necessary for make-before-break operations that are fundamental to the operation of the repositioning of LSPs during traffic engineering, needs a new mechanism in transport networks.

Bandwidth Is Less Granular

Traffic engineering in MPLS networks can theoretically be managed as bandwidth measured down to individual bytes per second. In practice (partly because of the floating point notation used to encode the bandwidths and partly for sanity) bandwidth is usually measured and reserved in larger units reflecting the type of service required. This may be 10 or 100 Kb/sec for a typical end-user service, but larger amounts are reserved for aggregated flows. A key aspect of MPLS traffic engineering is that multiple flows can be aggregated onto a single link to share the total available bandwidth.

In a transport network, as already described, the resources reserved for an LSP are associated with physical resources. Simple traffic engineering aggregation is not possible. Thus, if a WDM laser provides 2.5 Gbps, a 10-Kbps LSP that uses that laser (wavelength) will demand the full 2.5 Gbps and waste most of the bandwidth. The case is even worse if the laser provides a 10- or 40-Gbps service.

Traffic engineering in a transport network, therefore, requires careful consideration of bandwidth wastage, and needs new aggregation techniques to carry multiple traffic flows using the same resources. Note that traffic policing is not necessary in a transport network because a single flow is physically incapable of exceeding the bandwidth reserved for it.

Path Computation Needs More Constraints

The traffic engineering problem for transport networks is generally more complex than for packet networks simply because there is a tendency toward a greater number of constraints on the paths that can be selected. These constraints may be fixed, such as switching capabilities of the hardware, or the data encoding mechanism. Alternatively, the constraints may be dynamic, such as the optical impairments of the signals in the network.

To impose such constraints the computing node or workstation needs to obtain information about pertinent link attributes. Hence more traffic engineering information needs to be advertised. The increased volume of advertising causes scalability concerns; therefore, mechanisms to make the TE advertising more scalable are very much desirable.

Control Plane and Data Plane Channels Are Separated

The separation of control and data planes in transport networks means that there has to be a clean separation of the TE information advertised so that the topology built into the TED reflects the data plane connectivity and not the control plane connectivity.

Further, the routing and TE advertising protocols cannot be relied on to detect link failures, because the failures they will discover are failures in the control plane. The Link Management Protocol (LMP, see Chapter 6) is used to detect and correlate data plane TE links and to isolate failures, whereas failures in the control plane are usually allowed to happen without disruption to the data plane.

All these aspects cause fundamental conceptual differences in the TE mechanisms in transport networks compared to MPLS networks, where the control and data links are congruous.

Usage of Hierarchical LSPs

Hierarchical LSPs (referred to in this book as H-LSPs) provide a significant scaling advantage in TE networks where they allow multiple end-to-end LSPs to be clustered and tunneled down a single H-LSP. This results in considerable simplification and reduction of the control and data plane state at transit nodes. In packet switched networks, this is the limit of their benefit, but in transport networks H-LSPs play a much more important role.

Note that a transport network service can span links with different switching capabilities. For instance it can start on a segment with TDM links, go through several wavelength switches, and terminate within some other TDM segment (as shown in Figure 8.3).

In this example, the node that is located on the boundary between the first TDM network and the optical network (node C) cannot allocate individual timeslots on the link facing the optical network (link CD). The only reasonable option for the node C in this case is to create an H-LSP going through the optical segment (CDEF) and nest all TDM level LSPs within the H-LSP. The alternative would be to allocate a separate lambda channel for each TDM LSP and utilize only a fraction of the allocated resources, and as already discussed, this would result in a lot of wasted bandwidth.

H-LSPs define data links that traverse the network between nodes that are not necessarily physically adjacent, but rather, adjacent in a particular network layer. These data links are available to carry LSPs and form part of the network topology — that is, provide extra network flexibility — and are used during traffic engineering. In transport networks, H-LSPs form an important part of the TE mechanism and must be carefully planned (as is the case for the static topology) and advertised with their TE properties.

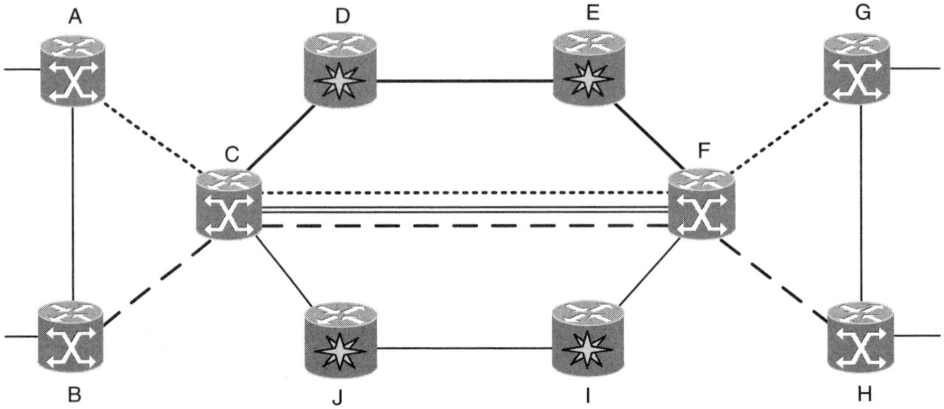

Figure 8.3 Multi-region transport network.

We will discuss the traffic engineering aspects of multi-region/multi-layer networks in greater detail in Section 8.6.

8.2.1 *Traffic Engineering in Photonic Networks*

Optical networks built of photonic cross-connects present additional challenges for traffic engineering. One of the problems with photonic cross-connects is that they cannot perform wavelength conversion; that is, they cannot convert a signal received with one wavelength to be sent out using a different wavelength. This limitation results in the wavelength continuity constraint for paths in such networks. That is, for a path to be considered a feasible candidate for some service, each data link of the path must have at least one lambda channel of the same frequency available for reservation. To honor such a constraint, a much larger volume of TE advertising is required (information about every individual channel on every link must be available for path computing nodes) and more complex path computation algorithms must be applied (paths have to be computed not in terms of TE links but in terms of lambda channels). On the other hand, signaling of such paths is simpler than signaling of conventional GMPLS LSPs: there is no need for label negotiation during the optical trail setup — the path computing node selects lambda channels and hence assigns all labels.

The other class of challenges in photonic networks comes from the fact that because of signal attenuation and optical impairments, and because the photonic network cannot regenerate the signal, the quality of the optical signal deteriorates while the signal travels over data links and cross-connects in the network. By the time the signal arrives at the service destination, it might not be possible to transform the optical signal back into an electrical signal with an acceptable quality. Path computation needs to account for all contributions to the signal degradation by all devices — fibers, amplifiers, cross-connects, DWDMs, DCMs, and so forth — that constitute the path. It needs to do this while deciding whether the path is feasible or not. It is a formidable task, because these contributions to the signal degradation are not always linear or cumulative. Sometimes the degradations are also wavelength dependent, and sometimes they are also a function of other signals going through the same devices or fibers.

From the traffic engineering point of view the challenges described here result in more advertisements (more TE link attributes), and a completely new class of path computation algorithms to be introduced. See Chapter 10 for further discussion of path computation with complex optical constraints.

8.3 GMPLS Traffic Engineering Definitions

Analyzing objectives, requirements, and peculiarities of traffic engineering in transport networks leads to an obvious conclusion: For a transport network, MPLS traffic engineering is good but not perfect. Numerous extensions, and brand new principles and paradigms are necessary for every aspect of the MPLS control plane to make traffic engineering attractive for transport Service Providers.

Fortunately, GMPLS technology is flexible enough to accommodate the necessary extensions in such a way that they work and are very useful in packet switching networks as well. To develop such extensions is exactly the goal of the GMPLS technology in general and GMPLS traffic engineering in particular.

This section describes the key terms and concepts necessary to enable traffic engineering in a GMPLS network.

It is convenient to decompose a transport network into the following abstract components: network, control channels, control interfaces, data switchers, data links, and data interfaces (see Figure 8.4).

The *Controller* is where all control plane intelligence (routing, TE and signaling protocols, and path computation elements) is located. Controllers communicate with each other over *control channels*. Locally, controllers are connected to control channels through *control interfaces*. For example, controllers C1 and C2 in Figure 8.4 use their control interfaces in order to establish an OSPF adjacency over control channel C1C2.

A *data switch* (also referred to as a *transport node*) is a component capable of terminating a data traffic flow and/or forwarding it on the route to its destination. A *data link* (or simply a *link*) is a construct used in network topology that characterizes a set of network resources that are used to deliver traffic between two data switches that are adjacent in a particular network layer. For example, the data

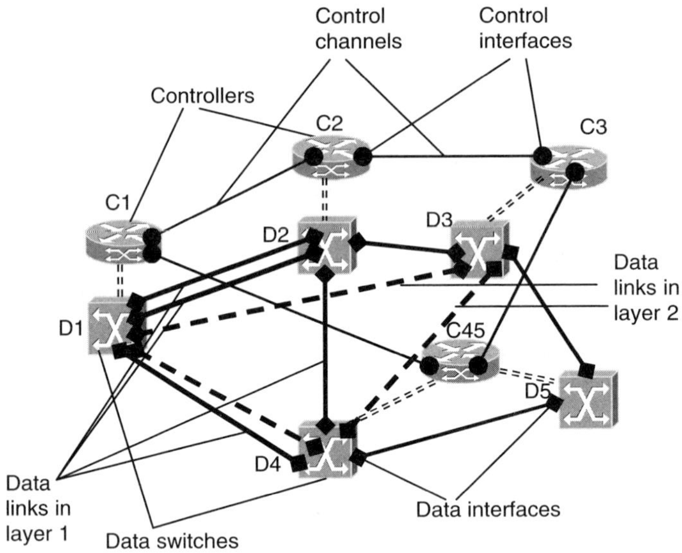

Figure 8.4 Transport network elements.

link D2D3 in Figure 8.4 delivers all traffic going from D2 to D3 in network layer 1, while the data link D4D3 carries data between D4 and D3 in network layer 2.

The *network layer* (or *layer*) is an abstraction representing a collection of network resources of the same type (see more details on network layers and regions in Section 8.6).

Data links on transport networks are usually bidirectional; hence data link D5D4 (which will sometimes be known as D4D5) also delivers traffic going from D4 to D5. A pair of data switches can be interconnected within the same layer by more than one data link. For instance, switches D1 and D2 are interconnected by two parallel data links in layer 1. And, of course, a pair of data switches could be interconnected by multiple data links in different network layers (like switches D1 and D4).

Locally, data switches are connected to data links through *data interfaces* (also referred to as *link interfaces* or simply *interfaces*). As we will see later, the most important characteristics of a data interface are its switching, termination, and adaptation capabilities. A data switch can be connected to the same data link via several data interfaces with one of them modeling the switching function, while the rest encompass different termination/adaptation functions.

A GMPLS-based control plane distinguishes data links of two types: *dynamic* data links and *static* data links. The former are completely under the control of the GMPLS control plane. Such data links could be added to or removed from the network topology of a particular layer by setting up or tearing down LSPs in different layers. What is important about dynamic data links from the GMPLS point of view is that they could be added/removed "on the fly" to achieve certain traffic engineering objectives like adding additional network flexibility to provide a path for a particular service. For example, data link D4D3 in layer 2 could be realized by establishing an LSP in layer 1 going through nodes D4, D5, and D3. As mentioned earlier, LSPs that are created to be used as data links in different layers are called *Hierarchical LSPs* (see more details on H-LSPs in Section 8.6). Static data links are those that are either manually provisioned (for example, ATM PVCs) or created by a non-GMPLS control plane (for example, ATM SVCs).

Controllers discover network resources that they manage (that is, local network resources) in the form of data links. Local data link ends are learned via configuration, whereas the information about the remote data link ends is provided by LMP (see Chapter 6) or configuration. However, network resources are advertised into the TE routing domain in the form of *TE links*. In contrast to a data link, which is a "real" network topology construct, a TE link is a *logical* grouping of network resources for the purposes of routing. It is important to keep in mind that paths for a particular service are computed in terms of TE links, whereas the LSPs onto which a service is mapped are provisioned over data links. One of the functions of a controller that takes part in setting up a particular LSP is to translate a local TE link found in the explicit path of the LSP Setup message into a local data link where resources must be allocated. Usually one TE link reflects exactly one data link. However, it is possible to advertise resources of two or more parallel data links (that is, data links connecting the same pair of data switches within the same network layer) as one TE link (this is called TE bundling — see Section 8.5 for more details). It is also possible to advertise any fraction of a data link as a separate TE link, while reserving the rest of the data link resources for other purposes, such as recovery.

The controllers managing the ends of a data link (and, hence, the associated TE link) need to have control plane connectivity with each other to make use of the link during dynamic LSP provisioning. Such connectivity could be achieved via a parallel control plane channel link (for example, link D2D3 in layer 1 has a parallel control plane link C2C3) or a sequence of control plane link (for link D1D3 in layer 2 control plane connectivity could be achieved via the link C1C2 and C2C3). The control plane connectivity is termed a *control channel*, and care should always be taken to ensure that such control plane connectivity exists.

However, there are some links for which control plane connectivity is guaranteed. Let us consider the link D1D3 in layer 2. This link could be constructed using an H-LSP established in layer 1 going over the links D1D2 and D2D3, and the link could be advertised as a TE link. An LSP advertised as a TE link is called *TE-LSP* and could be advertised into the same or a different instance of the control plane from that used for advertising the constituent links from which the TE-LSP was constructed. The former case is interesting because the TE-LSP has *guaranteed* control plane connectivity between its ends. The fact that the TE-LSP was successfully created means that each of its constituent links has control plane connectivity within the instance of the control plane that was used to provision the TE-LSP. Because the TE-LSP is advertised into the same instance of the control plane, the control plane connectivity between the TE-LSP ends is guaranteed to be at worst a concatenation of control plane connections connecting the end points of each of its links. In GMPLS such dynamic links that have intrinsic control plane connectivity between their ends are called *Forwarding Adjacencies* (*FAs*).

One controller can manage one or several data switches. For example, controller C45 manages two switches, D4 and D5. In most of the cases, controllers and the data switches they manage are arranged in a one-to-one relationship and are physically collocated within the same devices. It is fair to note, however, that, at least theoretically, the controller and the switches could be separate devices, even coming from separate vendors. It is possible to imagine, for example, a model where an intelligent protocol-rich control box controls one or several simple optical cross-connects, and this is often proposed as the migration path for including legacy (or dumb) switching equipment in GMPLS networks. In the case when a controller manages a single data switch it is useful to denote the combination of the controller and the switch as a *node*.

One of the most remarkable differences between transport and packet switching networks is the relationship between control channels and data links. On packet switching networks control packets are usually delivered over the same links as the data. This is possible because data switchers forward data on a packet-by-packet basis. To do so they need to understand packet boundaries, headers, and so forth. They can easily detect control packets destined to local devices and pass such packets to local controllers. Data switchers on transport networks, on the other hand, forward entire signals based on wavelengths or timeslots. They cannot distinguish the boundaries of individual packets. Hence, for control plane packets to be terminated at each switch, the control plane traffic must use separate channels specifically dedicated for this purpose. A control channel and associated data link represent totally different sets of network resources. It is important to understand why path computation for transport services must consider only network TE information and disregard IP related advertising: Data paths have nothing to do with control plane paths. *For a transport service, IP routing reachability between the service source and destination is of no importance*. The fact that two controllers can exchange control messages does not mean that the associated data switches are interconnected through a sequence of links with available resources (fibers, wavelength channels, timeslots) to deliver the traffic. Likewise, a sudden loss of control plane connectivity does not necessarily mean a user traffic hit. Also, there are no guarantees that a fiber cut disconnecting a service can be detected via the control plane.

Transport Service, Path, and LSP

Let us define a point-to-point transport service as a way to deliver user traffic of specified parameters with specified QoS between specified user-network interfaces. A transport service should be distinguished from a transport service path, which we define as a sequence of Service Provider network TE links that have appropriate resources to deliver the service. A transport LSP is the path that is adequately provisioned over data links (that is, all resources are allocated, bound, and committed) for the service delivery. A transport service is a routable object; that is, it can be placed on one or more LSPs. It can also be re-routed over different LSPs when the original ones become inoperable.

8.3.1 *TE Link Attributes*

TE link attributes as well as attributes of the data interfaces that connect associated data link(s) to a data switch are configured on and advertised by the associated controller. Let us assume that each data link in Figure 8.4 is advertised as a separate TE link. Thus, controller C2 in Figure 8.4 advertises attributes of TE link D2D3 and also attributes of the data interface that connects data switch D2 to the link D2D3. Likewise, controller C3 advertises attributes of TE link D3D2 and attributes of the data interface that connects data switch D3 to the link D3D2. From the perspective of any given controller in the network, a TE link is denoted as *synchronized* if the controller has received valid and consistent advertisements related to both sides of the link. Only synchronized TE links are installed as edges into the local TE network graph and, thus, made available for local path computation elements. (For a longer discussion of the TE network graph, see Chapter 10.)

The following link attributes are introduced for the purpose of link synchronization.

- Link type
- Link ID
- Local interface IP address (for numbered TE links)
- Remote interface IP address (for numbered TE links)
- Local link identifier (for unnumbered links)
- Remote link identifier (for unnumbered links)

The *Link type* attribute identifies the TE link type. Two link types are currently defined (1: point-to-point; 2: multi-access). Only links of type 1 are relevant for transport networks, since multi-access optical or TDM networks have not yet been deployed.

The *Link ID* attribute has a very confusing name. For point-to-point links it identifies a Router Address of a controller associated with the *other* side of the link. By a controller Router Address we mean some routable IP address configured on the controller, which is always available and associated with the data switch that originates/terminates the link. It could also be defined as an IP routable data switch identifier. Note that a controller needs to have several Router Addresses if it manages several data switches (one per data switch).

The end points of the TE link are identified by a local and a remote link identifier. A TE link can be either numbered or unnumbered. A TE link is numbered if its link identifiers on both sides are four-byte network-wide unique numbers (usually, but not necessarily, IPv4 addresses). A TE link is unnumbered if its link identifiers are four-byte numbers unique within the scopes of the two local controllers. Thus, in order to uniquely identify an unnumbered TE link within the whole network, one needs to augment its local identifier with the Router Address of the advertising controller.

The *Local interface IP address* and *Remote interface IP address* attributes identify, respectively, local and remote link identifiers for numbered TE links. These attribute names are also confusing. They are inherited from MPLS, where control channels and data links are inseparable, and the control interface IP address is used as an identifier of the associated TE link. In GMPLS, numbered TE link identifiers do not have to relate to associated control interfaces — there might not even be any associated control interfaces. The numbered TE link identifiers also do not need to be routable.

The *Local link identifier* and *Remote link identifier* attributes denote, respectively, local and remote link identifiers for unnumbered TE links. There are multiple ways that advertising controllers may learn about remote link identifiers. For example, they can learn about them the same way they learn about local link identifiers — through configuration. Remote link identifiers can also be learned via the LMP link auto-discovery mechanism. For more details about LMP, see Chapter 6.

TE link advertising is consistent if all the following conditions hold.

- TE link attributes are advertised by controllers associated with both ends of the link.
- The Link type attribute is the same in both advertisements and equal to one (point-to-point).
- The Link ID attribute in one advertisement matches the controller Router Address of the other and vice versa.
- The non-zero Local interface IP address attribute in one advertisement matches the Remote interface IP address attribute of the other and vice versa (only for numbered TE links).

- The non-zero Local link identifier attribute in one advertisement matches the Remote link identifier attribute of the other and vice versa (only for unnumbered TE links).

As was mentioned earlier, from the perspective of a controller on the domain, a TE link can be considered synchronized if both advertisements are consistent and valid. The advertisement validity means the following.

- TE link attributes that the processing controller can understand are advertised in a proper format defined by the TE protocol in use — OSPF-TE or ISIS-TE. Note that unknown link attributes are usually simply disregarded, as they do not prevent the link from becoming synchronized.
- There is always a way for the advertising controllers to withdraw their advertisements. That is, the processing controller is connected to each of the advertising controllers via a sequence of active routing adjacencies. This is necessary because once the processing controller loses routing connectivity with any of the advertising controllers, it might use stale information in its local path computations for a considerable period of time (up to 60 minutes in the case of OSPF) until the advertisements are withdrawn from the local TED due to their timeout.

All other GMPLS TE link attributes are intended for use in constraint-based path computation. The following attributes are standardized.

- Traffic engineering metric
- Administrative group
- Link protection type
- Shared Risk Link Group (SRLG)
- Interface Switching Capability descriptor

The *Traffic engineering metric* attribute is used as a cost of the arc that represents the TE link on the TE network graph in the direction *from* the data switch with which the advertising controller is associated. For example, controller C2 (Figure 8.4) may advertise the Traffic engineering metric attribute 10 for the TE link D2D3. This piece of information instructs every network controller to assign cost 10 to arc D2D3 in the direction from D2 to D3 on the locally built TE network graph. Note that controller C3 may advertise a different traffic engineering metric for TE link D3D2 (say, 15). For every path computing controller this will make the link more attractive in the direction D2D3 than in the direction D3D2.

The *Administrative group* attribute is a 32-bit number that may be advertised for a TE link. Each bit of the administrative group represents some network-wide

Table 8.1 Link Protection Capability Values

Link Protection Attribute	Link Protection Capability	
0 × 01	Extra Traffic	The link is currently provisioned to protect one or more other links. Other services may be mapped onto this link, but may be disrupted in case of a failure of any of the protected links.
0 × 02	Unprotected	There is no link that protects this link. Services that are mapped onto the link will be disrupted if the link fails.
0 × 03	Shared	There are one or more disjoint links with the "Extra Traffic" link protection capability that protect this link. The protection links are shared with some other links that also have the "Shared" link protection capability.
0 × 04	Dedicated 1 : 1	There is one disjoint link with the Extra Traffic link protection capability that is dedicated to protect this link. The protection is not shared with any other links.
0 × 05	Dedicated 1 + 1	There is one disjoint link that is dedicated to protecting this link. The protecting link is not advertised by the routing protocol and, therefore, is not available for any traffic other than of the services mapped on this link.
0 × 06	Enhanced	Some advanced protection scheme is provisioned for this link, which is more reliable than the "Dedicated 1 + 1" protection. For example, four fiber BLSR/MS-SPRING.

known quality of the link (link color), so that a path computation process can be constrained to avoid or force the use of TE links with particular colors, depending on the service for which the path is computed.

The *Link protection type* attribute represents the TE link protection capabilities. All currently defined link protection capabilities are presented in Table 8.1.

The link protection attribute is used to constrain the path computation algorithm to consider only links that can guarantee some acceptable level of protection on every link. The definition of acceptable will depend on the particular service; for example, if there is a need to compute a path for a service that expects shared protection, all links with the link protection attribute 2 or lower are supposed to be excluded from the path computation.

The *Shared Risk Link Group* attribute identifies all SRLGs to which the link belongs. As mentioned earlier, several links can constitute an SRLG if they share a network resource whose failure may affect all links in the group. For instance, if two fibers belonging to two separate data links are located within the same conduit, and there is a cut in the conduit, both links may fail. Hence, the two links belong to an SRLG associated with the conduit. Every SRLG on the network is identified by a 32-bit network-wide unique number. Any given TE link may belong to multiple SRLGs, thus the SRLG link attribute may include more than one SRLG ID.

The SRLG attribute is very useful for the computation of recovery paths. It is always desirable for a service recovery LSP to be as disjoint as possible from the service working LSP, so that a failure of a single network resource would not affect both LSPs. It is reasonable to instruct the path computation to make sure that the union of SRLGs of all links belonging to the resulting working path and the union of SRLGs of all links that belong to the resulting recovery path have zero SRLGs in common.

Unlike all other TE link attributes, the *Interface Switching Capability (ISC) descriptor* attribute describes the characteristics not of a TE link, but of a data interface. As we discussed earlier, a data switch is locally connected to the near side of an associated data link via a data interface. For example, data switch D3 in Figure 8.4 is connected to the link D3D5 via a data interface (marked as a black diamond). As part of advertising the TE link D3D5, controller C3 advertises parameters of the data interface connecting the associated data switch D3 to the link D3D5. Likewise, controller C5 advertises the characteristics of the data interface that connects switch D5 to the link D5D3.

The following information is provided by the ISC descriptor attribute.

- Interface switching capability type
- Data encoding type
- Maximum LSP bandwidth available for reservation for each (0–7) priority level

For packet switch capable interfaces the ISC descriptor additionally includes the following.

- Minimum LSP bandwidth
- Interface Maximum Transmit Unit (MTU)

For TDM capable interfaces the descriptor additionally includes the following.

- Minimum LSP bandwidth
- Indicator of whether Standard or Arbitrary SONET/SDH is supported

The most important data interface parameter is its switching capability type. This describes how and with what granularity data can be switched from/onto the link connected through the interface. Some interfaces can distinguish individual data packets within the data flow received over a connected link, look into packet headers, and make forwarding decisions depending on the headers' contents. Other interfaces may not be capable of distinguishing packet boundaries, but can switch individual channels within an SDH payload. There are also interfaces that can only

Table 8.2 Data Interface Switching Capability Type Values

Switching Capability Identifier	Switching Capability Type	
1	PSC-1	Packet Switch Capable (level 1)
2	PSC-2	Packet Switch Capable (level 2)
3	PSC-3	Packet Switch Capable (level 3)
4	PSC-4	Packet Switch Capable (level 4)
51	L2SC	Layer 2 Switch Capable
100	TDM	Time Division Multiple Capable (TDM)
150	LSC	Lambda Switch Capable
200	FSC	Fiber Switch Capable

switch individual wavelength channels, or entire traffic received over individual fibers. The importance of switching capabilities within GMPLS networks is described later in this chapter. It should be noted here that when a path is computed across a network it must use TE links that provide the right level of switching capabilities. See Section 8.6 for a description of multi-region and multi-layer networks.

All currently defined switching capabilities are presented in Table 8.2.

Data encoding type is another data interface attribute. It is always associated with a switching capability type within the ISC descriptor attribute and provides information about encoding supported by the interface. All currently defined data encoding types are presented in Table 8.3.

The data encoding type describes the format of data presentation to the transport medium. Fundamentally this is a characteristic of a traffic flow and not

Table 8.3 Data Interface Encoding Type Values

Data Encoding Type Identifier	Data Encoding Type
1	Packet
2	Ethernet
3	ANSI/ETSI PDH
4	Reserved
5	SDH ITU-T G.707/SONET ANSI T1.105
6	Reserved
7	Digital wrapper
8	Lambda (photonic)
9	Fiber
10	Reserved
11	Fiber channel

an attribute of a link or link interface. For example, the ANSI PDH type defines how DS1 or DS3 traffic is presented on the wire. One may find it particularly confusing to see this parameter among TE link and link interface attributes. For instance, if it is said that a link interface has *Lambda* for switching capability type and *Lambda* for the encoding type, what does it really mean? It means that the link interface can multiplex/de-multiplex entire wavelength channels, and it does not know how the data is structured within the channels. A link interface that has the *Packet* switching capability type and *Ethernet* data encoding type is capable of switching individual packets based on 801.3 headers. Thus, in the context of traffic engineering the data encoding type has a different meaning. This is the extent to which a data interface understands how data is encoded within the traffic flows they switch. Again, this is important information during path computation because consistent TE links must be selected.

Link interface switching capability type and encoding type parameters are always associated with the third component of the ISC descriptor attribute: *Maximal LSP Bandwidth available* at each of the eight priority levels. Some descriptors also include switching capability specific information. For example, the TDM descriptor additionally includes Minimal LSP bandwidth and indicates whether Standard or Arbitrary SONET/SDH concatenation is supported. This information along with the Data encoding type is particularly important for identification of network layers and layer boundaries within a single network region. For instance, a TDM region (identified by TE links with the TDM switching type) may be (and usually is) comprised of multiple layers. Each such layer is identified by a layer *switching capability* a combination of switching capability type, data encoding type, the arbitrary concatenation indicator, and the minimal LSP bandwidth — describing the data format and switching granularity of the links comprising the layer (see more details on network layers in Section 8.6).

There are several reasons why a data switch can be locally connected to a data link by more than one link interface. Suppose a data link carries 40 wavelength channels. It is possible that, say, 30 of these channels could be switched only as lambdas. In GMPLS this is modeled by connecting the link to the switch via a link interface providing the *switching* function. For the remaining ten channels, however, there could be termination and adaptation function in place, so that lambda channels can be terminated and individual TDM channels can be extracted from the SDH payload of the terminated lambda channels and switched onto separate TDM interfaces. This is modeled by connecting the link to the switch by an additional link interface providing the termination function for the lambda channels as well as adaptation of the TDM channels onto them.

It is not required for a data switch to be locally connected to all data links with link interfaces of the same switching capability or even the same switching capability type. An optical cross-connect, which is also an STS cross-connect, will be connected to some links via LSC interfaces and to others with TDM interfaces.

The ISC descriptor link attribute serves two purposes.

- To identify TE region and layer boundaries on the network.
- To constrain the path computation to consider only TE links with appropriate switching capability.

8.4 GMPLS Traffic Engineering Protocols

Controllers need to exchange control messages in order to operate signaling protocols to establish LSPs in the data plane. To do so, they encapsulate the messages within IP packets and use the IP infrastructure for message delivery. IP transport requires IP forwarding tables on all controllers, so that each of them knows how to forward IP packets. The forwarding tables must be built and updated in a dynamic way without management interference, since at any point of time new controllers might be added to or removed from the network, and control channels might go in and out of service. The dynamic management of forwarding tables is solved by running a link state IP routing protocol (OSPF or ISIS) on every controller. Specifically, each controller advertises information about itself and the control channels to which it is connected. The advertisements are distributed to all other protocol speakers in a reliable and efficient way. Thus, any given controller also receives similar advertisements from all other controllers, and builds the Link State Database (LSD) that contains a complete view of the network topology. Periodically, each controller runs the Shortest Path First (SPF) algorithm on the LSD and determines the shortest IP paths to all other controllers. Finally, it uses the SPF outcome to build and update the local IP forwarding table.

A controller component that applies TE policies also requires accurate network representation, only in this case it needs to view the topology not in terms of controllers and control channels, but in terms of data switches and TE links. This information is needed for building the TED. Once the TED is built, a local path computation element can run constraint-based path computation algorithms to determine optimal paths for any given data service.

It is tempting, and seems natural and straightforward, to use a link state IP routing protocol for the distribution of TE advertisements in the same way as it is used for IP forwarding-related advertisements. That is exactly how the Traffic Engineering protocols (OSPF-TE and ISIS-TE) were introduced in MPLS: the transport of respective protocols was exposed to the TE layer, so that it could distribute the TE-related information in a way that was opaque for the routing protocols.

One can find numerous statements in MPLS-related books or specifications saying that OSPF-TE is OSPF extended to support traffic engineering.

Conceptually this statement is not correct. It is true that OSPF-TE distributes its advertisements using OSPF mechanisms (for example, OSPF database synchronization, LSA flooding) and may share those mechanisms with a running instance of OSPF; however, this is the full extent of the commonality between the two protocols. They advertise completely unrelated information, which is used for entirely different purposes.

8.4.1 *OSPF-TE*

OSPF-TE makes use of the OSPF opaque LSA option introduced in RFC 2370 — *The OSPF Opaque LSA Option*. TE-related advertisements are encapsulated into OSPF opaque LSAs and presented for distribution to OSPF, which acts as a transport mechanism. The TE LSAs are of type 10 (area scope); thus, they are flooded only within the LSA originator's OSPF area, and their payload is delivered to the TE layer of every OSPF-TE speaker within the area. The TE layer is responsible for building and managing the local TED. It also produces the network TE graph with data switches represented as graph vertices and synchronized TE links as edges or arcs. It is this network graph that is used to compute paths through the network for data services (LSPs).

The TE LSA payload is structured as a set of Type-Length-Value blocks (TLVs). Top-level TLVs may nest other TLVs (sub-TLVs) within themselves. Two types of TE top-level TLVs are currently defined:

- Router Address
- TE Link

Only one top-level TLV is permitted per opaque LSA to facilitate small updates when one of the TLVs changes.

The Router Address TLV is used so that the advertising controller can specify one of its IP addresses that is always routable (for example, a loopback address). This address may be used to uniquely identify the advertising controller so that if both OSFP-TE and ISIS-TE are used to advertise TE links, a connection can be made between the two advertisements and they can be collected into a single TED. At the same time, the address provides a routable target for control plane messages (that is, signaling messages) that concern the resources associated with the TE links terminated on a locally managed data switch. As was mentioned earlier, it also provides a good candidate for the data switch identifier.

The TE Link TLV is used to advertise attributes of one TE link. Each TE link attribute is encoded as a separate sub-TLV.

Currently, there are several restrictions on the use of TE TLVs. No router may advertise more than one Router Address TLV, and there is no way to segregate the

TE links advertised by a router to apply to distinct data switches. Thus, if a router controller wishes to manage more than one data switch (as shown by C45 in Figure 8.4), it has two somewhat contrived options.

1. It can impersonate multiple routing controllers by having distinct Router IDs and Router Addresses for each controller. In this way, each controller can continue to control a single data switch. The disadvantage of this approach is that it does not fit well with the necessary topology in the control plane, but with some care and some virtual control plane connections between the distinct routers, this approach can be made to work.
2. The set of data switches that are managed by a single controller can be presented to the outside world as a single switch. That is, a composite logical switch can be constructed from the real component switches. Only the external TE links are advertised. Clearly a good degree of care must be taken to manage the effect on the externally visible TE links of switching data through component switches. The effect of depleting the resources on an "internal" link may be to remove the ability to establish an LSP across the composite logical switch, thereby introducing a horizontal switching constraint that is hard to explain to external path computation algorithms.

A more comprehensive solution is being worked out between the IETF's CCAMP Working Group and ITU-T Study Group 15. The ideal solution will allow for clear differentiation of data switches in the TE advertisements of a single routing controller, so that each router controller may advertise the capabilities and TE links belonging to more than one data switch.

For more information about MPLS OSPF-TE see the *Further Reading* section at the end of this chapter.

GMPLS extensions to OSPF-TE introduce additional TE Link sub-TLVs for the purpose of advertising the following new GMPLS TE link attributes (see Section 8.3 for more details on TE link attributes).

8.4.2 *ISIS-TE*

ISIS-TE serves exactly the same purpose as OSPF-TE. The choice between ISIS-TE and OSPF-TE depends simply upon which routing protocol, IS-IS or OSPF, is used in the control plane. In theory one could use one protocol to distribute IP reachability and the other to distribute TE information, but this would be unusual because there is no necessity to run both protocols.

To advertise their information to the network, IS-IS speakers use Link State Protocol Data Units that are composed of multiple TLVs. ISIS-TE defines two new types of TLVs: the Traffic Engineering Router ID TLV and the Extended

IS Reachability TLV. Both new TLVs contain the same information and are used for the same purpose as the OSPF-TE Router Address and Link TLVs, respectively.

GMPLS ISIS-TE introduces some new sub-TLVs for the Extended IS Reachability TLV to make it possible to advertise such TE link attributes as link local and remote identifiers for unnumbered TE links, link protection types, ISC descriptors, and SRLGs.

For more information about ISIS-TE, see the references in the *Further Reading* section at the end of this chapter.

8.5 Traffic Engineering Link Bundling

GMPLS constraint-based path computation requires more TE information to be advertised than in MPLS, and this causes legitimate scalability concerns. TE link bundling is one way to decrease the volume of TE advertisement as well as to control the TED size.

Consider the network represented in Figure 8.4. Suppose controller C3 determines a path in layer 1 going from switch D3 to switch D1 as D3-D2-D1. There are two parallel data links between D2 and D1, which could be advertised as separate TE links; however, provided that both TE links have equal TE metrics and satisfy all computation constraints, controller C3 would not normally care which of the data links the service takes. In fact, all it needs to know is that at least one of the two links satisfies the service requirements. It can be left for controllers C2 and C1 to agree upon which data link to use during the LSP setup. Thus, both data links can be advertised as a single TE link by both controllers without adversely affecting the accuracy of the path computation on controller C3 or any other network controller.

TE link bundling introduced in an IETF Internet-Draft *Link Bundling in MPLS Traffic Engineering* specifies a way of summarizing attributes of parallel data links and advertising the whole bundle as a single TE link (that is, within a single OSPF-TE link TLV or ISIS-TE Extended IS Reachability TLV).

A data link within a bundle is called a *component link*. Component link IDs are relevant only for controllers that handle switches on either side of the bundle and are of no importance to the rest of the controllers in the network, although there may be some value to diagnostic service mapping, to see which component link an LSP has actually used. According to the IETF Internet-Draft, the controller handling the upstream side (with respect to the direction of LSP establishment) of a TE bundle is responsible for choosing which component link to use to support the LSP. It signals the chosen component link ID to the controller handling the other side of the bundle in the LSP Setup message.

Perhaps surprisingly, there are currently no mechanisms to consistently let the transit controllers report which component links they use, or to allow negotiation between adjacent controllers about which component link to use (in the manner of GMPLS label negotiation). Considering severe limitations and binding constraints on transport data switches, one would think such mechanisms would be very practical mechanisms to have. Consider a situation where there is a bundle with ten component links, and the service requirements are such that the downstream controller (perhaps because of some switching limitations) can accept only one particular component link. Rather than signal to the upstream controller which of the component links is acceptable, it has the option only of rejecting successive setup requests and letting the upstream controller try again and again until it finally guesses the right component link.

The following conditions must hold for two or more component links to become a part of the same bundle.

- They must begin and end on the same pair of data switches.
- They must belong to the same network layer; that is, must have the same ISC descriptor.
- They must have the same traffic engineering metric attribute.
- They must have the same administrative group attribute.

Note that apart from the traffic engineering metric and administrative group, all other attributes of bundle components could be different. For instance, the component links may provide different protection capabilities, SRLGs, and so forth. A TE bundle advertisement includes the highest protection capability provided by any of the components, and the union of all SRLGs associated with each component.

Just like simple TE links, TE bundles could be numbered or unnumbered. Parallel TE-LSPs (see the following section) could also be bound into bundles provided that they satisfy the restrictions on what links can be components of the same bundle.

8.6 Traffic Engineering Regions and Switching Layers

Initial GMPLS implementation and deployment efforts targeted single, homogeneous transport networks. Those were networks built of elements with a single switching type. Examples of such networks are G.707 SONET/SDH and G.709 optical transport networks. The level of complexity of a GMPLS control plane that manages a homogeneous transport network is roughly equal to the level of complexity of an MPLS control plane working on a classical IP packet switching network. For example, TE link switching capability need not be a constraint during path computations on such networks; a single round-trip exchange of signaling messages is sufficient to establish a GMPLS LSP, and so forth. In general, the size of a homogeneous transport network is considerably smaller than an MPLS network.

Because the GMPLS control plane works equally well for many different types of network (packet and transport), it is realistic to consider how it may be applied to heterogeneous networks built from component networks that have different switching capabilities. In the transport data world this is known as network layering, and a network of one switching capability provides connectivity for a pair of nodes in a network of a different switching capability. There is generally considered to be a hierarchy of network layers, which follows exactly the hierarchy of GMPLS switching capabilities.

Consider the network represented in Figure 8.3, where two TDM network segments (built of digital cross-connects A, B, C and F, G, H) are interconnected with a wavelength switching network (built of optical switches D, E, J, and I). Although it is possible to use separate control planes for the TDM and wavelength networks, it would be cumbersome in such a small network, and would require significant error-prone configuration efforts for maintaining and integrating the two control planes — recall the IP/ATM overlays! Therefore, the idea of using a single unified control plane that can manage both networks at once is appealing.

A heterogeneous network managed by a single instance of the GMPLS control plane can be decomposed into TE regions and switching layers. A *TE region* (also referred to as an *LSP region* or simply a *region*) is a set of data links that are connected to data switches via interfaces of a particular switching type. In other words, a TE region is a set of data links associated with a particular data plane technology. Examples of TE regions are IP, ATM, TDM, photonic, and fiber switching. A *switching layer* (also referred to as a *network layer* or simply a *layer*) is defined as a set of data links with interfaces that have the same switching and data encoding types and switching bandwidth granularity. It is obvious from this definition that a single TE region can contain and manage one or more switching layers. Examples of switching layers are SDH VC12, SDH VC4, ATM VP, ATM VP/VC, Ethernet, and IP.

It is important to note that a network should not be viewed as a single stack of layers. Generally it is comprised of multiple independent stacks of layers where the server-client relationships can be established between layers within a stack, but not between layers that belong to different stacks. For instance, a single TDM device may support multiple SDH branches, with each of them representing a separate stack of layers, and with termination and adaptation functions existing only within the branches, but not across the branches.

Network decomposition into TE regions is significant only from the control plane point of view. Regions and region boundaries are important for the signaling sub-system of the control plane because connections (LSPs) are signaled somewhat differently (that is, they use different signaling object formats and semantics) in different regions. Furthermore, TE advertising, routing, and path computation could be performed differently in different regions. For example, computation of paths across photonic regions requires a wider set of constraints (for example, optical impairments, and wavelength continuity) and needs to be performed in different terms (for example, in terms of individual resources such as lambda channels, rather than in terms of TE links) from path computation in other regions like IP or TDM.

Regions and region boundaries, however, are of little (if any) importance from the data plane point of view. What is significant for the data plane is switching layers and the server-client relationships by which LSPs in one (server) layer may provide network flexibility (that is, data links) for other (client) layers. Whether the server and client layers belong to the same or different regions is insignificant. It is important to understand that an LSP is always provisioned within a particular switching layer despite the fact that it can trigger re-provisioning in multiple layers and even regions.

It should be noted that the level of the GMPLS control plane complexity increases when more than one switching layer is supported. This is because, from the control plane point of view, such networks require *vertical integration*. This can be defined as a set of collaborative mechanisms within a single instance of the control plane driving multiple (at least two) switching layers and the *adaptation* between the layers. The notion of vertical integration should not be confused with the notion of *horizontal integration*, which is defined as a way of handling the situation where a single instance of a control plane manages networks that belong to separate routing areas or autonomous systems, and hence have separate TE advertising domains. We will discuss horizontal integration later in this chapter. For now it is important to understand that horizontal integration happens within a *single* switching layer, whereas vertical integration involves *multiple* switching layers.

So, what exactly is vertical integration, where does it occur in the network, and which of the control plane sub-systems does it affect? In the examples described in this chapter it is assumed (unless explicitly stated otherwise) that each region has exactly one switching layer. This is done for reasons of simplicity, and the reader must keep in mind that all inter-layer relationships described in the examples are also true for layers that belong to the same multi-layer region.

Refer once again to the example network in Figure 8.3. Suppose no LSPs have been set up anywhere yet, and we need to place a service carrying SDH traffic from node A to node G. The path computation on node A needs to constrain the path selection to TDM switching capable links. Such links are AC, BC, FG, and FH. Thus, we have problem number one: No sequence of TDM switching capable links can be found that interconnects the source and destination nodes, and hence the path computation fails. Apart from this, even if we could somehow force the path computation to define a path (say, ACDEFG), the subsequent LSP setup could fail because either link CD or link EF might not have an adaptation function that could place or extract an SDH payload onto or from the wavelength channels on links CD and EF (problem two). Finally, suppose we are lucky, and the necessary adaptation function is available on both links, and the LSP is successfully established and carries traffic — in this case, the capacity of the wavelength channels allocated for the service will only be fractionally used, while the rest of the allocated channel's bandwidth will not be available for any other services and thus will be wasted. This is problem three.

All three problems can be solved through vertical integration. H-LSPs, introduced in MPLS as pure abstractions for the purpose of scalability improvements through the reduction of required control plane states, turn out to be a crucial tool for vertical integration.

Let us define a layer boundary node as a data switch that is connected to TE links with interfaces of multiple (at least two) switching capabilities and with an adaptation function to place/extract a layer corresponding to the lower switching capability into/from a layer associated with the higher switching capability. In our example the layer boundary nodes are C and F, assuming, of course, that they have the adaptation function.

Node A can solve the first problem during path computation simply by relaxing the switching capability constraint. Instead of limiting candidates to TDM links, it considers links that have the switching capability type numerically equal to or larger than the TDM switching capability type. Note that PSC links are still not considered. That is, it can compute an end-to-end path that crosses all three layers and changes switching capabilities at the boundary nodes (C and F). In a more complex network, the computation might be arranged to:

- make as much use of the original switching capability as possible;
- minimize the number of changes in switching capability;
- not attempt to use switching capabilities lower down the hierarchy than the source capability.

This third point is most important because, for example, a lambda service cannot be carried on a TDM link.

Such a path is highly dependent on the existence of suitable adaptation components at the layer boundaries. In our example, node C must be capable of adapting a TDM signal onto a lambda channel (not technically hard, but it does require special equipment), and node F must be capable of extracting the TDM signal from the lambda channel and sending it onward. As the second problem indicates, this method of end-to-end or *contiguous* LSP establishment in a particular layer that requires involvement of other layers is vulnerable to nodes that lie on layer boundaries that do not have the requisite adaptation capabilities. The obvious solution is for the node that performs the path computation to generate the LSP's route by excluding those boundary nodes that do not have the necessary capabilities. Unfortunately, there is currently no means for the boundary nodes to advertise their adaptation capabilities — the default assumption is that a node that has links of two different switching capabilities has the means to switch between those links, but that need not be a valid assumption. It is likely that further extensions will be made to the TE information advertised by the routing protocols so that the adaptation capabilities can be known.

Even if a contiguous LSP is set up and can carry the end-to-end data, the third problem shows how this is sub-optimal and can waste a high percentage of the bandwidth in the server layer (that is, a layer providing necessary network flexibility for the successful LSP setup). Consider the relatively reasonable example of an OC-48 service from A to G. As this crosses the LSC layer from C to F it will require a full lambda channel. Now, a single lambda channel can often carry 10 Gbps, but OC-48 only actually uses 2.488 Gbps, thus 7.5 Gbps (or 75%) of the lambda channel's bandwidth is wasted. Because the lambda channel cannot be subdivided (the transit switches are only LSC and so cannot switch subdivisions), what is clearly required is some way to multiplex additional TDM signals onto the lambda channel to make use of the spare bandwidth.

Real vertical integration happens on the layer boundary nodes and offers a solution to this third problem. When the LSP Setup message arrives at node C, it recognizes that the LSP is about to enter a layer of a coarser level switching capability. It suspends the setup of the end-to-end LSP and triggers the setup of an H-LSP (in this case an LSC LSP) across the LSC layer, between itself and the remote layer boundary node located on the path (node F). Once the H-LSP is established, it could be used as a data link of the TDM switching layer — the layer where our original LSP is provisioned — and node C can resume the setup of the original LSP. To do this it sends the LSP Setup message direct to the far end of the new link (node F), requesting a TDM label and resource reservation on the link. Finally, the two nodes provision their local adaptation functions so that the service traffic could be carried over the LSC layer within the dynamically created link. As we see, on layer boundary nodes, vertical integration involves both control and data planes.

Note that an explicit path supplied in the LSP Setup message must not reference nodes or links entirely within the server layer. This is because the H-LSC LSP is going to be used as a data link in its own right, and it will constitute a single hop in the end-to-end LSP.

Since the H-LSP is now used as a TDM data link, the nodes at its two ends can (but do not have to) advertise the LSP to the TE routing domain as a TE link with TDM switching capability. This makes the LSP (which becomes a TE-LSP) more generally available for use by other end-to-end LSPs. Let us consider what happens if, some time later, node B decides to establish a TDM LSP going to node H. First, there will be no problems for path computation on node B, since both TDM segments are now interconnected by a TDM TE link that has resources available for an additional LSP; that is, the TE-LSP advertised by nodes C and F.

Secondly, when the second LSP Setup message arrives at node C, it will realize that it does not have to establish a new LSC LSP for this LSP, because there is already a suitable TDM link in place (provided by the TE-LSP). All that it has to do is to continue the LSP setup by sending the LSP Setup message direct to node F and requesting a label and resource reservation within the dynamic TDM link. Thus, the third problem is resolved as well.

The process that is responsible for placing finer grained tunnels within a coarser grained tunnel is called *traffic grooming*. It allows for efficient network utilization when the bandwidth on links can be allocated in chunks of a significant size. Layer boundary devices are particularly well suited to traffic grooming.

8.6.1 *Virtual Network Topology*

In our example an LSC LSP provided a necessary connectivity to deliver TDM traffic over the optical layer. Generally speaking, a set of such H-LSPs provides a *Virtual Network Topology* (VNT) for routing the traffic for higher layers requiring a finer switching granularity. For example, a set of LSC H-LSPs can provide a TDM VNT. Likewise, TDM LSPs can also be used as H-LSPs and constitute a VNT for PSC or L2SC traffic, and so forth. Note here that in the hierarchy of switching types, fiber switch capable (FSC) is usually referred to as the highest switching type with packet switch capable (PSC) the lowest type. However, in layered networking, the layer that supports other layers (that is, the server layer) is the lowest layer; thus FSC networks form the lowest layer and PSC networks the highest layer.

There are four ways in which a TE link supported by an H-LSP can be added to the VNT, and the choice has some impact on the way the network operates. As described in the example above, an H-LSP can be created on demand by the boundary node that provides access to the lower layer. The associated TE link can then be advertised for use by other end-to-end LSPs. This technique is effective, but it requires the node that computes the path to make assumptions about the behavior of the two boundary nodes that it selects to provide ingress to and egress from the server layer. There is an implicit cooperation between the ingress and the boundary nodes so that the H-LSP is established. The mechanism also requires that the computing node has full visibility into the topology of the server layer so that it can be reasonably certain that it is actually possible to establish the desired LSP in the server layer.

An alternative approach is to pre-establish a set of H-LSPs that traverse the server layer and to ensure that these are advertised as TE links so that they can be used for path computation. This brings us to the situation in the second half of the example where the H-LSP has already been established. Such a network of H-LSPs is clearly useful and simplifies the path computation problem, but it requires an element of network planning and configuration. Which boundary nodes will need to be connected? How much bandwidth will be required — that is, how many parallel H-LSPs are needed? Note that in an LSC network where there are multiple parallel lambda paths across a layer, the H-LSPs do not need to be advertised as individual TE links. Instead, they can be formed into a bundle that is advertised as a single TE link in its own right using the techniques described in Section 8.5.

In practice, such network planning questions are likely to give rise to the construction of a full mesh of H-LSPs between all boundary nodes. Low bandwidth requirements will be assumed, and some trigger mechanism will be used to ensure that further H-LSPs are set up as the resources on the existing ones become depleted. This technique is all very well, but it actually wastes considerable bandwidth in the core of the server layer — resources are reserved for H-LSPs that carry no traffic, and they could be allocated for other services.

What we need is some way to trigger the H-LSPs on demand, but to make the associated TE links visible to the computing node *before* the LSPs are actually created. This is achieved through the third method of managing the VNT — the use of *virtual H-LSPs*. The H-LSPs are configured at the boundary nodes and are advertised as TE links as part of the VNT, but the H-LSPs themselves are not signaled until an LSP Setup message arrives for an end-to-end LSP that needs to use the H-LSP. Obviously, there is some risk that the H-LSP will fail to establish, but apart from that, this technique gives the flexibility of easy computation through a richly populated VNT without the consequent resource wastage in the server layer.

One interesting alternative to virtual H-LSPs on which the CCAMP community has begun to work is the concept of *soft H-LSPs* (method number four). These are dynamic links provided by H-LSPs that are only half-pre-provisioned. The necessary resources are allocated on all links, but are not bound into the LSP cross-connects. Such soft H-LSPs can share resources with other soft H-LSPs. Additionally, their resources could be used to support protection LSPs and can even carry extra traffic. When the LSP Setup message of the first, higher layer LSP to be nested inside a soft H-LSP arrives at the ingress node for the soft H-LSP, the soft H-LSP is activated — an LSP Modify message is sent hop-by-hop to every controller that is involved in the soft H-LSP requesting that the H-LSP resources are bound into the cross-connects. Thus, two goals are achieved: the resources allocated for a soft H-LSP are not wasted when the H-LSP is idle, and the resources are guaranteed to be available and in place when they are actually needed.

Note that a virtual H-LSP requires more configuration and management coordination than a real (also referred to as hard) or a soft H-LSP because the latter is able to allocate and signal interface identifiers when it is set up, but the virtual H-LSP must have these identifiers configured in matching pairs (just as for a physical link that does not use LMP). The interface identifiers are needed, of course, so that the TE links can be advertised to form part of the TED.

Ultimately, a network operator may choose some mix of all four mechanisms. That is, the TED used in the higher layer will include TE links associated with static data links that belong to this layer as well as any H-LSPs (hard, soft, and/or virtual) contributed by the VNT. The balance between the four modes of operation will obviously depend on the predicted network usage.

Routing of user traffic over a transport network depends on the network topology in general and VNTs in particular, and can be impaired if the topology changes too frequently. For example, if TE links are frequently added and removed from the TED, there will be a continual need to flood new TE state information and repeated attempts may be made to re-optimize the active LSPs to make better use of the available resources. In our example there is one aspect that we have not considered yet: When should the TE link associated with LSC H-LSP be removed? One may guess that the H-LSP should be torn down and the associated TE link advertisement should be withdrawn from the domain immediately after the last nested end-to-end LSP is removed. Imagine the situation when for some reason a single TDM LSP ACFG (Figure 8.3) is set up and torn down in quick succession. This would cause the LSC H-LSP to be constantly set up and torn down as well, and the associated TE link will also be frequently advertised, removed, re-advertised again, and so on, which is not good. It would be much better to apply some hysteresis to the H-LSP removal. Thus, routing robustness must be traded with adaptability with respect to the change of incoming traffic requests.

On the other hand, it may actually be optimal to tear down an H-LSP even when it is carrying end-to-end LSPs that have active traffic. Recall that an unused H-LSP wastes resources in the server layer and that those resources might be better used for a new H-LSP between some other pair of boundary nodes. In the same way, an H-LSP that carries an end-to-end LSP that uses only a small percentage of the H-LSP's resources is also wasting server layer resources. In the first instance it may be possible to *re-groom* the end-to-end LSP onto some other existing H-LSP between the two boundary nodes — this can be achieved by using make-before-break on the end-to-end LSP. If no such second H-LSP is available between the boundary nodes, it is possible that a different path is available through the higher layers and over the server layer using another H-LSP between a different pair of boundary nodes. Again, make-before-break can be used to re-position the end-to-end LSP. As a final resort, preemption may be used within the transit network so that a low priority H-LSP may be displaced by a higher priority service request. When this happens, the end-to-end LSPs carried on the displaced H-LSP are broken and must be repaired or discarded.

8.6.2 *Hierarchical LSP Protection*

When a layer boundary node decides to establish an H-LSP, it may choose for recovery purposes to set up two disjoint H-LSPs rather than one. The first will carry higher layer LSPs, while the other will stand by, so that if the first H-LSP fails, the nested tunnels can be rapidly re-routed onto the second H-LSP. Note that in this case, despite there being more than one H-LSP, only one TE link will be advertised. The Link Protection Capability attribute of the TE link will depend on the nature of the second H-LSP (whether it is 1 + 1, dedicated 1 : 1, shared, and so forth). It is also possible to have a configuration where two or more parallel H-LSPs are advertised as a single TE link (that is, a bundle) with the Link Protection attribute set to "Shared M:N." In this case, in the steady (fault-free) mode, the protecting H-LSPs may nest extra traffic LSPs. The latter are subject to preemption during protection switchover. It is important to keep in mind that TE links associated with H-LSPs are no different from "normal" (static) TE links, and hence parallel H-LSPs bundled into TE links can provide all types of link protection as described in Chapter 7.

Alternatively, the layer boundary node could form two parallel links based on each of the H-LSPs and advertise two separate TE links (let us call this scheme 2). Although it is similar in spirit — the nested tunnels can be switched onto the parallel H-LSP if the working one fails — conceptually it is different from the model of a single link associated with two H-LSPs (scheme 1) for the following reasons.

- In scheme 1, the second H-LSP cannot be used for unprotected nested tunnels (with the exception of extra traffic tunnels in some link protection schemes; see Chapter 7 for details); all its resources are entirely dedicated to protecting the nested tunnels carried by the first H-LSP. In scheme 2 both H-LSPs can be used to carry unrelated unprotected nested tunnels.
- In scheme 1 it is guaranteed that if there are available resources on the first H-LSP sufficient to nest a particular tunnel, there are also resources on the second H-LSP to carry the same nested tunnel during protection. This is not the case in scheme 2, because other tunnels may have been nested into the second H-LSP and so depleted the resources.
- In scheme 1, service recovery is realized on the link level, whereas in scheme 2 it is achieved on the level of nested tunnels (that is, path level).

8.6.3 *Adaptation Capabilities*

At this stage it should be absolutely clear that at least one TE link attribute of great importance is currently missing. This is the attribute advertising interface *adaptation* capabilities. We may call it the Interface Adaptation Capability (IAC) Descriptor (similar to the ISC Descriptor). For example, the fact that a node has some TDM interfaces and some LSC interfaces does not necessarily mean that on a particular LSC interface the node can:

- originate/terminate a TDM-level H-LSP (for example, there is no suitable transceiver on the link);

- adopt/extract a particular TDM traffic flow onto/from the H-LSP (that is, the transceiver may not be able to cross-connect to the proper SIM card, or there may simply be no hardware capable of performing the necessary adaptation).

We need this attribute to constrain the hierarchical (that is, multi-layer) path computation to those links that can actually provide such adaptation that will decrease LSP setup blocking probability. At a minimum an IAC Descriptor entry should include the following fields.

- Switching layer (which is identified via switching and bandwidth encoding types, and by switching bandwidth granularity) of the signal to be adopted/extracted (inner LSP traffic parameters).
- Switching layer of the H-LSP to be created.
- Bandwidth (on per-priority level) available for termination/adaptation purposes.

This problem is an example of a vertical binding constraint. It is not to be confused with a horizontal binding constraint — a limited ability to bind together data links of the same switching level that might exist in some switching platforms, for example, where the hardware is implemented as "switchlets." Horizontal constraints might also need to be advertised, but on a TE node basis (rather than on a TE link basis as for the IAC Descriptor).

As multi-region/multi-layer traffic engineering work is extended within the IETF, it is likely that both the vertical and horizontal constraints will need to be added to the TE advertisements.

8.7 Inter-Domain Traffic Engineering

A GMPLS LSP may span different routing areas or even administrative domains. As was mentioned earlier, such LSPs require horizontal integration on area/domain borders. From the traffic engineering perspective, provisioning inter-domain LSPs implies an environment of partitioned TE advertising domains. It has both path computation and signaling challenges.

8.7.1 *Path Computation with Limited TE Visibility*

Let us consider a very simple multi-area network presented in Figure 8.5. Suppose there is a request to establish a service going from node A to node M. As the service

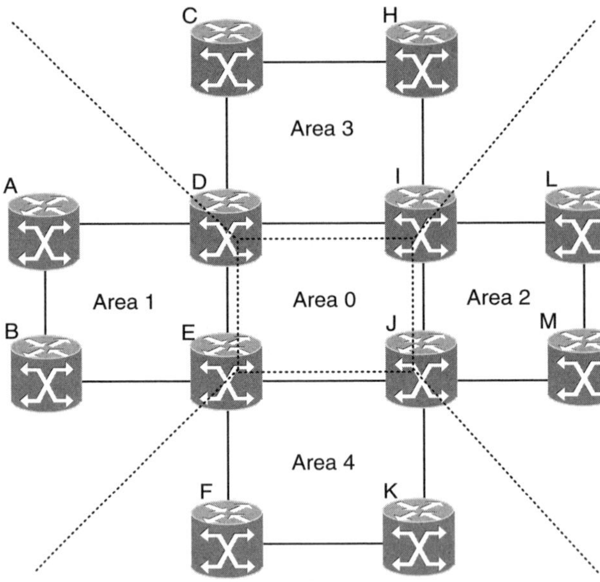

Figure 8.5 Multi-area network.

head-end node, node A attempts to compute a path for the service. Recall that TE advertisements are only of area scope; hence node A knows only about the four TE links AD, DE, EB, and BA. Thus, it cannot compute a full path. It does not even know where the path should exit from the first area.

There are two ways that path computation can be performed under these conditions of limited TE visibility.

- Using distributed path computation (method 1)
- Using remote path computation element(s) (method 2)

In method 1, the service ingress node (node A) first requests from its local routing sub-system a list of nodes that advertise IP reachability to the service destination. If the list is empty, the path computation request and the service setup are failed with the reason code "unknown service destination." Otherwise, node A assumes that the nodes in the list are area/domain border nodes with a wider TE network view and will be capable of determining the service path over the next area/domain (fortunately, this assumption is true in most of the cases). The ingress node computes the TE paths to those list members (border nodes) that have entries in the local TED (in our example nodes D and E), and selects the shortest path to signal the LSP Setup message. The message contains detailed path information only up to the selected border node (node D), although the destination is obviously also part of the message.

When the message arrives at the border node, it attempts a path computation to extend the path to the service destination. If this is still not possible, the border node performs the same operations as the ingress node. Specifically, it determines its own set of next area/domain border nodes (nodes I and J), computes paths to them, and sends the LSP Setup message toward the closest one (say, node I). The process repeats itself on all border nodes that lie on the path until one of them (node I) sees the destination in its local TED and is able to complete the path computation and the service setup.

A protected service requires one or more paths disjoint from the working path. When a service spans multiple TE domains, each domain is usually responsible for recovery of the service LSP segment that belongs to the domain. That is, recovery paths are computed and provisioned between the border nodes within domains. If in our example the service working LSP is ADILM, the recovery path in areas 1, 0, and 2 would be ABED, DEJI, and IJM, respectively. In this mode of protection, inter-domain services do not present additional challenges from the point of view of recovery path computation, because each recovery path is computed with full TE visibility. However, such a recovery scheme makes border nodes single points of failure, and can lead to over-provisioning of resources on links that run between border nodes (such as the link DE). One way to address this problem was described in Chapter 7: Applying the segment recovery technique, it is possible to install additional recovery schemes to protect against border node failures. However, there are also reasons why some services require end-to-end node disjoint recovery paths rather than allowing protection to be performed per domain. One way to compute such paths is by using the distributed path computation mechanism just described, but with the following modifications.

- The ingress node computes disjoint paths to all border nodes returned by the routing sub-system.
- The ingress node selects the closest border node (the one with the shortest path) and sends the LSP Setup message to it.
- The message includes the path to the selected border node as the working path as well as paths to all other border nodes as alternate paths.

In our example the LSP Setup message going out of node A would contain path AD as the working path and path ABE as the alternate path.

When the message arrives at the first border node, it expands the working and alternate paths. To do so it computes disjoint paths from each of the last nodes found in the working and alternate paths to all of the next domain border nodes returned by the local routing sub-system. In our example node D computes a pair of shortest disjoint paths, one from node D to one of node J or node I, and the other from node E to the other of node J or node I. One of the paths (DI) extends the working path, while the other (EJ) extends the alternate path. Similar path computations are repeated on each border node on the working path. When the LSP Setup message reaches the destination, the alternate path is copied into the LSP Accept message (RSVP Resv) and thus sent back to the ingress. When the ingress node receives the LSP Accept message for the working path, it will have complete path information to set up the end-to-end recovery path.

Note that this algorithm will miss alternate paths that go through domains other than those traversed by the working path. To compute such paths using distributed path computation is quite a challenging task and is likely to involve a degree of trial and error. Note also that the mechanism described is suitable for domains where there are no confidentiality issues (such as IGP areas), but may be seen as a concern in inter-AS traffic engineering, since the alternate path provides information about the topology of the neighboring AS.

In method 2, paths for inter-domain services are computed using remote path computation elements (PCEs). PCEs can be collocated with domain border nodes (border nodes have a wider TE view of the network than other nodes and hence are a good choice for hosting PCEs), or they can be placed on off-line servers. Path computing nodes learn about the location of PCEs either through configuration or dynamically. In the latter case nodes hosting PCEs may advertise their ability to accept remote path computation requests by making use of protocols similar to the TE information distribution protocols (see Section 8.4). For example, there are proposals within the IETF to introduce a way for OSPF speakers to advertise their PCE capability within OSPF areas or across an entire AS using the OSPF opaque LSA.

When path computation on some node fails because the path request destination cannot be found in the local TED, the node performing the path computation may select a remote PCE and request a remote path computation. This process obviously requires a protocol for communication between the LSR controller and the PCE, and the IETF is currently working to develop such a protocol.

Suppose, in our example, node A learns that it can use nodes D and E as remote PCEs. In order to compute one or several disjoint paths to node M it can send an appropriate path computation request to node D or node E, or to both. Once node A receives path computation responses from all PCEs, it picks the optimal set of paths and sets up working and, if necessary, recovery LSPs.

A PCE, while trying to satisfy a path computation request, might use other PCEs. The PCE on node D, for example, will not be capable of computing a path from node A to node M on its own, because node M is not in its local TED. Thus, it might send a request to, say, the PCE on node I to compute path(s) from itself and/or from node E to node M. Once node D receives a response with the requested path(s), it is capable of building the proper response for node A's request.

The advantage of method 1 is simplicity: there is no need to support yet another communication protocol. It will also usually provide better service setup times because there is no need to wait for remote PCEs to respond. Method 2 also has a problem with PCEs as potential bottlenecks and single points of failure. However, method 2 produces paths of a better quality: They are potentially more efficient and the setup of the paths is less likely to be blocked; hence service setup time on some configurations can be even better than the setup time for services that take paths computed with method 1.

8.7.2 *Provisioning of Inter-Domain LSPs*

When a service LSP Setup message arrives at a domain border node, the latter is supposed to perform the integration of LSP segments that belong to the neighboring domains. This procedure is called *horizontal LSP integration*. Its complexity depends on the similarity of signaling protocols running in each domain and on local policies.

When both domains run the same signaling protocols, the border node is likely to continue the service LSP setup as a contiguous LSP. It performs the usual functions of an intra-domain transit node. In this case no special integration is necessary. If the signaling protocols are slightly different (for example, each or one of them is using a set of domain proprietary signaling objects), the LSP is still likely to be set up as a contiguous LSP. However, in this case the border nodes might remove the objects specific to the previous domain, and add the objects specific to the next domain to the signaling messages.

It is also possible that neighboring domains run entirely different signaling protocols, or that one of them uses only static provisioning. In such cases a mechanism called *LSP stitching* is used for the horizontal integration. In this model some or all intra-domain LSP segments could be pre-provisioned, while the provisioning of others could be induced by receipt of inter-domain LSP Setup messages. In any case, when an inter-domain LSP Setup message arrives, the border node conducts the following operations.

- It performs data plane binding of the inter-domain LSP with a suitable intra-domain LSP segment that starts on the processing border node and terminates on the next domain border node.
- It tunnels the inter-domain LSP Setup message to the next domain border node, so that the latter could perform data plane binding on the remote end of the LSP segment and continue the setup of the inter-domain LSP.

Inter-domain LSP Accept messages (RSVP Resv) are tunneled between domain border nodes in the opposite direction.

It could be that the neighboring domains are built of devices with different switching capabilities. In this case the border node needs to perform both horizontal integration and vertical integration (that is, the integration between data layers). The vertical integration is accomplished via H-LSPs (see Section 8.6). The only peculiarity about H-LSPs established on border nodes is that they could be provisioned statically or by using a signaling protocol that is different from the one used for the provisioning of nested (in our case inter-domain) LSPs. Note that the latter are likely to be contiguous in this case. But they can also be stitched if, for example, intra-domain stitching LSP segments are pre-provisioned within H-LSPs.

8.7.3 *Handling Inter-Domain LSP Setup Failures*

The goal of constraint-based path computation is to produce paths that have a good likelihood of successful service established. However, despite that, a service LSP setup can fail. There are numerous reasons for that. For example:

- The local TED on a path computing node might not adequately reflect the current state of the network resources.
- The path computation request might not take into account all necessary constraints, perhaps because not all link attributes were advertised.
- Unexpected hardware problems might be detected during programming of the data plane on some links.

Normally the LSP ingress node handles LSP setup failures by re-computing the path with a constraint to exclude all previously failed links, and re-attempts the LSP establishment over the new path. This is quite straightforward to do in the single TE domain environment, where information about all network TE links is available.

It is not so simple when paths are computed in a distributed way under conditions of limited TE visibility. Suppose the setup of an inter-domain service LSP was attempted over path ADILM (Figure 8.5), and the setup failed because of some problem with link DI. When node A computes a new path, it cannot exclude the failed link (or rather, excluding the link will make no difference), because the latter belongs to a different area. But node A can constrain the path computation to avoid using node D. Suppose it does this and attempts to set up the LSP over intra-domain segment ABE. Unfortunately, by the time the LSP Setup message arrives at node E, the information about the previously failed link is lost (that is, it is known by node A but not by node E), and nothing prevents node E from selecting a path that traverses the failed link DI for the LSP segment going though area 0. Thus, the setup will repeatedly fail despite the existence of paths that would lead to the successful LSP setup.

The solution to inter-domain setup failures was proposed in two IETF Internet-Drafts that define Crankback and Route Exclusion (see the references in the *Further Reading* section at the end of this chapter). The former introduces a way to carry summarized or detailed information about all link failures in the LSP Upstream Error message (RSVP PathErr). It also suggests recovering LSP setup failures on domain border nodes before attempting end-to-end recovery. In our example, the first attempt to re-establish the LSP would happen on node D. This seems to be the correct thing to do because node D is responsible for path computation of the LSP segment over area 0, and it can exclude the failed link from the computation of an alternate path. If node D fails to compute the new path or to setup the LSP over the new segment, it is supposed to send the LSP Upstream Error message upstream, adding itself to the crankback information as a point of blockage. According to the proposed solution, the next computation recovery attempt happens on the next closest upstream border node or, as in our example, on the ingress node (node A). Computation is constrained to avoid using the nodes and links in the crankback information (node D). Provided that an alternate path segment can be computed (segment ABE), a new LSP Setup message will be sent out over the new path.

The route exclusion proposals allow the LSP Setup message to contain a list of all links and nodes that must be excluded from subsequent path computations. Thus, when node E computes the LSP path segment over area 0, it will not consider the failed link DI.

8.8 Service Path Re-Optimization

It is possible that after a service has been established, a more efficient path for the service becomes available, perhaps because one or more new TE links have been advertised or because some other services have been torn down causing resources in the network to be released. A path computation element could be designed so that it keeps track of all path requests and paths it has determined for all locally collocated and remote applications. When a better path can be found for one of the previously computed paths, the node or component that originally requested the path can be notified. In order to take advantage of the new path, the service ingress node must re-route the service onto the new path using the *make-before-break* technique.

Such optimization is simpler to do in the single TE domain environment, where service path computation is normally performed only once on the service ingress node. In the TE multi-domain environment it is the responsibility of every PCE that has participated in the distributed path computation to notify the ingress node about availability of better paths for its LSP segments. A further proposal in the IETF introduces signaling and procedural extensions to RSVP-TE to provide this information and allow the control of head end path re-optimization from remote nodes.

Service path re-optimization is not always desirable because it may also impose a traffic hit even using make-before-break techniques. Therefore, it is important to be able to provision a service as *pinned.* Once established, a pinned service cannot be re-routed away from the paths taken during the setup.

Frequent service path re-optimizations, especially involving multiple services, could also be dangerous for network stability. Hence there should always be a configurable limit on how often service path re-optimization can be triggered on a particular node.

8.9 Further Reading

The following IETF RFCs and Internet-Drafts provide additional information about traffic engineering in MPLS and GMPLS networks and describe some of the extensions proposed for enhancing traffic engineering for more complex networks.

RFC 2702 — Requirements for Traffic Engineering Over MPLS
RFC 2370 — The OSPF Opaque LSA Option
RFC 3630 — Traffic Engineering (TE) Extensions to OSPF Version 2
RFC 3784 — Intermediate System to Intermediate System (IS-IS) Extensions for Traffic Engineering (TE)
RFC 4203 —
OSPF Extensions in Support of Generalized Multi-Protocol Label Switching
RFC 4205 —
IS-IS Extensions in Support of Generalized Multi-Protocol Label Switching
RFC 4201 —
Link Bundling in MPLS Traffic Engineering
RFC 4206 —
LSP Hierarchy with Generalized MPLS TE
draft-ietf-ccamp-crankback
Crankback Signaling Extensions for MPLS Signaling
draft-ietf-ccamp-rsvp-te-exclude-route
Exclude Routes - Extension to RSVP-TE
draft-ietf-ccamp-inter-domain-framework
A Framework for Inter-Domain MPLS Traffic Engineering

CHAPTER 9

GMPLS Path Computation

In this chapter we will define GMPLS path computation, and why and when it is required by other sub-systems of the GMPLS control plane. We will show how a transport network can be presented as a weighted, connected graph, and how graph theory can be used to determine efficient paths on to which GMPLS services can be mapped. We will describe some basic popular unconstrained path computation algorithms and, after that, we will show which constraints must be considered in order to determine optimal paths in real networks.

9.1 Definitions

We define a transport service as a way of delivering user traffic of a certain type from the service source point to the service destination point with a certain quality. The user traffic characteristics, as well as the service quality, are agreed upon by the user and the Service Provider. We define a path as a sequence of Service Provider network resources, which, if properly provisioned, can realize the service. Once a path is determined it can be signaled between control elements that manage the selected resources to perform the provisioning (resource allocation, building of the cross-connects, and so on).

Path computation is the process of selecting or determining the path, and can be performed either at the time of, or ahead of service provisioning. The former is called *on-line path computation* and the latter, *off-line path computation*. The hybrid case is also possible where some (usually initial) path computation is performed off-line and some is performed on-line. Off-line path computation is beyond the scope of this book because it is not considered to be a component of GMPLS systems. If all paths for the service are computed on one node, such path computation is called *centralized path computation*. A *distributed path computation* is performed by several cooperating computation entities either to provide a single complete path in response to a single request, or when a series of requests is issued by controllers along the path as the service is established.

9.2 Transport Network Graph Representation

A transport network is usually presented as a connected weighted graph G(V,A), where $V = \{v0, v1, \ldots, vN)$ are vertices representing transport nodes (cross-connects, add-drop multiplexers, and so forth) that are capable of originating, terminating, and/or switching user data traffic; and $A = \{a0, a1, \ldots, aM\}$ are arcs representing TE links in a particular network layer (see the definitions of TE link and network layer in Chapter 8) needed to deliver user traffic between adjacent nodes in one direction (see Figure 9.1).

A *path* is a sequence of contiguous arcs that interconnects a pair of vertices. For example, XCY and XBDFY are different paths between vertices X and Y. A path contains loops if there is at least one vertex that it crosses more than once. For example, the path XBEDBCY contains a loop — node B is crossed twice. A path is called *simple* or *elementary* if it does not contain loops.

For every arc, an integer number is assigned indicating the preference of using this arc versus using other arcs (for example, it can be a function of the arc usage dollar cost). This number is called the *arc weight* (it is also called the *arc metric*) and may have positive, zero, or negative value. The less the arc weight, the more preferable this arc is, and the more likely it will appear in the selected path.

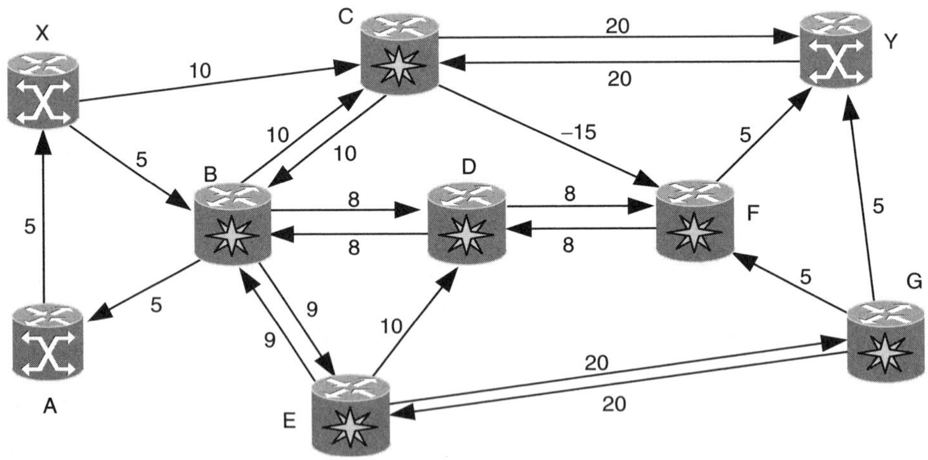

Figure 9.1 A transport network as a connected graph.

The path cost is the sum of weights of all arcs that constitute the path. For example, the cost of path XCY is 30. Suppose two paths — P1 and P2 — exist between the same pair of vertices, and path P1 has a lesser cost than path P2. We say that path P1 is *shorter* than path P2.

There are several problems that can be solved by path computation.

- *Single-source shortest path problem*: finding the shortest paths from a given vertex to all other vertices.
- *Single-destination shortest path problem*: finding the shortest paths to a given vertex from all other vertices.
- *Single-pair shortest path problem*: finding the shortest path between two given vertices.
- *All-pairs shortest path problem*: finding the shortest paths between every pair of vertices.

The last three problems can be reduced to the first one. For example, the single-destination shortest path problem can be transformed into the single-source shortest path problem by changing the direction of every arc on the graph. If one finds the shortest paths between a particular vertex S and all other vertices, one finds the shortest path between vertex S and any other given vertex; that is, one solves the single-pair shortest path problem. In fact, as will be shown later, most of the algorithms that address the single-pair shortest path problem cannot guarantee that the computed path between vertex S and vertex D is indeed the shortest one until the shortest paths between vertex S and all other vertices are computed. The Dijkstra algorithm has an advantage over other algorithms for the average case because it can be terminated as soon as the first path between the given pair of vertices is found. Finally, running a single-source algorithm once for every vertex can solve the all-pairs shortest path problem. However, as will be shown later in this chapter, an algorithm that is designed specifically to address the all-pairs shortest path problem can solve the problem significantly faster.

It is important that negative arc weights be assigned with caution. If arc CF had weight −45 the shortest path between nodes X and Y simply would not exist because the more times a path crosses nodes B, C, F, D, and B, the less it costs. Such loops as B-C-F-D-B are called negative loops. Negative weights are an important tool and are intensively used in arc- and vertex-diverse path computation algorithms. Apart from the Dijkstra algorithm, all single-source algorithms allow for and properly handle negative weights as long as they do not produce negative loops that are reachable from the source vertex.

The graph in Figure 9.1 is usually simplified in the following way: If two vertices are connected with two arcs that run in opposite directions and that have equal weights, the arcs are replaced with single undirected lines — called *edges* — that have the same weight as the arcs. The simplified graph is shown in Figure 9.2.

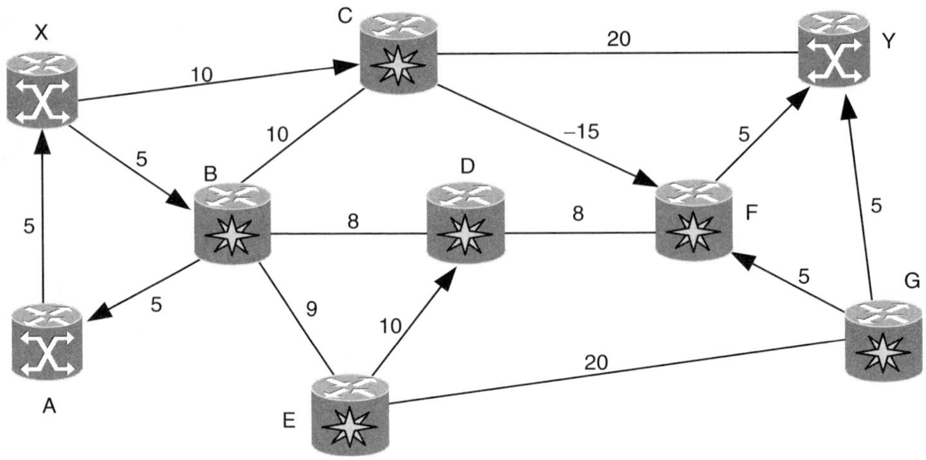

Figure 9.2 A transport network as a graph with arcs and edges.

9.3 Basic Single Source Algorithms

There is a great variety of published single source algorithms. In the literature they are often referred to as Short Path First (SPF) algorithms. The four most popular ones, used intensively in constraint-based path computations, are described here. They are the Bellman-Ford, the Dijkstra, the Modified Dijkstra, and the Breadth First Search algorithms. We will first describe some important qualities of a shortest path that all of the algorithms rely on, and some variables and procedures that all of them use.

Optimal Structure of a Shortest Path

All single source algorithms rely on the fact that the shortest path between any pair of vertices is composed of shortest paths. In other words, if P(s,d) is the shortest path between vertices s and d, and it crosses vertices x and y, than path P(s,d) goes through the shortest path between vertices x and y.

Shortest Path does not Contain Loops

As was mentioned earlier, a shortest path cannot contain negative loops. But can it contain non-negative loops? Let us assume that a path P(s,d) is the shortest path between nodes s and d and contains one or more non-negative loops. If we remove the loops, we will produce a path P′(s,d) with the cost of path P(s,d) minus the costs of the removed loops. Thus, the assumption that shortest paths do not contain any loops is safe.

Common Variables

There are two variables (d[v] and π[v]) that a single source algorithm associates with every vertex v on the graph. d[v] is called *path estimate*, and upon termination of a single source algorithm it contains the cost of the shortest path between source vertex s and vertex v. π[v] is called *predecessor*, and it contains the ID of a vertex that is the penultimate vertex on the path from s to v. Thus, at the end of a single source algorithm it is possible to build shortest paths between source vertex s and any vertex v that is reachable from vertex s by defining the predecessor of vertex v (π[v]), the predecessor of the predecessor of vertex v ($\pi[\pi[v]]$), and so forth. In fact, the set of predecessors of all vertices that belong to the graph G(V,E) identify an important sub graph $G'(V',E')$, where V' is the subset of vertices reachable from the source vertex s, and E' is the subset of edges that interconnect vertex s with every reachable vertex v via the shortest path between vertex s and vertex v. The graph $G'(V',E')$ is called the *Shortest Path Tree* (*SPT*).

Common Procedures

There are two procedures that are performed by all single source algorithms: *initialization* and *arc/edge relaxation.* During initialization d[v] and π[v] are set to the following values.

$$d[v] = \infty \text{ for every vertex v except s}$$

$$d[s] = 0$$

$$\pi[v] = \text{NIL for every vertex v}$$

The value ∞ is some large positive number that must be larger than the cost of the longest path between vertex s and any reachable vertex v. In practice it is usually set to the sum of weights of all edges/arcs of the graph.

To describe the arc relaxation procedure let us consider an arc a with weight w(a) that interconnects a pair of adjacent vertices u and v. The process of relaxing arc a involves testing whether the selected shortest path from vertex s to vertex v can be improved by going through vertex u, that is, by traversing arc a. If this condition holds, it is said that arc a is *relaxed.* This is the only procedure that may change the values stored in d[v] and π[v] and can be summarized as follows.

$$\text{if } (d[u] + w(a) < d[v])$$

$$\text{then } d[v] = d[u] + w(a);\ \pi[v] = u.$$

9.3.1 *Bellman-Ford Algorithm*

The Bellman-Ford algorithm solves the single source problem in the most general way. That is, for a given graph G(V,A) it produces shortest paths from any given vertex s to all other vertices reachable from vertex s. It allows negative metrics for some arcs provided that they do not produce negative loops reachable from vertex s. One valuable quality of the Bellman-Ford algorithm is that it can detect the presence of negative loops rather than assuming that there are no such loops on the graph (as the Dijkstra or Breadth First Search algorithms do).

The Bellman-Ford algorithm shown in Table 9.1 is very simple to implement because it does not require complex data structures like the min-priority queue, as in the case of the Dijkstra algorithm (see the next section). The only disadvantage of the Bellman-Ford algorithm is that other algorithms, if properly implemented, run asymptotically faster.

The following notes apply to the Bellman-Ford algorithm shown in Table 9.1.

- Lines 1–3 — Initialization.
- Lines 4–6 — Body: Walking through all arcs and performing arc relaxation for every arc. The process is repeated $|V|-1$ times, where $|V|$ is a total number of vertices on graph G.
- Lines 7–8 — Test for negative loops: Walking through all arcs and verifying if there is still an arc, for which the arc relaxation would re-label (modify the distance estimate of) the arc terminating vertex. The presence of such an arc at this stage indicates the presence of a negative loop.
- Line 9 — Completion: The algorithm notifies the calling application that there are no negative loops. The costs of the shortest paths from the source vertex s to all vertices are stored in d[v], and an actual path from vertex s to some vertex v can be built via walking from vertex v back to vertex s using

Table 9.1 The Bellman-Ford algorithm

```
BELLMAN-FORD (G,s)
1. do for every vertex v ∈ V
2.    d[v] = ∞; π[v] = NIL
3. d[s] = 0
4. do for every i ∈ (0, 1, . . . ,|V| − 1)
5.    do for every arc a(u, v) ∈ A
6.    if d[v] > d[u] + w(a) then d[v] = d[u] + w(a); π[v] = u
7. do for every arc a(u, v) ∈ A
8.    if d[v] > d[u] + w(A) then return FALSE /* negative loop is present */
9. return TRUE /* no negative loops */
```

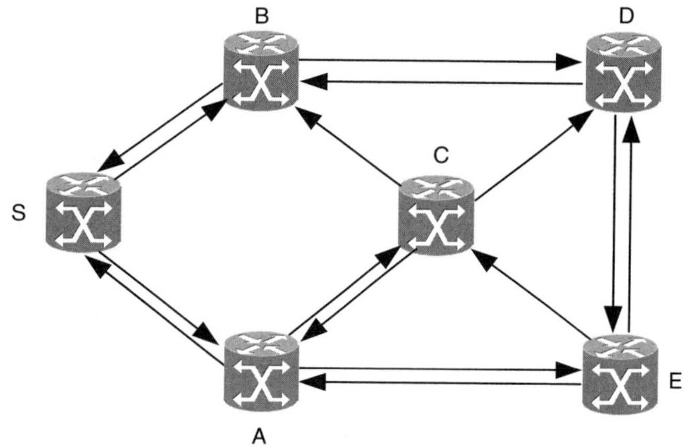

Figure 9.3 Network graph for the Bellman-Ford algorithm.

predecessors stored in $\pi[v]$. Distance estimates of vertices that are not reachable from vertex s will be equal to ∞.

The Bellman-Ford algorithm runs in $O(|V||A|)$ time: The initialization takes $\Theta(|V|)$ time, each of the $|V|-1$ passes over the arcs (lines 4 and 5) takes $\Theta(|E|)$ time, and the final loop required for the negative loop detection takes $O(|A|)$ time.

By way of an example, let us run the Bellman-Ford algorithm to define shortest paths from vertex S to all other vertices on the graph presented in Figure 9.3. Let us assume that information about the graph's arcs is stored as shown in Table 9.2. The progress of the algorithm is shown in Figure 9.4. A vertex is highlighted every time its distance estimate is updated (in order: S, A and B, D and E, C and E).

9.3.2 *Dijkstra Algorithm*

The Dijkstra algorithm (see Table 9.3) efficiently solves the single-source and the single-pair shortest path problems on the weighted directed graph G(V,A) for the case where there is no arc $a \in A$ that has a negative weight ($w(a) < 0$). The algorithm makes use of an auxiliary data structure, the min-priority queue, that contains graph vertices keyed by their distance value estimate and allows for the following operations on its components: INSERT_ENTRY, DECREASE_ENTRY_KEY and EXTRACT_MIN_KEY_ENTRY. The efficiency of the Dijkstra algorithm depends heavily on the type/implementation of the min-priority queue.

Table 9.2 Arc Weights for the worked example of the Bellman-Ford algorithm

Arc Originating Vertex	Arc Terminating Vertex	Arc Weight
B	D	14
D	B	8
D	E	10
E	D	10
C	B	5
C	D	8
E	C	−10
E	A	13
A	E	13
A	C	−8
C	A	12
A	S	6
S	A	12
S	B	10
B	S	10

The algorithm maintains two sets of vertices.

1. L — vertices for which the shortest path from the source vertex s has been already determined (labeled vertices).
2. U — vertices for which the shortest path from the source vertex s has not been determined yet (unlabeled vertices).

All vertices $v \in U$ are kept within the min-priority queue keyed by distance estimate d[v]. Originally L is empty, all vertices $v \in V$ are inserted into U with $d[v] = \infty$ for every v except source vertex s, and $d[s] = 0$. The algorithm repeatedly removes the vertex u with the smallest d[u] from U, and inserts it into L and relaxes all arcs originating from u and terminating on vertices $v \in U$. As a result of the arc relaxation some of the vertices $v \in U$ change (decrease) their distance estimates. The algorithm for the single-source shortest paths problem is terminated when U becomes empty.

One feature of the Dijkstra algorithm is that once a vertex v is removed from U and placed into L, its distance estimate never changes; that is, the shortest path from vertex s to vertex v is fully determined. This means that if there is need only to determine the shortest path from source vertex s to some vertex v (the single-pair shortest path problem) and vertex v is labeled already (that is, placed into set L), there is no need to determine shortest paths to all other vertices, and the algorithm

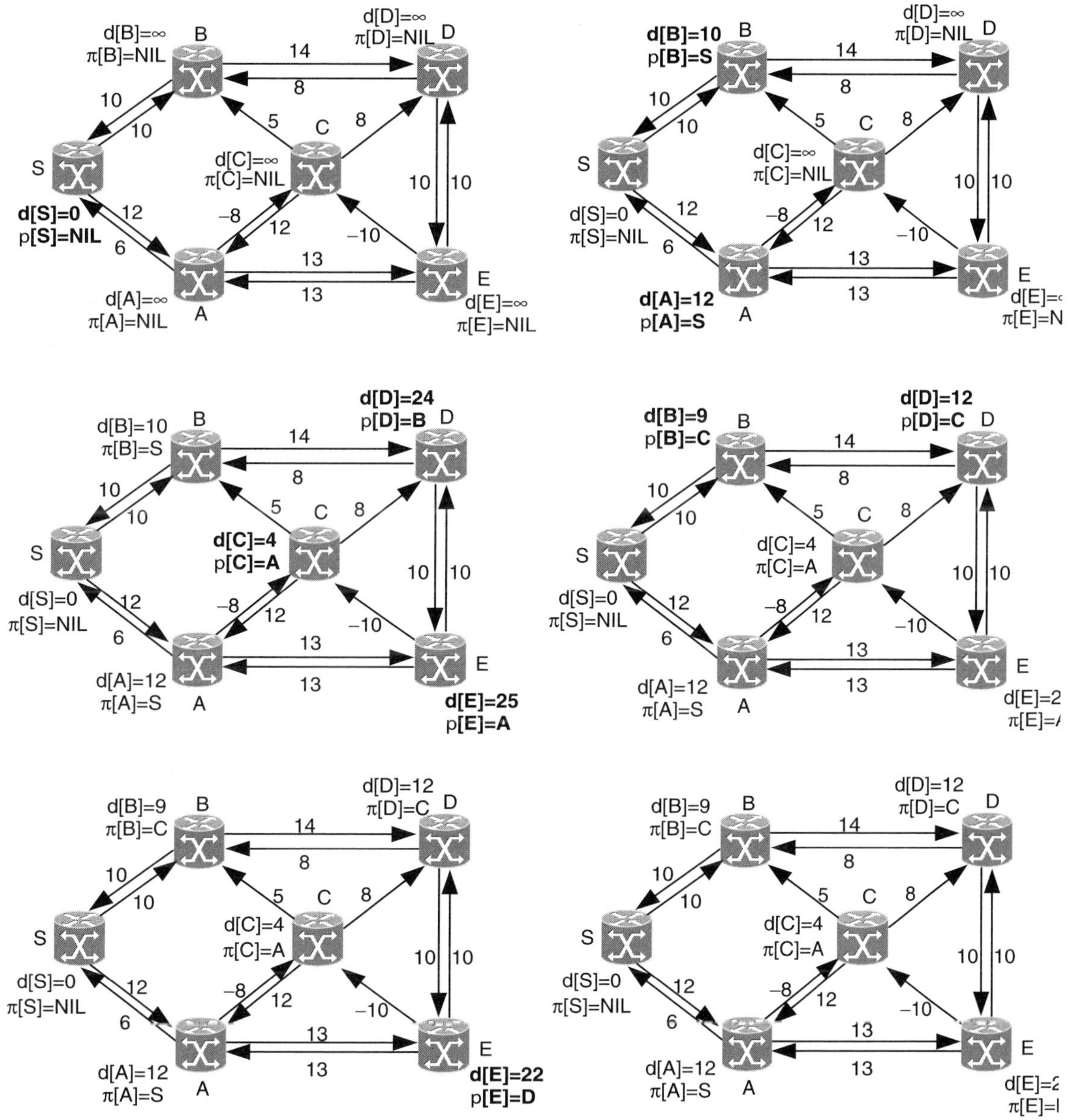

Figure 9.4 The progression of the Bellman-Ford algorithm.

Table 9.3 The Dijkstra algorithm

```
DIJKSTRA (G,s) /* for the single source shortest paths problem */
 1.  do for every v ∈ V
 2.     d[v] = ∞, π[v] = NIL
 3.  d[s] = 0
 4.  L = 0, U = V
 5.  do while U! = 0
 6.     u = EXTRACT_MIN_KEY_ENTRY(U)
 7.     L = L + u
 8.     do for each arc a(u, v) ∈ Originating[u] /* Originating[u] = arcs originating from vertex u */
 9.     if v ∈U && d[v] > d[u] + w(a)
10.     then d[v] = d[u] + w(a), π[v] = u, DECREASE_ENTRY_KEY(U, v)
```

can be terminated immediately. Thus, the Dijkstra algorithm can be optimized for the single-pair shortest path problem.

The following notes apply to the Dijkstra algorithm shown in Table 9.3.

- Lines 1–4 — Initialization: The set of labeled vertices is made empty, and all vertices are placed into min-priority queue U keyed by vertex distance estimate d[v].
- Lines 4–10 — Body: Extracting from the min-priority queue U a vertex u with smallest d[u]; walking through all arcs originating from vertex u and performing the arc relaxation for the arcs that connect vertex u to vertices that are still in the min-priority queue U. As a result of the arc relaxation some vertices get re-labeled and moved within the min-priority queue U. The algorithm is terminated when the min-priority queue U becomes empty. By this time shortest paths from the source vertex s to all other vertices are determined. Their costs are stored in d[v], and an actual path from vertex s to some vertex v can be built by walking from vertex v back to vertex s using predecessors stored in π[v]. Distance estimates of vertices that are not reachable from vertex s will be equal to ∞.

As was discussed above, the Dijkstra algorithm for the single-pair shortest path problem — define the shortest path between vertex s and vertex z — can be modified by adding a new line (6a) in the following way in order to terminate the algorithm once the destination vertex has been moved from the min-priority queue U.

6a. **if** (u = = z) **then** exit

As was mentioned before, the running time of the Dijkstra algorithm depends on how the min-priority queue is implemented. Note that the

DECREASE_ENTRY_KEY function is called many more times than the EXTRACT_MIN_KEY_ENTRY function. Therefore, any min-priority queue implementation that reduces the amortized time of each DECREASE_ENTRY_KEY operation without increasing the time of the EXTRACT_MIN_KEY_ENTRY operation would make the Dijkstra algorithm run faster. A running time of O(|V|lg|V| + |A|) can be achieved for the Dijkstra algorithm by implementing the min-priority queue with a Fibonacci heap. This is a significant improvement on Bellman-Ford's running time of O(|V||A|). Readers interested in specifics of Fibonacci heap implementations as well as in methods for evaluating algorithm complexity are referred to *Graphs and Algorithms* listed in the *Further Reading* section at the end of this chapter.

9.3.3 *Modified Dijkstra Algorithm*

Note that the Dijkstra algorithm fails on graphs where some arcs have negative weights. The reason for this is that a vertex once removed from the min-priority queue U never gets re-labeled and never gets re-inserted into U. This is correct for graphs with non-negative arcs; however, every time a negatively weighted arc is relaxed, it may yield a better distance estimate for a vertex it terminates, even if the vertex is already permanently labeled (that is, has been removed from U). (The value of negatively weighted arcs in certain computations was mentioned in Section 9.2 and will be discussed in detail in Section 9.5.)

The Modified Dijkstra algorithm (see Table 9.4) handles arcs with negative weights by allowing labeled vertices to be re-labeled. Such re-labeling may affect

Table 9.4 The Modified Dijkstra algorithm

```
MODIFIED DIJKSTRA (G,s)
do for every v ∈ V
   d[v] = ∞; π[v] = NIL
d[s] = 0
L = 0, U = V
do while U! = 0
   u = EXTRACT_MIN_KEY_ENTRY(U)
   L = L + u
   do for each arc a(u, v) ∈ Originating[u]
   if d[v] > d[u] + w(a) then
   d[v] = d[u] + w(a), π[v] = u
   if v ∈ U
   then DECREASE_ENTRY_KEY(U, v)
   else L = L − v, INSERT_ENTRY (U, v)
```

distance estimates of other labeled vertices, and, therefore, every time a labeled vertex is re-labeled, it must be inserted back into U.

Note that when the Modified Dijkstra algorithm is used for the single-pair shortest path problem, it cannot be terminated once the destination vertex is removed, because there is no guarantee that the destination vertex has obtained its final distance estimate until the shortest paths to all other vertices have been determined.

Note that the differences between the Modified Dijkstra algorithm shown in Table 9.4 and the Dijkstra algorithm shown in Table 9.3 begin on line 9. Vertex v is allowed to get re-labeled even if it does not belong to U, and once it is re-labeled it is inserted back into U.

9.3.4 *Breadth First Search Algorithm*

The Breadth First Search (BFS) algorithm (see Table 9.5) is yet another simple SPF algorithm that, for a given graph G(V,A), produces shortest paths from any given vertex s to all other vertices reachable from vertex s. It allows negative metrics for some arcs provided that they do not produce negative loops reachable from vertex s. Unlike the Bellman-Ford algorithm, it cannot detect negative loops and does not converge if run on a graph with negative loops reachable from vertex s. In sharp contrast to the Dijkstra algorithm it does not re-label vertices from a single selected vertex. Rather, it maintains a set F of vertices re-labeled in the previous iteration and repeatedly tries to re-label all vertices reachable from every vertex that belongs to F.

Like the Dijkstra algorithm, the BFS algorithm can be optimized for the single-pair shortest path case. Specifically, a vertex v does not need to be relabeled and, therefore, considered in the next iteration if the new distance estimate d[v] is larger than the one determined for the destination vertex d[z].

Table 9.5 The Breadth First Search algorithm

```
BFS (G,s)
do for every vertex v ∈V
   d[v] = ∞; π[v] = NIL
d[s] = 0, F = s
   do while F! = 0
   do for every u ∈F
   do for every arc a(u, v) ∈ A
   F = F − u
   if d[v] > d[u] + w(a)
   then d[v] = d[u] + w(a), π[v] = u, F = F + v
```

One interesting quality of the BFS algorithm is that where several equal cost shortest paths exist between source vertex s and some vertex v, the algorithm always chooses the one that has the smaller number of arcs that interconnect the vertices. This is a valuable feature for the GMPLS control plane because it speeds up dynamic service setup, modification, and teardown and minimizes the number of control plane states to maintain. On the other hand, the number of hops is not always the most desirable tiebreaker.

The following notes apply to the Breadth First Search algorithm shown in Table 9.5.

- Lines 1–3 — Initialization: Set F is initialized to contain only source vertex s.
- Lines 4–9 — Body: Walking through all vertices that belong to F. For every such vertex u the following procedures are performed: vertex u is removed from set F; for every arc originating from vertex v an attempt is made to relax the arc; and if the arc relaxation succeeds, the arc terminating vertex (that is, the re-labeled vertex) is added to set F.

The BFS algorithm terminates when set F becomes empty.

For the single-pair shortest path problem the algorithm can be optimized by modifying line 8 to read:

8. **if** $d[v] > d[u] + w(a)$ && $d[u] + w[a] < d[z]$

Arc a is not relaxed if the new distance estimate for the arc terminating vertex v is larger than d[z] — the current distance estimate of the destination vertex z. This optimization significantly reduces the algorithm's convergence time for the average case.

The BFS algorithm running time is $O(V + E)$, which is better than any other algorithm described above. In practice it is widely used as a basic SPF algorithm for all problems but the single-pair shortest path problem on graphs with non-negatively weighted arcs, where the Dijkstra algorithm on average performs better because of its ability to terminate immediately once the destination is reached. Note that many simple networking path computations resolve to precisely this case.

9.3.5 *Johnson Algorithm*

Sometimes there is a need to define paths between all pairs of vertices $u, v \in V$ for a graph G(V,A). This is the all-pairs shortest paths problem. Obviously it can be solved by running a single source algorithm for every $v \in V$ as a source vertex. The Johnson algorithm (see Table 9.6) solves the all-pairs shortest paths problem for a

Table 9.6 The Johnson algorithm

```
JOHNSON (G)
create new vertex s
G′ = G + s; A′ = A
do for every v ∈ V
    create a(s, v) with w(s, v) = 0, A′ = A′ + a
if (BELLMAN-FORD(G′, s) == FALSE)
    then exit /* negative loop is detected */
do for every a ∈ A
  w(a) = w(a) + d′[u] – d′[v] /* d′[u] and d′[v] are distance estimates of u and v determined
    by BELLMAN-FORD */
do for every v ∈ V
  DIJKSTRA(G, v)
    do for every u ∈ V store δ[v, u] /* shortest path from v to u computed by DIJKSTRA */
```

graph $G=(V,A)$ with some arcs having negative weights in $O(|V|^2 lg|V| + |V||A|)$ time, which is better than repeated iterations of any single source algorithm. It performs a transformation from graph G into graph G′ that does not have arcs with negative weights, and then runs the Dijkstra algorithm on graph G′ to determine the shortest paths between every pair of vertices $u, v \in V$. This graph transformation must be such that the shortest path between any two vertices u and v on graph G′ is also the shortest path between the two vertices on graph G. The graph transformation according to the Johnson algorithm is performed as follows.

- A new vertex s is added to the graph. It is connected to all other vertices $v \in V$ with zero-weighted arcs. Thus, $V' = V + s$; $w(s,v) = 0$ for every $v \in V$; $A' = A + a(s,v)$ for every $v \in V$.
- The Bellman-Ford algorithm is run on graph G′ for vertex s as a source. It determines distance estimates $d'[v]$ for all vertices $v \in V$.
- All arcs $a \in A$ are re-weighted according to the formula:

$$w'(u, v) = w(u, v) + d'[u] - d'[v]$$

where

w'	is the new weight of arc a(u,v);
w	is the original weight of arc a(u,v);
$d'[u]$ and $d'[v]$	are distance vectors determined by the Bellman-Ford algorithm for the originating and terminating vertices of arc a.

As a result of such a transformation all arcs $a \in A$ obtain new non-negative weights, and SPTs rooted from any vertex $v \in V$ on the graph with re-weighted arcs match ones on the graph with original (possibly negative) arc weights.

The following notes apply to the Johnson algorithm as shown in Table 9.6.

- Lines 1–4: A new vertex s is added and it is connected to every vertex v with arc(s, v) that has zero weight.
- Lines 5 and 6: The Bellman-Ford algorithm is called to compute shortest paths from vertex s to all other vertices. The algorithm terminates if the Bellman-Ford algorithm detects a negative loop.
- Lines 7 and 8: Arc re-weighting is performed to get rid of arcs with negative weights.
- Lines 9–11: The Dijkstra algorithm is called for every vertex $v \in V$ as a source; returned shortest paths from vertex v to all other vertices are stored in the matrix $\delta[v, u]$ that is available for the calling application.

9.4 K Shortest Paths Algorithm

The shortest path is not necessarily the optimal path on which a transport service can be placed. As will be discussed later in this chapter, there are numerous constraints and preferences that a user may express for path selection of a particular service: available bandwidth on every selected link/arc, link protection quality, and a minimal number of optical-electronic-optical (OEO) conversions. It may be the case that the shortest path does not satisfy some constraints, while some longer path does. One way to select a path subject to some vector of constraints is to compute several shortest paths between the service source and destination vertices, and then determine which of them is the shortest path that satisfies all constraints. Thus, the k ($k = 1, 2, 3, \ldots.$) shortest paths (KSP) problem — determine k shortest paths between some pair of nodes sorted in path cost increasing order — must be solved.

The most straightforward and obvious way to solve the KSP problem is as follows.

1. Choose a single-pair shortest path algorithm.
2. Compute and return the first shortest path by running the algorithm on the initial graph.
3. If $k > 1$, compute the next shortest path between source and destination nodes by removing from the graph one arc $a \in A$ and running the algorithm again on the modified graph. Repeat this step until k distinct paths with minimal cost have been computed.

This solution is simple, but not practical because it is computationally very intensive. On a large graph it may produce a lot of useless paths and their duplicates. Besides, no matter how many shortest paths are requested (k > 1), all possible paths will be computed — some of them many times.

There is a variety of published k shortest paths algorithms and heuristics that try to avoid computing all possible paths — only "good" paths are found, and only if they are needed. One such algorithm maintains a list of previously returned paths as well as a min-priority queue of computed but not yet returned path candidates keyed by their costs. The algorithm uses a technique called *branching of previously returned paths*: if there is a need to compute the jth ($j > 2$) path, and it is determined that the previously returned $(j - 1)^{th}$ path has several first arcs in common with all other previously returned paths, then the following steps are carried out.

- A branching point status is assigned to a vertex that terminates the common part of the path returned in the previous iteration and all other previously returned paths (this common part is called a *stem*).
- All arcs that originate from the branching point and belong to any of the $j - 2$ previously returned paths are removed from the graph.
- One or more paths are computed between the branching point and the destination vertex by removing one arc at a time from the segment of the $(j - 1)^{th}$ path that interconnects the branching point and the destination vertex.
- New path candidates are created by pre-pending the stem to the newly computed paths. If a new path candidate is not a duplicate of one of the previously computed paths — that is, it is neither in the list of previously returned paths nor in the min-priority queue of path candidates — it is added to the min-priority queue.
- A path candidate with minimal cost is removed from the min-priority queue and returned as the jth path.

The KSP algorithm described here uses the procedure shown in Table 9.7. The variables are first initialized as shown, and then the function KSP_NEXT_SHORTEST_PATH is called repeatedly to compute new candidate paths.

The following notes apply to the description of the function KSP_NEXT_SHORTEST_PATH(G, s, z) that returns the next shortest path as shown in Table 9.7.

- Lines 1–3: The first shortest path is computed and returned.
- Lines 4–6: All previously returned paths stored in P are broken by removing arcs originating from the branch point. This forces the algorithm to produce new paths in subsequent path computations.
- Lines 7–12: New path candidates are computed: Arcs of the path returned in the immediately previous iteration are removed one at a time, the BFS algorithm is run on modified graphs, paths returned by BFS are pre-pended with the stem

Table 9.7 The K Shortest Paths algorithm

```
Variable initialization
P = 0                  /* P is set (list) of previously returned paths */
Q = 0                  /* Q is min-priority queue of path candidates */
p_prev = 0             /* p_prev is a path returned in the previous iteration */
branch = 0             /* branch is current branching point */
stem = 0               /* stem is a path segment that starts at source vertex
                          and common to all previously returned paths */

KSP_NEXT_SHORTEST_PATH(G, s, z)   /* G is graph G(V, A) without negative loops,
                                     s — source vertex,
                                     z — destination vertex */

if p_prev == 0
      then p_prev = BFS(G, s, z)
      return p_prev
do for every p ∈ P
      do for i = 0; i < number_of_arcs(p); i = i + 1 /*
         number_of_arcs(p) is a total number
         of arcs that constitute path p */
      if v_orig(a(p, i)) == branch
      then A = A − a(p, i) /* v_orig(a)
         is a vertex that originates arc a, a(p, i)
         is the i-th arc of path p starting from the path head */
do for i = 0; i < number_of_arcs(p_prev); i = i + 1
      A = A − a(p_prev, i)
      p = stem + BFS(G, b, z)
      if p!∈ P && p!∈ Q
      then INSERT(Q, p); A = A + a(p_prev, i)
if Q == 0 then return 0
p_new = EXTRAC_MIN(Q)/* p_new
   is a path that will be returned in current iteration */
do for every p ∈ P
      do for i = 0; i < number_of_arcs(p); i = i + 1
      if v_orig(a(p, i)) == branch then A = A+ a(p, i)
if |P| == 0 then stem = p_prev
do for i = 0; i < number_of_arcs(p_new); i = i + 1
      if a(p_new, i)! = a(stem, i) then break
branch = v_orig(a(stem, i))/* branch is set
   to be the originating vertex of the first diverting arc */
do while i < number_of_arcs(stem)
   stem = stem − a(stem, i)
P = P + p_prev
p_prev = p_new
return p_new
```

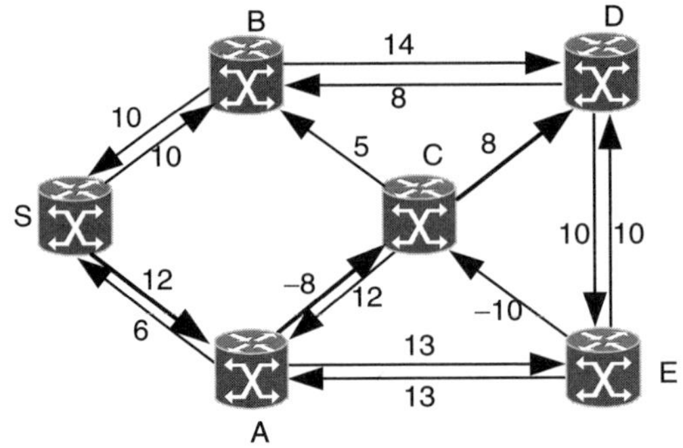

Figure 9.5 State of the KSP algorithm after returning the first shortest path. P_prev = SACD(12), P = 0, stem = undefined, branch = undefined, Q = 0.

and added to the min-priority queue Q of path candidates provided that they are not duplicates of already known paths.

- Line 13: The path candidate with minimal cost is extracted from min-priority queue Q. This is the path that will be returned as a result of the current iteration.
- Lines 14–16: All previously returned paths stored in P and broken by lines 4–6 are restored.
- Lines 17–23: New branch point and stem are determined: If this is a request to return the second shortest path (that is, second iteration), the stem is initiated to be the first shortest path; a new branch point is defined by identifying a common part of the path to be returned and the current stem starting from vertex s; and after the new branch point is defined, the stem is cut up to the branching point.
- Lines 23 and 24: The path returned in the previous iteration is added to P; the new path is copied into the previous path.
- Line 25: The new path is returned to the requesting application.

By way of example, let us run the KSP algorithm to define four shortest paths between vertex S and vertex D on the graph presented in Figure 9.3. The progress of the algorithm is shown in Figures 9.5 to 9.8. The shortest paths that are determined in each iteration are shown with thick arrows.

9.5 Diverse Path Computation

Today, in an environment of fierce competition between Service Providers, users have come to expect very high quality from the services they are paying for.

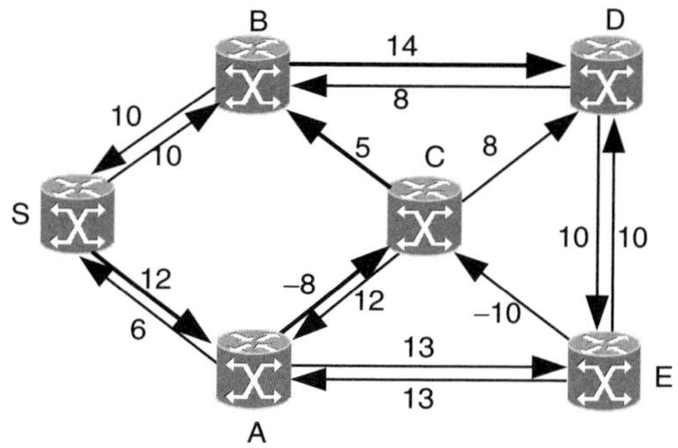

Figure 9.6 State of the KSP algorithm after returning the second shortest path. P_prev = SACBD(23), P = {SACD(12)}, stem = SAC, branch = C, Q = {SAECD(23), SBD(24), SAED(35)}.

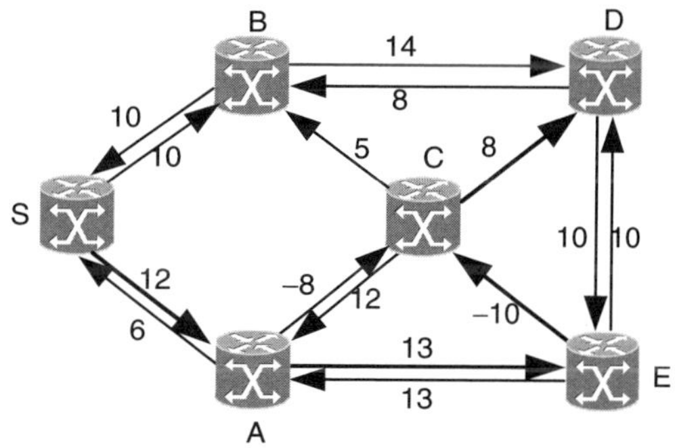

Figure 9.7 State of the KSP algorithm after returning the third shortest path. P_prev = SAECD(23), P = {SACD(12), SACBD(23)}, stem = SA, branch = A, Q = {SBD(24), SAED(35)}.

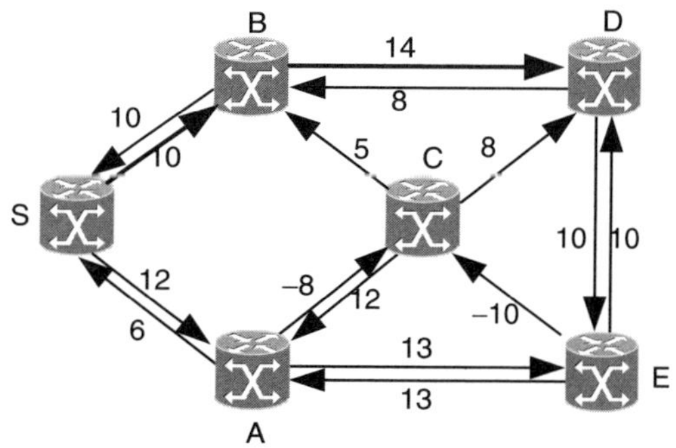

Figure 9.8 State of the KSP algorithm after returning the fourth shortest path. P_prev = SBD(24), P = {SACD(12), SACBD(23), SAECD(23)} stem = 0, branch = S, Q = {SAED(35)}.

In particular, they do not tolerate service disruption for time intervals of more than a few tens of milliseconds. The reality is, however, that elements of Service Provider networks do fail: communication cables get broken, switches get damaged, and so on. The only way to guarantee an undisrupted service in such conditions is to provision some sort of redundancy. A service is usually mapped to more than one path, so that if the primary path fails, the user traffic can be switched swiftly to one of the secondary paths. The secondary path can protect an entire working path or the failed segment of the working path. Note that even in this case some service disruption is unavoidable; however, the order of magnitude of the disruption will be much less than in an unprotected service where the path has to be entirely re-computed and re-signaled after the fault has been detected. The paths must be diverse — that is, use different network resources — otherwise a single network failure may make several paths inoperable, and the service may be disrupted anyway. That is why computation of several diverse paths between a pair of vertices on the graph representing a GMPLS network has such great practical importance.

In this section we will discuss different diverse path computation algorithms. We will start with the most practical ones: computing two edge-, vertex-, and best-disjoint paths between a pair of vertices of graph G(V,E). They cover the requirements of the great majority of currently deployed service recovery schemes. Some of them, however, require provisioning of more than two paths (for example, in case of M:N protection). Therefore, we will show how the algorithms that compute two diverse paths can be modified to produce k (k > 2) diverse paths.

9.5.1 *Simple Two-Step Approach*

It is not wise to compute two edge-disjoint paths by running a single-pair shortest path algorithm (for example, Dijkstra) to determine the first path, pruning out the edges taken by the first path from the graph, and running the algorithm again to determine the second path.

To demonstrate why this approach does not always work, let us consider computing two edge-disjoint paths from vertex S to vertex Z on the graph presented in Figure 9.9.

A run of the function DIJKSTRA(G, S, Z) yields the path SCEZ with cost three. If we prune out edges SC, CE, and EZ, we will make vertex Z unreachable from vertex S. Thus, according to the two-step approach, two edge-disjoint paths between vertices S and Z do not exist. However, the paths do exist. They are SCDGZ(31) and SBFEZ(31). It can also be shown (see *Survivable Networks — Algorithms for Diverse Routing* in the "Further Reading" section at the end of this chapter) that even if the two-step algorithm does produce paths, they may be sub-optimal; that is, there may be another pair of edge-disjoint paths whose sum cost

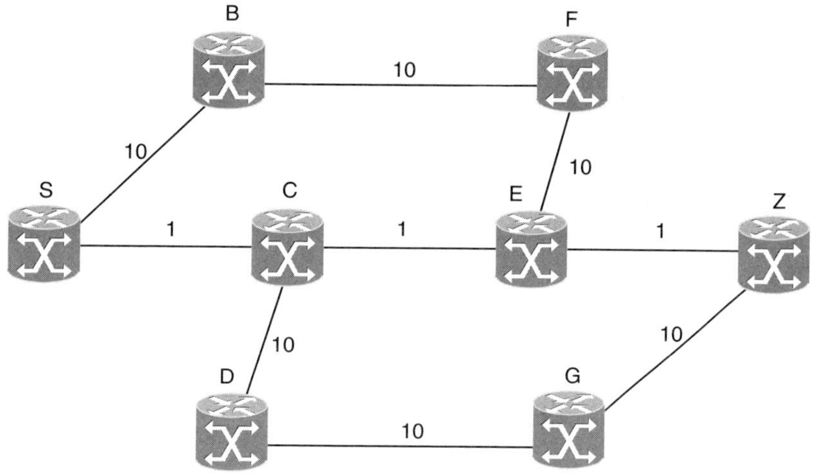

Figure 9.9 Sample network graph to demonstrate edge-disjoint path computation.

will be less than the cost of the paths determined by the algorithm. Thus, the two-step algorithm cannot be trusted.

9.5.2 *Computation of Two Edge-Disjoint Paths*

One of the algorithms that is widely used to compute two edge-disjoint paths for a protected transport service assumes that the network graph G(V, E) does not contain edges with negative weights.

1. Run the Dijkstra algorithm to compute the shortest path from the source vertex S to the destination vertex Z.
2. Split all edges taken by the shortest path into their component arcs. Remove arcs that are taken by the shortest path. Change the sign of the weights of the corresponding oppositely directed arcs (that is, make their weights negative). This graph transformation prepares for the second path computation and accomplishes two things.
   - It guarantees the edge-disjointedness of the second path from the first path — arcs of edges of the shortest path directed towards the destination are removed and, therefore, cannot be selected for the second path.
   - It encourages the use of edges of the first path in the opposite direction (because edge arcs for opposite direction have negative weights), which is claimed to guarantee the optimality of the resulting pair of paths because it forces the resulting paths to be as close as possible to the absolute shortest path (computed in step 1).

3. Run an algorithm that can handle negatively weighted arcs (for example, BFS) on the modified graph to compute the shortest path between the source and destination vertices.
4. Post-process the computed paths in the following way (sometimes called *untwisting*).
   - Walk through the paths and determine the edges that are used by both paths in opposite directions.
   - Every time such an edge is detected, remove it from both paths and swap the path tails (path segments starting on one of the edge vertices up to the destination vertex Z).
5. Restore the original graph, and return the resulting paths to the calling application.

Note: According to the algorithm, the second path computation should be performed on a graph with some arcs having negative weights. As we discussed earlier, this is possible only if there are no negative loops reachable from the source vertex. It is easy to prove that there are no such loops provided that the original graph does not contain arcs with negative weights. Suppose this were not true, and the graph transformation described above did produce a negative loop: This would mean that there is a path segment P(x,y) outside of the shortest path (returned by the first path computation) interconnecting a pair of vertices x and y that lie on the shortest path that is shorter than the segment of the shortest path Pshortest(x,y) interconnecting the two vertices. If this were true, we could replace the segment Pshortest(x,y) of the shortest path with P(x,y) and we would obtain a path that is shorter than the shortest path. This is not possible, because the Dijkstra algorithm guarantees that there is no path shorter than the one that it determines. Thus, the assumption about the possibility of a negative loop is not correct.

For strict proofs of the correctness of the algorithm described above, see *Survivable Networks — Algorithms for Diverse Routing*, listed in the *Further Reading* section at the end of this chapter.

To illustrate the operation of this algorithm, let us use it to define two edge-disjoint paths from vertex S to vertex Z on the graph in Figure 9.9. The progress of the algorithm is shown in Figures 9.10 to 9.12.

9.5.3 *Computation of Two Vertex-Disjoint Paths*

When a transport service is mapped to two edge-disjoint paths, it may still be the case that the failure of a single network element brings the service down on both paths. Consider, for example, a network with the graph shown in Figure 9.13.

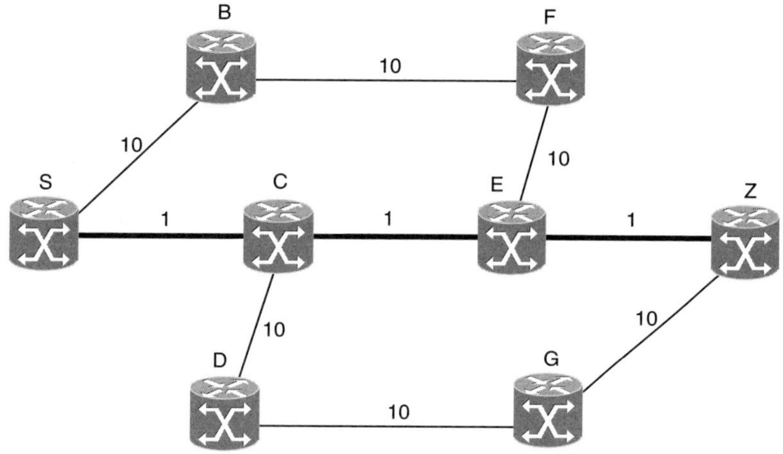

Figure 9.10 Progress of the computation of two edge-disjoint paths. The first path (SCEZ) is computed.

If a GMPLS service is mapped onto a shortest pair of edge-disjoint paths from vertex S to vertex Z — SACDZ(4) and SBCEZ(4) — and the network node represented by vertex C fails, both paths will be affected because they cross vertex C. Such a problem would not exist, however, if the service was mapped onto two vertex-disjoint paths SADZ(12) and SBCEZ(4). Thus, there is a need for vertex-disjoint path computation.

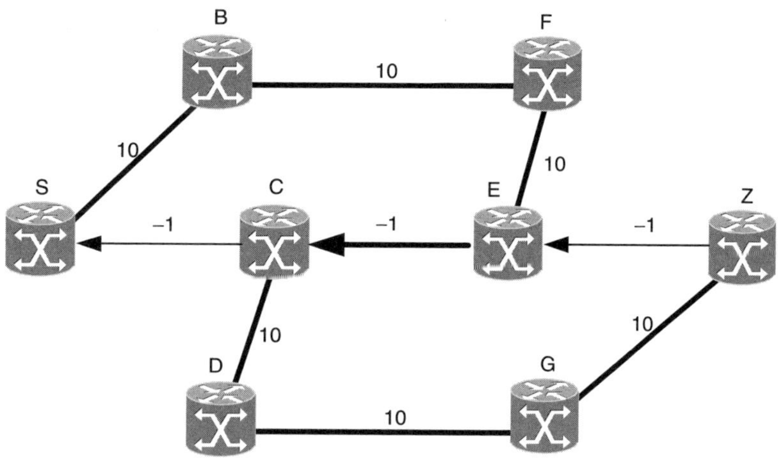

Figure 9.11 Progress of the computation of two edge-disjoint paths. Graph transformation is performed. The second path (SBFECDGZ) is computed.

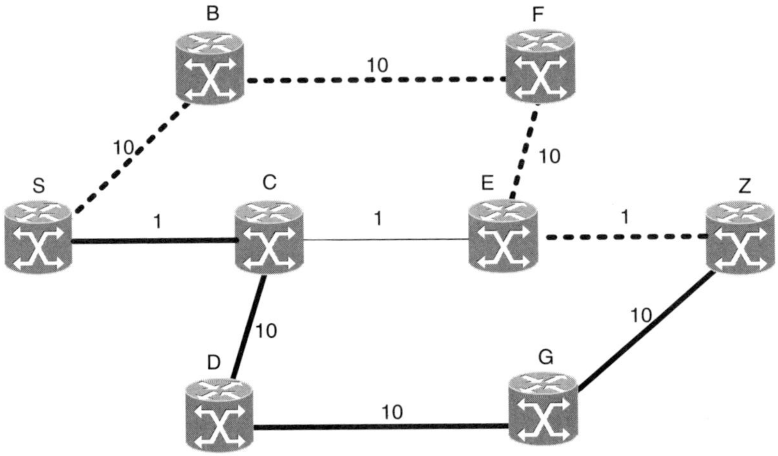

Figure 9.12 Progress of the computation of two edge-disjoint paths. Path post-processing is performed. The resultant paths are SCDGZ and SBFEZ.

Let us call the number edges that are originated/terminated on vertex v the *degree* of vertex v; for example the degree of vertex S on Figure 9.13 is two, whereas the degree of vertex C is four. One can make two general observations regarding vertex-disjoint paths. First, they are also edge-disjoint paths, and, thus, the problem of computing two vertex-disjoint paths can be solved by modifying the algorithm described in Section 9.5.2 to constrain the resulting paths so they will not cross common vertices. Secondly, only vertices with the degree four or

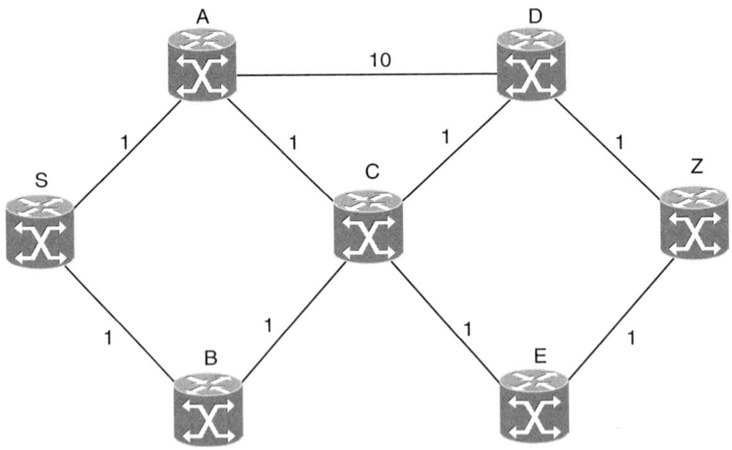

Figure 9.13 Sample network graph to demonstrate vertex-disjoint path computation.

more (for example, vertex C) need to be the subject of such a constraint, because only these vertices can be shared by edge-disjoint paths.

To compute two vertex-disjoint paths the algorithm described in Section 9.5.2 is modified in the following way.

1. Run the Dijkstra algorithm to compute the shortest path from the source vertex to the destination vertex.
2. Split all edges taken by the shortest path into their component arcs. Remove arcs that are taken by the shortest path. Change the sign of the weights of the corresponding oppositely directed arcs (that is, make the weights negative).
3. Find vertices that lie on the shortest path apart from the source and destination that originate/terminate two or more edges external to the shortest path (that is, vertices with the degree of more than or equal to four). Split every such vertex V into two sub-vertices V′ and V″. Connect the two with a single zero-weight arc (V″V′) that is opposite to the direction of the shortest path. Split all edges of vertex V external to the shortest path into their arc components. Have all outgoing external arcs originate from the sub-vertex V″ and all incoming external arcs terminate on the sub-vertex V′.
4. Run an algorithm that can handle negatively weighted arcs (for example, BFS) on the modified graph to compute the shortest path from the source to the destination.
5. Post-process computed paths in the following way.
   - Remove arcs that connect the split sub-vertices, and collapse them into original vertices.
   - Walk through the paths and determine the edges used by both paths in opposite directions.
   - Every time such an edge is detected, remove it from both paths and swap the path tails (path segments starting on one of the edge vertices up to the destination vertex).
6. Restore the original graph, and return the resulting paths to the calling application.

9.5.4 *Computation of Two Best-Disjoint Paths*

It may be that two paths from a source vertex s to a destination vertex d exist, but full path disjointedness cannot be achieved. Consider, for example, the network represented in Figure 9.14.

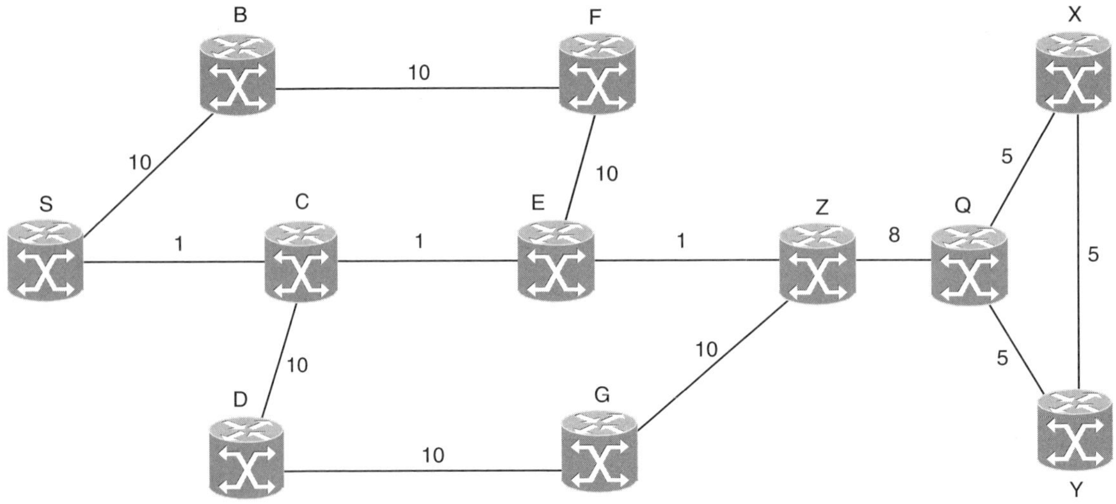

Figure 9.14 Bridged network configuration.

Any path going from vertex S to vertex X will always go through the edge ZQ (the bridge), and, therefore, edge-disjoint paths between S and X do not exist. A GMPLS service going from S to X, however, must still be as resilient to network failures as possible. The requirement for path computation for this service is to determine an optimal pair of maximally edge-disjoint paths — that is, paths that have the smallest number of edges that are used by both paths. For example, paths SCDGZQX(44) and SBFEZQYX(49) are maximally edge-disjoint paths that have a single edge (ZQ) in common. Usually the probability of the situation when a single network failure disrupts the service traffic is smallest if the service is mapped on maximally disjoint paths.

Computation of Two Maximally Edge-Disjoint Paths

Recall that during the edge-disjoint path computation we removed from the graph the arcs taken by the first shortest path before computing the second one (see Figure 9.15b). This graph transformation guarantees that the second path will not share the edges of the first path in the same direction.

Suppose that, instead of removing the arcs we keep them in place, but assign for their weights some very large positive number ED (Figure 9.15c). This would make the arcs available for the second path computation but less preferable to other arcs. If the value ED is greater than the sum of the weights of all graph edges, then such arcs will be used by the second path only if there is no other choice; that is exactly what we want to achieve.

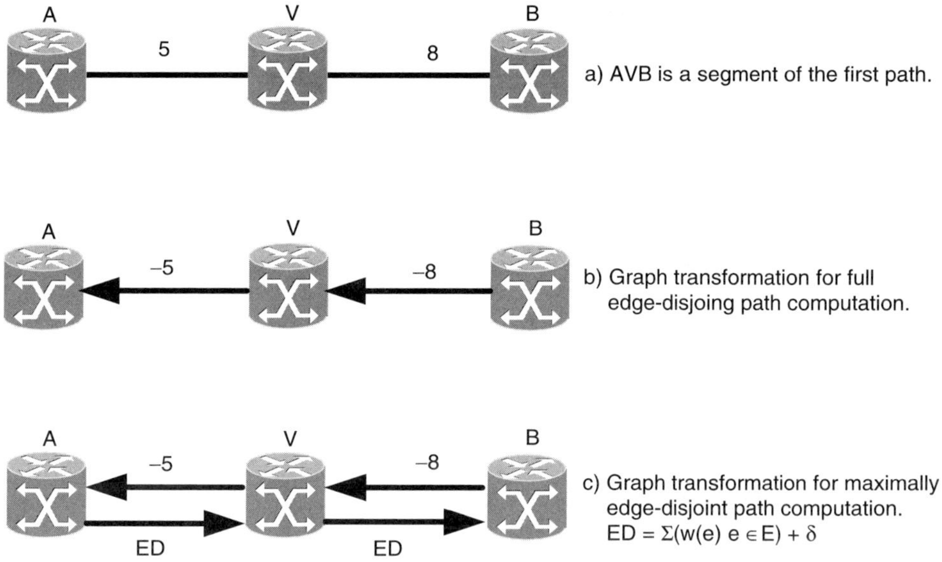

Figure 9.15 Graph transformation for edge-disjoint path computation.

Thus, the part of the algorithm to compute two edge-disjoint paths that prepares the graph for the second path computation should be modified as follows.

2. Split all edges that belong to the shortest path into their component arcs. Change the sign of weights of the arcs oppositely directed to the path. Re-weight the arcs that are taken by the path by assigning for each of them weight ED, where

$$\mathrm{ED} = \sum(\mathrm{w(e)}\ \mathrm{e} \in \mathrm{E}) + \delta$$

Note: δ is some positive number. It is needed to cover the case when all edges have weight of 0.

Computation of Two Maximally Vertex-Disjoint Paths

There are reasons why the user would want to have a transport service placed on two vertex-disjoint paths, but this cannot be achieved in every network configuration. On bridged configurations, once the paths have to share some edges, they will also have to share vertices on either side of these edges. Apart from bridges, there are cases where two edge-disjoint paths can be determined only

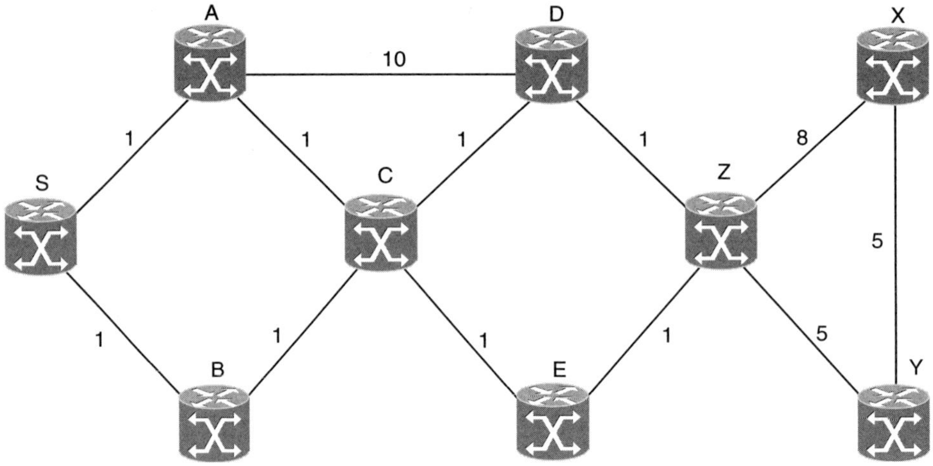

Figure 9.16 Network configuration to demonstrate the computation of two maximally vertex-disjoint paths.

if they share some vertices. Consider, for example, the network represented in Figure 9.16.

Notice that any path going from vertex S to vertex X will always cross vertex Z, and, therefore, two fully vertex-disjoint paths from vertex S to vertex X cannot be determined. Because common vertices are single points of failure, the user may request to place its service on two paths that have a minimal number of common vertices. To address this problem we will modify the algorithm used to compute two vertex-disjoint paths as we did for the algorithm to compute two maximally edge-disjoint paths.

Recall that to impose vertex-disjointedness of the second path, we split all vertices that lay on the first path (apart from the source and the destination vertices) and which had degree of four or more, into two sub-vertices. We connected the sub-vertex that originated all external outgoing arcs (V″) with the sub-vertex that terminated all external incoming arcs (V′) using a single zero-weighted arc. Because of the absence of an arc in the opposite direction, this operation made sure that the second path would never enter any split vertex on one of its external incoming arcs and exit it on one of its external outgoing arcs, and, as a consequence, it would never be used simultaneously by both paths.

Let us relax this constraint and add arcs that connect sub-vertices V′ to sub-vertices V″ with a weight of some large positive number VD (Figure 9.17c). These new arcs will be available for the second path computation. However, because of the large weight, they will be less preferable than all other arcs. Thus, if VD is large enough, they will be used only where there is no other choice — where the second path cannot avoid using common vertices in order to reach the destination.

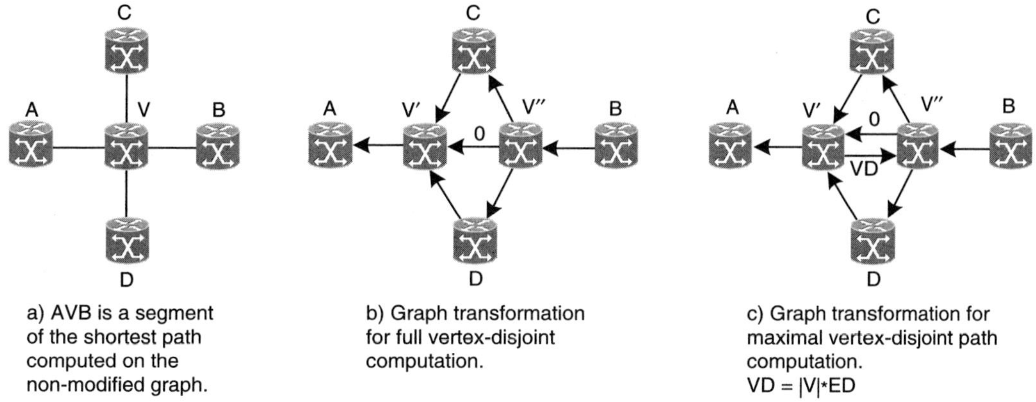

Figure 9.17 Graph transformation for edge-disjoint path computation.

In other words, the addition of these arcs will not affect the second path computation on network configurations where full vertex-disjointedness can be achieved, but will help to produce a path with a minimal number of vertices shared with the first path when the full vertex-disjointedness does not exist.

Thus, the part of the algorithm for computing two vertex-disjoint paths that splits vertices lying on the first path is modified as follows:

3. Find vertices that lie on the shortest path apart from the source and destination with the degree more than or equal to four. Every such vertex V split into two sub-vertices V′ and V″. Connect sub-vertex V″ to sub-vertex V′ with a zero-weighted arc (V″V′) that is directed toward the destination (opposite to the direction of the shortest path). Connect sub-vertex V′ to sub-vertex V″ with an arc with a positive weight VD. Split all edges of vertex V external to the shortest path into their arc components; have all outgoing external arcs originate from the sub-vertex V″ and all incoming external arcs terminate on the sub-vertex V′.

Note: In order for the algorithm to behave properly on configurations containing bridges, it is recommended that the following value for the VD be used:

$$VD >= ED * |V|$$

where ED is the value to ensure maximal edge-disjointedness, and |V| is the total number of vertices on the graph.

Computation of Two Best-Disjoint Paths

A user may ask to place a transport service onto two best-disjoint paths, which implies that he just wants to minimize the number of single points of failure.

Such a request can be interpreted in several ways. For example, the GMPLS path computing entity can be called to compute two fully edge-disjoint, maximally vertex-disjoint paths. Alternatively, in configurations with bridges, the path computing entity will be requested to compute two maximally edge-disjoint, maximally vertex-disjoint paths. Finally, the request to determine two best-disjoint paths can be interpreted as the computation of two maximally edge-disjoint, maximally vertex-disjoint paths as long as the cost of disjoint paths does not significantly exceed the cost of paths that share some edges and/or vertices. The latter is called the diversity versus cost case. One can observe that the greater the disjointedness of paths, the higher their sum cost may be. Indeed, if we did not impose constraints for the second path computation, the resulting second shortest path would be identical to the first shortest path; that is, we would receive the cheapest (albeit non-disjoint) paths.

The user may express the desire to tolerate a higher probability of service interruption owing to network failure if he gets significant savings on the service cost. Consider, for example, the network configuration represented in Figure 9.13. There are two full vertex-disjoint paths from S to Z, SADZ and SBCEZ, with the sum cost of sixteen. However, if the user will tolerate that vertex C is shared by the paths, then his service could be placed on the full edge-disjoint paths SACDZ and SBCEZ with the service total cost of eight. Thus, by tolerating a single point of failure, the user will have to pay less for the service.

Fortunately, by applying the algorithm to compute two maximally edge-disjoint and maximally vertex-disjoint paths, and by properly assigning the values of ED and VD, we can handle all types of best-disjoint path computation. Specifically, if the commonness of edges cannot be tolerated, ED must have a value of ∞ (that is, the arcs that are taken by the first path must be removed from the graph). If edge commonness can be accepted only in the case of configurations with bridges, ED must, as was discussed, be calculated as $ED = \Sigma(w(e)\, e \in E) + \delta$. Finally, for the edge-disjointedness versus cost case, ED can be assigned to have some positive value $0 < ED < \Sigma(w(e)\, e \in E) + \delta$ and will be interpreted by the second path computation as a cost penalty for sharing edges with the first path so that the arcs with weights of ED will appear in the second path only if their usage yields a better cost than edges that are not shared with the first path.

Likewise, if vertex commonness between the two paths cannot be accepted, VD must be given the value ∞ (that is, there should be no arcs interconnecting v' and v'' sub-vertices of a split vertex v). If the vertex commonness can be accepted only when a pair of full vertex disjoint paths cannot be determined, VD should be greater than or equal to $|V| * (\Sigma(w(e)\, e \in E) + \delta)$. For the vertex-disjointedness versus cost case, VD should be within the range $0 <= VD <= |V| * (\Sigma(w(e)\, e \in E) + \delta)$.

9.5.5 *Computation of K (K > 2) Edge-, Vertex-, Best-Disjoint Paths*

For a transport service to be resilient to multiple network failures, the user may want to place the service on more than two diverse paths. Thus, the GMPLS path computing entity must be capable of computing k (k > 2) edge-, vertex-, and best-disjoint paths. A natural way to accomplish this would be to expand corresponding algorithms for computing two edge-, vertex-, or best-disjoint paths to compute more than two paths. Fortunately, we can do just that.

Let us consider, for example, the request to compute three edge-disjoint paths between some source vertex S and destination vertex Z. Suppose the algorithm to compute two edge-disjoint paths has just completed the second path computation. To prepare the graph for the third path computation we must perform some graph transformation that would ensure that the third shortest path will be edge-disjoint with the previous two, and the triplet of paths will be the optimal one; that is, there will be no other three edge-disjoint paths with a lesser sum cost. Note that this is exactly the same situation we faced after the first path computation, when we needed to prepare the graph before computing the second path. Recall that by removing the arcs taken by the first path we ensured that the path returned by a subsequent path computation would never use the edges of the first path in the same direction. By making the weights of the corresponding oppositely directed arcs negative, we encouraged the second path to go through the same edges as the first path but in the opposite direction, and thus achieved the minimal sum cost of the two paths. All we need to do is to perform the same operations for the edges that lie on the second path. Thus, the algorithm to compute k (k > 2) edge-disjoint paths should be modified as follows.

1. Run a single-pair shortest path algorithm (Dijkstra the first time, BFS all subsequent times) to compute the shortest path between source vertex S and destination vertex Z.
2. If the number of path computations already performed equals the number of required paths, post-process the computed paths in the following way.
   - Walk through all computed paths and determine any edges that are used by any two of the paths in opposite directions.
   - Every time such an edge is detected, remove it from both paths and untwist the paths by swapping the path tails (path segments starting on one of the edge vertices up to the destination vertex Z).
   - Restore the original graph and return the resulting paths to the calling application.

3. Otherwise:
   - Spit the edges taken by the most recently computed path into their arc components.
   - Remove all arcs that belong to the path except the arcs with negative weights.
   - Change the sign of the weights of the corresponding oppositely directed arcs (that is, make them negative).
   - Go to step 1.

Applying the same logic to the two vertex-disjoint path computation algorithm we will obtain an algorithm to compute k (k > 2) vertex-disjoint paths:

1. Run a single-pair shortest path algorithm (Dijkstra the first time, BFS all subsequent times) to compute the shortest path between source vertex S and destination vertex Z.
2. If the number of path computations already performed equals the number of required paths, collapse the sub-vertices of all split vertices into the original ones and post-process the computed paths in the following way.
   - Walk through the paths and determine any edges that are used by any two paths in opposite directions.
   - Every time such an edge is detected, remove it from both paths and swap the path tails (path segments starting on one of the edges up to the destination vertex Z).
   - Restore the original graph and return the resulting paths to the calling application.
3. Otherwise:
   - Split the edges taken by the most recently computed path into their arc components.
   - Remove all arcs that belong to the path except the arcs with negative weights.
   - Change the sign of the weights of the corresponding oppositely directed arcs (that is, make them negative).
4. Find vertices that lie on the most recently computed path apart from the source and destination vertices with the degree of four or more.
   - Split every such vertex V into two sub-vertices V′ and V″.
   - Connect the two with a single zero-weight arc (V″V′) that is directed opposite to the direction of the path.

- Split all edges of vertex V external to the path into their arc components.
- Have all outgoing external arcs originate from the sub-vertex V″ and all incoming external arcs terminate on the sub-vertex V′.

5. Go to step 1.

9.5.6 *Computing Physically Disjoint Paths*

Vertex-disjoint paths do not necessarily guarantee the disjointedness of the physical optical fibers (represented on the network graph by edges) that interconnect transport nodes (represented by vertices). One reason for this is that fibers interconnecting different nodes may be distributed within the same conduits, and a breakage of a single conduit may affect multiple fibers, which may cause multiple paths to fail. If a service is mapped onto two paths that share the broken conduit, it may be disrupted for a considerable period of time. None of the algorithms described above can address this problem, because it was always assumed that there was complete independence of each edge from the others.

One way to solve the problem is to introduce the notion of a Shared Risk Link Group (SRLG). This is a network unique number that identifies a physical device, set of devices, or even physical location upon which the operational status of multiple physical fibers depends. One SRLG may be associated with multiple arcs. For example, a conduit ID number may be associated with all arcs for the physical fibers that are carried by the conduit. An arc may be associated with multiple SRLGs. The union of SRLGs of all arcs that constitute a path describes the vulnerability of the path to failures like conduit breakages, flooding of buildings containing network equipment, and so on. Thus, the physically disjoint path computation problem can be described as defining two or more vertex-disjoint paths that have non-overlapping unions of SRLGs.

Unfortunately, there is no way to solve this problem by simple modifications to one of the algorithms described above, because the union of SRLGs of a particular path is not known until the path is determined. The constraint of non-overlapping SRLGs is a constraint of a path type and must be handled in a general way along with other path type constraints like overall path length, or end-to-end delay. We will discuss how paths for transport services are calculated with the consideration of path type constraints when we consider constraint-based path computation in the next chapter.

9.6 Further Reading

There are many books on graph theory and path computation algorithms. Some which the author have found particularly useful are listed below.

Graphs and Algorithms by M. Gondran and M. Minoux (1984), John Wiley & Sons.

Introduction to Algorithms by Thomas H. Cormen, Charles E. Leiserson, Ronald L. Rivest, and Clifford Stein (2001), The MIT Press.

Survivable Networks — Algorithms for Diverse Routing by Ramesh Bhandari (1999), Kluwer Academic Publishers.

Design of Survivable Networks with Bounded Rings (Network Theory and Applications Volume 2) by Bernard Fortz (2000), Kluwer Academic Publishers.

CHAPTER 10

Constraint-Based Path Computation

The GMPLS path computation entity is expected to consider all user preferences regarding the selection of paths, and to determine one or more optimal paths that have a good likelihood for successful service establishment and that will be operable even when some network resources fail to perform their functions. This chapter looks at why the path computation algorithms described in the previous chapter are not sufficient to handle arbitrary constraints requested by the user, and what can be done to derive suitable algorithms.

What is wrong with the algorithms already described in the previous chapter? For one thing, the user has very little control over the path selection. The algorithms return one shortest path or several disjoint shortest paths. But what if the user does not want shortest paths? For instance, there are multiple reasons why the user would want to avoid using certain arcs or vertices, even if this would make the resulting paths longer. One good example is handling crankbacks. Suppose one or more unsuccessful attempts to set up a service have already been made, and the path computing controller has been notified about all links where the service failed to set up. Arcs representing the failed links must be disregarded in a subsequent path computation; otherwise, the same paths used for the previous attempts will be determined, and the service will fail to set up again. There can also be policy-driven reasons why the user would like to divert a particular service away from certain network nodes and/or links. Likewise, the user may explicitly request the paths to use certain links, despite the fact that it would make the paths longer. Thus, the path computation entity must be prepared to handle user requests to exclude or include certain arcs and/or vertices.

Secondly, not every path that topologically connects service source to service destination is a good candidate for every service. For example, if one of the arcs represents a link that does not have enough resources to carry the traffic between adjacent nodes, then the service will fail to set up over this path.

Likewise, the service will fail to set up over links that do not have proper switching capabilities. For example, a link cannot be a part of an optical trail when it can only carry a SONET/STS payload.

Therefore, there is a need for *constraint-based path computation* algorithms that allow things like the bandwidth available on links, link protection capabilities, and type of network resources associated with the links, to be taken into consideration during the path selection process. Additionally such algorithms should factor in user preferences with regard to which links or nodes are to be included or excluded from the resulting paths, the criteria for the path optimization, and so forth.

In this chapter we will develop the concept of the link attribute first discussed in Chapter 8, and introduce the notions of path attribute and path computation constraint. We will discuss different types of constraints and ways they can be handled in constraint-based path computation.

10.1 Attributes Within the Network

10.1.1 *Link Attributes*

Up to now, the only number that we have used to characterize the preference for using a particular link during path selection was the weight of the arc representing the link on the network graph. It is impossible to express all user requirements for path selection in just one value per link. A vector of multiple attributes must be allowed to be associated with every link. Recall from Chapter 8 that a set of attributes can be associated with a TE link (in this chapter we use terms *link* and *TE link* interchangeably) and advertised via the TE routing protocol (OPSF-TE or ISIS-TE). The following are examples of attributes that are usually associated with a link.

- Protection type. This is a value that describes which protection capabilities exist for the link; so path selection can be constrained to links that have some acceptable protection capability.
- Shared Risk Link Groups (SRLGs). As was mentioned earlier, a set of links may constitute a shared risk link group where there is a network resource whose failure may affect all of the links in the group. An SRLG is identified by a 32-bit number, which is unique within the network. By associating each link with every SRLG upon which it depends, the path selection may be constrained to consider only paths that do not share any network resources — that is, to determine paths that are completely disjoint.
- Link Switching Capabilities. A link interconnecting two adjacent nodes may be capable of carrying some types of traffic and not others. For instance, it may be

able to carry an SDH payload, but not individual data packets. By configuring the Link Switching Capabilities attribute for every link, the path computation may be constrained to selecting paths that are appropriate for a particular service type. For example, a path for a 10G Ethernet service from vertex S to vertex Z will likely be different from a path for an SDH service from vertex S to vertex Z, because the paths will go over links with different switching capabilities: L25C and TDM, respectively.

- Data Encoding Type. This is a value that describes the format in which the user traffic is encoded when delivered over the link. This link attribute allows the path selection to be constrained to considering only those links that "understand" user data in the specified format. For example, if a service is to deliver an SDH payload, it must take a path built of links with the data encoding type SDH, and avoid using links with, say, the data encoding type Ethernet 802.3.
- Maximum Unreserved LSP Bandwidth. This is a value that identifies how much bandwidth is available on a link for a new service at a particular priority level. It allows the path computing entity to consider only those links that have sufficient bandwidth at the setup priority level of the new service to be provisioned.
- Resource Class. This is a link attribute that identifies certain qualities of a link and makes it possible to force the path computing entity to consider only links of a particular type, or, to the contrary, to disregard links of a particular type.

Note that a path computation algorithm does not need to consider all link attributes in every path computation — only those that are related to the constraints (see Section 10.2) specified in a given path computation request.

10.1.2 *Path Attributes*

Path attribute is a characteristic of a path or a segment of a path, which can influence the path acceptance/rejection decision and/or optimization process. Usually all path component links contribute to the path attribute value and, therefore, path attribute can be calculated according to:

$$\mathrm{Pattr}(p) = \sum f(\mathrm{Latr}(a))\ a \in p,$$

where Latr(a) is the attributes of a link used by path p and represented on the graph by arc a.

Examples of path attributes are the total length of links that constitute the path, the end-to-end delay and delay jitter of traffic going over the path, the total number of OEO conversions on the path, and the union of SRLGs of all links that constitute the path.

10.2 Path Computation Constraints

In theory every link or path attribute, or any combination of them, may be a subject for optimization during path selection. In practice, however, a simpler approach is usually taken. The path computing entity is still requested to determine one or several *shortest* paths, but with the condition that the resulting paths satisfy all specified path computation *constraints*. In other words, it is not necessary to compute paths that are optimal from the point of view of multiple criteria. Rather, we want to determine paths that consume the minimum network resources and are "good" enough for a particular service.

A path computation constraint is a way of telling the path computation algorithms why a particular link, node, path, or path segment must not (or must) be accepted as a candidate for the path computed for a particular service. All path computation constraints can be broken into four types.

- Exclusions: Do not consider certain links and/or nodes during the path selection.
- Inclusions: Make sure that specified links and/or links of specified nodes appear in the selected path(s) in the specified order.
- Link-type constraints: Do not consider links for which one of the link-evaluating functions specified by the user returns FALSE. For example, do not consider links with the maximum unreserved LSP bandwidth attribute at priority p ($0 <= p <= 7$) less than the specified value.
- Path-type constraints: Disregard paths or path segments, for which one of the path-evaluating functions specified by the user returns FALSE. For example, disregard paths with a total length of all component links greater than the specified value.

10.2.1 *Handling of Exclusions*

Generally speaking, the path computing entity may be requested to compute one or more edge-, vertex-, or best-disjoint paths with an additional requirement to exclude an unordered list of links and/or nodes from any resulting path (global exclusions), an unordered list of links and/or nodes from path number one (first path exclusions), an unordered list of links and/or nodes from path number two (second path exclusions), and so forth.

The problem of computing k (k >= 2) disjoint paths each with its own private set of exclusions is quite complex. It cannot be solved by the algorithm described in the previous chapter (see Section 9.5) because the algorithm assumes some path segment exchanges between the paths (recall the path tail swapping or path untwisting in the case where two paths share some edge in the opposite direction). Because of these possible exchanges only global exclusions can be honored. The problem of private exclusions can be solved the same way as that of path-type constraints, which is computationally very expensive (the problem and the solution will be discussed later in this chapter). Fortunately, in the vast majority of cases only global exclusions need to be handled — that is, different exclusions are not applied to the different paths in a computation set.

Global exclusions can be handled by pruning out from the network graph arcs and vertices that represent links and nodes that are to be excluded, and then running the appropriate diverse path computation algorithm (see Section 9.5) on the modified graph.

Example

Let us compute two edge-disjoint paths from vertex S to vertex Z on the graph in Figure 10.1 with the edge AC specified as an exclusion for some policy-driven reason. After pruning out edge AC we will run the two edge-disjoint path computation algorithm on the remaining graph.

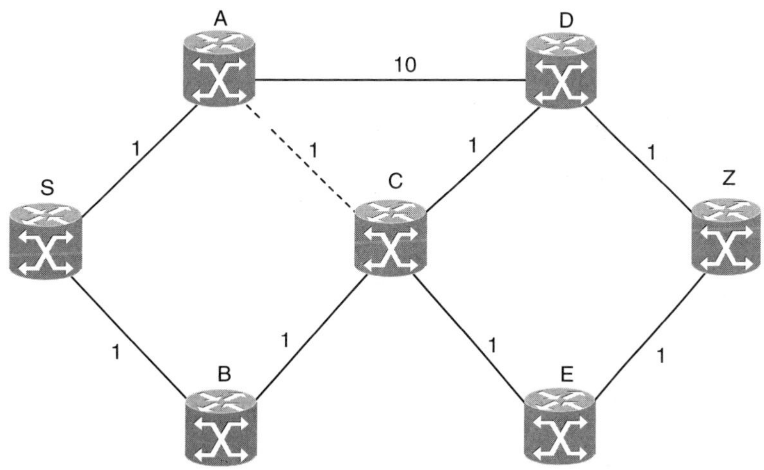

Figure 10.1 Network graph with an edge to be excluded.

The resulting paths are SADZ (12) and SBCEZ (4). Note that they are more expensive than paths SACDZ (4) and SBCEZ (4) that would be computed on the unmodified graph. Note also that if the edge CE is specified as an exclusion as well, a path computation request to compute two edge-disjoint paths from vertex S to vertex Z would fail.

10.2.2 *Handling of Link-Type Constraints*

The user may specify link-type constraints by augmenting a request with a set of link evaluation functions, and use this to compute a single path, or two or more edge-, vertex-, or best-disjoint paths. Each such evaluation function takes one or more attributes of a link as input, and returns TRUE if the link is a good candidate for one of the paths for the service to be provisioned, or FALSE otherwise. For example, the link bandwidth evaluation function takes a link's Maximum Unreserved LSP Bandwidth attribute as an input, and returns TRUE if the attribute's value for the specified priority level is larger than or equal to the bandwidth required for the new service.

Link-type constraints can be handled in a similar way to global exclusions. Specifically, during the initialization stage, an additional walk through all arcs of the graph should be performed. For every arc, all link evaluation functions should be called specifying, as input attributes of the link represented by the arc. If at least one of the functions returns FALSE, the arc should be pruned out of the graph. The execution of k (k >=2) edge-, vertex-, or best-disjoint algorithms (see Chapter 9) on the modified graph will yield optimal paths that honor the specified link-type constraints.

Note that this operation could also be performed during the path computation phase without requiring an additional walk across the graph, but this would be unwise. Link evaluation functions are not necessarily trivial, and calling each of them every time a link is evaluated (especially in multi-path computations) is less practicable than just walking through the links to discard unsuitable ones before starting the actual path computation. In other words, the choice is between evaluating each link just once using a separate walk across the graph to prune out all the unsuitable links (recommended), and evaluating each link each time it is examined by the algorithm.

10.2.3 *Handling of Inclusions*

Generally speaking the path computing entity may be requested to compute one or more edge-, vertex-, or best-disjoint paths with an additional requirement to include an ordered list of links and/or nodes in path number one (first path inclusions), an ordered list of links and/or nodes in path number two (second path inclusions), and so forth. The problem of computing k (k >= 2) disjoint paths each with its own private set of inclusions cannot be solved with the algorithms described in the previous chapter for the same reason that the problem of private exclusions cannot be solved (see Section 10.2.1). Specifically, the algorithm assumes some possible exchanges of path segments between the computed paths, and, therefore, the inclusions are guaranteed to be part of the resulting paths only if they are specified globally — that is, they are required for every path.

In many cases, however, the user just wants the service to go through a specified ordered list of nodes. This is the global inclusions path computation problem that can be formulated as a request to compute one or several edge- or best-disjoint paths, each of them crossing the specified ordered list of nodes. The global inclusions path computation problem can be solved by modification of the corresponding unconstrained diverse path computation algorithm.

Single Path Computation with Inclusions

Let us first consider computing a single path from source vertex S to destination vertex Z crossing an ordered list of nodes A, B, C, . . . , M. Considering the optimal structure of the shortest path, it is easy to prove that the shortest path from S to Z will be the shortest path from S to A appended by the shortest path from A to B appended by the shortest path from B to C, and so forth, appended by the shortest path from M to Z.

Thus, to accommodate inclusions in a single path computation we must replace shortest path computation from the service source to the service destination with multiple shortest path computations: first, from the source to the first inclusion, then, from the first inclusion to the second inclusion, and so on until the shortest path from the last inclusion to the destination. By splicing the computed paths together we will obtain the shortest path from the source to the destination that crosses the specified ordered list of vertices.

There is an issue with path computations with inclusions, however, that makes things more complicated. One may notice that nothing prevents the described algorithm from returning a path with loops.

Why can loops appear in the resulting path? First of all, the user may specify (perhaps by mistake) the list of inclusions in such a way that one or several inclusions appear in the list more than once. In this case the path computation would have no choice but to return the resulting path with a loop.

Secondly, path computations to determine segments between inclusions are performed independently, and therefore nothing prevents the segments from crossing each other. This would not happen if the subsequent segments were computed with exclusions of all vertices taken by the paths of previous segments.

Finally, if the path computation for a particular segment is constrained to exclude vertices taken by previous segments, its failure does not necessarily mean that the path for this segment and resulting path from the source to the destination does not exist. If the previous segments had taken different paths, different vertices would have been excluded from the path computation, and the path computation might have succeeded. Thus, after the failure to compute a path for a segment i, an attempt should be made to recursively re-compute all previous segments starting from segment i−1. One arc at a time should be removed from segment i−1 to force the segment path re-computation to consider other paths. Once a new path is computed for segment i−1, the path vertices should be added to the list of exclusions for segment i path computation, and a new attempt to re-compute the path for segment i should be made. If none of the new paths for segment i−1 can result in a successful path computation for segment i, new paths for segment i−2 should be considered that can ensure a successful path computation for both segments i−1 and i. This process should continue until either the paths for all segments up to and including segment i are successfully computed, or it is detected that none of the paths for the first segment can make it possible to compute non-crossing paths for all segments up to and including segment i. In the latter case the algorithm should be terminated with the "Path does not exist" return code. In the former case an attempt should be made to compute a path for segment i + 1 and so forth until a path from the last inclusion to the destination is successfully computed.

Considering all these observations, the algorithm to compute a single shortest path from source vertex S to destination vertex Z that goes through vertices A, B, . . . , M can be described as follows.

1. Make sure that the list of inclusions does not have entries that appear more than once.
2. Run a single-pair shortest path algorithm (for example, BFS) to determine the shortest path from the source to the first inclusion.
3. If the destination for the previous segment path computation is also the destination of the entire path (that is, vertex Z), terminate the algorithm and return the resulting path as the splice of all paths computed for all segments.
4. Otherwise, add vertices taken by the path determined for the previous segment to the list of exclusions. Run a single-pair shortest path algorithm that can handle exclusions to determine the path for the next segment.
5. If the path computation in step 4 is successful, go to step 3.
6. Otherwise, recursively re-compute paths for all previous segments starting from the most recent successful one, so that the path computation for the current segment succeeds.
7. If step 6 was successful, go to step 3.

8. Otherwise, terminate the algorithm and return with the "Path does not exist" return code.

Diverse Path Computation with Global Inclusions

Let us consider now how the computation algorithm for k (k >= 2) edge-disjoint paths can be modified to accommodate global inclusions (that is, an ordered list of vertices that all paths should go through).

Recall the algorithm described in Section 9.5.2. One may guess that all that has to be done is to modify step 1, leaving all other steps unchanged. Step 1 should read:

1. Run a single path computation algorithm capable of handling inclusions (like the one described above) to compute the shortest path between source vertex S and destination vertex Z that crosses the inclusion vertices A, B, ..., M in the specified order.

This guess is correct with one caveat. The algorithm requires graph transformation between path computations. Specifically, edges of the most recently computed path must be replaced with oppositely directed negative arcs. Recall that this can be done with the guarantee that such graph modifications will not introduce negative loops only if the computed path is the *shortest* path. A single path computation algorithm that honors inclusions does not guarantee, however, that the computed path is shortest. In fact, most likely it will be longer than the path computed by Dijkstra or BFS without inclusions. Thus, an adjustment is needed to make sure that the path with inclusions is no longer than any other path from the same source to the same destination. It can be done in the following way.

Suppose a path with inclusions is longer than the shortest path returned by Dijkstra or BFS by some positive value δ. Then, if we find the first edge where the shortest path diverts from the path with inclusions and increase the edge weight by δ, we will guarantee that at least this path is no shorter than the path with inclusions. We can repeat this trick several times until the cost of the shortest path returned by Dijkstra or BFS will be the same as one of the paths with inclusions. Thus, the modified algorithm that can compute k (k >= 2) edge-disjoint paths with each of them crossing an ordered list of inclusions can be stated as follows.

1. Run a single path computation algorithm capable of handling inclusions to compute the shortest path between source vertex S and destination vertex Z that crosses the inclusion vertices A, B, ..., M in the specified order.
2. If the number of path computations already performed equals the number of required paths, post-process the computed paths in the following way.
   - Walk through all the computed paths and determine all the edges that are used by any two of the paths in opposite directions.

- When such an edge is detected, remove it from both paths and swap the path tails (path segments starting on one of the edge vertices up to the destination vertex Z).
- Restore the original graph and return the resulting paths to the calling application.

3. Otherwise, make sure that there is no shorter path than the one that is computed in the most recent path computation with inclusions. For this purpose run the BFS algorithm to compute the shortest path from the source vertex S to the destination vertex Z without inclusions. If the shortest path is shorter than the path with inclusions by some value δ, find the first edge where the shortest path diverts from the path with inclusions and increase the edge weight by δ. Repeat this one or more times until the path returned by BFS algorithm is no shorter than the path with inclusions.
4. Split the edges taken by the path with inclusions into their arc components. Remove all arcs that belong to the path, excluding the arcs with negative weights; change the sign of the weights of the corresponding oppositely directed arcs (that is, make them negative).
5. Go to step 1.

Note: Swapping path tails as described by step 2 will not violate the inclusion constraint because all computed paths cross the inclusions in the same (specified) order.

The k (k >= 2) best-disjoint path computation algorithm can be modified to accommodate global inclusions exactly the same way as the k (k >= 2) edge-disjoint algorithm.

10.2.4 *Handling of Path-Type Constraints*

The user may specify path-type constraints by augmenting a request to compute one or more edge-, vertex-, or best-disjoint paths with a set of path evaluation functions. Each such function takes one or more attributes of a path as input and returns TRUE if the path is a good candidate for the service to be provisioned, or FALSE otherwise.

Path-type constraints are very important for path computation of optical trails that go over transparent networks. We will discuss such path computation in detail later in this chapter. One of the biggest challenges in computing paths over transparent networks is that the quality of the optical signal may change dramatically on its way from one point of regeneration to the next one. However, if the distance between two subsequent points of regeneration is short enough, it is reasonable to assume that the quality of the signal remains the same on the entire segment. Thus, one way to handle optical impairments is to constrain the path computation to produce the desired paths such that the length of each path segment between signal regeneration points is always less than a certain value.

Another example of path computation with path-type constraints is computing two or more paths with non-overlapping sets of SRLGs. Such paths can be considered as completely diverse and guarantee the best resilience of a transport service against network failures.

Until now all algorithms we have described have handled path computation constraints according to the following scheme: Pre-process the network graph to disallow (or, to the contrary, force) use of certain arcs and/or vertices by an unconstrained path computation algorithm; run the unconstrained path computation algorithm on the modified graph to produce resulting paths. Unfortunately, this scheme does not work for path constraints because the input for path evaluating functions — path attributes — is not defined before the path is computed. In other words, we cannot just remove "bad" arcs from the graph because arcs are bad or good only in the context of a particular path that has yet to be determined. Thus, in order to handle path-type constraints, an entirely different approach must be taken.

In the following sections we will discuss three methods that can handle path-type constraints. The first one modifies an unconstrained single-pair shortest path algorithm (say, Dijkstra or BFS) by including calls to the specified path evaluation functions that approve or the path dismiss or path segments. The second method makes use of the KSP algorithm, which is capable of determining multiple paths from the service source vertex to the service destination vertex in increasing order of path costs. Paths returned by the KSP algorithm can be evaluated by the path-evaluating functions so that the shortest path that satisfies the path constraints can be determined. Note that neither the first nor the second method works for diverse path computation. The third method is based on the Optimal Algorithm for Maximal Disjointedness. This algorithm grows all possible paths, pairs of paths, triplets of paths, and so forth, concurrently, while discarding those that violate at least one of the path-type constraints. It is computationally very expensive, although it does work for the computation of k (k >= 2) diverse paths and can handle any type of constraint, including path-type constraints, exclusions, and inclusions.

Handling Path-Type Constraints Using a Modified Single-Pair Shortest Path Algorithm

When there is a need to compute a single path from some source vertex S to destination vertex Z that satisfies the specified set of path-type constraints, a single-pair shortest path algorithm (Dijkstra or BFS) can be used, provided the algorithm is modified as described below.

Let us consider, for example, the Dijkstra algorithm. Recall that the shortest path tree is built through the process of arc relaxation, during which an arc a connecting a permanently labeled vertex u (that is, a vertex for which the shortest path has been determined already) to a non-permanently labeled vertex v is considered. If it turns out that the distance estimate of vertex v can be decreased by going through arc a because the current value $d[v] > d[u] + w(a)$. Vertex v is relabeled by assigning it the new distance estimate $d[v] = d[u] + w(a)$. Suppose, we have the algorithm call all specified path evaluation functions immediately before the re-labeling of vertex v to verify whether the path from source vertex S to vertex v going through vertex u violates any of the path-type constraints. If it does, we can block the vertex v re-labeling and thus dismiss the bad paths. With this modification it will be guaranteed that once the destination vertex D is labeled, the shortest path from vertex S to vertex D satisfies all specified path-type constraints.

One can notice that the method described here works for those path attributes/constraints for which each link on the network contributes a value of the same sign. For example, every added link will always make the path longer. If one of the constraints is that the path length must not exceed a specified value, then, once it is discovered that a path segment already exceeds the specified length, there is no point in considering the whole path any longer. The same is true for other constraints like the end-to-end delay constraint. However, there are path attributes for which links contribute differently. A good example is the end-to-end optical dispersion of the optical trail: Some links increase the dispersion, but ones that use dispersion compensation fibers and/or dispersion compensation modules (DCMs), on the contrary, decrease the dispersion. Thus, if the dispersion introduced by some path segment exceeds the specified maximum end-to-end value, it does not necessarily mean that the entire path will violate this constraint. Therefore, the path-evaluating functions for such attributes must be called only when the vertex v to be re-labeled is, in fact, the destination vertex D.

Handling Path-Type Constraints Using the KSP Algorithm

The path computation algorithm to compute a single path from some source vertex S to destination vertex Z under some set of path-type constraints can be described as follows.

1. Initialize the KSP algorithm for generating paths from vertex S to vertex Z.
2. Request the KSP algorithm to return the next shortest path from vertex S to vertex Z.
3. Compute all relevant path attributes for the retuned path and call all path-evaluating functions specified by the user. If all of the functions return TRUE, terminate the algorithm and return the path as the resulting path.
4. Otherwise, go to step 2.

Handling Path-Type Constraints Based on the Optimal Algorithm for Maximal Disjointedness

Observe that there is a common pattern in all of the path computation algorithms described above: perform some operations (for example, edge pruning) on the network graph, call some single-pair shortest path computation algorithm (for example, Dijkstra or BFS) to compute the first path, perform some more graph modifications, call BFS again to determine the second path, and so forth.

In sharp contrast with this pattern, the algorithm based on the Optimal Algorithm for Maximal Disjointedness "grows" all possible paths or combinations of paths concurrently, immediately discarding those that already violate specified path-type constraints.

Let us first consider computing a single path from some source vertex S to destination vertex Z on graph G(V,A) under some set of path-type constraints. The algorithm for such computation can be described as follows.

1. Walk through all arcs emanating from vertex S and initialize all possible paths according to the following rule: Every arc that does not violate any of the specified path-type constraints initializes a new path candidate with path cost equal to the arc weight. For example, if some arc with weight ten represents a link that has a length of 50 miles, and one of the constraints specifies that the resulting path must be no longer than 30 miles, this arc will not initialize a path candidate. Otherwise, a path candidate with cost ten will be initialized provided that other specified constraints are not violated as well.
2. Insert all path candidates into a min-priority queue keyed by path cost.
3. If the min-priority queue is empty, return with the "Path is not found" return code.
4. Otherwise, extract from the queue a path candidate with minimal path cost.
5. If the extracted path candidate is terminated by vertex Z, return the path candidate as a resulting path.
6. Otherwise, walk through all arcs emanating from the vertex that terminates the extracted path candidate and generate new path candidates by augmenting the path candidate with each arc. Verify that new path candidates do not form a loop and satisfy all constraints. Discard those that do not pass the verification, and insert the rest into the min-priority queue.
7. Go to step 3.

Note: Just as in the method described earlier that uses a modified single-pair shortest path algorithm, path attributes/constraints must be differentiated depending on whether all links contribute to the path attribute in the same way. If not, paths cannot be discarded when the path constraint is violated until they reach the destination.

Now let us consider computing k (k >= 2) paths from some source vertex S to destination vertex Z on graph G(VA) with a specified type of path-disjointedness and under some set of global path-type constraints (that is, constraints that should be satisfied by every resulting path). The algorithm for such computation can be described as follows.

1. Walk through all arcs emanating from vertex S. Discard those that violate specified path constraints. Initialize out of the rest of the arcs all possible path group candidates (duplets, triplets, and so forth, depending on k) according to the following rule: Every arc combination that does not violate the specified path-type constraints initializes a new path group candidate with sum path cost equal to the arc group sum weights. For example, if one of the specified constraints is non-overlapping with the resulting path's SRLGs, and two of the arcs have an SRLG in common, then no path group candidate will be initialized that includes the two arcs.
2. Insert all path group candidates into a min-priority queue keyed by the sum path cost.
3. If the min-priority queue is empty, return with the "Paths are not found" return code.
4. Otherwise, extract from the queue a path group candidate with minimal sum path cost.
5. If all paths of the extracted path group candidate are terminated by vertex Z, return the path candidate group as resulting paths.
6. Otherwise, generate new path group candidates by augmenting the paths of the extracted group that do not terminate on vertex Z with arcs emanating from the path-terminating vertices. Verify that none of the paths of new path group candidates forms a loop and that all of them satisfy the requested path disjointedness and specified constraints. Discard those path group candidates that have at least one path that does not pass the verification, and insert the rest into the min-priority queue.
7. Go to step 3.

Note: Generally speaking, the resulting paths will reach the destination vertex in different iterations. The rule is that after one of the paths within some path group candidate reaches the destination, it stops growing, while other paths within the group continue to grow in the following iterations until all of them reach the destination.

Handling Sets of Constraints

The approach of concurrently growing all paths toward the destination is very powerful (albeit computationally expensive). It allows us to accommodate almost any user requirement regarding the path selection. Suppose the user wants to specify a separate set of constraints for each of the paths to be determined for his service (perhaps because he has different requirements for the working and protection paths). Because all paths are determined concurrently on the *same* graph, the constraints do not have to be specified globally. If, for instance, we are computing two paths, all we need to verify before we add a new path group candidate into the min-priority queue is that one of the paths within the group satisfies one of the sets of constraints while the other path satisfies the other set. In order to handle sets of constraints we need to modify step 6 of the algorithm described in the previous section in the following way:

6. Otherwise, generate new path group candidates by augmenting paths of the extracted group that do not terminate on vertex Z with arcs emanating from the path terminating vertices. Verify that none of the paths of the new path group candidates forms a loop and that all of them satisfy the requested path disjointedness and *each of them satisfies all global constraints and a separate set of constraints*. Discard those path group candidates that have at least one path that does not pass the verification, and insert the rest into the min-priority queue.

Note that we are not talking here only about path-type constraints. Recall that when we discussed algorithms that can handle exclusions or inclusions (Sections 10.2.1 and 10.2.3) we repeatedly stated that the algorithms could handle only global exclusions/inclusions because they require the operation of "path tale swapping" — an exchange of path segments between the paths. Under these circumstances only global exclusions and inclusions can be honored. The algorithm that grows paths concurrently does not assume exchanges of path segments between the paths at any stage, and therefore can handle sets of exclusions and/or inclusions. In fact, a constraint of any type — exclusion, inclusion, link-type, or path-type — can be part of a set of constraints.

10.3 Optical Trails in Transparent Networks

Networks that include transparent optical switches present additional challenges for transport service path computation. First of all, transparent optical switches cannot perform wavelength conversion. This fact is translated for path computation into the wavelength continuity constraint: It is not sufficient for a path that has available lambda channels on every link to be considered as a candidate for a particular service — at least one channel of the same wavelength must be available on every link of the path within every isle of transparency (that is, between adjacent points of signal regeneration). Secondly, because of impairments introduced by optical fibers, amplifiers, WDM devices, and switches, the quality of the optical signal may change dramatically within isles of transparency up to a point where the signal becomes unusable. This is translated into multiple path-type constraints for the paths to be taken by services that traverse one or more isles of transparency. In the following sections we will describe what changes must be made in path computation algorithms so that the resulting paths satisfy these constraints.

Handling of Wavelength Continuity Constraint

Let us consider a network with transparent switches using the graph shown in Figure 10.2. Suppose the switches represented by vertices A, B, and C are transparent switches. What does it mean that a switch cannot perform wavelength conversion? It means that if some service traffic enters the switch over some link on a particular lambda channel (say, green), it can only exit the switch over some other link on a lambda channel of the same wavelength (also green). From the path computation point of view it also means that the switch is not a single switch. In fact, it is a group of physically collocated but independent switches, and each of them can handle links with exactly one lambda channel. Therefore, it can be presented on the network graph as a group of independent vertices (one per channel ID) with every arc associated with a link that has at most one lambda channel available. Let us call such graph a *colored graph* (see Figure 10.3). (Note that the limitations of black and white printing mean that we have to be a little creative in our representation of a colored graph on the pages of this book. The key in the bottom left corner of the figure shows how four distinct lambda channels are received at a single transparent switch, R, and how that switch may be considered as four component vertices, R–gr, R–re, R–pi, and R–bl.)

The single shortest path with the wavelength continuity constraint can be computed by running any single-pair shortest path algorithm on the network

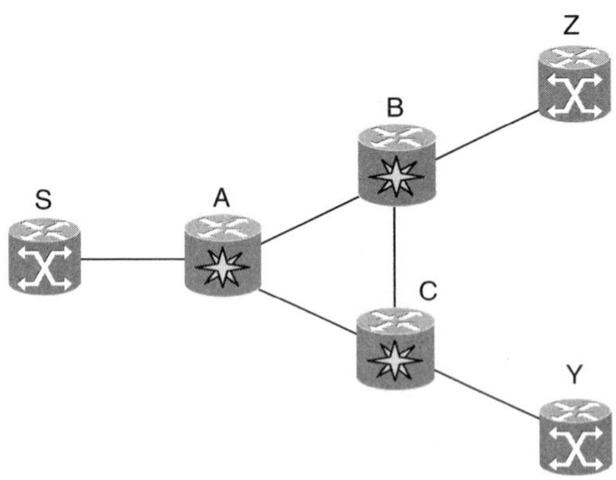

Figure 10.2 Network with transparent switches.

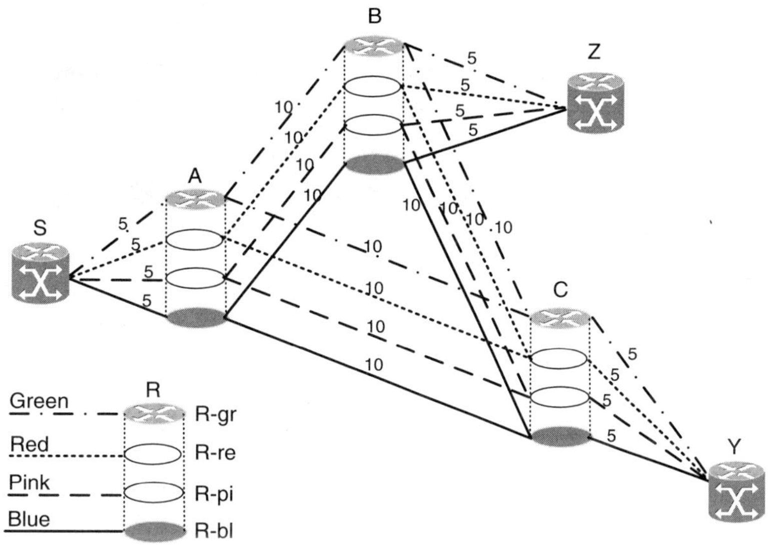

Figure 10.3 Transparent network colored graph.

colored graph. For example, one of the shortest paths from vertex S to vertex Z could be determined by the Dijkstra algorithm as SA(green)–AB(green)–BZ(green). Note that the path is determined in terms of lambda channels because every edge on the colored graph is associated with exactly one channel. The process of determining paths in terms of lambda channels is often called individual lambda routing. One remarkable feature of such computation is that paths are determined not just as sequences of links; all resources to be used on each link are identified as well. This makes the process of service setup much simpler because the biggest part of it, resource ID negotiation between every pair of adjacent nodes, is not needed. It also makes dynamic service provisioning more predictable because all network resources that are going to be allocated for the service can be known *a priori* on the service path computing node.

Unfortunately things get more complex when we try to compute k (k >=2) edge-, vertex-, or best-disjoint paths with the wavelength continuity constraint. It may seem obvious to run one of the diverse path computation algorithms on the colored graph, but recall that all these algorithms require that, starting from the second path, edges taken by previously computed path must be replaced with oppositely directed negatively weighted arcs before computing the next path. Suppose we are in the middle of the computation of two edge-disjoint paths, and a segment of the first computed path is AB(red)–BC(red) (see Figure 10.4a).

According to the algorithm for computing two edge-disjoint paths we must replace edges AB(red) and BC(red) with arcs as shown in Figure 10.4b. The question is, what must be done with the parallel colored edges that are associated

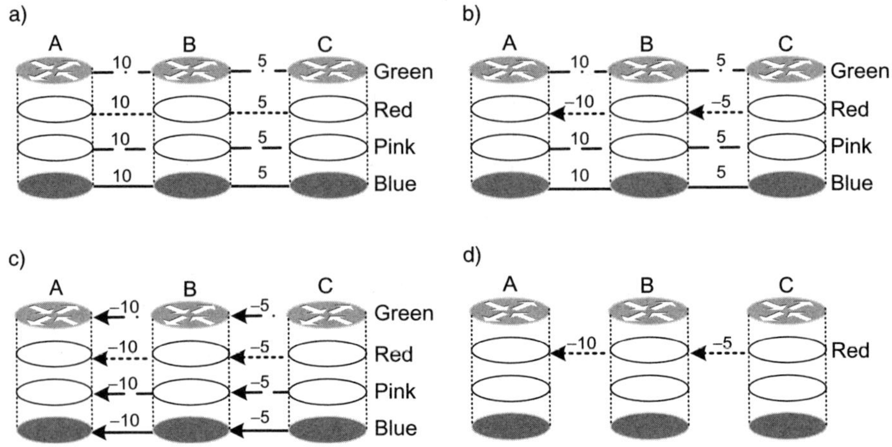

Figure 10.4 Graph transformations for the edge-disjoint path computation on the lambda channel level.

with the other channels of the links taken by the first path: edges AB(green), BC(green), AB(pink), BC(pink), and so forth?

Something must be done; otherwise, nothing would prevent the second path computation from selecting some of them for the second path, and, as a result, a service would be mapped on two paths that share some fibers, which is exactly what we want to avoid.

Maybe we should replace the edges with negatively weighted arcs as we did for edges taken by the first path (Figure 10.4c). But this would not work either, because this would encourage the second path computation to use the edges in the opposite direction. Recall that the algorithm requires detecting the edges taken by two paths going in opposite directions, removing them, and swapping the path tails. The path tail swapping would be a problem in our case, because the computed paths would use channels of different wavelengths and the resulting paths would violate the wavelength continuity constraint.

One possibility is removing the parallel edges entirely from the graph (Figure 10.4d). Such a graph transformation would encourage the second path computation to take the edges of the first path in the opposite direction only if the channel of the same wavelength is going to be assigned for the second path as it was assigned for the first path. In all other cases the second path computation would have to select links that are not taken by the first path. In our example the second path computation would be encouraged to use links CB and BA for the red channel only. This would work, but there are cases where the path computation fails when proper paths actually exist. Consider, for example, the transparent network colored graph in Figure 10.5.

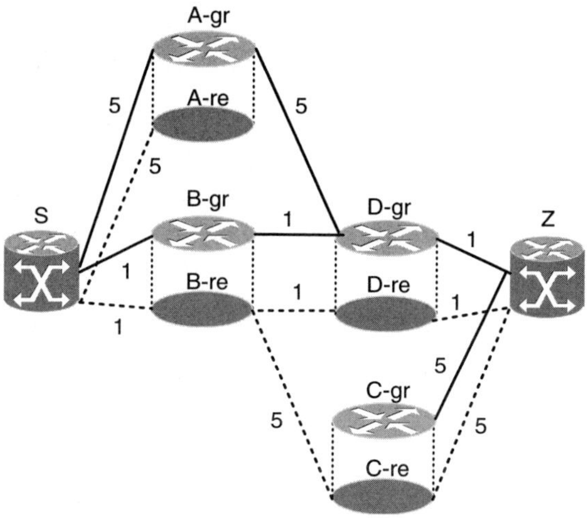

Figure 10.5 Transparent network colored graph.

Suppose links AD and BC have just one channel available, green and red, respectively. It is easy to see that if we allow only one channel of the first path's links to participate in the second path computation (Figure 10.4d), the path computation would fail. However, two edge-disjoint paths from vertex S to vertex Z satisfying the wavelength continuity constraint *do* exist: SADZ(green) and SBCZ(red). This means that we have to allow the parallel edges to participate in the second path computation (that is, we have to use the scheme in Figure 10.4c), but perform some additional graph transformations that will guarantee that the path tails can be swapped without loss of wavelength continuity on either of the paths.

The algorithm to compute two edge-disjoint paths with the wavelength continuity constraint can be described as follows.

- Compute the first shortest path on the colored graph using the Dijkstra algorithm.
- Walk along the first path from the destination to the sources; replace all the edges taken by the first path with oppositely directed arcs and make the arc weights negative. Perform the same operation for the parallel edges associated with the other channels of the first path's links on condition that *the corresponding channel is also available on the next link toward the destination* (this will guarantee that the second path segment common to both path segments could be stitched to the first path tail should the second path computation assign the channel in question to the second path). For those parallel edges that were replaced with negatively weighted arcs, perform additional operations on the arc-terminating sub-vertices.

- Connect them with the corresponding sub-vertices that belong to the first path with a single zero-weighted arc (for example, the arc B—gr–B—re in Figure 10.7).
- Remove all originating arcs external to the first path (for example, the arc D—gr–A—gr).

The last operation will guarantee that the second path segment common to both path segments could be stitched to the first path head should the second path computation assign the channel in question to the second path.

- Run the BFS algorithm to compute the second path.
- Post-process the two paths by detecting the segments that are used by both paths in opposite directions; remove such segments from both paths and swap their tails.

The progress of the algorithm to compute two edge-disjoint paths is shown in Figures 10.6 through 10.8.

Fortunately, no modifications specific to vertex-disjoint path computation are necessary because the vertex disjointedness is imposed in a way orthogonal to the wavelength continuity constraint. The algorithm for computing two vertex-disjoint paths on a colored graph can be stated as follows.

- Compute the first path using the Dijkstra algorithm.
- Perform all graph transformations as described for the edge-disjoint path computation.

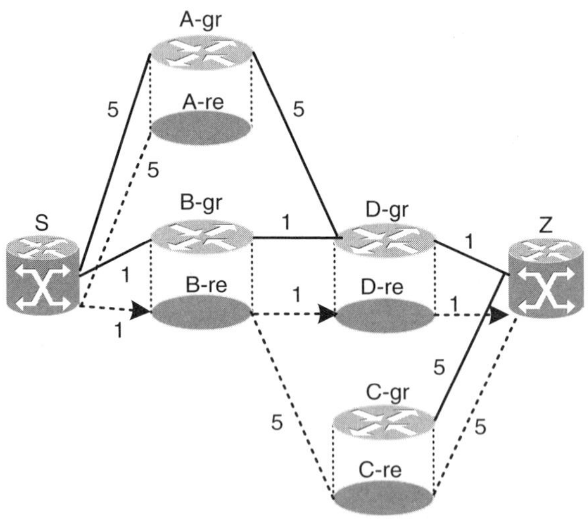

Figure 10.6 Progress of the computation of two edge-disjoint paths. First path is determined: SBDZ(red).

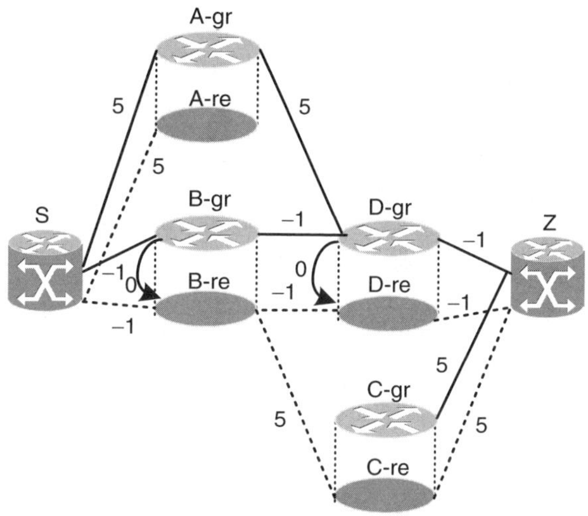

Figure 10.7 Progress of the computation of two edge-disjoint paths. Graph transformation is performed, second path is determined: SADB(green)BCZ(red).

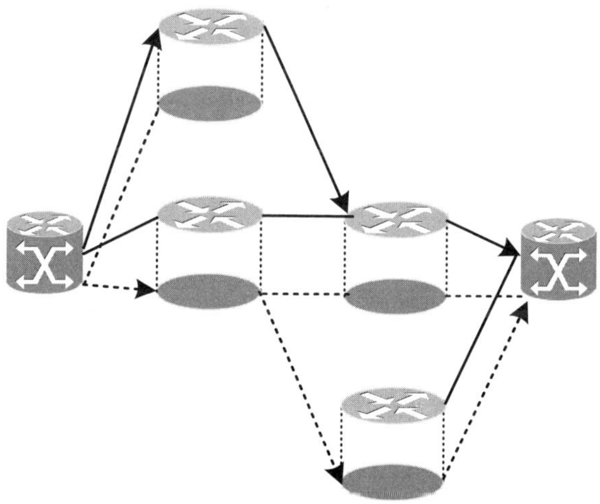

Figure 10.8 Progress of the computation of two edge-disjoint paths. Resulting paths are SADZ (green) and SBCZ (red).

- Split all sub-vertices that terminate negatively weighted arcs introduced in the previous step following the rules described in Section 9.5.3.
- Run the BFS algorithm to compute the second path.
- Collapse the split sub-vertices.

- Post-process the two paths by detecting the segments that are used by both paths in opposite directions; remove such segments from both paths and swap their tails.

An alternative approach to handling the wavelength continuity constraint is to consider it as a path-type constraint (like the SRLG non-overlapping constraint) and run a path computation algorithm that can handle path-type constraints. The algorithm described in Section 9.6.7 is a good choice for this task. Although it is computationally more expensive compared to the algorithm described in this section, it is simpler because it does not require complex graph modifications. Besides, it can handle other path-type constraints, which, as we shall see in the following section, are always required when computing paths over transparent networks.

Optical Impairments

The quality of an optical trail signal is usually characterized by two metrics: optical signal noise ratio (OSNR), and end-to-end dispersion (optical impulse widening). The two parameters directly affect the service bit error ratio (BER) — the QOS parameter visible to the user.

The quality of an optical trail signal deteriorates as the trail travels across a transparent network because of impairments introduced by the optical trail components. The OSNR and end-to-end dispersion values, however, must remain within acceptable margins by the time the signal arrives at the receiver in order to guarantee that the service BER is acceptable. This fact presents an additional challenge for optical trail path selection. It is not sufficient for a path to be considered feasible for a particular service if the path source and destination are topologically connected, and all path links satisfy the wavelength continuity constraint. It is also required that parameters identifying optical signal degradation along the path must not exceed some specified values.

One way to address the optical impairments problem is to set a limit on path segment length over isles of transparency. This means that it can be assumed with sufficient accuracy that the signal quality remains the same on the receiver as it was on the transmitter. In networks with small isles of transparency, paths can be computed either without additional constraints or with a single path-type constraint that makes sure that selected paths do not have transparent segments longer than some specified value. Such network design, however, assumes the deployment of multiple expensive wavelength converters. Networks can be much cheaper if they are totally transparent or have large isles of transparency. This comes with a price: The need to consider optical impairments during path selection.

Generally speaking, the influence of an impairment of a certain type on optical signal quality can be described as a non-linear function of the signal's initial power level, service bit rate, path link attributes, channel wavelength, and parameters describing effects of other optical signals that go through the same links or nodes as the signal in question. It would be a formidable task to account for all impairments of all types. Fortunately, ones that contribute the most to the signal quality degradation (attenuation, noise, and dispersion) tend to be cumulative and can be described as follows:

$$\text{Dimp} = \sum F(P, B, \lambda, A\varepsilon) \text{ for all } \varepsilon \in p,$$

where

Dimp is an effect of optical impairment of a particular type (for example, chromatic dispersion);

$A\varepsilon$ is a set of attributes of the εth link of path p;

P is the initial signal power level;

B is the signal bit rate;

λ is the channel wavelength;

F is a function of some level of complexity depending on the available computation resources, path computation time, required accuracy of computation, and so forth.

Important impairments to be considered are set out below.

- *Attenuation (power loss)*. Every time an optical signal goes through a passive element (fiber, wavelength multiplexer, wavelength cross-connect), it loses some power because of light absorption. For example, the standard SMF-28 fiber imposes roughly 0.25 dB/km of power loss. If, by the time the signal arrives at the receiver, its power level is too low, intrinsic receiver noise (mostly thermal noise) will introduce bit errors. Note that the original power level cannot be too high because fiber non-linearities will impair the signal. Attenuation can be considered as not dependent on the wavelength.
- *Amplified spontaneous emission (ASE) noise*. The way to fight power loss is to periodically recover the signal by optical amplification. However, this always comes with the price of added random optical noise (ASE noise), which, as it eventually accumulates, becomes the dominant noise mechanism and limits the attainable reach. Usually amplifiers are gain-locked and flattened to remove the wavelength dependence of gain. Amplifier noise is proportional to gain, roughly speaking, and, therefore, a series of low-power amplifiers is far superior in terms of added noise than a series of fewer, high-power amplifiers. For example, two 10-dB ($G = 10$) amplifiers have one-fifth the net added noise of one 20-dB ($G = 100$) amplifier.

- *Dispersion*. This is the process of optical trail broadening during light propagation within some media. Dispersion causes widening of optical impulses, and if it exceeds some threshold, adjacent bits may interfere with each other, and, as a result, the receiver may introduce additional bit errors. Dispersion happens for several reasons. The major contributor is *chromatic dispersion* — a result of having different spectral components of an optical signal traveling with different velocities. It is a function of fiber type and proportional to fiber length; for example, the standard SMF-28 fiber accrues +18 ps/nm/km. Chromatic dispersion can be managed to an extent by using dispersion-compensating fibers and installing DCMs on some links. Chromatic dispersion can be considered as independent of the choice of wavelength. One example of a minor contributor to dispersion is *polarization mode dispersion* (*PMD*). It is caused by different group velocities of the two transverse modes (x and y) of the electric field of the electro-magnetic wave during light propagation through a non-circular (elliptical) core fiber. The separate arrival of polarizations at the receiver causes additional broadening of optical impulses. PMD is wavelength dependent. Fortunately, its impact is insignificant compared to that of chromatic dispersion, and, therefore, almost always can be safely ignored.
- *Cross-talk*. This represents a collective effect of other optical signals on the signal in question. Cross-talk can be created in different components of an optical path: filters, wavelength multiplexers, wavelength cross-connects, and so forth. Cross-talk is very difficult to account for in path computation, mainly because signals going through non-local links and nodes are not known to the path computing nodes. One way to handle the cross-talk effect is to decrease path OSNR and dispersion budgets by tightening other constraints in order to make room for signal degradation related to cross-talk.

Table 10.1 lists some of the optical path elements. For each element it lists the optical impairments that the element may introduce and thereby contribute to signal degradation.

Table 10.1 List of all contributors to optical signal degradation due to optical impairments

Optical Path Element	Parameters that Influence Optical Signal Degradation
Transmitter	Power level, bit ratio
Wavelength multiplexer-de-multiplexer	Power attenuation, cross-talk
Fiber	Power attenuation, dispersion, non-linearities
Amplifier (EDFA)	Power gain, noise (ASE)
Wavelength cross-connect	Power attenuation, cross-talk
Dispersion-compensating module (DCM)	Power attenuation, dispersion compensation
Receiver	Thermal noise, bandwidth multiplication noise

Handling of Optical Impairments

To compute one or k (k >= 2) diverse paths that guarantee a certain level of optical signal quality, the following actions must be performed.

- Link attributes that affect optical signal quality must be made available to the path computation engine for every link via configuration or advertising. Examples of such attributes are fiber length, fiber type, and parameters of EDFAs and DCMs.
- The path computation request must be accompanied by a set of path-type constraints. Examples of such constraints are acceptable dispersion, power level, and noise.
- The path computation request must be accompanied by a set of path-evaluating functions. Each of them must take as parameters the current path attributes, candidate link attributes, and return new path attributes assuming that the link will be augmented to the path, and must also indicate whether the path will still satisfy one or more of the specified constraints.
- A path computation algorithm that can handle path-type constraints must be run. The algorithm described in Section 10.2.4 is a good choice for this task.

10.4 Further Reading

Further information about path computation in optical networks can be found in the following texts:

Multiwavelength Optical Networks: A Layered Approach by Thomas E. Stern and Krishna Bala (1999), Prentice Hall PTR.

Optical Networks: A Practical Perspective by Rajiv Ramaswami and Kumar Sivarajan (2001), Morgan Kaufmann.

Mesh-based Survivable Transport Networks: Options and Strategies for Optical, MPLS, SONET and ATM Networking by Wayne D. Grover (2003), Prentice Hall PTR.

Survivable Optical WDM Networks (Optical Networks) by Canhui (Sam) Ou and Biswanath Mukherjee (2005), Springer.

Survivable Networks—Algorithms for Diverse Routing by Ramish Bhandari (1999), Kluwer Academic Publishers.

CHAPTER 11

Point-to-Multipoint GMPLS

GMPLS is a very young and rapidly growing technology. Users and providers of transport services, and vendors of transport network equipment and management systems watch all areas of the development of GMPLS very closely. Features, applications, frameworks and architectural solutions, protocol standards, interoperability events, and scientific and marketing research all contribute to the rapid forward motion of GMPLS. The enthusiasm with which new directions are developed within GMPLS, and the importance placed on these developments by the Service Providers and equipment vendors, arise because of the potential revenues and services that the technology promises to deliver if it is successful.

In this chapter we will discuss an example of such an application — GMPLS Point-to-Multipoint (P2MP) Traffic Engineering. It relies very heavily on the concepts, principles, solutions, and techniques described in the previous chapters. At the time of writing, Point-to-Multipoint GMPLS is in the early stages of discussion and standardization.

Chapter 12 describes Layer One Virtual Private Networks, another example of a GMPLS application that is in the early stages of development.

11.1 GMPLS Point-to-Multipoint Traffic Engineering

So far, while discussing transport services, we have always assumed that each service had exactly one source and exactly one destination. However, there are applications that require data delivery from a single source to multiple destinations. Examples of such applications are IP Multicast, VPN Multicast, Content Distribution, Interactive Multimedia, and many others. These applications need point-to-multipoint transport services — that is, services that can deliver data from a single source to multiple destinations. Hence there is an opportunity for transport Service Providers to sell very complex and valuable services that could deliver significant revenues.

Should point-to-multipoint services be traffic engineered? Yes, without a doubt. Traditionally such services have relied on multicast routing protocols (for example, PIM). Just as in the case of point-to-point services, the hop-by-hop data delivery paradigm provided via forwarding tables built by the routing protocols does not account for network resource availability on TE links, nor any other path computation constraints such as resource colors, SRLGs, link protection, and switching capabilities. Hence the only QoS class that can be offered is best effort. Also there is no way for a network operator to exclude or impose the use of certain links and nodes in the data distribution tree. Furthermore, service recovery from network failures cannot be achieved within acceptable time limits — the only option is to rely on routing protocol convergence.

All of these problems are successfully addressed for point-to-point services by using GMPLS-based Traffic Engineering (see Chapter 8). Therefore, the first solution that might come to mind is to break a point-to-multipoint problem into multiple point-to-point problems: specifically, to establish a set of point-to-point TE tunnels from the source to each of the destinations. This solution will work, but only in some cases, and even when it does, it could be sub-optimal. To understand this, let us consider the optical transport network presented in Figure 11.1.

Suppose we need to provide a service that delivers the same data from node A to each of nodes B, C, D, E, H, and I. We can map the service onto six point-to-point tunnels: A-B, A-B-C, A-B-C-D, A-F-G-E, A-F-G-I, and A-F-H, respectively. One can see that such a mapping would require, for example, four optical channels on link AF, each of them carrying the same data traffic (this is the same service). Let us assume that link AF has only one channel available. Could the service be successfully established and functional in this case? Yes, provided that we abandon the attempt to operate six point-to-point LSPs, and that node F is capable of performing replication of the data received over link AF onto links FH and FG.

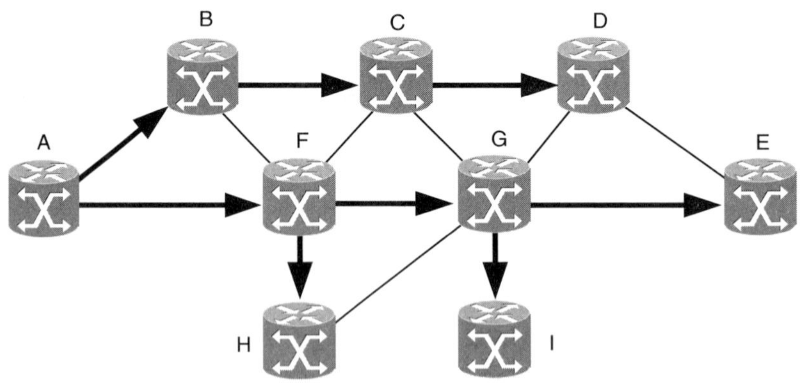

Figure 11.1 A point-to-multipoint service delivered in a mesh network.

In general, if all nodes involved in a point-to-multipoint data distribution are capable of replicating data, there is no reason why there should be more than one channel allocated per link per service. Thus, instead of establishing distinct tunnels resulting in data replication on the source, a better solution is to set up tunnels that share resources on common links. Then, with appropriate path computation, all components of a point-to-multipoint data distribution tree could be determined in such a way that data replication points (such as nodes B, C, F, and G in our example) will be as close as possible to the destinations, making more efficient use of network resources.

Fortunately the RSVP-TE signaling protocol provides resource sharing for LSPs that are signaled with the *Shared Explicit* reservation style and a common SESSION object. The question arises as to what to assign for the Session Tunnel End-Point Address. In point-to-point GMPLS, the field is used to specify the address of the egress node for the tunnel (that is, the LSP destination address). Obviously, several LSPs with different destinations cannot have a common SESSION object, and cannot share resources. Thus the individual LSPs supporting the point-to-multipoint service (each to a different destination) would be unable to share resources. One solution would be to use the destination address of one of the LSPs for the Session Tunnel End-Point Address of the SESSION object used by all of the LSPs. However, such an approach would make this LSP somehow distinct from the others and special. For instance, what would happen if the destination associated with the SESSION object needed to be disconnected from the service? Its removal would make the Session Tunnel End-Point Address value semantically unrelated to the service, or would require the entire set of LSPs supporting the service to be re-signaled with a new SESSION object. Note that in the latter case the make-before-break operation is not an option because it relies on the persistence of the SESSION object. Besides, from an application perspective, a service is required to be permanently and unambiguously identified network-wide throughout the lifetime of the service.

A clear alternative is to use some arbitrary identifier of the group of destinations in the Session Tunnel End-Point Address of the SESSION object for all of the LSPs. However, this would contradict the current semantics of that field, which should contain a routable address of the egress of the tunnel. Therefore, the team designing the P2MP protocol extensions decided to introduce a new format (a new c-type) for the SESSION object for the purposes of point-to-multipoint signaling. The new object has a 32-bit P2MP ID in place of the Session Tunnel End-Point Address, and this must be set to some number (for example, a multicast group ID) that is unique within the context of the Extended Tunnel ID (which is usually set to the source address, making it globally unique), and that is not modified across the lifetime of the point-to-multipoint service (that is, as long as there is at least one destination still connected to the service).

The idea of resource sharing among LSPs associated with the same point-to-multipoint service and the introduction of the new semantics for the SESSION object are the two most important concepts of the framework for point-to-multipoint traffic engineering, which was developed by the joint efforts of the MPLS and CCAMP IETF Routing Area Working Groups. The major objectives of the framework were as follows.

- To introduce a way of dynamically provisioning traffic engineered point-to-multipoint services in the same or a similar way, and subject to the same set of constraints, as for point-to-point services, so that the required QoS can be guaranteed to:
  - efficiently map point-to-multipoint services onto network resources
  - provide an efficient and scalable way of adding new, and removing existing, destinations to/from active point-to-multipoint services
  - make it possible for point-to-multipoint services to recover from network failures within acceptable time limits
  - provide a way for point-to-multipoint service re-optimization (full or partial) in the event that better paths become available after the service setup has completed.

11.1.1 *TE Point-to-Multipoint Related Definitions*

Let us define a *Point-to-Multipoint* (*P2MP*) *tunnel* as a service that delivers data traffic with specified characteristics from a single source (*P2MP tunnel root* or simply *root*) to one or more destinations (*P2MP tunnel leaves* or simply *leaves*) with an agreed-upon quality of service, blocking probability, and resilience against network failures.

A *P2MP tree* (see Figure 11.2) is a graphical representation of all TE links that are committed for a particular P2MP tunnel. In other words, a P2MP tree is a representation of the corresponding P2MP tunnel on the network TE graph. A *P2MP sub-tree* is a part of a P2MP tree describing how the root or an intermediate node is connected to a particular subset of leaves. A *P2MP branch* is a part of a P2MP sub-tree describing how a particular branch node that belongs to the sub-tree is connected to a subset of leaves.

A *P2MP LSP* could be defined as a sequence of network resources interconnected in a certain way so that they can provide data delivery from LSP ingress (one of the tunnel nodes that is usually, but not necessarily, the root) to all LSP egresses (some of the tunnel nodes that are usually, but not necessarily, leaves).

A P2MP tunnel could be mapped onto (that is, supported by) one or multiple P2MP LSPs. The case of mapping a P2MP tunnel onto more than one P2MP LSP is defined as the *P2MP tunnel decomposition*. It is accomplished by decomposing

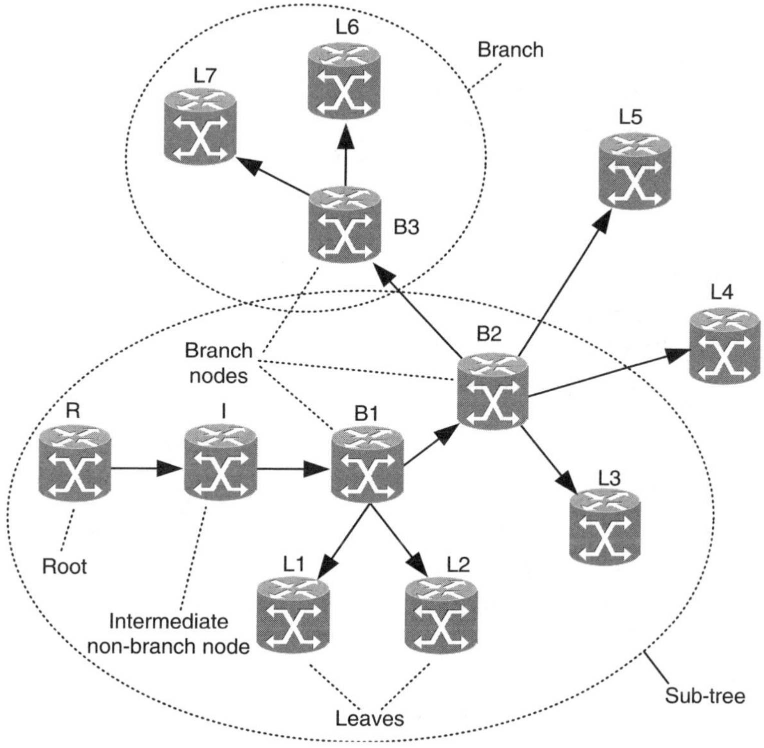

Figure 11.2 Point-to-multipoint tree components.

the corresponding P2MP tree into multiple sub-trees. Each sub-tree starts at the root or at an intermediate node and terminates at a subset of intermediate nodes or leaves. Each sub-tree is provisioned as a *separate* P2MP LSP, which could be managed — modified, re-optimized, torn down, and so forth — independently from other LSPs related to the same tunnel. P2MP LSPs may have distinct or overlapping sets of egresses. In our example in Figure 11.1, the P2MP tunnel could be mapped onto a single P2MP LSP: (A-B-C-D, A-(F-(G-E, G-I), F-H)); or, for example, two separate P2MP LSPs: A-B-C-D and A-(F-(G-E, G-I), F-H).

A *P2MP branch node* (or simply a *branch node*) is a node that performs data replication for the P2MP tunnel. Note that *branching* is a data plane function only and should not be confused with origination of a separate P2MP LSP (which can be seen as branching in the control plane). Nodes B1, B2, and B3 (see Figure 11.2) are examples of branch nodes. Note that the root could be also a branch node (for instance, node A in Figure 11.1). Furthermore, a leaf can also be a branch node (for example, node B in Figure 11.1). Such leaf-and-branch nodes are called *P2MP buds* or simply *buds*.

It is important to keep in mind that all P2MP LSPs of a particular P2MP tunnel share resources on common links, but have separate distinct control plane states. It is also very important to understand that from the data plane viewpoint a P2MP tunnel is always mapped onto a single monolithic data distribution tree, irrespective of the number of P2MP LSPs that have been provisioned for the tunnel. In other words, the provisioning of a single P2MP LSP with a full set of leaves results in the same tunnel data plane state as the provisioning of multiple P2MP LSPs, each with a single leaf or a subset of leaves.

In addition to the usual provisioning operations such as tunnel setup, teardown, and optimization, there are several operations that are unique to P2MP tunnels. They are grafting, pruning, leaf-initiated join, and leaf-initiated drop. *Grafting* is defined as the process of connecting one or more additional leaves to an operational P2MP tunnel by the initiative of the root or an intermediate node. *Leaf-initiated join* (*LIJ*), on the other hand, is the process of connecting a new leaf to a P2MP tunnel by the initiative of the leaf. Likewise, *pruning* is the procedure by which the tunnel root or an intermediate node disconnects one or more leaves from the tunnel, and *leaf initiated drop* (*LID*) is a way for a leaf to disconnect itself from the tunnel.

11.2 Point-to-Multipoint Tree Computation

A P2MP tree may be determined in a variety of ways. It could be fully computed or fully specified via configuration. It is also possible that a network operator specifies a P2MP tree as a root, a set of leaves, and an ordered lists of intermediate nodes and/or links that the tree should traverse from the root to all or some of the leaves. In the latter case the entity that computes the P2MP tree is expected to fill the "gaps" between the specified nodes/links, and thus produce a P2MP tree that satisfies the specified preferences. The path computation entity could also be requested to compute diverse paths for some or all segments of the resulting tree to provide recovery segments for the tunnel.

In general the path computation problem for a traffic engineered P2MP tunnel can be stated similarly to that for a point-to-point (P2P) tunnel: Compute a P2MP tree subject to a set of constraints for a tunnel that is designed to carry traffic with a set of parameters from the tunnel root to a set of leaves.

In Chapter 10 we discussed in detail the aspects, techniques, and algorithms of the constraint-based path computation of traffic engineered P2P tunnels. One way to solve the P2MP tree computation problem is to break it into multiple P2P path computations with an additional constraint of encouraging selected paths to share common links.

Let us consider the weighted network graph presented in Figure 11.3.

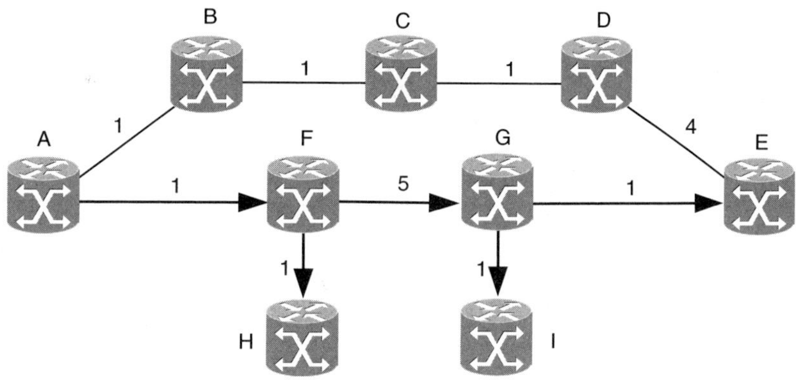

Figure 11.3 P2MP tree from A to I, H, and E.

Suppose there is a need to compute a P2MP tree from node A to nodes I, H, and E. This could be done according to the following algorithm.

- Compute the shortest path subject to all constraints from the root (node A) to the first leaf (node I). The resulting path is A-F-G-I.
- Assign cost 0 to all arcs taken by the first path and compute the shortest path from the root to the second leaf (node E). The resulting path is A-F-G-E. Note that such cost assignment seems to be a reasonable thing to do, because once traffic is delivered over a link for one leaf, there is no extra cost (that is, no extra resources required) to deliver the data over this link to another leaf, and hence the path selection process should be encouraged to use the links that are already selected for the tunnel.
- Assign cost 0 to all arcs taken by the second path and compute the path from the root to the third leaf (node H).
- Repeat the process until paths are computed from the root to every leaf in the specified set.

This algorithm is simple and has another valuable quality: It does not require knowledge of all leaves during tree computation; thus, additional leaves can be incrementally added to the tree after it is originally computed. Equally important is the fact that these additions do not alter the paths to the existing leaves and hence do not cause the reconfiguration of the entire tunnel every time a new leaf is added.

The major problem with this approach is that the tree it produces depends on the order in which the component paths are computed and could be sub-optimal. For example, what would happen if the first leaf in the set is node E

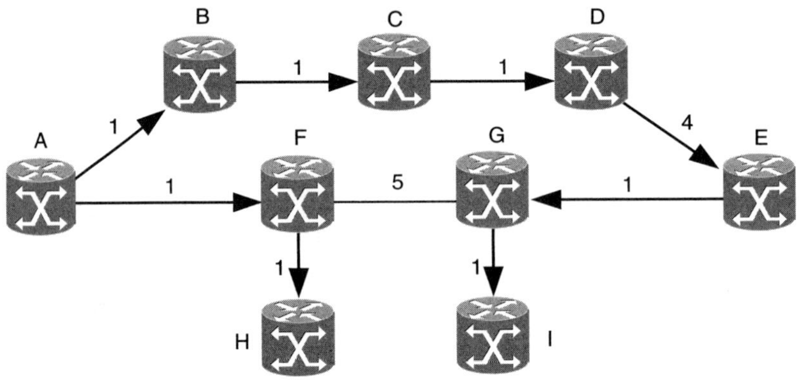

Figure 11.4 P2MP tree from A to E, I, and H.

instead of node I? The resulting tree in this case would be as shown in Figure 11.4.

To overcome the dependency on leaf ordering, the tree could be computed as a *Steiner* tree — a tree in a weighted graph that spans a given subset of vertices (*Steiner Points*) with the minimal total weights on its edges.

Formally the Steiner tree computation problem (the Steiner Problem) could be stated as follows:

Let $G=(V, E, d)$ be an undirected graph in metric space, where V is the set of vertices in G, E is the set of edges in G, and d is the metric distance method. Let S be a subset of V.

Let $D(g) = \text{sum } d(ei)$, where g is a graph with indexed edges ei. Let X be the set of trees in G which span S.

Find the element of X, $T=(V',E',d)$, such that $D(T) = inf\{D(x) : x \text{ element of } X\}$

The Steiner problem is NP-complete. Matters are even more complicated because the resulting tree must satisfy TE constraints. However, one can find in the literature and at Internet sites numerous heuristic algorithms that approximate the result within polynomial time (for more details about Steiner trees see the references in the *Further Reading* section at the end of this chapter).

Steiner tree computation guarantees the cheapest resulting tree. However, adding or removing a single leaf to/from the set may result in an entirely different tree. This is not much of a problem if leaves are seldom added to or removed from the tree, and if the additions and removals occur in large batches. However, if they are added or removed frequently and one at a time, the tunnel reconfiguration provisioning may prove to be too heavy, and may even cause network destabilization.

Therefore, a good compromise could be achieved if the tree is computed as follows:

- Use Steiner tree computation to compute a tree for the initial set of leaves known at the time of the tunnel setup.
- Every time a new leaf needs to be connected to the tunnel, compute appropriate sub-tree(s) using the incremental tree computation algorithm described at the beginning of this section.
- Every time a leaf needs to be disconnected from the tunnel, remove the corresponding sub-tree(s) of the tunnel without tree re-computation.
- Run Steiner tree computation periodically, and re-optimize the tunnel accordingly.

11.2.1 *P2MP-Related Advertisements*

Tree computation for P2MP TE tunnels requires additional path computation constraints to those used in the point-to-point constraint-based path computation (see Chapters 8 and 10 for details). This is because some nodes cannot participate in all or some aspects of P2MP tunnel provisioning or data distribution due to hardware limitations or lack of proper software. For instance, some nodes can terminate a P2MP LSP and hence function as P2MP leaves, but cannot provide data replication — that is, cannot work as branch nodes. A node may not be upgraded with proper signaling software (supporting P2MP), and thus could not be root, branch, or leaf, and could only function under certain limited circumstances (see below) as a non-branch intermediate node. Ignoring these facts during tree computation would lead to a higher blocking probability during P2MP tunnel provisioning. Therefore the IETF is working on a way for a node to advertise whether or not it supports P2MP signaling, and, if so, which of the roles (root, branch, leaf, bud) it can play in the data plane.

Note that a node that does not have P2MP signaling capabilities may still function as a transit node of a P2MP tunnel. However, this is only possible if it is placed inside a hierarchical or stitched LSP (see Chapter 8) interconnecting P2MP-capable nodes. Consider node C in Figure 11.4. It may know nothing about P2MP, yet still be a part of the P2MP tunnel presented in the figure. This is possible if, for example, nodes B and D are

- P2MP capable
- Capable of terminating a hierarchical LSP or stitching segment going through node C.

Therefore, the capabilities of nodes that originate and terminate hierarchical LSPs and stitching segments is also a very important piece of information that must be available to P2MP tree computation entities and needs to be advertised.

11.3 Signaling Point-to-Multipoint Tunnels

11.3.1 *P2MP Tunnel Setup*

It may seem that the problem of P2MP tunnel provisioning could be addressed in a very simple way. Consider the network presented in Figure 11.5. Suppose a P2MP tree with a root at node A and leaves at nodes H, M, and J is computed to follow the path shown (bold lines with arrows) in the figure. It may seem that all that has to be done is to signal separate point-to-point LSPs from node A to nodes H, M, and J, respectively, with the *Shared Explicit* reservation style and a common SESSION object. Indeed, according to RFC 3209, all three LSPs will share resources on links AD and DI, making data replication happen on branch node I. This seems to meet our requirement to push data replication points as close as possible to the tunnel termination points. There is also a useful byproduct of such signaling. If some time later, after the tunnel has been established and

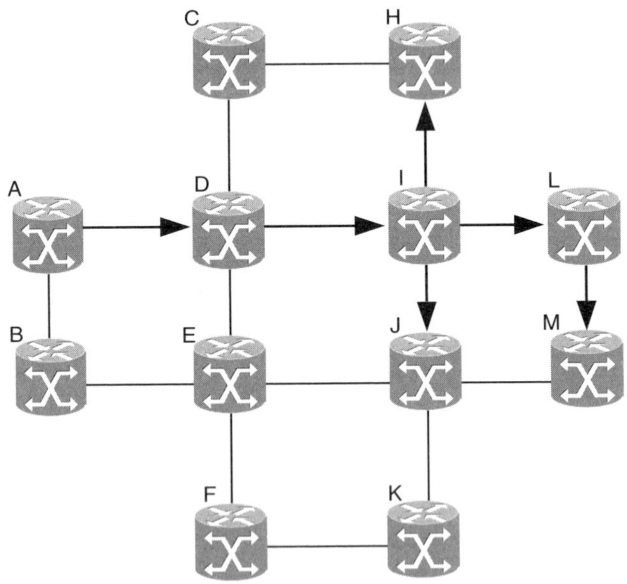

Figure 11.5 P2MP tunnel signaling.

is functioning, there is a need to remove from the tunnel, say, leaf M, or to add leaf K, there will be no problem in doing so. The corresponding LSPs could be torn down or set up using regular, well-defined procedures independently from each other as well as from other LSPs related to the tunnel.

The major problem with such an approach is in the control plane. Consider the tunnel provisioning and management from the viewpoint of, say, node D. Note that it has to keep full states for all three LSPs. The states are almost identical, with the requested/recorded path tails (ERO/RRO) as the only exception. Thus, there is an obvious sub-optimality in the RSVP state memory usage. Besides, each of the states must be separately updated by RSVP Path and Resv refresh messages, and each of the updates must be processed. This results in unnecessary control channel bandwidth and controller CPU consumption. And what if there are 10,000 leaves instead of three? The approach of keeping full state on every controller for each leaf of each P2MP tunnel does not scale particularly well.

An alternative solution is to signal a single P2MP multi-leaf LSP instead of multiple P2P LSPs. The IETF is currently working on a solution that does just this by introducing three new objects. These are the Leaf ID object, the SUB-ERO, and the SUB-RRO (not to be confused with the SEROs and SRROs used in LSP segment recovery signaling; see Chapter 7 for details). Leaf ID objects are used in the P2MP LSP Setup (RSVP Path) message to identify each of the leaves signaled for the LSP. SUB-EROs are used to specify paths toward all but the first leaf. Each SUB-ERO path runs from an intermediate node present in the ERO or another SUB-ERO, so that the full path to the leaf can be deduced. At a minimum, these paths include path-originating nodes and corresponding leaves (as loose hops), but may also (and are likely to) include all or some other nodes or links that have been computed and/or configured to be part of the paths. Note that the first leaf of a P2MP LSP does not require identification, and the path from the root toward the first leaf is specified in the ERO object. The Leaf ID and SUB-ERO association is called the *Leaf Descriptor* in this book. The processing rules for Leaf Descriptors are not trivial (see the next section).

Let us now go back to our example. When a P2MP LSP is signaled for the tunnel presented in Figure 11.5 (root, node A; leaves, nodes H, M, and J), node D receives a single P2MP LSP Setup message containing the ERO {A-D-I-H} and two Leaf Descriptors {M, I-L-M} and {J, I-J}. Note that such signaling contains a concise set of information needed for tunnel provisioning without any repetition. For instance, the signaling session and sender identifications, bandwidth, and protection requirements are specified only once (not three times as in the case of the single leaf LSP approach). Node D creates and manages a single state (not three states) for the tunnel.

Node D detects zero local Leaf Descriptors; therefore, it originates no new branches. Node I, on the other hand, realizes that both Leaf Descriptors are local and originates two additional P2MP LSP Setup messages: one for branch I-J and another for branch I-L-M. Node I removes both Leaf Descriptors from the incoming message. Thus, node L, for instance, while processing the incoming P2MP LSP Setup message, will encounter none of them. In the data plane, node I works out that it needs to receive data on one link (D-I) and send it out over three links (I-H, I-L, and I-J). Therefore, it allocates the necessary resources (for example, optical channels) on all four links and programs the cross-connect so that necessary data replication can be achieved.

When the P2MP LSP Setup message reaches a leaf, the latter triggers a P2MP LSP Accept (RSVP Resv) message in the opposite direction in the usual way (as in the case of P2P signaling). When the P2MP LSP Accept message arrives at a branch node, the node has a choice either to forward the message upstream toward the root, or wait for some time to collect P2MP LSP Accept messages for all or some of the other branches and send a single aggregate P2MP LSP Accept message upstream. Clearly, in the latter case fewer P2MP LSP Accept messages are required and the solution will scale better, but the delay to the establishment of the P2MP tunnel to some of the leaves may be an unwarranted trade-off. An option is to delay the first P2MP LSP Accept message for only a very short period, but to delay subsequent ones for longer. The first P2MP LSP Accept message will ensure that data flows to the branch node (and hence to all leaves that have sent P2MP LSP Accept messages) and other leaves can be added at the branch without being impacted by the delay to their own P2MP LSP Accept messages.

It is usually important for each node involved in P2MP signaling to obtain information about the actual tree taken by the tunnel. As in the case of P2P signaling, this is achieved through the use of RROs. However, when P2MP LSP Accept messages are aggregated on branch nodes, the RROs from incoming P2MP LSP Accept messages are copied into the SUB-RROs of outgoing aggregates. Suppose node I (Figure 11.5) receives three P2MP LSP Accept messages from each of the leaves and decides to send the P2MP LSP Accept aggregate to node D. Let us assume that the label recording was not requested. The RROs of each of the received message are updated by prepending the IDs of corresponding local links. Thus, the resulting RROs will be as follows: IL-LM; IJ; IH. One of the RROs (say, the first) is used as an RRO of the aggregate; two others are encoded in the outgoing message as SUB-RROs.

It is important to be able to establish P2MP LSPs in an alarm-free manner. As in the case of P2P LSP provisioning, this can be achieved by setting up the LSPs with alarm detection initially disabled on all nodes, and enabling the alarm after the first P2MP LSP Accept message arrives at the root by sending a P2MP LSP Modify message with an appropriately modified AdminStatus object. A minor challenge is not to enable alarms prematurely on the branches for which the P2MP LSP Accept message has not yet been received. One way to solve this is for the branch nodes to block the propagation onto such branches of all P2MP LSP Modify messages.

To assist in the data plane trouble-shooting process, the P2MP capable control plane should be capable of signaling alarms detected by any P2MP LSP nodes among other nodes of the LSP. This can be achieved strictly following the procedures in the IETF's Alarm Propagation specification: There are no differences compared with P2P LSP management.

11.3.2 *Processing Leaf Descriptors*

A node that processes a P2MP LSP Setup message starts the processing of encoded Leaf Descriptors by dividing them into two groups: *local* (those whose first SUB-ERO sub-object is associated with a locally configured IP address) and *pass-through* (all others or those that cannot be classified as local).

For each local Leaf Descriptor the following logic is applied. First, a path computation is performed for the purpose of expanding its SUB-ERO if necessary (as usual, such computation is needed if the first sub-object associated with a non-local IP address is flagged as *loose*). The subsequent processing depends on whether the expanded SUB-ERO describes a path whose head matches one of the existing LSP branches or not.

In the former case the SUB-ERO is modified in the following way: Its leading sub-objects are removed up to (but not including) the sub-object that is associated with the node where the path described by the SUB-ERO diverts from the matching branch, or that has its immediate *next* sub-object flagged as loose. By doing so the Leaf Descriptor's status is changed from local to non-local and the Descriptor is moved into the outgoing P2MP LSP Setup message associated with the branch.

In the latter case (where the path described by the SUB-ERO diverts from all of the existing branches locally), the processing node realizes that it needs to start a new branch; hence an additional P2MP LSP Setup message is originated. The new message inherits all objects from the incoming message with the exception of the ERO and Leaf Descriptors. The contents of the SUB ERO are copied into the ERO of the new message. Some pass-through Leaf Descriptors are left in the original message and some are moved into the new one.

The distribution depends on the P2MP tree topology; specifically, on whether the first node of a pass-through Leaf Descriptor's SUB-ERO is located on the branch associated with the original (incoming) or the new P2MP LSP Setup message. Generally speaking, such separation is not a trivial task and may require iterations through the message processing functions. It is possible, however, to impose certain rules on how Leaf Descriptors should be originally encoded. For instance, it is possible to oblige a node originating a P2MP LSP Setup to encode all Leaf Descriptors in the tree using *depth-first* ordering according to the algorithm in Table 11.1.

Making the assumption that SUB-EROs are encoded in depth-first order significantly simplifies matters, because a node that processes a P2MP LSP Setup message is able to sort pass-through Leaf Descriptors according to their position in the incoming message, and place them into proper outgoing messages.

Table 11.1 Algorithm to perform depth-first ordering of leaf descriptors

```
ENCODE_SUB_TREE(branch node b, leaf l, leaves L)
1. encode SUB_ERO(b, l)
2. do for every branch node b′ in the SUB_ERO starting from the closest to b
3.     select any leaf l′ from L that has a path from b
4.     call ENCODE_SUB_TREE(b′, l′, L)
ENCODE TREE (root r, leaves L)
1. Select any leaf l from L
2. encode ERO (r, l)
3. do for every branch node b in the ERO starting from the closest to r
4.     select a leaf l′ from L that has a path from b
5.     call ENCODE_SUB_TREE(b, l′, L)
```

11.3.3 *P2MP Tunnel Teardown*

To tear down a P2MP LSP, the LSP originator sends a P2MP LSP Release (RSVP PathTear) message. If the message contains an empty list of Leaf IDs, the entire LSP is torn down. However, if the message contains a non-empty list of Leaf IDs, only resources that were *exclusively* allocated for the purpose of provisioning paths toward the associated leaves are released (and the corresponding control plane states are removed).

Graceful P2MP LSP shutdown could be achieved by disabling alarm reporting on all LSP nodes and then triggering the LSP teardown.

11.3.4 *Handling of Failures*

Signaling or resource reservation of a P2MP LSP may fail on one or more nodes or links during LSP establishment. This may happen because of hardware problems, software crashes, configuration errors, lack of proper protocol support, and so on. It also may happen because the P2MP tree was computed without considering all necessary constraints, or because the Traffic Engineering Database (TED) used for tree computation did not contain some important advertisements or was not updated in a timely manner. As in the case of P2P signaling, nodes located upstream from the point of failure (that is, closer to the root) and having the necessary level of flexibility (usually those that participate in the distributed tree computation) may try to recover from failure(s) by re-computing alternative paths or segments of paths, hopefully taking into account the crankback information provided by failure-detecting nodes.

How should we handle the situation where the P2MP LSP fails to set up to one or more leaves, while the LSP is successfully established to other leaves? Normally, when a setup failure is detected, resources are released and control plane states are removed only as far as the nearest upstream branch node. The P2MP LSP is still considered to be successfully established as long as a data plane path is provisioned from the LSP ingress node to at least one of the leaves. However, it is possible to signal a P2MP LSP with a P2MP Integrity attribute. This causes the entire LSP to fail if the path to any one of the leaves fails to set up.

As will be discussed in the next section, a P2MP tree can be decomposed into several sub-trees with each of them signaled as a separate P2MP LSP. Note that nothing prevents us from signaling some of the LSPs with and some without the P2MP Integrity attribute. This could result in some LSPs connecting all specified leaves to the tunnel, while other LSPs provide data paths to only some leaves (or possibly just one leaf) from the set.

11.4. P2MP Tunnel Decomposition

Signaling a single P2MP LSP with all leaves specified in a single message is obviously a better approach from the scalability point of view (number of messages, CPU time, memory, and so on) than signaling of multiple single-leaf LSPs. Unfortunately P2MP multi-leaf signaling has problems of its own, and some of them are quite unusual.

For instance, a P2MP LSP Setup or Accept message that is necessary to provision a P2MP LSP with a large number of leaves spanning a large network topology may not fit into a single IP datagram. Note that a similar problem in the P2P context could be discarded as unrealistic.

The general solution for such a problem is to rely on IP fragmentation; however, it is widely recognized that this does not perform well and may cause numerous problems. Therefore, P2MP Traffic Engineering, like many other network applications that rely on IP connectionless communication, explicitly requires all provisioning messages to fit within a single IP datagram.

Furthermore, a P2MP tunnel signaled as a single P2MP LSP is awkward to manage. Consider changing the route to some leaf, or adding a leaf to an existing tunnel with 1000 leaves. This could be done by issuing a P2MP LSP Modify (a new RSVP Path) message from the root, but would result in potentially extensive processing at every transit LSR along the path to the final branch as each node checks through all of the SEROs to see whether there is a change to the tree for which it must take action. Further, some implementations might cause such P2MP LSP Modify messages to be propagated throughout the whole tree causing all LSRs to perform extra work. What is more, there could be a requirement to apply

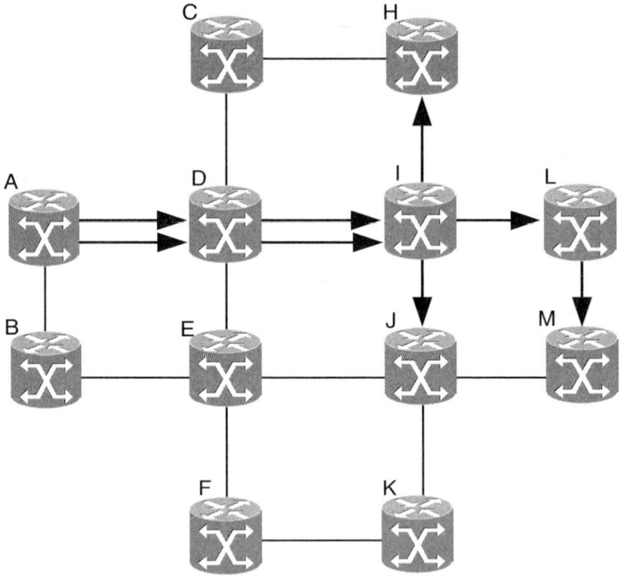

Figure 11.6 P2MP tunnel decomposition.

different policies to different sets of leaves, making the use of a single P2MP LSP undesirable.

In this respect the approach of signaling separate LSPs for each destination is better, because any management operation applied to a particular leaf will result in the processing of a small message, and each leaf can be provided with individual treatment. On the other hand, a management change intended to apply to a set of leaves would require multiple P2MP LSP Modify messages, one to each leaf.

To achieve an optimal trade-off between the granularity with which the tunnel can be managed (number of messages) and the amount of work (CPU resource, amount of control state, and so forth), the P2MP tree can be decomposed into multiple sub-trees with (possibly overlapping) subsets of leaves. Each sub-tree is signaled as a separate P2MP LSP.

Thus, a P2MP tunnel could be mapped onto several multi-leaf P2MP LSPs. For example, the P2MP tunnel in Figure 11.5 could be mapped onto two P2MP LSPs in the way shown in Figure 11.6.

P2MP tunnel decomposition also easily solves the problem of large signaling messages. The rule is simple: The tree must be decomposed at least to a point when signaling messages required for provisioning of each P2MP LSP could be carried within single IP datagrams. Because the expansion of SUB-EROs may happen at transit nodes, and because the control plane MTU size may vary across the network, intermediate nodes must be ready to further decompose the P2MP tunnel or to return an error to the ingress in such a way that it can work out how to decompose the P2MP tunnel to successfully get past the problem. This intermediate node decomposition is discussed in more detail below.

Recall that in the context of P2P TE tunnels there is also a situation where a tunnel is mapped onto more than one P2P LSP sharing resources on common links. This may happen during *make-before-break* tunnel modification. The make-before-break operation is also legitimate and useful on P2MP tunnels. Imagine that after the tunnel shown in Figure 11.5 is established, it needs to be re-routed onto a new, freshly computed tree. This could be accomplished by setting up new P2MP LSPs that share resources on common links with the old LSPs, and once the new LSPs are successfully established, the old ones can be torn down.

11.4.1 *Tunnel Re-Merge*

There is a fundamental difference between LSPs created for make-before-break purposes and LSPs created because of P2MP tunnel decomposition. The co-existence of the former is transient and supposed to be short-lived, while the co-existence of the latter is normal and could be permanent. In a PSC environment, make-before-break LSPs may have identical or different labels on common links, while sub-tree LSPs must have identical labels on common links. Certain problems that could be ignored in the case of the make-before-break LSPs should be resolved for the sub-tree LSPs. A good example of such a problem is the *re-merge* problem — re-merging of P2MP LSPs carrying data to non-matching sets of leaves onto the same links. An example of the P2MP re-merge situation is shown in Figure 11.7. The paths from root A to leaves H, J, and M are A-D-I-H, A-D-I-L-M, and A-B-E-D-I-J and, clearly, they re-merge at node D. At a minimum the re-merge indicates a sub-optimality in network resource usage and, although it could be ignored during make-before-break procedures, it should be avoided in the case of sub-tree LSPs.

Clearly there is a need for a P2MP signaling message-processing node to be able to tell whether a new P2MP LSP is being created for the make-before-break operation or for the purpose of P2MP tunnel decomposition.

Therefore, it was decided for the purposes of P2MP signaling to introduce a new format for the SENDER_TEMPLATE and FILTER_SPEC RSVP signaling objects. The new format of both objects includes an additional field — Sub-Group ID. The field is set to some P2MP tunnel scope unique number by the P2MP LSP ingress nodes. Thanks to this field, a P2MP LSP Setup message processing node can distinguish make-before-break LSPs from sub-tree LSPs. Specifically, if there are more than one LSP state associated with the same P2MP SESSION object, the decision on whether these LSPs are intended for

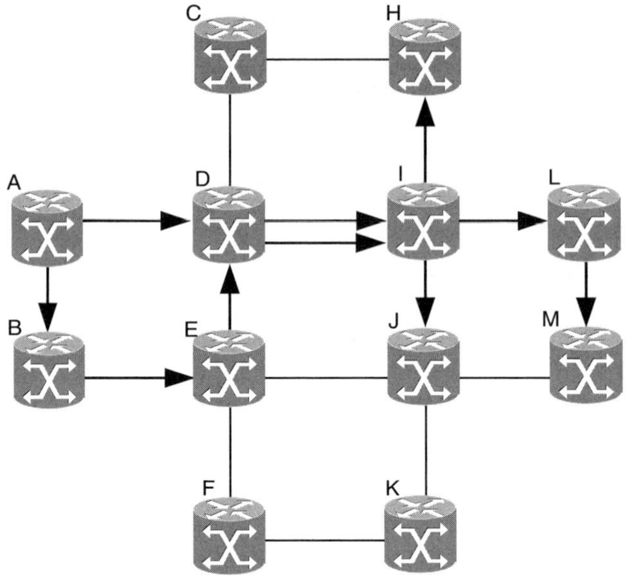

Figure 11.7 P2MP re-merge problem.

make-before-break operations or provisioned due to the P2MP tunnel decomposition is made as follows.

- If SENDER-TEMPLATE objects related to each of the LSP states are different in the Sender ID or LSP ID fields, then, regardless of the content of the Sub-Group ID fields, these LSPs are the make-before-break LSPs and will not co-exist for long.
- If SENDER_TEMPLATE objects are different *only* in the Sub-Group ID fields, then the LSPs represent P2MP separate sub-trees.

As mentioned earlier, a P2MP tunnel can be decomposed at the root and/or at intermediate node(s). In the case of *root P2MP tunnel decomposition* the root is aware of it. The most likely reason for such decomposition is an instruction from the management plane that the tree should be decomposed in a certain way because, for example, there is a need to manage each set of destinations separately. In the case of *non-root P2MP tunnel decomposition* an intermediate node decides for some reason to originate an additional P2MP LSP. The root may not be aware of such decomposition. In fact, it may not even be aware of leaves that are connected to the tunnel via the new LSP.

One of the reasons for non-root P2MP tunnel decomposition is an attempt to avoid signaling message IP fragmentation on an intermediate node. Consider the situation where the root issues a P2MP LSP Setup message that barely fits within one IP datagram. Suppose also that an intermediate node, while processing the message, needs to perform an additional path computation because it encounters a loose next hop in the ERO. One can see that in this case the expanded ERO might make the outgoing P2MP LSP Setup message too large to fit within one IP datagram. One way to handle this is to have the processing node send a notification to the root (via an RSVP PathErr message) with the instruction to move some leaves from the LSP to some other LSP and repeat the setup. This, however, would undoubtedly increase the tunnel setup time, especially if it would take several attempts to identify acceptable root P2MP tunnel decomposition. A better approach is to have the processing node perform the decomposition; specifically, to clone a new P2MP LSP Setup message from the received one and split the leaves between them so that each of the messages could fit within a single IP datagram.

Another reason for non-root P2MP tunnel decomposition is the hierarchical provisioning of P2MP tunnels (see Section 11.6.1).

Let us refer once again to the example in Figure 11.6. The P2MP tunnel {A, (H, M, J)} that is decomposed on the root into two P2MP LSPs {A, H} and {A, (M, J)}, could be further decomposed on node D. The resulting P2MP LSPs that the tunnel is mapped onto are shown in Figure 11.8.

A P2MP tunnel decomposed in a certain way does not have to stay that decomposed throughout its lifetime. It is simple to merge one or more sub-trees

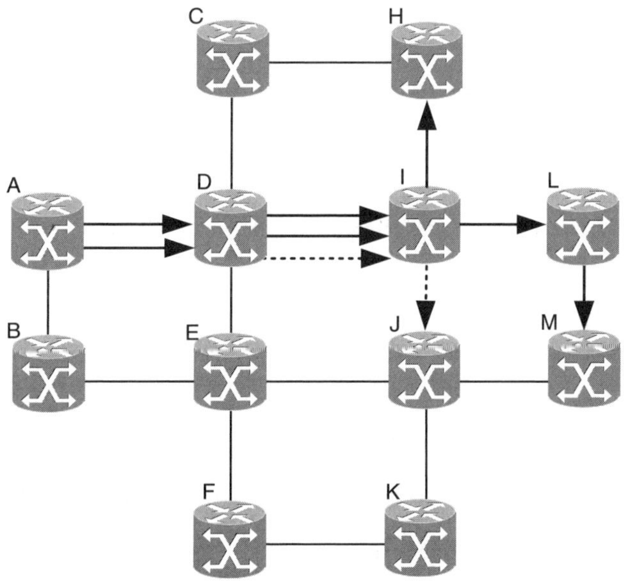

Figure 11.8 Root and non-root P2MP tunnel decomposition.

into a single sub-tree and replace multiple corresponding P2MP LSPs with a single one. Such a merger of the LSPs causes no impact on the tunnel data plane state (and hence on traffic delivery). For example, the tunnel mapped onto two P2MP LSPs as shown in Figure 11.7 could be re-mapped onto a single P2MP LSP (as shown in Figure 11.5) via the following provisioning procedures from the root.

- Step 1: Send a P2MP LSP Modify (RSVP Path) message for one of the LSPs specifying the full set of the tunnel's leaves.
- Step 2: Wait for a P2MP LSP Accept (RSVP Resv) message to arrive and then send a P2MP LSP Release (RSVP PathTear) message for the second LSP.

Note that there is a period of time (between Step 1 and Step 2) when there are two LSPs that have overlapping sets of leaves (those leaves that originally belonged to the second LSP are in common). Also note that the procedures cause no actions in the data plane on any of the nodes. Finally note that this is not a make-before-break procedure — adding/removing leaves does not require modification of the Sender-ID/LSP-ID fields of the SENDER_TEMPLATE object. However, this operation could be seen as a special P2MP-specific case of the make-before-break operation — make-before-break on the leaf level.

Using similar procedures it is also possible to split a single P2MP LSP into two or more LSPs.

In general it is important to note that P2MP tunnel decomposition is a powerful technique. It allows provisioning of different recovery schemes for different sets of destinations. It is even possible (at least, theoretically) to signal different resource color preferences, COS, QOS, or even bandwidth requirements for different destinations within the same P2MP tunnel.

11.4.2 *Limited Branching Capability Problem*

So far we have identified two reasons for P2MP tunnel decomposition.

- To address the signaling message fragmentation problem.
- To provide the flexibility of setting up and managing different sub-trees independently.

There is another problem that can be solved by P2MP tunnel decomposition. A node may be capable of replicating data onto no more than some small number of outgoing links because of a hardware or data plane technology limitation. Even when the hardware is capable of replicating, for example, packets, onto an unlimited number of ports, each replication may introduce a small delay so that

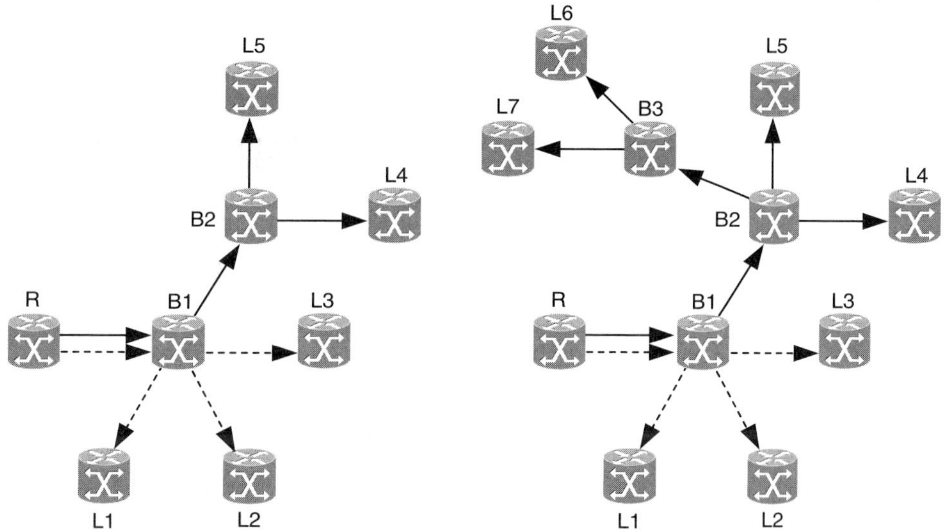

Figure 11.9 A P2MP tunnel may be run over nodes with limited branching capability.

an unacceptable delay is introduced to the nth branch. Imagine that in the network presented on the left-hand side of Figure 11.9, each node is capable of replicating data onto no more than three outgoing links.

In this case a P2MP tunnel with root R and leaves L1...L5 cannot be set up as a single P2MP LSP the way it is in the figure (because of node B1).

One way to solve this problem is to constrain the tree computation appropriately so that there will be no nodes on the resulting tree with the branching degree more than three. However, because of the topology constraints, this might not be feasible.

Fortunately it is possible to decompose the tree into two sub-trees — (R, {L1, L2, L3}) and (R, {L4, L5}) — and signal each of them as a separate P2MP LSP. When node B1 processes the second P2MP LSP Setup message, it will realize that it cannot add the new outgoing resource to the existing cross-connect. Hence, it will allocate a new incoming resource, bind it with the new outgoing resource into a separate cross-connect, and return a label to node R distinct from the label assigned for the first LSP. Thus, there will be two sets of resources allocated on link R-B1 for the same tunnel.

If, sometime later, there is a need to add a new set of leaves, L6, L7 (see the right-hand side of Figure 11.9), an additional P2MP LSP could be signaled. Node B2 will not experience the same problem as node B1; hence, it will return the same label for the third LSP as for the second one, and resources on link B1–B2 will be shared.

11.5 Grafting and Pruning

The set of leaves of a P2MP tunnel is likely to vary during the tunnel lifetime. It is a strict requirement from Service Providers for a P2MP capable control plane to provide a way to add new leaves and remove existing ones to/from an operational P2MP tunnel. The operations of adding/removing leaves to/from an operational P2MP tunnel via instructions from the root or an intermediate node are called *grafting* and *pruning*, respectively. It is worth noting that grafting and pruning are not the only operations through which leaves could be added/removed to/from the tunnel. The Leaf Initiated Join and Drop procedures provide an alternative way.

The requirement of grafting/pruning operations in the data plane is to cause minimal (ideally, zero) effect on traffic delivery to the leaves that are not involved in the operations. The requirement on the control plane is to be non-intrusive, cheap, and scalable; that is, to require the minimal number of signaling messages to be exchanged and only between nodes located on the paths toward the affected leaves. Finally, it is also required that the ability to perform the grafting/pruning causes no additional complexity (for example, number and size of states) in the control and management planes.

Those are potentially conflicting requirements. There is more than one way to perform grafting and pruning; each method satisfies some requirements better than others. Therefore, optimality trade-offs are required depending on the total number of leaves in the tunnel, the network topology, the frequency with which leaves are added/removed to/from the tunnel, and so forth.

Consider the P2MP tunnel {A, (H, M, J)} in Figure 11.5. Suppose that, after it was originally provisioned as a single P2MP LSP, there is a need to add two more destinations to the tunnel — for example, nodes E and C. There are at least three options to achieve this.

- Option 1: Add new leaves to the existing LSP. This is accomplished by issuing a P2MP LSP Modify (RSVP Path) message from the root that includes two new Leaf Descriptors in addition to ones describing the existing leaves. The new Leaf Descriptors include the addresses of corresponding leaves (E and C) and paths to them from the root (A-D-E and A-D-C).
- Option 2: Set up a new P2MP LSP for each of the new leaves. This is accomplished by issuing two P2MP LSP Setup (RSVP Path) messages from the root with the same SESSION object as was signaled for the first LSP. Paths from the root to each of the leaves are encoded in the EROs of the corresponding messages.
- Option 3: Set up a single new P2MP LSP that connects the root to both new leaves. This is accomplished by sending a P2MP LSP Setup message from the root with the same SESSION object as was signaled for the first LSP. A path

from the root to one of the leaves (say, E) is encoded in the ERO. The message contains a single Leaf Descriptor that includes the address of the second leaf (C) and the path to it from the root.

As was mentioned earlier, the disadvantage of Option 1 is that the operation requires processing of larger signaling messages compared to the other two options. Even though such extra processing does not affect the data plane state, it may be desirable to avoid it because it consumes unnecessary bandwidth on the control channel and requires additional CPU resources. However, after the leaves have been added to the tunnel, option 1 results in just a single control plane state dedicated to the entire tunnel on each of the nodes. Thus, if there is a need to modify the tunnel parameters (for example, boost holding priority or increase bandwidth requirements) or discontinue the entire service, a single message issued from the root — P2MP LSP Modify or Release, respectively — will do the job.

Option 2, on the other hand, requires processing of many, smaller signaling messages. Leaves can be connected or disconnected with no effect on the remaining leaves even in the control plane. However, this method does add two more control plane states on every node involved in the path to the new leaves. Also, after the new leaves are connected to the tunnel, any tunnel-wide management operation will require one provisioning message to be sent from the root for each leaf, rather than just one for the whole tree as in Option 1.

Probably a good trade-off could be achieved by adding leaves in clusters of a configurable size through the setting up of a separate P2MP LSP for each of the clusters (which is Option 3). Also, two, several, or all of the P2MP LSPs of a particular tunnel can always be merged into one single LSP with a superset of all the leaves. Or a P2MP LSP perceived to be too large to manage could be split into one or more LSPs, each with a subset of leaves of the original LSP.

Similarly, there are several ways to perform pruning.

- Tear down a P2MP LSP by sending a P2MP LSP Release (RSVP PathTear) message from the LSP ingress node that contains an empty list of Leaf ID objects. This would disconnect all the leaves with which the LSP was provisioned.
- Remove specific leaves from a P2MP LSP by sending a P2MP LSP Release (RSVP PathTear) message from the LSP ingress node with the list of Leaf ID objects identifying the leaves to be removed.
- Remove specific leaves from a P2MP LSP by sending a P2MP LSP Modify (RSVP Path) message from the LSP ingress node, excluding from the list of Leaf Descriptors the ones associated with the leaves to be removed.

Note that as a result of a pruning operation a node that used to perform data replication may stop doing so and become a "regular" non-branch intermediate node. Likewise, after grafting, a node may be "promoted" to become a branch node. In our example node D was originally a non-branch intermediate node. After node C or node E is added to the tunnel, node D becomes a branch node and converts back into a non-branch node once the leaf is removed.

11.6 Advanced Features

11.6.1 *Hierarchical P2MP Tunnels*

When a P2MP tunnel has only a small number of leaves, the leaf management — connecting and disconnecting leaves to/from the tunnel, changing (re-optimizing) paths toward the leaves, and so forth — can be accomplished via provisioning messages sent from the root. But what if there are 10,000 leaves in the tunnel? Should the root know about every one of them, or might it be possible to arrange things in such a way that the root will know about 100 distribution points, with each of them handling 100 leaves? The latter approach is highly desirable, because it allows for growing and managing large tunnels (especially those that span multiple traffic engineering domains) in a very scalable manner.

Fortunately, the P2MP tunnel decomposition on intermediate nodes and/or leaves can easily provide such hierarchical leaf management. Let us consider the tunnel presented on the right-hand side of Figure 11.9. It is possible to provision the tunnel in such a way that a P2MP LSP originated from the root establishes data paths only up to nodes B1, B2, and B3, which would be the tunnel leaves as far as the root is concerned. We will discuss later how the root learns about the leaves to be added to the tunnel, but let us assume for now that node B1 learns about leaves L1, L2, and L3; node B2 about leaves L4 and L5; and node B3 about leaves L6 and L7, all in the same way that the root learns about leaves B1, B2, and B3.

Provided that the root has authorized nodes B1, B2, and B3 to autonomously handle their subsets of leaves, they can set up three additional P2MP LSPs — (B1, {L1, L2, L3}), (B2, {L4, L5}), and (B3, {L6, L7}), as shown in Figure 11.10 — connecting the leaves to the tunnel. Leaves L1–L7 in their turn could serve as distribution points for their subsets of leaves and so forth.

The root can authorize such hierarchical leaf management or prohibit it by setting a flag while signaling its own LSPs.

11.6.2 *Inter-Domain P2MP Tunnels*

A P2MP tunnel may span multiple TE domains. In this case its root and at least some leaves are located in separate TE domains, which presents an additional

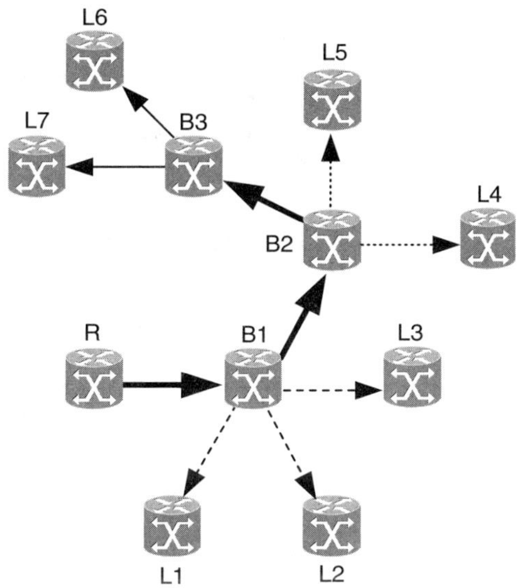

Figure 11.10 Hierarchical leaf management.

challenge for tree computation since the tree computation entity on the root does not have enough TE visibility to compute paths to all leaves.

One approach to solving this problem is to request the tree computation from a remote Path Computation Entity (PCE) as described in Chapter 9. PCEs are usually located on nodes with wide TE visibility (ABRs, ASBRs) and can also request cooperation of other PCEs. The PCE is expected to return a complete tree connecting the route to all the leaves. Once the tree is determined, the provisioning of the inter-domain tunnel is no different from the provisioning of a tunnel located entirely within a single TE domain (that is, an intra-domain tunnel).

It is also possible to compute a P2MP tree in a distributed way. Imagine, for example, that there is a need to provision a P2MP tunnel spanning several OSPF areas, as shown in Figure 11.11. With this approach the original tree computation is performed on the root (node A). The computation produces a *partial tree*: Paths toward leaves that are not located in the root's local TE domain (nodes H, M, and N) are defined only up to the domain border node (node D), and contain single loose hops from there on to the leaves.

Accordingly, a P2MP LSP Setup (RSVP Path) message that is sent from the root includes ERO {A-D-(loose)H} and two SUB-EROs: {A-D-(loose)M} and {A-D-(loose)N}. When the message arrives at node D, it performs additional path computations, completing the path to leaf H (it is capable of doing so because it has access to the TED of area 3 where leaf H is located) and expanding the paths toward leaves M and N up to the next domain border node on the paths — node I.

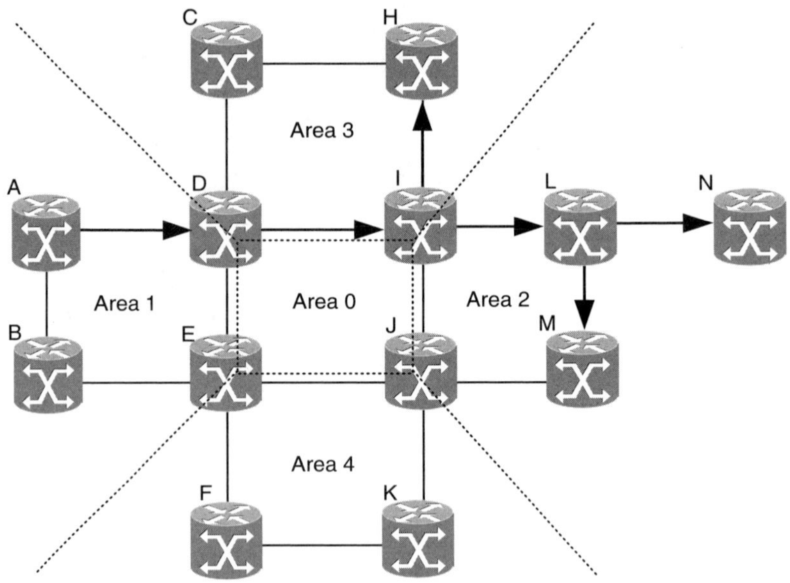

Figure 11.11 An inter-domain P2MP tunnel.

The latter, as a part of P2MP LSP Setup message processing, also performs path computations and completes the paths to leaves M and N.

Distributed tree computation is simple, but has some problems. First, it can never be guaranteed that the resulting tree is optimal; in other words, provided that all necessary TE information is available, a centralized tree computation is likely to produce a better tree. Secondly, the P2MP re-merge problem that was mentioned in Section 11.4.1 could easily occur during tunnel provisioning with distributed tree computation. To understand this, let us first consider how a TE tree or path computation entity decides which TE domain border node to select for a partial tree or path toward destinations located outside the local TE domain. Whenever it is discovered that a destination does not have a record in the local TED, the local routing sub-system is usually requested to determine which ABR or ASBR advertises the destination's IP reachability. Once the ABR/ASBR is identified, the path to the latter from the source is determined in the hope that the ABR/ASBR advertising reachability to the destination (and hence knowing about the shortest IP path to the destination) can also compute an optimal (or at least some) TE path to the destination.

In our example we implicitly assumed that IP routes to all leaves are advertised by node D. But there is another ABR in area 1 — node E. It is equally possible that the IP route to node M is advertised by node E, while IP routes to the rest of the leaves are advertised by node D. The distributed tree computation under such conditions could result in the tree shown in Figure 11.12.

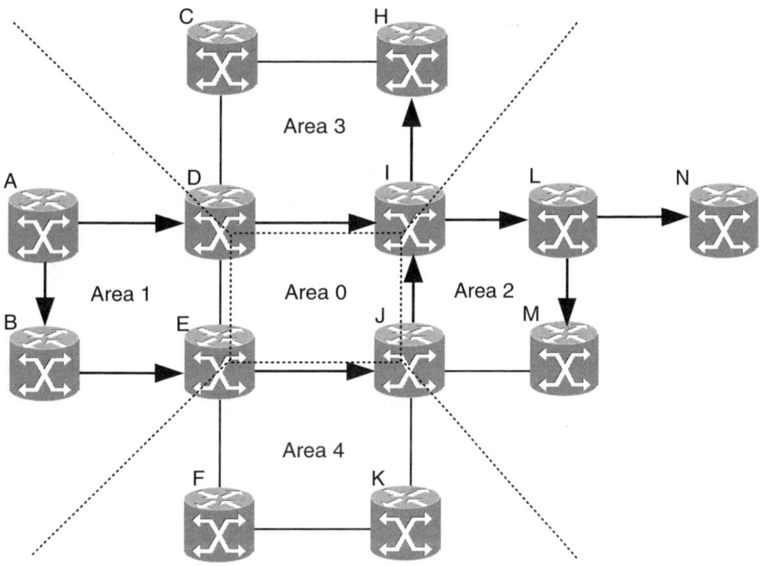

Figure 11.12 Inter-domain P2MP tunnel demonstrating the re-merge problem.

This might happen because the root would signal two sub-trees (A, {H, N}) and (A, M) as two separate P2MP LSPs. While processing the P2MP LSP Setup messages, node D would perform path computations to determine paths to leaves H and N, and node E would compute a path to leaf M. Because nodes D and E would perform the path computations independently of each other, it is quite possible that the resulting paths might merge onto some links (link I-L in our example) or even a sequences of links.

In packet networks the re-merge situation is highly undesirable and should be prevented because it may cause data duplication toward the affected leaves (nodes M and N in our example). In non-packet networks, however, although the re-merge represents a sub-optimal use of upstream resources, it does not present a problem of data duplication toward the downstream nodes. Node I, for example, should certainly be capable of receiving the same data from two links — D-I and J-I — and of sending a single copy out of link I-L. In fact, this is no different from terminating a 1+1 service protection scheme (see more details on service recovery schemes in Chapter 7). Having said that, it should be noted that resources on links A-B, B-E, E-J, and J-I are used unnecessarily and wasted (presumably unintentionally). Therefore, the re-merge-detecting node (node I) is obliged to notify the originator of the second LSP (the root in our case) that it would be more optimal to combine the LSPs.

It is also worth noting that sometimes the re-merge is intentional and desirable. In order to mitigate the consequences of a single ABR crash, for example,

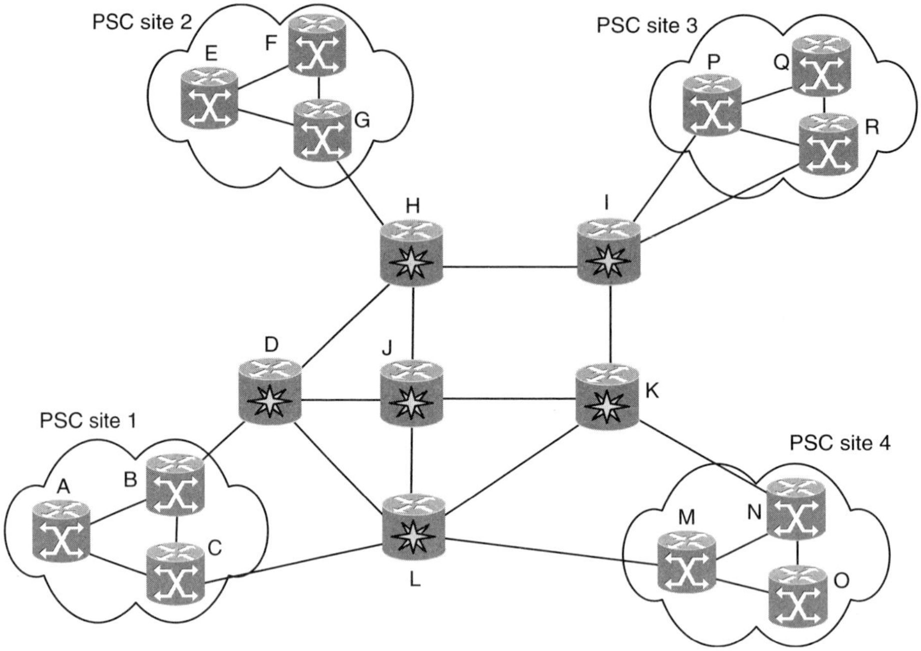

Figure 11.13 A multi-layer network.

an inter-domain P2MP tunnel could be provisioned to distribute data through two or more ABRs (for example, nodes D and E), actually *relying* on the re-merge to happen somewhere after (hopefully close to) the TE visibility boundary.

Finally, there is a third option for how an inter-area P2MP tunnel could be provisioned. It is possible to "grow" the tunnel hierarchically as described in Section 11.6.1. Specifically, it is possible to set up one or more P2MP LSPs connecting the root to one, several, or all known TE domain border nodes and authorize the latter to autonomously manage their own subsets of leaves and/or data distribution points.

11.6.3 *Multi-Layer P2MP Tunnels*

A P2MP tunnel may span networks with different switching capabilities. Consider the network topology in Figure 11.13. It includes four PSC sites and a TDM network providing transport services to interconnect the PSC sites. Suppose it is required to establish a P2MP tunnel connecting root A to leaves E. F, P, Q, M, and O.

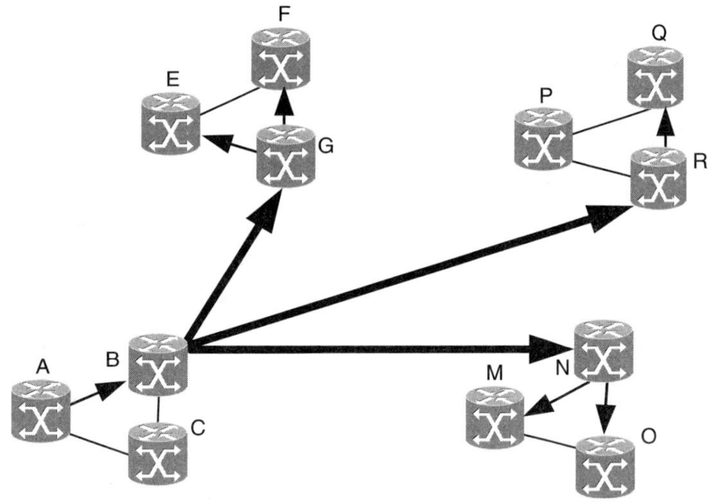

Figure 11.14 P2MP tunnel over P2P transport tunnels.

One way to accomplish this is to establish several P2P transport tunnels providing interconnectivity between the sites, present these P2P transport tunnels as TE links between the PSC sites, and then set up the requested P2MP tunnel over resulting PSC topology as shown in Figure 11.14. Note that in this case the tree computation entity would see no difference between links provided by the transport network (B-G, B-R, B-N) and static intra-site links like A-B or G-F. Furthermore, node B would perform a regular branch node function — receive data over link A-B and replicate it over links B-G, B-R, and B-N.

Such an approach would work, but we should try to do better because the resources in the transport network are not used efficiently. The reason why it is desirable for a P2MP service to use a single P2MP tunnel instead of multiple P2P tunnels is that the P2MP tunnel moves data replication points from the service root to the service destinations, and thus makes use of network resources more efficiently. The transport network needs to provide a P2MP service connecting root B (which is where the PSC P2MP tunnel enters the network) and leaves G, R, and N (the tunnel's exit points).

Applying this logic, we can replace the three P2P transport tunnels with a single P2MP transport tunnel. In other words, the PSC P2MP tunnel could be mapped onto a single P2MP TDM tunnel (see Figure 11.15).

It is important to note that the multi-layer tunnel bandwidth utilization problem that was discussed in Chapter 10 is also relevant for P2MP tunnels. Specifically, the question arises of how to make use of the extra bandwidth allocated on lower-level switching capability links because of the difference in granularity of bandwidth allocation. Imagine that our P2MP PSC tunnel requires

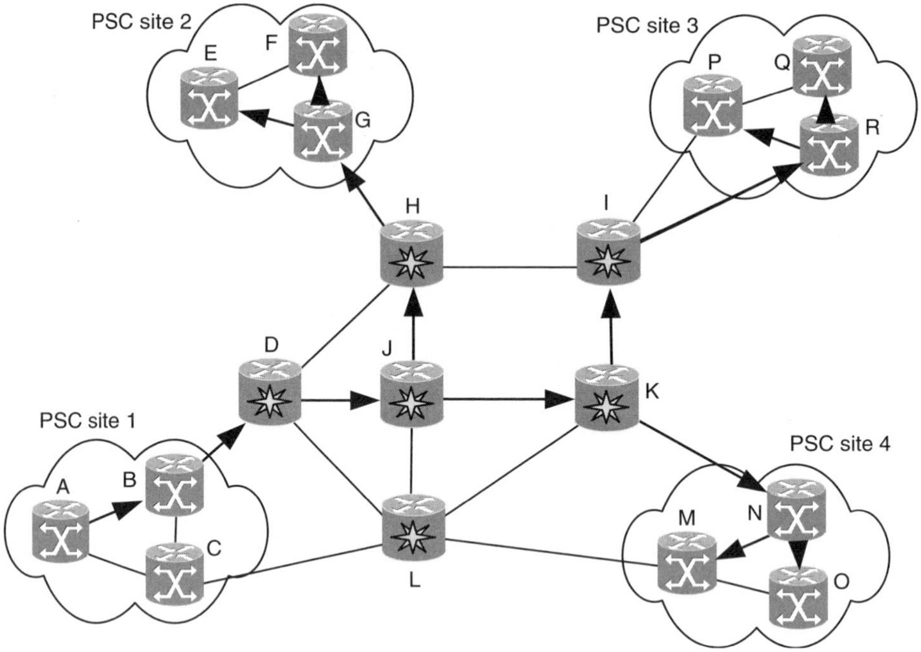

Figure 11.15 A multi-layer P2MP tunnel.

a bandwidth reservation of 100 Mbbps on each link, whereas the bandwidth on the TDM links could be allocated only in chunks of 2.5 Gbps. The resources allocated on transport links in this case would be far more than needed by the service.

Recall that in the P2P context this problem is resolved using the concept of hierarchical LSPs (H-LSPs); specifically, by advertising lower-level switching capability LSPs as higher-level switching capability links with some relatively small numbers for TE metrics and unreserved bandwidth equal to the difference between the bandwidth originally allocated and reserved so far for nested LSPs. Such advertising encourages path computation entities to place higher-level LSPs within existing H-LSPs rather than trigger establishment of new ones.

Currently, the concept of an H-LSP can be applied only to P2P tunnels. There is no way for the entity that computes a PSC P2MP tree on node C, for instance, to learn about the P2MP tunnel created in the TDM network. Hence it cannot route a new PSC P2MP tunnel in such a way that it uses the TDM P2MP tunnel and takes advantage of the allocated TDM bandwidth.

It may seem that the problem could be resolved simply by having roots of lower-level P2MP tunnels advertise multiple H-LSPs as P2P TE links — one per root-leaf pair. For instance, node B could advertise three H-LSP TE links: B-G, B-R, and B-N. This would make the network topology graph look as it does in

Figure 11.14, despite the fact that, in reality, a single P2MP tunnel is set up in the TDM network (rather than three P2P tunnels). Thus, tree or path computation entities could consider the H-LSP TE links in new P2MP and P2P path computations.

This approach has a drawback, which makes it unacceptable. Suppose there is a request to provision a unidirectional P2P tunnel going from node C to node E. The PCE on node C may decide to place the tunnel on link C-B, H-LSP B-G, and link G-E. Unfortunately, B-G is not an independent link — it is part of a P2MP tunnel. Hence the data sent from node C to node E will also arrive at nodes R and N, which are not the intended receivers. Such a situation is classified as a misconnection and is usually explicitly prohibited because it may breach confidentiality or lead to a node being swamped by spurious data.

This suggests the need to introduce a P2MP TE link (or a multi-access TE link). Its advertisement must contain, among other information, the IDs of the underlying H-LSP's root and all its leaves. The advertisement processing should result in the installation on local TE network graphs of multiple arcs connecting the H-LSP's root to each of the leaves. Furthermore, these arcs could *only* be considered during P2MP tree computations (that is, pruned out from the graph when P2P paths are computed), and accepted for the resulting tree only if the tree enters the lower-level network layer and exits out of it on the same root and the *identical* set of leaves as was advertised for the P2MP TE link.

11.6.4 Leaf-Initiated Join and Drop Procedures

At this time the MPLS IETF Working Group is discussing how the root of a P2MP tunnel should be notified about leaves it needs to add to or remove from the tunnel, and whether LIJ and LID procedures should be realized within the P2MP Traffic Engineering framework.

Some argue that P2MP TE tunnels should always be considered in the context of the applications for which they are used. These applications normally invoke numerous protocols that could provide, as a byproduct, all necessary leaf-related information. For example, when a P2MP TE tunnel is owned by an IP multicast application, the tunnel's root can access such information by querying the PIM routing protocol. Likewise, in the context of a multicast VPN, the leaves to be added to or removed from the tunnels could be learned from BGP. Even when there are no protocols to provide such information (as in the case of Layer 2 Multicast over MPLS/GMPLS), and leaves need to be added or removed via configuration, the question is why not configure them directly on the root? This would mean that there would be no need for LIJ and LID procedures, which would only unnecessarily complicate matters; it is sufficient to perform all leaf management via grafting/pruning from the root.

Others believe that there are serious reasons why it is important for a new potential leaf of a P2MP tunnel to discover dynamically which nodes in the local TE domain could connect the leaf to the tunnel, select one that could do it in the most efficient way, send it an appropriate notification, and thus get connected to the tunnel without using any external protocols. Some simple way should also be provided for a leaf to get disconnected from the tunnel if it wants to do so.

One of the reasons is that LIJ mechanisms embedded in the GMPLS P2MP signaling protocols could be used as a tool to grow and manage hierarchical tunnels (see Section 11.6.1), so that intermediate nodes could autonomously manage their subset of leaves without tunnel roots knowing about the leaves' existence.

Secondly, the LIJ procedure allows a leaf to be connected to a P2MP tunnel in the most efficient way. This is because the leaf, while deciding which node to send an LIJ notification to (out of several candidates it learned about), can select the candidate that can originate the most optimal TE path to the leaf. This is not always possible when a root learns about potential leaves from external protocols. Consider the situation when the root of a P2MP tunnel is instructed to add a leaf located outside the local TE domain. In this case the root would signal the request to an ABR or ASBR that advertises IP reachability to the leaf, but this ABR or ASBR might not be capable of connecting the leaf (perhaps because it might not be able to originate a TE path to the leaf) or might join the leaf in a sub-optimal way.

The LIJ procedures could be realized in a relatively simple way. Recall that P2MP nodes are already obliged to advertise their P2MP capabilities; for example, whether they are capable of performing branching or not (see Section 11.2.1). It should not be a problem to extend the format of the advertisement to include a list of P2MP tunnels for which the advertising node is authorized to perform an LIJ operation. This would allow all nodes within a local TE domain to discover potential targets for LIJ Notify requests. A leaf willing to be connected to a particular tunnel can select one such target by running an inverse CSPF on the local TE network graph so that the candidate capable of originating the most optimal TE path to the leaf could be determined. Once the candidate is selected, the leaf could send the LIJ Notify (GMPLS RSVP Notify) message specifying its ID as well as the ID of the P2MP tunnel it wishes to be connected to.

Curiously, in the existing protocol specifications, nothing prevents a leaf of a particular P2MP tunnel from sending a P2MP LSP Upstream Release message (RSVP PathErr with the path state removal flag set). The closest branch node in this case would disconnect the leaf from the tunnel while processing the message. Hence, the LID procedure can be provided within the current framework with no additions or modifications.

11.6.5 *P2MP Service Recovery*

A P2MP service should be capable of recovering from network failures within an acceptable period of time. Recall, from Chapter 7, that the required resilience for a P2P service could be achieved via over-provisioning — additional network resources could be allocated for the service along paths disjoint from the working path, and the service traffic could be switched over onto the disjoint paths as soon as a failure on the working path is detected. Recall also that a recovery scheme for a P2P service could be either end-to-end or use local repair. In the former case the entire working path is protected via a single recovery path. In the latter case different pieces of the working path are protected independently via several recovery paths.

Let us consider the P2MP service presented in Figure 11.16. The service connects root R to leaves L1 and L2. Could end-to-end recovery be provisioned for the service? Certainly. While computing the tree it is possible to determine alternative paths from the root to all leaves. These paths can be disjoint from the corresponding working paths. As a result, it is possible to provision recovery P2P LSPs at the same time as the working P2MP LSPs (as shown on the left-hand side of Figure 11.16).

The question is whether end-to-end P2MP service recovery is practicable. The answer is yes, but only if we are talking about either service restoration, or whether the protection LSPs could be reused for extra traffic or could be shared with other P2MP and P2P services (for example, participate in a full mesh restoration scheme).

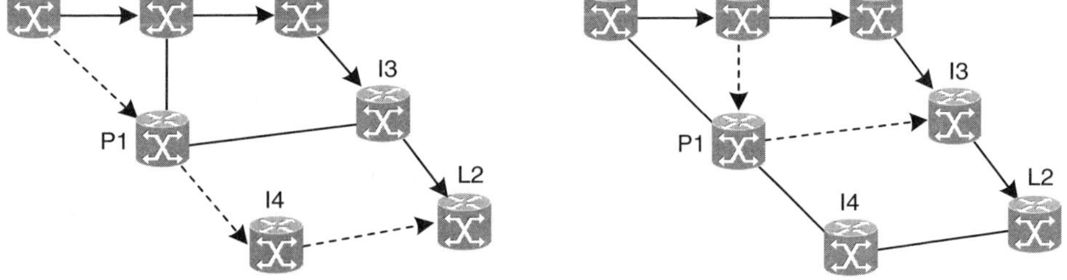

Figure 11.16 P2MP service recovery.

Dedicated, end-to-end protection for a P2MP service does not make any practical sense. Indeed, by its provisioning we end up with multiple P2P LSPs provisioned for a single service, and recall that the whole purpose of a P2MP LSP is to avoid using multiple P2P LSPs.

On the other hand, a scheme that provides dedicated local repair for a particular P2MP service is certainly worth consideration. The idea is to mitigate the consequences of network failures by protecting "important" nodes and/or segments of a P2MP tree. Good targets for dedicated local repair are branch nodes that start branches with large numbers of leaves or large numbers of sub-branches. An example of a P2MP service, for which dedicated local repair is provisioned, is shown on the right-hand side of Figure 11.16.

Fortunately, the path segment recovery model (discussed in Chapter 7) works nicely for provisioning local repair for P2MP PSC and non-PSC services. The same tree computation entity that determines a P2MP tree for a particular service can also identify segments of the tree to be protected, as well as appropriate recovery paths. This could be done after the tree is computed or, even better, concurrently with the tree computation. The recovery LSPs could be provisioned along with P2MP LSP(s) by signaling the recovery paths and associated types of recovery in the SEROs of the P2MP LSP Setup (RSVP Path) message. Note that the SEROs should not be confused with SUB-EROs that encode branches of the working tree and are signaled in the P2MP LSP Setup message as well.

It is also possible to use the *dynamic* form of path segment recovery, letting the network identify which branch nodes and/or segments need to be protected and set up the necessary recovery paths. Regardless of whether the dynamic or static approach is taken, the P2MP LSP ingress node can learn the entire topology taken by the working tree and recovery paths by looking into the RRO, SUB-RROs, and SRROs of the P2MP LSP Accept (RSVP Resv) message.

One interesting peculiarity of P2MP tunnel local repair is that that all recovery LSPs (unless they are of the 1+1 protection type) protecting against a failure of a particular branch node should originate on the *same* node. Consider that local repair against the failure of branch node B is provisioned as shown in Figure 11.17. Recall that a branch node, when starting a branch, originates an additional P2MP LSP Setup message that inherits most of the objects from the incoming P2MP LSP Setup message. This includes the stack of NotifyRequest objects. If one of the recovery paths starts on node R and another on node I1 (as shown in the figure), the P2MP LSP Setup message arriving at node B will contain two NotifyRequest objects: the first one associated with node I1 and the second with node R.

The incoming P2MP LSP Setup messages on nodes I2 and I3 will contain the same stack of the NotifyRequest objects.

Let us assume that at some point in time node I3 detects a failure on link B-I3. In this case it will send an FIS message to an address found in the first NotifyRequest object in the stack, which would be the address of node I1. In the best case scenario the latter will realize (by looking into RRO or Sub-RROs, or by

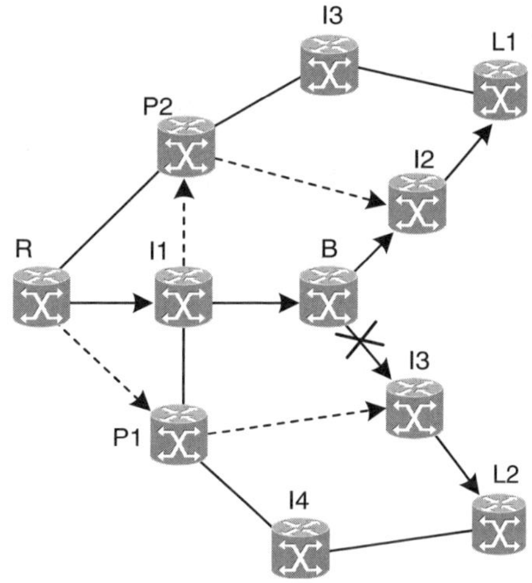

Figure 11.17 P2MP tree segment recovery might not always work.

examining the local TED) that it cannot recover from the indicated failure and will redirect the FIS to node R. This would work but would take more time for the service to recover. In the worst case node I1 will blindly (and uselessly) trigger the switchover onto recovery path I1-P2-I2. Therefore, the intended recovery scheme should be provisioned as shown on the right-hand side of Figure 11.16.

It is important to note that in cases when a P2MP tunnel is mapped (decomposed) onto several P2MP LSPs, each of the LSPs is provisioned independently. Hence it is possible to signal different recovery requirements, SEROs, and so forth, for different LSPs and provide different service availability for different sets of service destinations.

11.6.6 *P2MP Tunnel Re-Optimization*

It is possible that a more optimal P2MP tree becomes available for an operational tunnel. In this case it is desirable to re-map the tunnel onto new P2MP LSP(s) with minimum (ideally zero) effect on the traffic delivery. This is usually done using a make-before-break operation. Specifically, new P2MP LSPs are created that share resources on common links with the old LSPs, and once this is successfully accomplished the old LSPs are torn down. Such tunnel re-optimization is simple to perform in the case where the tree is computed in a centralized way (either locally on the tunnel's root or using a remote tree computation entity).

However, if some of the tunnel's P2MP LSPs span multiple TE domains and the tree is computed in a distributed way, tunnel re-optimization could be trickier to perform. The situation may occur when an intermediate node that performed a partial tree computation during the LSP setup identifies a more optimal sub-tree. The node cannot start the make-before-break procedure because the procedure could not be started on a non-ingress node. The ingress node, on the other hand, is likely to be located in a different TE domain, and hence will not be aware of the better sub-tree.

This problem is resolved the same way as for P2P tunnels. Specifically, the intermediate node is recommended to send a notification (RSVP PathErr or GMPLS RSVP Notify message) to the LSP ingress node requesting the make-before-break operation.

Tunnel re-optimization should not be performed too often, in order to avoid control plane destabilization. Each P2MP capable node is usually configured with a parameter defining how frequently it is allowed to re-optimize P2MP LSPs originated on the node.

It is worth remembering that a P2MP LSP ingress node is not necessarily the associated P2MP tunnel's root. If the tunnel is decomposed (as in the case of hierarchical tunnels), its P2MP LSPs could start on any node of the tree. Each of the LSPs could be re-optimized autonomously without necessarily involving the root of the tunnel in the process.

11.7 Further Reading

Two books provide a good examination of path computation for point-to-multipoint trees:

The Steiner Tree Problem by Frank K. Hwang, Dana S. Richards, and Pawel Winter in *The Annals of Discrete Mathematics, Vol. 53* (1992), North-Holland.

Steiner Trees in Industry (Combinatorial Optimization) by Xiuzhen Cheng and Ding-Zhu Du (2001), Springer.

Several Internet-Drafts produced by the MPLS and CCAMP working groups of the IETF are also relevant.

draft-ietf-mpls-p2mp-sig-requirement

Signaling Requirements for Point to Multipoint Traffic Engineered MPLS LSPs draft-ietf-mpls-rsvp-te-p2mp

Extensions to RSVP-TE for Point to Multipoint TE LSPs

draft-vasseur-ccamp-te-node-cap

Routing extensions for discovery of Traffic Engineering Node Capabilities

CHAPTER 12

Layer One Virtual Private Networks

GMPLS enables multiple applications that could be sold as transport-related services. In the previous chapter we discussed one such application — Multi-Layer Point-to-Multipoint TE tunnels. In this chapter we will concentrate on Point-to-Point Layer One services, in particular, on Layer One Virtual Private Networks (L1VPNs). We will identify the service as it is seen from the Service Provider's and service user's perspectives: service components; building blocks; deployment scenarios; requirements for and separation of responsibilities between data, control, and management planes; and finally, the reference models that are needed to satisfy the requirements. After that we will analyze how and to what extent the GMPLS technology can be used to provide L1VPNs, and what additions/extensions are required.

12.1 Layer One Point-to-Point Services

The following definitions are used in this chapter.

Provider: An organization that has administrative control over a Layer One network.

Provider network: A Layer One network.

Customer: An organization that uses services provided by the Provider.

Customer site: A segment of the Customer network built from Customer network devices whose interconnection is realized by means not related to the services provided by the Provider. Customer site 1 and Customer site 2 in Figure 12.1 are two examples of Customer sites.

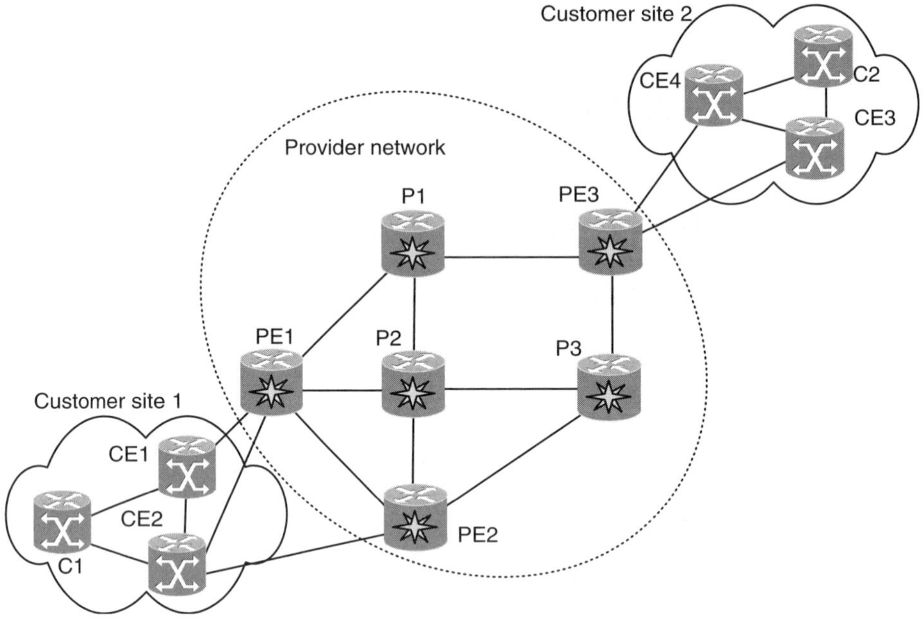

Figure 12.1 Layer One service components.

Customer network: Two or more isolated Customer sites interconnected via the Provider network.

Provider device (*P*): A Provider network node that has links only to other Provider network nodes. Examples of Provider devices are nodes P1, P2, and P3 in Figure 12.1.

Provider Edge device (*PE*): A Provider network node that has at least one link interconnecting the node with a Customer site. Examples of Provider Edge devices are PE1, PE2, and PE3 in Figure 12.1.

Customer device (*C*): A Customer network node that has links only to other Customer network nodes. Examples of Customer devices are nodes C1 and C2 in Figure 12.1.

Customer Edge device (*CE*): A Customer network node that has at least one link interconnecting the node with the Provider network. In other words, a CE has one or more links interconnecting it with one or more PEs. Examples of CEs are CE1, CE2, CE3, and CE4 in Figure 12.1. Note that a single CE could be connected to multiple PEs, and a single PE could be connected to multiple CEs.

In Chapter 7 we defined a *transport service* as a way of delivering user (Customer) traffic with specified characteristics between two boundaries of the Provider network (that is, between a pair of PEs) with an agreed upon quality of service, blocking probability, and resilience against network failures. Thus, the Customer sees a transport service as a set of the following basic services.

- Data plane connectivity between two sites (for example, between CE1 and CE3)
- Capacity in terms of bit rate
- Format of data encoding (for example, SONET/SDH overhead bit transparency)
- Quality of Service (for example, number of error seconds per month)
- Availability (percentage of time when the service meets agreed parameters)

From the Traffic Engineering point of view, transport services enable TE links between the interconnected CEs. Suppose there are three transport services provisioned over the Provider network interconnecting CE1 with CE4, CE2 with CE4, and CE2 with CE3, respectively. In this case the TE network graph on C1 would look as shown in Figure 12.2.

A transport service could be mapped to permanent, soft-permanent and/or switched LSPs. For permanent LSPs, the control plane is not involved in LSP provisioning/management either on the Customer or on the Provider side: Network Management Systems (NMSs) on both sides agree on the LSP parameters and independently manage local sides of the CE-PE links. In addition the Provider NMS provisions each link of the PE-PE segment of the LSP.

Switched LSPs, on the other hand, are provisioned/managed end-to-end through the cooperation of the Customer and Provider control planes with zero

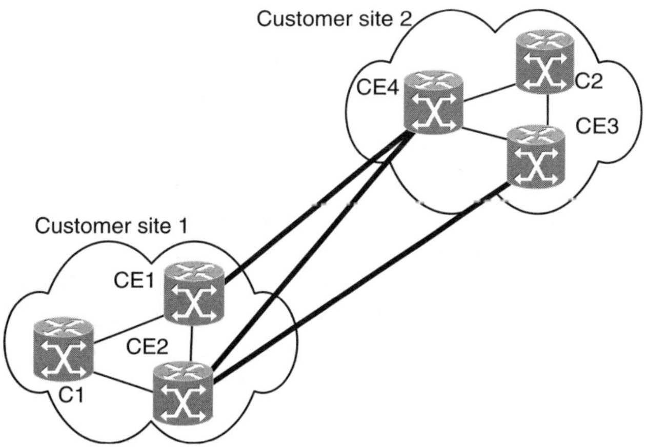

Figure 12.2 The TE network graph seen from a Customer node.

involvement of the management plane. In the case of the soft-permanent LSPs, the responsibilities between the control and management planes are split in the following way: PE-PE segments are managed by the Provider control plane, while CE-PE links are managed by the management plane in the same way as permanent LSPs. It is worth noting that soft-permanent LSPs are a very attractive mechanism for Providers, because they do not force the Providers to open their control networks up to security concerns as much as fully switched LSPs do; there is no direct signaling interface to the Customer when soft-permanent LSPs are used. Considering the fact that the focus of this book is on the use of the dynamic GMPLS control plane, and also that soft-permanent LSPs do not present additional issues that have not been considered in the previous chapters of this book, we will not discuss permanent and soft-permanent LSPs in this chapter and will assume that the CE-CE LSPs are always dynamically provisioned.

Let us define a *Layer One service* as a full set of services that could be provided by the Provider network. This includes services in both the control and data planes. A transport service could be defined as a data plane component of a Layer One service. Although it is an important part of a Layer One service, it is not the only one.

How does a CE know about CEs in other sites? Should the Customer implement or outsource the service that could provide such knowledge, or could it be a value-added service from the Provider? The latter is more convenient for the Customer (one-stop shopping) and for the Provider (all necessary building blocks are available for an additional service that could be sold to the Customer). Likewise, how can the IP reachability and TE information be distributed between the Customer sites? Note that the appropriate mechanism is neither trivial nor immediately apparent, because transport services interconnecting the sites provide only data plane connectivity not necessarily suitable for delivering control plane information between CEs. Channels for out-of-band control plane connectivity are likely to be required.

Furthermore, it should be noted that the Customer would like to see no difference between its static intra-site links and inter-site links based on Layer One services. This requires, among other things, out-of-band control plane connectivity to provide a transport for the exchange of *arbitrary* control plane information between CEs (not just flooding of routing/TE advertisements). For instance, the control channels should make it possible to establish signaling (RSVP-TE) adjacencies, LMP sessions, or to run any other protocols between the CEs. Needless to say, such control channels are a valuable additional service that could be offered by the Provider. The requirement for out-of-band control plane connectivity is a very important distinction between Layer One and, for example, Layer Two services in general, and between L1VPNs and Layer Two VPNs in particular. We will discuss in detail what services comprise a Layer One service and a VPN later in this chapter.

Purchasing Layer One services could be attractive for the Customer: It makes outsourcing of the management of the transport network and the links interconnecting the Customer sites possible, so that the Customer can concentrate on providing services in the area of its expertise. Usually, more than one Customer will use Layer One services provided by a Provider; therefore, one can say that any given Customer makes a relatively small use of the Provider network by sharing the Provider network resources, and hence costs, with other Customers.

For the same reason, selling Layer One services could be good business for the Provider, especially if the services are dynamic and on-demand: In this case the Provider has full or partial control over how the services are placed on its network resources and therefore can use them most efficiently. For instance, the Provider can place the services in such a way that they will share backup paths or reuse idle protection resources.

In previous chapters we have implicitly assumed that point-to-point services are independent from each other. We did this for the sake of simplicity: While discussing signaling and routing protocol aspects, and considering TE and path computation problems, the relationships between the services are not significant. However, there are multiple ways that the services could be offered to the Customer. For instance the Customer may want to ask the Provider to interconnect *several* sites, or *several sets* of sites, applying different policies and paying different costs for each such set. Therefore, the ITU-T Study Group 13 identified two categories of Layer One services:

- Category 1: Single service (one Customer, two CEs)
- Category 2: Multiple service (one Customer, three or more CEs)

Furthermore, the L1VPN is defined as a Layer One service of Category 2, with the following additions.

- The set of CEs that is involved in the service is restricted in the sense that CEs that belong to a particular Customer can be interconnected only if they are members of the same VPN.
- The service membership information is distributed between the CEs.
- A separate policy could be applied by the Customer on a per-service basis (that is, per-VPN) for each service component. An example of such a policy is the level/type of service protection against network failures.

An L1VPN also could be defined as a VPN whose data plane operates at Layer One. A connection between CEs located in different sites of an L1VPN is called a *Layer One VPN connection*. L1VPN connections enable inter-site CE-CE links. An example of two L1VPNs is shown in Figure 12.3. The network TE view of one of the VPNs (VPN 1) is shown in Figure 12.4.

It is important to note that CE-PE separation is logical: The entities could be collocated within a single network device; however, conceptually they are still two

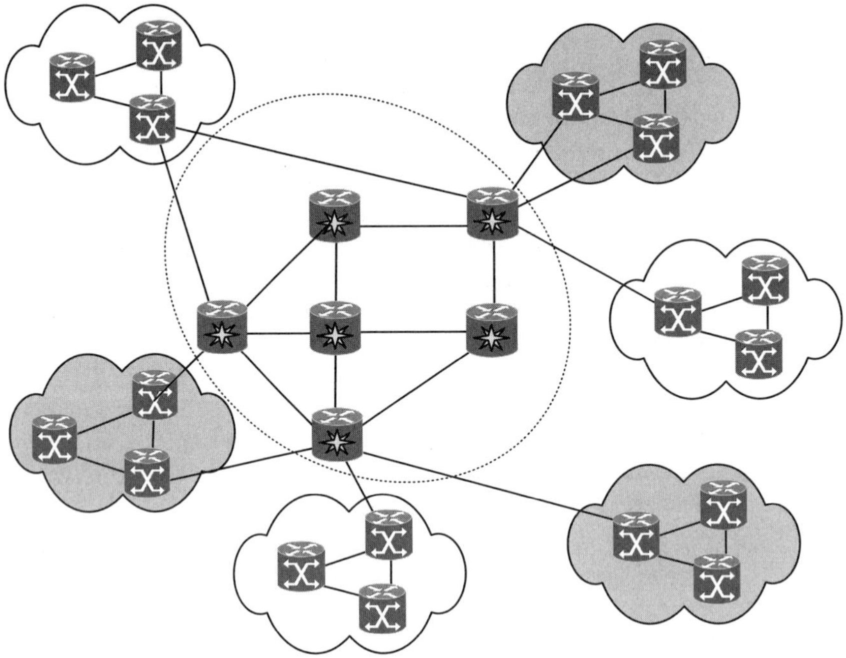

Figure 12.3 Layer One VPNs.

separate network elements interconnected with at least one CE-PE link which may not physically exist.

CE-PE links could be managed by the Customer or by the Provider or by some third party. A CE-PE link could be a static link or enabled by a network connection (possibly an L1VPN connection) provided by the same or some other Provider.

12.2 Layer One VPN Deployment Scenarios

In this section we will analyze several L1VPN deployment scenarios. This analysis will help to clarify different service models and the full spectrum of requirements for an L1VPN application from both Provider and Customer perspectives.

12.2.1 *Multi-Service Backbone*

Let us consider a large Provider network delivering multiple services to its Customers (see Figure 12.5). One way to manage such a network is to divide it

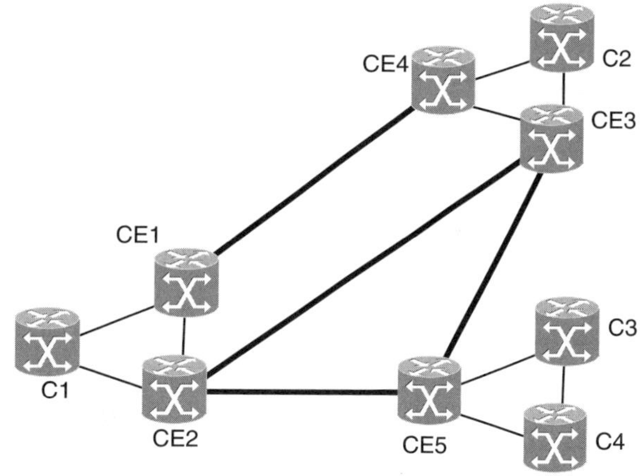

Figure 12.4 The TE network view seen by VPN 1.

administratively into several departments. Let us assume that department A is responsible for providing service A (say, TDM) to the Customers, while department B provides service B (say, IP). Furthermore, let us assume that a third department — Layer One Core — provides Layer One services (connectivity, capacity, protection, and so forth) for departments A and B so that they can transfer user traffic between their physical locations. The traffic delivered over the Layer One Core could be of any type, and so the same transport resources could be shared between multiple higher-layer services. One way to organize such a division of responsibilities between the departments is for the Layer One Core department to provide internal L1VPN services to the other departments. The customers of these L1VPN services (that is, nodes P-CE1, P-CE2, P-CE3, and P-CE4 in the figure) can automatically discover which of the P-CE nodes can be interconnected, and can establish appropriate Layer One connections to provide links for the higher-layer services.

What is significant about this deployment scenario is that one can assume complete trust between the parties (all of them belong to the same organization). This means that the amount of information about the internal resources of the Layer One Core that is advertised to the rest of the network is limited only by scalability concerns and internal policies. For instance, matters could be organized in such a way that every Provider network node outside of the Layer One Core would know about every Layer One Core resource.

Considering these circumstances one may wonder why we would ever need internal L1VPN services. Suppose there is a requirement to deliver IP traffic between CE4 and CE8. Assuming that all Provider nodes are GMPLS capable, it would be possible to take advantage of the GMPLS multi-region/multi-layer concept (see Chapter 8 for details). Specifically, PE4 could compute a multi-layer

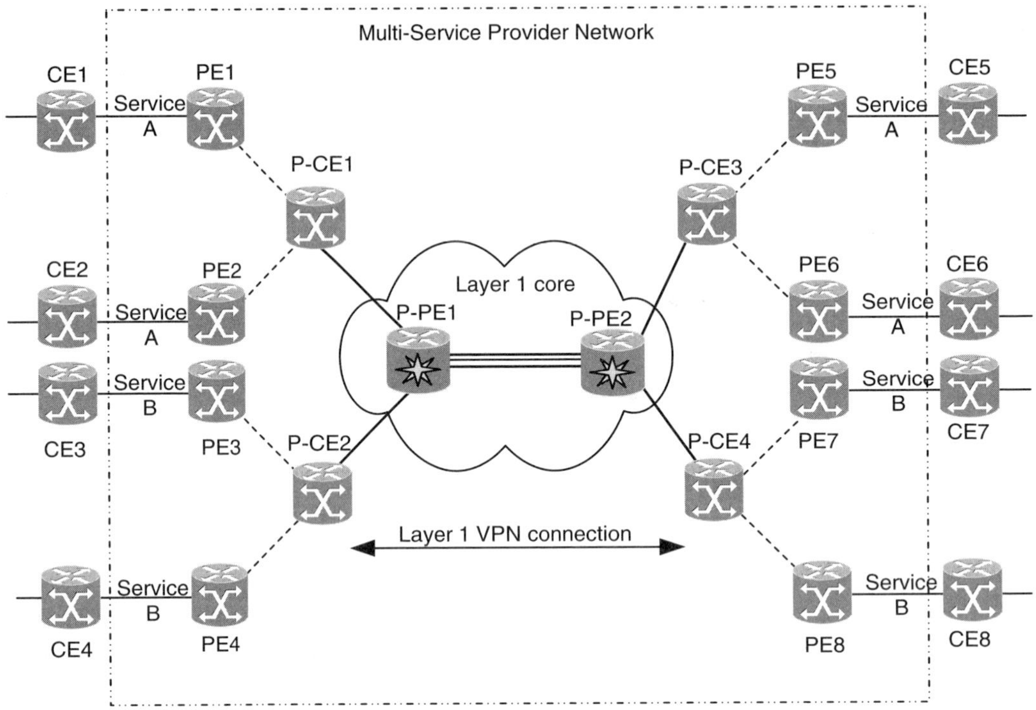

Figure 12.5 Multi-service backbone scenario.

path from itself to PE8. The LSP setup would trigger the establishment of a hierarchical LSP (H-LSP) and advertisement of the associated TE link between P-CE2 and P-CE4. Provided that the H-LSP has sufficient unreserved resources, it could carry other LSPs; for example, one going from PE3 to PE7.

There are several reasons why the internal L1VPN approach is better. The first reason is the control plane connectivity. PE8 holds information about the reachability and TE links within the Customer site to which it provides access, and PE4 needs to get access to this information. Transport connections over the Layer One Core guarantee only data plane connectivity; hence the control plane connectivity requires additional service(s), configuration/management effort, and possibly out-of-band network resources. As was mentioned earlier and as will be discussed in detail later, L1VPNs provide a broad set of services including arbitrary control plane data exchange between CEs that belong to the same VPN. Hence an L1VPN, for example, makes possible the establishment of an IGP adjacency between P-CE2 and P-CE4 for the purposes of routing and TE information exchange.

The second reason for using internal L1VPNs is the flexibility they offer for applying different policies per VPN. For example, the view of Layer One Core internals could be controlled on a per-VPN basis, encouraging the use of transport resources differently for, say, TDM and IP services. Likewise, the transport connections could be provisioned to recover from network failures in different ways depending on which VPN sites they interconnect.

The third reason is that the internal L1VPN service eliminates any requirement for homogeneity of the control plane managing different networks. For example, ATM services could be provided using an ATM control plane with transport connections interconnecting remote ATM sites realized via GMPLS.

12.2.2 *Carrier's Carrier*

Consider a situation where a Layer Two/Layer Three Service Provider network has several geographically separated sites interconnected via Layer One services received from a Layer One Service Provider. Note that both Providers are separate players — that is, entities under separate administrative and corporate control. The major difference from the previous scenario is the level of trust between the Layer One Service Provider and the Customers. The Layer One services include the necessary data plane and control plane connectivity between the connected sites; however, the Layer One Service Provider is likely to expose neither its internal topology nor information about the resources currently available in the network. In this case a node within the Layer Two/Layer Three Service Provider network — for example, node PE1 in Figure 12.6 — views the entire Layer One Service Provider network as a single node (called the *virtual node* or *logical node*). When PE1 computes a path and considers a physical node (say, node P-CE1) to be a part of the path, it can control which TE links the path uses to enter and exit the node. However, it does not know about P-CE1's internal resources and cannot control the way that the inbound and outbound TE links will be interconnected, nor can it know how the path could be protected from internal resource failures. Similarly, PE1 can control how the computed path crosses the Layer One Service Provider network (the virtual node) only in terms of CE-PE links; that is, it cannot influence the path selection within the transport network.

It is fair to note that the Layer One Service Provider may advertise some limited information about the internal state of its network. Such information could be leaked into the Customer network sites in terms of abstract links interconnecting pairs of PEs on a per-VPN basis and could be used, for example, in diverse path computation.

12.2.3 *Layer One Resource Trading*

Let us assume that the Layer Two/Layer Three Service Provider can use external Layer One services from not one but two or more Layer One Service

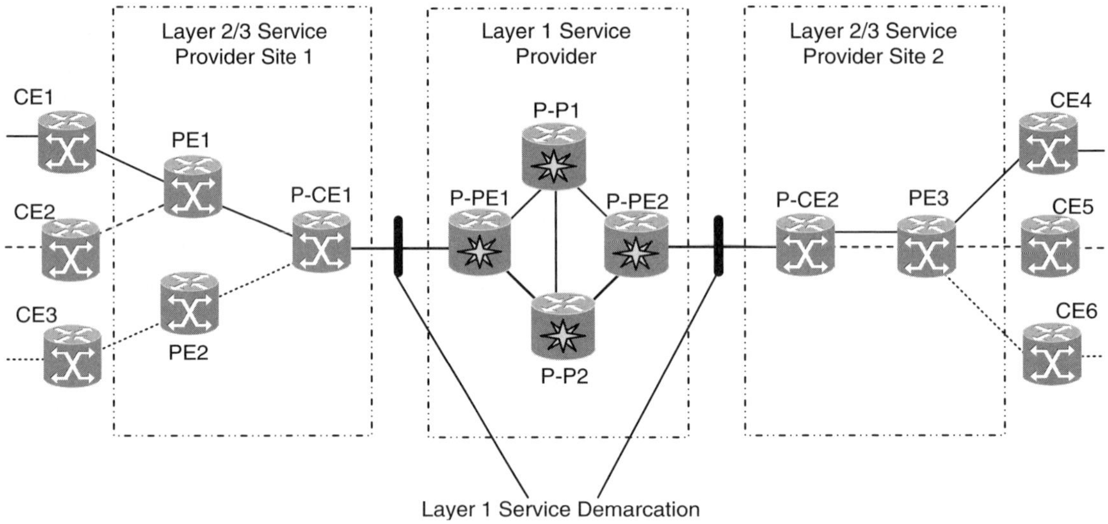

Figure 12.6 Carrier's carrier scenario.

Providers (see Figure 12.7). Such *multi-homing* is useful because at any point in time it is possible to select a service from one of the Layer One Service Providers depending on the cost of a suitable L1VPN connection, its availability, capacity, and so forth. In such a scenario Layer One Service Providers must be more "open" than in the Carrier's Carrier case. Specifically, they need to expose to the Customers (to a certain degree and on a per-VPN basis) information about services they provide and, possibly, some view of the internal state of their network, and provide timely notifications about changes so that the Customers can choose from which Layer One Provider to obtain the service. The term *resource trading* means that a particular Customer, by looking at information published by the Providers, continually decides how to make best use of the services they offer. For instance, at some point in time a Customer may decide to switch from one Provider to another if the latter can better satisfy the Customer's needs. Note also that an additional Provider could be used just for backup.

12.2.4 *Complex Layer One VPN*

In each of the previous examples, an L1VPN connection always contained three components at any point in time.

- Static link interconnecting the CE of the source site and the adjacent PE (for example, P-CE1–P-PE1 in Figure 12.6)

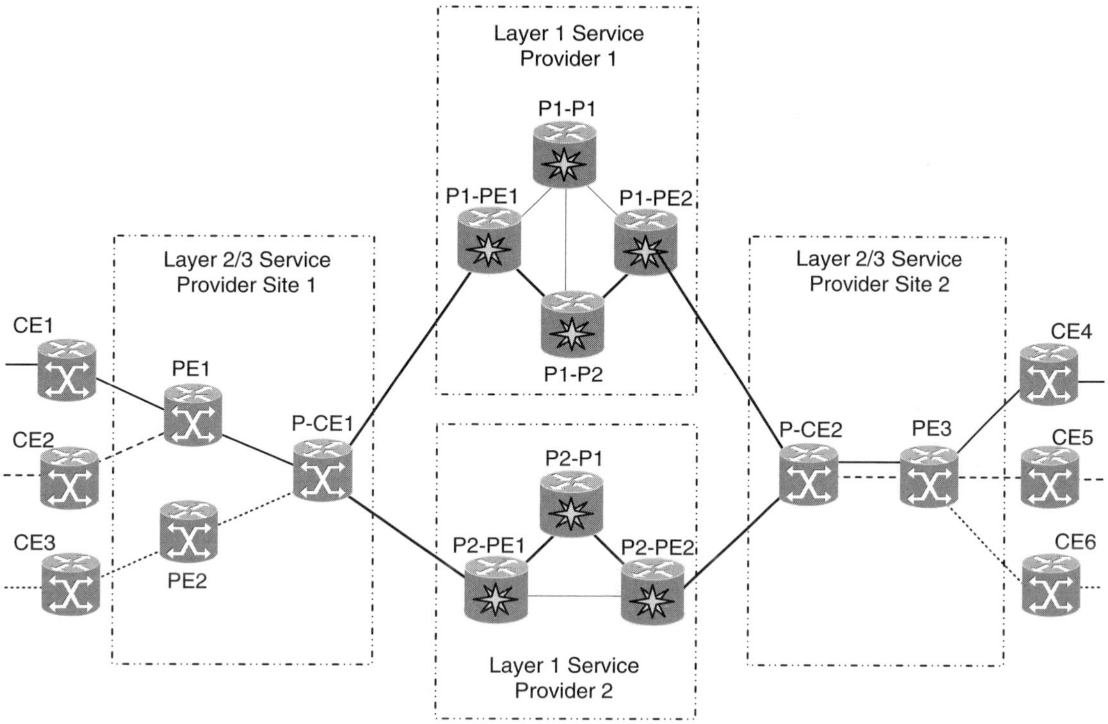

Figure 12.7 Resource trading scenario.

- Dynamic connection across the Provider network (P-PE1–P-PE2 in the same figure)
- Static link interconnecting the CE of the destination site and the adjacent PE (P-PE2–P-CE2, again in Figure 12.6)

However, it is possible for an L1VPN connection to have a more complex structure. Examples of such connections are inter-SP and nested L1VPN connections. Such connections require much more complex L1VPN services.

Consider the situation where the Layer One Service Provider in Figure 12.6 cannot provide the requested L1VPN service connecting P-CE1 to P-CE2 on its own and uses the cooperation of one or more other Providers to satisfy the request. The result of such cooperation is an inter-SP L1VPN Service providing data and control plane connectivity between Customer sites across multiple Layer One Service Provider networks (see Figure 12.8).

Let us assume now that the P-CE1–P-PE1 connection in Figure 12.6 is not a static link, but rather a link enabled by an L1VPN connection in its own right

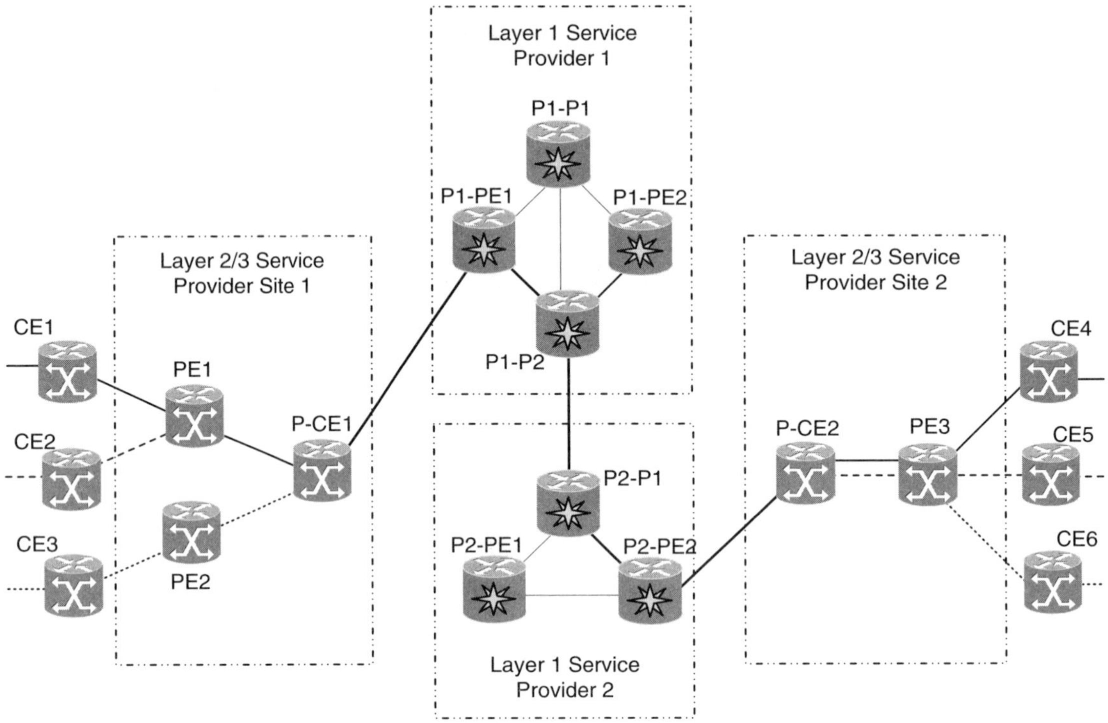

Figure 12.8 Inter-SP Layer One VPN.

resulting from a different L1VPN service received from the same or some other Provider. This would be an example of nesting L1VPNs (see Figure 12.9). The service that provides control and data plane connectivity between P-CE1 and P-CE2 is called *nesting* because it encompasses another service — one that interconnects P-CE1 and P-CE3 and is used as a base for the P-CE1–P2-PE1 link. Another example of nesting L1VPNs is shown in Figure 12.10. In this case the L1VPN Service Provider network has several isolated geographical sites and uses L1VPN services of other Providers to interconnect them, so that one or more links participating in the PE-PE segments of the L1VPN connections provided to the Customer are themselves enabled by L1VPN connections.

Despite some similarity between inter-SP and nested L1VPN services — both involve more than one Provider at the same time — they are fundamentally different and drive different requirements for service by Customers and Providers. From the Customer viewpoint an inter-SP service is no different from a single-SP service. The Provider is fully responsible for identifying other Providers with which it needs to cooperate, establishing peering relationships with them, and providing necessary end-to-end splicing in the data and control planes. Thus, for example,

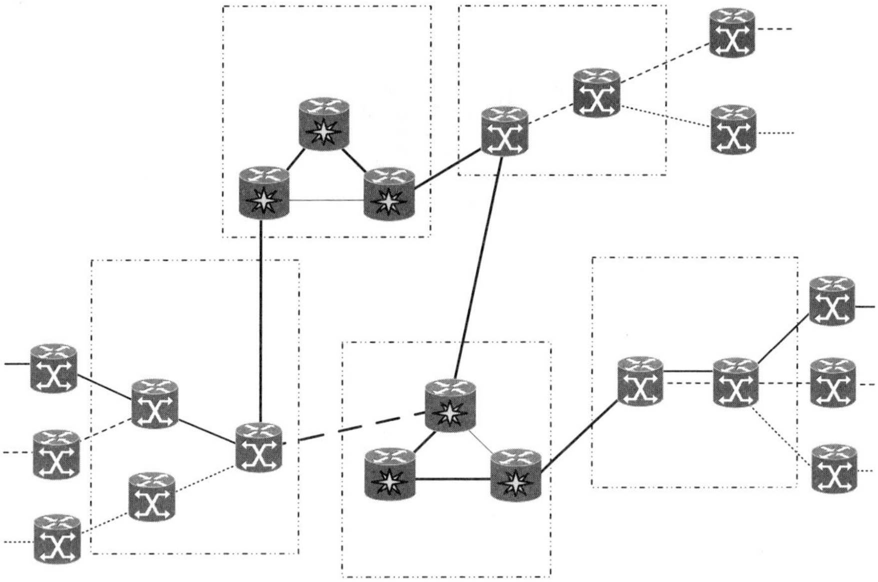

Figure 12.9 Nesting Layer One VPNs. One of the CE-PE links of a VPN connection is provided by a different VPN service.

directly attached Customers could receive membership information about VPN members that are connected with the help of other Providers.

On the other hand the Provider does not understand or perceive the relationship between nesting and nested L1VPN services: they are completely independent as far as it is concerned. It is the Customer who should provide all the necessary logic to enable the use of an L1VPN connection as a link for another L1VPN connection. For example, it is the responsibility of P-CE3 (see Figure 12.9) to relay the nesting VPN membership information received from P-PE1 to P-CE1 (possibly by using the transparent control plane exchange service provided by the nested VPN). Likewise, it is the responsibility of P-CE3 to provide the necessary splicing in the data plane for the purpose of P-CE1–P-CE2 data plane connectivity.

12.3 Resource-Sharing Models

Different requirements could be drawn for Customer and Provider views of L1VPN service implementation depending on how the control and data plane resources of

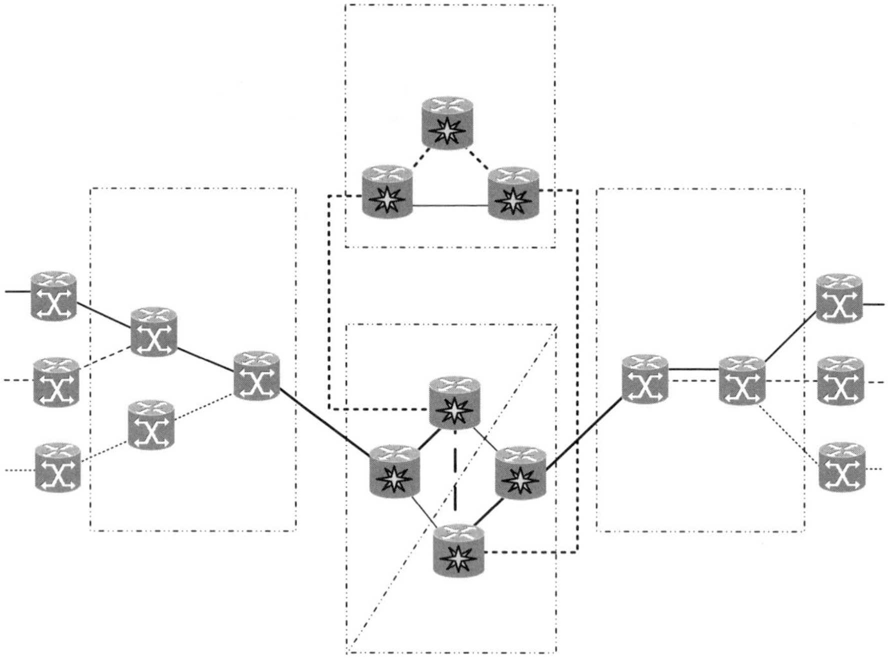

Figure 12.10 Nesting Layer One VPNs. One of the links of a PE-PE segment of a VPN connection is provided by a different VPN service.

the Provider network are distributed between different VPNs. The following data plane resource sharing models could be considered:

- Shared
- Dedicated
- Hybrid

In the shared model any Provider network resource can be allocated to any of the VPNs. The advantage of this model compared with the dedicated model is that a particular resource is available for all VPNs as long as it is not allocated to any VPN. In other words there cannot be a situation in this model where there is an unused resource within the Provider network that cannot be allocated for use by one VPN because it is dedicated for use by some other VPN(s). However, in this model it can never be guaranteed that a particular resource will be available for a certain VPN at a certain point in time. The only guarantee is that some minimum capacity (agreed upon in the service contract) is always available to provide connectivity between any pair of CEs. There is no reason to advertise shared resources to the Customers in this model, because this information cannot be used as a constraint in the path selection process.

In the dedicated resource-sharing model the Provider network resources are statically split between VPNs and can only be used to support L1VPN services for the VPNs to which they are dedicated. A resource may be dedicated for a single VPN or may be available for use by some subset of the total number of VPNs. In the hybrid model there is a pool of shared resources available for general use by any VPN, while some of the Provider network resources are dedicated for use in specific VPNs.

The Customers can take advantage of per-VPN resource publication in the dedicated or hybrid models because they can have full (dedicated model) or limited (hybrid model) control over path selection and can establish, for example, L1VPN connections that are disjoint from each other. The Provider can publish the dedicated resources as they are — as they are seen by the Provider network nodes — or can provide some sort of summarization/aggregation (for instance, by advertising abstract links that interconnect PEs).

The Provider control plane resources are likely to be shared between VPNs, although it is reasonable to consider the dedicated and hybrid models for control plane resources (for example, control channels) as well.

12.4 Layer One VPN Functional Model

It should be obvious from the L1VPN application point of view only CEs and PEs are important: C-devices, for instance, do not see any difference between static links interconnecting them within Customer sites and CE-CE links realized via L1VPN connections. Likewise, P-devices participate in the provisioning of the PE-PE segments and CE-CE control plane data transfer, but are not aware of the L1VPNs, do not maintain VPN-related states, and do not perform any VPN-related processing. Therefore, the ITU-T Study Group 13 has identified two functional "players" in L1VPNs — CEs and PEs. They are supposed to realize the functionality of dynamic L1VPN applications as required from the Customer and Provider sides, respectively. Functions that are expected from each of the sides are summarized in Tables 12.1 and 12.2; message exchanges between the sides are shown in Figure 12.11. It is important to bear in mind that the PE and CE are logical entities that could be physically co-located within the same network device.

It was mentioned earlier, but is worth highlighting again, that the demand for CE-CE out-of-band control plane connectivity is an important distinction between L1VPNs and Layer Two/Three VPNs, because in the latter case the inter-site data plane connectivity guarantees inter-site control plane connectivity.

Table 12.1 Functions to be provided by PEs

Function	Mandatory/Optional
Maintaining policies per VPN and per CE/per VPN	Mandatory
Providing authorization and authentication of VPN join requests	Mandatory
Providing authorization and authentication of VPN policy modification requests	Mandatory
Distributing VPN membership information between VPN PEs (VPN membership auto discovery)	Mandatory
Providing authorization/authentication of VPN connection requests	Mandatory
Managing Traffic Engineering Database state on a per-VPN basis for publishing per-VPN resource view of the Provider network to the Customer	Optional and only for resources dedicated to be used in particular VPNs
Limiting connectivity to the set of CEs that currently belong to the VPN of the requested connection	Mandatory
Identifying remote PE (P-space) address associated with the requested connection remote CE (VPN-space) address	Mandatory
Identifying parameters of the requested connection PE-PE segment by deriving them from the request received from the local CE and applying per-VPN and per-CE/per-VPN policies (capacity, link colors, recovery type, and so forth)	Mandatory
Computing one or more paths to the remote PE	Mandatory
Signaling (setting up, modifying, tearing down) of one or several PE-PE segments that are capable of providing agreed upon basic transport services (connectivity, capacity, data type encoding, and availability) for the requested VPN connection	Mandatory
Forwarding local CE control plane information to the remote PE so that it could be forwarded further to the remote CE	Optional
Maintaining connectivity information on a per-VPN basis to be ready to respond to Customer Network Management (CNM) requests	Optional
Collecting VPN connection related statistics (failures, rejections, data plane alarms, and so forth), gathering performance monitoring data	Optional
Accounting (recording the Provider network resource usage)	Optional

12.5 Layer One VPN Service Models

The main objective of this chapter is to analyze how GMPLS technology could be used to provision and manage L1VPN services. The discussion depends heavily

Table 12.2 Functions to be provided by CEs

Function	Mandatory/Optional
Selecting class of L1VPN services	Mandatory
Identifying destinations of L1VPN connections (that is, remote CEs)	Mandatory
Defining per-CE/per-VPN policies	Optional
Selecting parameters of L1VPN connections (bandwidth, link colors, requirements for recovery, and so forth)	Optional
Computing paths to be taken by the connections over the Provider network	Optional and only if the Provider publishes a per-VPN resource view of its network

on what service model is used for building the L1VPNs, especially on how the Customer and Provider control planes are involved in the provisioning process, and what expectations the L1VPN application has of the control plane.

One can distinguish the following three service models which drive how the L1VPNs could be implemented:

- Management-based
- Signaling Only
- Signaling and Routing

In the *Management-based* service model, Customer and Provider communicate only via the management plane; specifically, the Customer NMS sends requests to the Provider NMS to establish L1VPN connections between specified pairs of CEs. The Provider NMS responds with information about the status of current L1VPN connections: whether their setup has succeeded or not, what are the reasons for failures, what data plane problems have been detected, what recovery actions have been taken, how the QoS performance evaluation looks compared with the parameters agreed upon in the SLAs, and so forth. PE-PE segments of the connections could be provisioned either statically (via the management plane) or dynamically (soft-permanent LSPs via the control plane). In the latter case GMPLS could be used. However, even in this case, the L1VPN application does not place any new requirements on GMPLS — most currently available GMPLS implementations can do soft-permanent LSPs. CE and PE do not talk to each other via the control plane, and because of this the service model is of no further importance for our discussions.

In the *Signaling Only* service model the scope of the CE-PE control plane communication is limited to the signaling message exchanges; that is, CE uses the User-Network Interface (UNI) to dynamically request, modify, and tear down

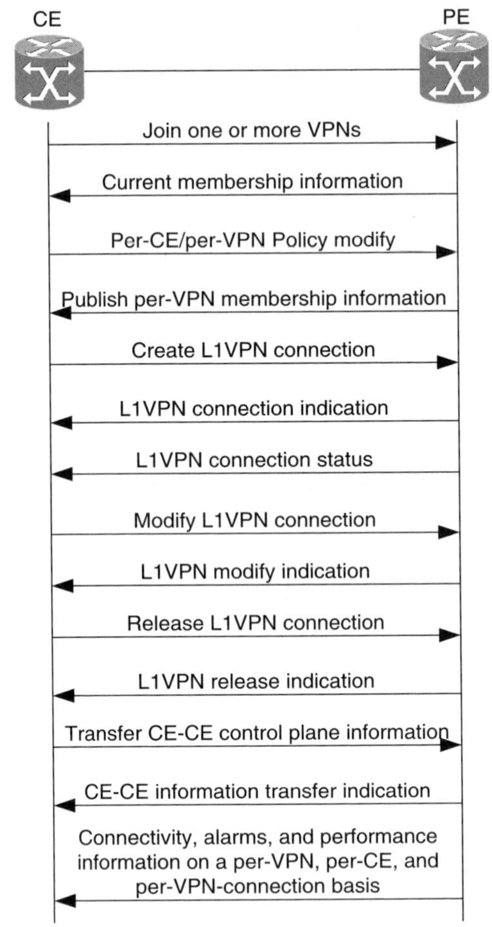

Figure 12.11 Message exchange between CE and PE during L1VPN management.

L1VPN connections. There is no other control plane information exchange over the UNI. PEs, for example, do not expose the Provider network resources to CEs in any form. Likewise, CEs are supposed to use static configuration, the management plane, or other services to learn about CEs located in remote sites and to exchange routing and TE information with them.

The *Signaling and Routing* service model is the most interesting model because the UNI between CE and PE is used for all L1VPN application needs. In other words, this service model enables the most complete integration of on-demand L1VPN services and is, therefore, a major target for the use of GMPLS — the combination of GMPLS and L1VPNs in this model provides another way to translate technology into revenue. The exchange of control information across the UNI between CE and

PE is not limited to signaling message exchanges. Routing message exchanges between CE and PE are the main way for a CE to learn about other CEs belonging to the same VPN, and to receive the routing and TE information from remote VPN sites. The PE uses the UNI to publish information about the Provider network resources available for new connections within a particular L1VPN. In this respect this service model is further broken into three models:

- Virtual Node
- Virtual Link
- Per-VPN Peer

In the *Virtual Node* model PEs leak no resource information to the attached CEs apart from describing the state of remote PE-CE links. Thus, CEs view the entire Provider network as a single node that can be entered and exited by LSPs over CE-PE links associated with the particular VPN. The CEs have no concept of, nor influence over, how the services that interconnect them are mapped onto the Provider network. This model is most suitable for the case where all Provider network resources are shared between the VPNs.

The Virtual Node model might seem to be the simplest of the three; however, it is not without problems. To make C and CE controllers perceive the Provider network as a single transport node, PEs have to synchronize their advertisements into the VPN routing protocol. Specifically, they need to advertise not only local PE-CE TE links, but also all remote PE-CE TE links associated with the same VPN (fortunately, this information is available as a result of the VPN auto-discovery process). Furthermore, all PEs that belong to a particular VPN should use the same advertising router ID and should advertise the same TE Router Address in the top level TE RTR TLV of the TE LSA/LSP. In other words, all of the PEs should advertise roughly the same set of LSAs/LSPs into the VPN routing protocol. Another problem is that a C or CE controller, while performing a path computation, will treat the vertex representing the Virtual Node on the VPN TE graph just as it would treat any other vertex. Specifically, the path computation engine will assume that a path can enter and exit the vertex via any pair of edges that terminate on the vertex. However, there is no guarantee that an internal path of the required quality exists between any pair of PEs across the Provider network. Hence, there is a need for additional information to be advertised synchronously by each of the PEs of a particular VPN. We need a matrix of internal connectivity or connectivity limitations between any pair of PE-CE links in the context of the VPN in question. This information (although it is not trivial) could be taken into consideration by the path computation engine, so that the resulting path will enter and exit the Virtual Node over a pair of CE-PE links that can be interconnected internally across the Provider network. All of these problems are quite new for GMPLS and need to be solved in the context of L1VPN applications.

In the *Virtual Link* model, PEs, in addition to advertising all VPN PE-CE TE links, also provide advertisement of virtual (also called abstract) TE links interconnecting all or some pairs of PEs. This information helps the Customer to understand how its sites could be interconnected efficiently because, for example, the cost of transferring data between a particular pair of PEs (and hence CEs) is clearer. The Virtual Link model might require more information to be leaked by PEs into the VPN routing compared with the Virtual Node model; however, each PE in the Virtual Link model is viewed by the VPN as a separate transport node. Hence, the problems discussed above for the Virtual Node model (the PE advertising synchronization, the advertising of internal connectivity) are not an issue in the Virtual Link model.

The *Per-VPN Peer* model is useful when some or all Provider network resources are dedicated for use in particular VPNs. PEs in this case may choose to publish the state of the dedicated resources to all or some VPN Customers. One can guess that the Customers will "like" such a model the most because they can exert a fairly strong influence on how their L1VPN connections cross the Provider network are achieved. For example, the Customer can select different P-links for different L1VPN connections so that there will be less chance of both failing at the same time. Another example of how the per-VPN view of Provider network resources could be used is in the computation of a path to interconnect two C-devices (not necessarily CEs) located at different sites: The published information could be considered while selecting a pair of CEs to be used, possibly triggering the establishment of an addition L1VPN connection. The Provider, on the other hand, will not like this model, because the Provider would prefer to organize matters in such a way that its resources could be shared between VPNs, and it would like to retain full control over how the resources are used. In other words, the Provider will prefer the Virtual Node model.

The way in which support for the trade-offs between these models is expressed within the standards bodies is very interesting. Currently, many Layer One Providers are seeking to influence the discussion heavily in favor of the Virtual Node model and are trying to preclude other models. Although this places L1VPNs within their comfort zone, it may not be very forward-thinking, because other Providers are more openly considering the potential revenue streams that can be generated by offering to meet the Customer's needs and desires.

12.6 GMPLS-Based Layer One VPN Offerings

In this section we will provide a brief analysis of two currently available GMPLS-based L1VPN solutions: Generalized Virtual Private Networks (GVPNs) and GMPLS Overlays.

Understandably, the two solutions have many things in common because they are both based on GMPLS. This includes CE-PE link addressing, CE-PE signaling, and dynamic provisioning of the PE-PE segments of CE-CE L1VPN connections. The major difference is in the mechanism used for VPN membership auto-discovery: how PEs learn about remote CEs, which VPNs they belong to, and what PEs are attached to them.

Both solutions make the following assumptions regarding CE-PE link addressing.

- The CE side of a CE-PE link (CE port) has a VPN space address (that is unique within a particular VPN) assigned by the Customer. Let us call it the CE_ID.
- The PE side of a CE-PE link (PE port) has two addresses. The first one, the PE_ID, is assigned by the Provider and is unique within the Provider address space. The second, the PE_VPN_ID, is assigned by the Customer and is allocated from the same address space as CE_ID.
- The PE port is also aware of a VPN ID — a number that unambiguously identifies VPN within the Provider domain.

For every related VPN, a PE maintains a table that keeps associations between <CE_ID, PE_VPN_ID, PE_ID> triplets and the state of the corresponding CE-PE links that it has discovered locally (for example, from configuration) and from remote sites via VPN auto-discovery procedures.

Both approaches use GMPLS to signal between CE and PE for the purpose of initiating, modifying, and releasing L1VPN connections with remote CEs. Furthermore, the GMPLS control plane is used in both cases for everything that is required for provisioning and maintenance of the PE-PE segments of the L1VPN connections: resource advertisement, path computation, provisioning of working and recovery LSPs, protection/restoration from network failures, and so on. Surprisingly, the current GMPLS toolkit includes all the necessary tools for this purpose with just one exception: There is no support for per-VPN resource management. If the Provider decides to dedicate a particular P-link for use in only one or a subset of VPNs, there is no easy way to let all PEs know about this fact. Thus it is hard for the PEs to publish the per-VPN resource view of the Provider network to the Customers for them to include in path computations.

12.6.1 *GVPNs*

The idea behind the solution shown in Figure 12.12 is to extend the BGP-VPN framework that was successfully used for Layer Three and Layer Two VPNs onto L1VPNs. It is assumed that the BGP routing protocol is running at least within the Provider domain (I-BGP) and preferably between CEs and PEs (E-BGP).

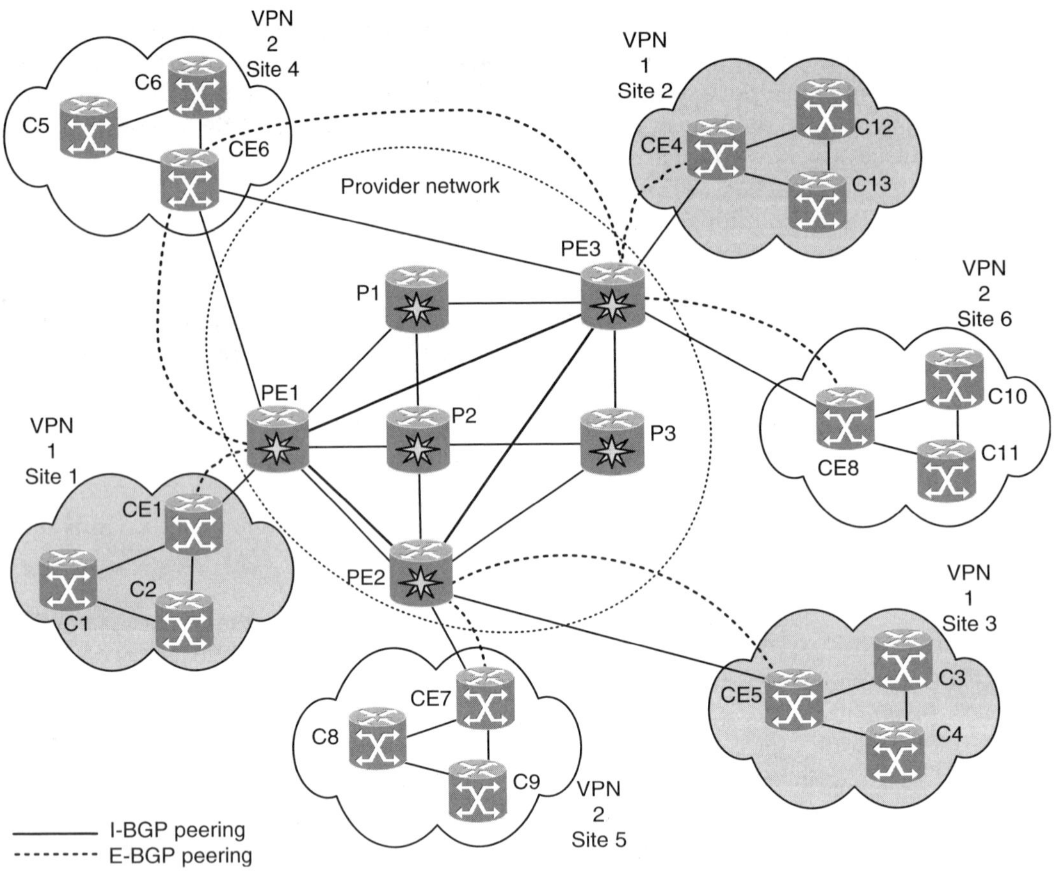

Figure 12.12 Generalized VPNs (GVPNs).

In the context of GVPN, the table containing the CE-PE address bindings along with the state of the corresponding CE-PE links is called the *Generalized Virtual Switching Instance* (GVSI). The GVSIs are maintained by PEs on a per-VPN basis. A GVSI is populated from two sources. Information related to local CE-PE links (called *local* information) is learned from configuration optionally in conjunction with the data received from the attached CEs (via E-BGP). Information regarding remote CE-PE links (called *remote* information) is obtained via the BGP-based VPN auto-discovery process that can be described as follows.

- All PEs are interconnected by a mesh of I-BGP sessions or via Route Reflectors (see Figure 12.12).

- Each GVSI is configured with one or more BGP Route Target Communities called export Route Targets. They are used for tagging the local information (that is, associating the information with local CE-PE links) whenever the information is sent to other PEs over I-BGP.
- Additionally, each GVSI is configured with one or more BGP Route Target Communities called import Route Targets. They are used for constraining the information to be installed in the GVSI. Information received in a BGP update is installed only in those GVSIs that have at least one import Route Target matching one of the export Route Targets found in the BGP message.
- Each PE sends the local information from all GVSIs to all other PEs. This information, however, ends up installed only in proper remote GVSIs because of the filtering mentioned above. Thus, every PE for each associated VPN possesses information about all CEs currently available in the VPN. This information is synchronized on a per-VPN basis with all other PEs.

It is not specified how a CE learns about the availability of other CEs within a particular L1VPN; however, there is a recommendation to use BGP multi-protocol extensions for this purpose. PEs should establish E-BGP sessions with all attached CEs (as shown in Figure 12.12) and use them for sending updates of their VPN membership information. The use of other sources of membership information is not precluded; for example, local configuration.

VPN membership information is sufficient for a CE to originate L1VPN connections with other CEs; however, it is not sufficient to interconnect C-devices located in different VPN sites. To make this possible the Provider network should participate in the VPN routing. It should:

- Establish IGP (for example, OSPF) adjacencies between PEs and attached CEs
- Use these adjacencies for advertising the TE attributes of all PE-CE links pertinent to a particular VPN
- Flood Customer TE information between VPN sites

To achieve this, each PE runs multiple instances of the IGP-TE protocol(s): one for the discovery of the Provider network topology and resources (for talking to P-devices and other PEs) and one for each associated VPN (for every GVSI) for flooding the VPN information. GVSIs that belong to the same VPN establish direct IGP adjacencies with each other for the purpose of synchronization of the information received from different VPN sites. The underlying transport for such adjacencies are IP tunnels within the control plane (for example, IP-in-IP, GRE, or IP/MPLS tunnels) that could be configured/established every time a local GVSI learns about the existence of a new GVSI. Note that the configuration/establishment of the tunnels is decoupled from the auto-discovery process. In particular, it is bound neither to the moment nor to the way remote GVSIs are discovered.

It is important to note that this solution is designed only for the Virtual Node service model. Recall that in this model all Customer network nodes are supposed to view the entire Provider network as a single node. As was discussed earlier, to achieve this, *all* PEs need to advertise all PE-CE TE links belonging to the same VPN using the same *advertising Router ID* and *TE Router Address* (both values could be configured on each of the PEs on a per-VPN basis). Also, recall that in the Virtual Node model it is highly desirable that PEs advertise information about the internal connectivity between all pairs of CE-PE links.

The solution can be extended to support the Virtual Link model by making PEs and virtual TE links interconnecting them within particular VPN visible to the Customer. Specifically:

- Advertisements of PE-CE TE links terminating on different PEs should contain a distinct VPN-scope unique Router ID and TE Router Address. The IP part of the PE_VPN_ID of the advertising PE is a good candidate for this purpose.
- Advertisements of virtual PE-PE TE links should be leaked into some or all VPNs. Both sides of the links should be advertised by each of the ends (PEs). Each PE should use the same advertising Router ID/TE Router Address for advertising PE-CE and PE-PE TE links that belong to the same VPN.

When a CE decides to set up a VPN connection, it originates a GMPLS LSP Setup (RSVP Path) message and sends it to the attached PE over the CE-PE control channel. It is assumed that the channel cannot be shared between multiple VPNs; thus, the PE can figure out for which VPN the connection is requested (and hence the associated GVSI) without needing the VPN ID to be explicitly signaled by the CE. The SENDER_TEMPLATE object of the original LSP Setup message is associated with the source CE_ID; and the SESSION object with the destination CE_ID.

When the ingress PE receives the LSP Setup message it looks up the destination CE_ID in the GVSI and determines the PE_ID of the PE attached to the destination CE. It also defines the attributes of the PE-PE segment such as bandwidth, data encoding type, recovery requirements, and resource colors. Some of the attributes are deduced from the incoming message, and the rest by applying VPN and/or CE policies. After that, one or more paths are computed for the PE-PE segment and its recovery.

The question arises: How should the ingress PE proceed with the provisioning of the L1VPN connection? There are two possible options.

- Option 1: to provision the connection as a simple contiguous end-to-end LSP built of three segments: source CE to ingress PE, ingress PE to egress PE, and egress PE to destination CE.
- Option 2: to provision the ingress PE–egress PE segment as a separate tunnel and use it as an H-LSP for the CE-CE LSP.

Option 1 simply assumes that the provisioning of the PE-PE segment is a continuation of the provisioning of the LSP originated on the source CE and going to destination CE. To proceed with the LSP setup several things have to be accomplished. First, external (CE-PE) and internal (PE-P/PE) signaling protocols could be different; hence, the PE should make sure that the objects used in the external signaling can be tunneled through the Provider network to the remote PE for delivery to the remote CE. Secondly, the SENDER_TEMPLATE and SESSION objects of the original message should be modified. Specifically, the ingress PE_ID should replace the source CE_ID in the SENDER_TEMPLATE object, and the egress PE_ID should replace the destination CE_ID in the SESSION object. However, the two objects must be restored back to their original contents on the egress PE before the message is sent to the destination CE, which requires the information to be tunneled across the Provider network to the remote PE. Why are such replacements necessary? Indeed, while the setup proceeds over the Provider network, the objects are not going to be used for any purpose other than LSP identification; specifically, the Destination ID field of the SESSION object will not be used as an input for routing decisions since the message contains an explicit path encoded in the ERO.

Such replacements are necessary because the CEs have VPN scope addresses. Consider the situation where two CEs located in different VPNs originate two L1VPN connections. It is quite possible that both LSP Setup messages would contain identical SESSION and/or SENDER_TEMPLATE objects because addresses for the CEs are allocated from independent spaces that may contain the same address values. This would not cause any problems on PEs because the PEs are aware of VPNs through the VPN IDs and signaling relationships with CEs. However, P-nodes know nothing about the VPNs, and if the two LSP Setup messages happen to cross the same P-node, it will not be capable of associating them with different LSPs. To eliminate such a possibility it is necessary for the SESSION and SENDER_TEMPLATE objects to contain addresses from the Provider address space as the LSPs transition the Provider network.

Unfortunately, RSVP-TE does not react well to the situation where the SESSION and/or SENDER_TEMPLATE objects are modified along the path of the LSP Setup message. Consider the situation when a PE has lost (for some reason) the control state of a L1VPN connection LSP whose SESSION or SENDER_TEMPLATE objects were modified on the PE. In this case the PE would not be able to use network cooperation to make a direct mapping between

LSP segments while restoring the LSP control state because there would be no easy way to associate messages received from the upstream (for example, CE) and downstream (for example, P) neighbors.

Option 2 is more complex. It requires two stages. It must first establish a (or find an existing) PE-PE H-LSP and, after that, resume the provisioning of the CE-CE LSP using the H-LSP as a link interconnecting ingress and egress PEs. The good news is that this option does not have the protocol-related problems of Option 1. The CE-CE LSP Setup message is sent as it is from the ingress PE to the egress PE as a directed or targeted message, and P-nodes do not participate in processing it. Thus, there is no need to tunnel signaling objects across the Provider network. For the same reason the modification and restoration of the SESSION and SENDER_TEMPLATE objects is not required.

Note that LSP stitching could be used if the CE-PE links have the same switching capability as the PE-P and P-P links. However, if the Provider network resources are from a lower switching layer than the CE-PE links (for example, the Customer is connected by TDM CE-PE links to the Provider network built of OXCs), then using H-LSPs produces an additional useful byproduct — an ability to reuse the extra bandwidth allocated for other L1VPN connections because of the difference in bandwidth allocation granularity.

Now let us consider how the GVPN solution addresses other (non-signaling) control plane functions expected by L1VPN services. It was mentioned earlier that it is recommended that PEs use E-BGP to send VPN membership updates to attached CEs. The same transport (that is, the multi-protocol BGP extensions) could be used for sending CEs additional information such as VPN connectivity, performance monitoring, and data plane alarms.

One of the expected services is the propagation of arbitrary control plane information between CEs. The CEs need such control channels for the purpose of establishing signaling adjacencies, LMP sessions, and so forth. One way to realize the CE-CE control channels is via a combination of using E-BGP on the CE-PE links, and IP tunnels that interconnect GVSIs within the same VPN (the same tunnels that are used as underlying transport for GVSI-GVSI IGP adjacencies). It should be noted that the flooding of routing and TE information between the VPN sites could be achieved via routing adjacencies built on top of the control channels and could be transparent for the Provider network. However, it is beneficial to realize the flooding as a separate L1VPN service. This would make it possible for the Provider network to participate in the Customer routing in the following way. Consider the situation where a PE receives an L1VPN connection setup request to some C (not a CE) network node located in the remote VPN site. If the Provider network provides a special service for the flooding of TE and routing VPN information, the PE is aware of the VPN TE topology and can select the optimal path toward the destination C, rather than only up to the egress PE/CE.

Finally, the support for the Per-VPN Peer service model needs to be addressed. First, TE information describing internal Provider network TE links cannot be propagated beyond CEs. This is because Cs are not aware of VPNs and could be confused by these advertisements because addresses of the Provider network TE links may collide with addresses of the Customer network TE links. For the same reason, CEs are the only entities that can make use of such information while selecting paths to be taken by L1VPN connections across the Provider network. Therefore, a reasonable solution would be to have PEs publish the VPN view of the Provider network by sending to the attached CEs *link-scope* TE LSAs that describe the Provider network TE links (real and/or virtual) that are dedicated for use in the corresponding VPNs. The LSAs could be sent over the same adjacencies that are used for flooding Customer routing and TE information between VPN sites. As mentioned earlier, there is a need for an additional TE Link sub-TLV — VPN ID sub-TLV — so that PEs could internally discover which Provider network TE links are dedicated to which VPNs.

12.6.2 *GMPLS Overlays*

BGP is a vector-style routing protocol primarily designed for distribution of reachability information over large IP networks. The protocol has found several uses in IP/MPLS networks and may be considered part of the GMPLS protocol family for PSC networks. But BGP is not considered part of a non-PSC network control plane — link state style IGPs (OSPF or ISIS) are sufficient and more suitable for traffic engineering needs.

BGP is seen by many Layer One Service Providers as a complex protocol that is difficult to manage. They have no deployment experience of BGP and the optical equipment currently on the market does not support the protocol, but BGP plays an important role in the GVPN solution described in the previous section. This makes GVPN less attractive for Layer One Service Providers: It is one thing to build an application on top of well-known and deployed protocols, but it is a totally different thing to implement a new complex protocol just for the sake of a single application.

GMPLS Overlays (also known as GMPLS UNI) provide another GMPLS-based solution for L1VPNs. It models the Provider network as a core network and the VPNs as overlay networks (or simply overlays), whose otherwise isolated sites are interconnected by means of the core network. Overlays are connected to the core network in the data plane by CE-PE links and in the control plane via CE-PE control channels. Neither CE-PE links nor control channels can be shared between different overlays.

The services provided by the core network to overlays are dynamically provisioned CE-CE LSP connections of particular capacity, availability, and data encoding type. The CE-PE channels are to be used for the signaling exchanges between CEs and the attached PEs. The CE-PE signaling protocol is fully compatible with (in fact, identical to) the standard GMPLS RSVP.

CE-PE TE link addressing is the same as for the GVPN solution; specifically, a CE port address is assigned by the Customer and is unique within a particular overlay network. A PE port has two addresses. The first one is assigned by the Customer from the same space as the CE port addresses and hence is also unique within the overlay network. The second address is assigned by the Provider from the core network address space (the space of addresses for internal core links). The core address space could be the same as the overlay network address space, but this is not necessary, and it is unlikely to be implemented in this way.

For the purpose of computing paths for the PE-PE segments of the CE-CE connections, each PE must be able to translate the destination CE address into an egress PE address. This is accomplished by maintaining a table per overlay on each PE containing the CE-PE address bindings and CE-PE TE link attributes for all CE-PE TE links that are configured for the overlay in question. The information related to local CE-PE TE links is learned via configuration. The mechanism by which a PE learns about remote CE-PE TE links is not limited to the BGP-based auto-discovery described for GVPNs. There are multiple ways the information could be obtained: configuration, automated management plane tools, or a variety of auto-discovery techniques. The latter could be based on some control plane protocol(s) that are available or are made available in the core network. One example of such protocols is LDAP. It is also possible to use TE extensions to the internal core IGP-TE (OSPF-TE or ISIS-TE) for the purpose of auto-discovery in a way similar to how IGP extensions are already used to advertise router capabilities. It is fair to note, though, that the BGP-based auto-discovery paradigm scales better because it does not require core non-PE nodes to participate in the discovery process. However, considering the relatively small size of existing transport networks, IGP-based auto-discovery is recognized as acceptable and may not be a problem.

The dynamic provisioning of CE-CE connections is almost identical to the process described for GVPNs. The source CE originates the GMPLS-UNI Setup (GMPLS RSVP Path) message, and specifies its own address and the address of the destination CE in the SENDER_TEMPLATE and SESSION objects, respectively, and sends the message to the attached PE. From the point of view of the PE, the CE-CE LSP setup is a two-stage process: First, it identifies the egress PE and establishes the H-LSP to it or finds a suitable existing H-LSP, and after that uses the H-LSP to carry the CE-CE LSP. Thus, the end-to-end CE-CE LSP always has exactly three hops: source CE to ingress PE, ingress PE to egress PE, and egress PE to destination CE.

An important requirement for the utility of an L1VPN model is that the control planes in the separate VPN sites should be able to communicate so that they can establish services that use the L1VPN connections. In some configurations (such as PSC overlays with a non-PSC core) this is easily achieved by the CEs, because these nodes are responsible for encapsulating packet traffic into the non-packet CE-CE LSPs. It is no extra burden to pass control plane traffic in the LSP together with the payload data. In this respect a link realized via the CE-CE L1VPN connection is no different from any other PSC link.

In other configurations where the overlay network is at a different switching layer from the core network, it may also be possible for the CE to encapsulate control plane traffic within the L1VPN connection; for example, by using overhead bytes within the encapsulation, or by withholding a timeslot within a lambda. But other configurations make this process hard or impossible, so another solution must be found to enable control plane communication between the overlay network sites.

One way to resolve this is to take advantage of the control channels that exist between the CEs and PEs and within the core network itself. These control channels (in-band or out-of-band) are packet-based and are capable of carrying the control plane traffic between the overlay sites. Because of addressing problems (overlay networks may use different address spaces from the core network), the easiest way to manage this is to establish IP tunnels between CEs within the control plane. Because the core network devices are unlikely to be able to support MPLS packet forwarding in the control plane (they are optical devices) the most likely tunnel technologies are IP-in-IP and GRE.

It would also be possible to tunnel the exchange of routing information in the same way so that all overlay sites could participate in the same IGP. Some care would be needed to make sure that the routing information in the core, and between CEs and PEs, did not get mixed up with the routing information that is specific to the overlay networks.

Note that the LSP Setup message originated by a CE over the GMPLS UNI might either not include an ERO at all, or might include one with sub-objects associated with ingress and egress PEs but not with any of the P-nodes or any links internal to the core network. This provides a way to support the Virtual Node and Virtual Link VPN Service models. On the other hand, if the Per-VPN Peer model is used, the ERO could be present and could indicate which core resources should be used to support the CE-CE LSP based on the per-overlay resource information published by the PE.

The GMPLS Overlay solution is simple and sufficient for implementing L1VPNs in the Signaling Only service model. It is harder to imagine its use in service models that include the exchange of routing information, but some controlled leaking of core routing information to the CEs is acceptable and the model begins to look more like the augmented model described in Chapter 13.

12.7 Further Reading

The ITU-T has described the functional requirements for L1VPNs in the following Recommendations.

Y.1312: Layer One Virtual Private Network Generic requirements and architecture elements, ITU-T Recommendation, September 2003

Y.1313: Layer One Virtual Private Network service and network architectures, ITU-T Recommendation, July 2004

The following Internet-Drafts and RFCs provide descriptions of the architectural models and proposed solutions for L1VPNs

draft-ietf-l1vpn-framework
  Framework for Layer One Virtual Private Networks

draft-ietf-l1vpn-applicability
  Applicability of GMPLS protocols and architectures to Layer One Virtual Private Networks

draft-ouldbrahim-ppvpn-gvpn-bgpgmpls
  GVPN Services: Generalized VPN Services using BGP and GMPLS Toolkit

RFC 4208
  Generalized Multiprotocol Label Switching(GMPLS) User-Network Interface (UNI): Resource ReserVation Protocol-Traffic Engineering (RSVP-TE) Support for the Overlay Model

CHAPTER 13

Architectural Models

This chapter describes the architectural models that can be applied to GMPLS networks. These architectures are not only useful for driving the ways in which networking equipment is deployed, but they are equally important in determining how the protocols themselves are constructed, and the responsibilities of the various protocol components.

Several distinct protocol models have been advanced and the choice between them is far from simple. To some extent, the architectures reflect the backgrounds of their proponents: GMPLS sits uncomfortably between the world of the Internet Protocol and the sphere of influence of more traditional telecommunications companies. As a result, some of the architectures are heavily influenced by the Internet, while others have their roots in SONET/SDH, ATM, and even the telephone system (POTS).

The supporters of the different architectures tend to be polarized and fairly dogmatic. Even though there are many similarities between the models, the proponents will often fail to recognize the overlaps and focus on what is different, making bold and forceful statements about the inadequacy of the other approaches. This chapter does not attempt to anoint any architecture as the best, nor does it even try to draw direct comparisons. Instead, each architecture is presented in its own right, and the reader is left to make up her own mind.

Also introduced in this chapter is the end-to-end principle that underlies the IETF's Internet architecture and then describes three different GMPLS architectural models. The peer and overlay models are simple views of the network and are natural derivatives of the end-to-end architectural model: They can be combined into the third model, the hybrid model, which has the combined flexibility of the two approaches. The architectural model specified by the International Telecommunication Union (ITU) for the Automatically Switched Optical Network (ASON) presents a different paradigm based on significant experience deploying and managing transport networks; it is presented at the end of the chapter and is followed by a discussion of the various ways to realize the architecture and the attempts to bridge the gap between the two architectures.

13.1 The Internet's End-to-End Model

The architectural principles of the Internet are described in RFC 1958, but, as that document points out, the Internet is continuously growing and evolving so that principles that seemed safe and obvious ten years ago are now no longer quite as straightforward. As new technologies and ideas are developed, it is possible to conceive of new architectural frameworks within which the Internet can continue to expand. Still, it is important to note that the Internet cannot be dismantled and rebuilt into a new network — it is a live network that must continue to operate in the face of innovation, and so new architectural paradigms must be integrated into the existing concepts in order to ensure a gentle migration.

The basic premise underlying the Internet's architecture is the delivery of end-to-end connectivity for the transport of data using intelligence that, as much as possible, is placed at the edges of the network. That is, an application wishing to supply a service across the Internet looks into the network to make an intelligent decision about how to achieve the service, and then makes specific directed requests to facilitate the service. The end-to-end principle means that information is only made available within the network on a "need-to-know" basis; the core of the network should be spared knowledge about the services that it is carrying, thus making the Internet massively more scalable. It also allows transit nodes to implement only basic protocols associated with data delivery, and avoid awareness of application protocols required to realize specific services. This makes the core nodes simpler to implement and, more important, means that new services and applications can be delivered over the Internet without the need to upgrade the core network.

A secondary determination is to make the Internet as independent as possible of the underlying physical technology; that is, it must be possible to construct the Internet from a wide variety of devices and connections that support a huge range of data speeds and very different switching granularities. The protocol layering architecture that is often described goes a long way to resolve this, and one of the key purposes of IP itself is to build up all data link layers to a common level of service for use by transport and application technologies.

In summary, the purpose of the nodes within the Internet is to deliver (and arrange for the delivery of) IP datagrams. Everything else should be done at the edges.

13.1.1 *How Far Can You Stretch an Architectural Principle?*

The origins of the end-to-end principle are rooted in discussions of where to place the "smarts." Where should the function of the communication system be placed? The answer was at the edges. But as the Internet evolved, grew larger, and became more complex, the question was extended to the consideration of where to store and maintain the protocol state associated with achieving end-to-end connections and services. The desire for scalability and flexibility drove this state to the edges of the network as well, and was reinforced by the growth of importance of network robustness and survivability. To recover from a partial network failure there should be no reliance on state held within the network, because that might be lost during a failure.

This model speaks loudly in favor of datagram services, because each datagram is independent and carries its own state information. However, more recent trends for traffic engineering in MPLS networks move away from datagram- or packet-based delivery and tend toward the provision of virtual circuits across the Internet. With GMPLS and the control of transport networks we are fully in the realm of logical and physical connections that are "nailed up" across the network. Connections require state: At the very least they require data plane state in the form of cross-connects. Where, then, does this leave the end-to-end architectural principle that tries to remove intelligence and state from the core of the network?

Even the IP packet network required some state to be held within the network. Not the least of this is the routing information needed for next hop forwarding of IP packets, but originally all of this information was independent of the transmitted data streams. Thus the core of the network did not need to know what applications or services it was delivering. Over time, however, the boundaries became fuzzy: QoS guarantees and session-based protocols were introduced and, although every effort was made to ensure that these protocols used "soft state" and were adaptive to network changes, these new protocols started to require the installation of state within the Internet. New rules were expressed stating that this state was acceptable, but must be kept to an absolute minimum.

Hard state — a state that is required for the proper operation of applications and that cannot be dynamically changed and reconstructed within the network — was still frowned upon and held at the edges of the network. Thus, RSVP (a session-based protocol that requires resources associated with individual data flows to be specifically reserved along the path of the data flow) is carefully designed as a soft state protocol. In the event of a failure of part of the network, RSVP heals itself to move the state to the new path of the traffic and to automatically discard state along the old path.

Although one may describe MPLS traffic engineering as the establishment of virtual circuits through the Internet, the use of RSVP-TE as the signaling protocol ensured that the necessary state was kept as soft as possible. In particular, the failure of a link or node is automatically detected and causes the removal of control plane and forwarding state. Further, the ability to place path computation function at the edge of the network based on information advertised from within the network but stored at the edges clearly fits well with the end-to-end principle.

The problem is complicated somewhat by the requirements of traffic engineering in a multi-domain environment. In this case where is the end of the service? Where is the edge of the network? Two models are currently being considered. In the first, each domain is considered a network in its own right, the service is "regenerated" at each domain boundary, and it is reasonable (and necessary) for additional state information to be held at those points. This model fits well with the demands of the GMPLS and optical network architectures described later in this chapter. The second approach uses the Path Computation Element (PCE) discussed in Chapter 9, and attempts to keep state out of the network by making more information available to the initiator of the service either direct or with the assistance of the PCE.

GMPLS, with its control of other switching capabilities, adds a further complication to our considerations. GMPLS is used to provision connectivity through transport networks and these networks employ special considerations for dynamic behavior and survivability. In particular, circuits in transport networks apply different rules to the definition of robustness. For example, the failure of control plane or management plane connectivity is not usually allowed to disturb the data plane — the data is king and connectivity must be preserved at all costs. On the other hand, a protected service may be happy to retain provisioned resources even in the event of a data plane failure, so the control plane must not withdraw state even when traffic can no longer pass through the connection. Although still based on RSVP-TE, GMPLS signaling has become much closer to being a hard state protocol.

In summary, the Internet architecture remains founded on the end-to-end principle. As far as the delivery and forwarding of IP traffic is concerned, the rule still holds fairly well, but as new services such as traffic engineering are considered, the policy becomes diluted. In practice, the end-to-end principle must be qualified by the phrase "as far as is reasonably possible." Thus MPLS TE places some state within the network but is still built on soft state techniques. But the application of GMPLS to transport networks relies on a more permanent "hardish" state retained at transit nodes. Nevertheless, the design goal remains that, wherever possible, state and functionality should be moved to the edges of the network to protect innovation and future developments while supporting reliability and robustness in the core.

13.2 GMPLS Service Models

To understand the different GMPLS service models we must first understand that the integrated Internet is constructed from disparate networks with different switching capabilities and different service paradigms. Thus, the Internet that we participate in as end-users is actually constructed from a large collection of physically remote network segments that contain IP packet routers. These IP router networks may be interconnected by networks of MPLS-capable routers, which in turn may be connected over metro or access networks, and these networks may rely on core transport networks for connectivity. Thus there is a hierarchy of dependency to connect the end-users at the edges of the IP networks.

The GMPLS service models examine how the resources of the lower-layer networks can be managed to provision connectivity in support of the end-user's services.

13.2.1 *The Peer Model*

The most basic service model is called the *peer model*, or sometimes the *unified service model*. It relies on end-to-end provisioning of services across the different network types. Most important, there is an assumption of full visibility of the routing protocols so that the head end of a service is aware of the topology and resources across all of the network hierarchy. Further, this model uses a single common signaling protocol so that the end-to-end service can be provisioned without any function-mapping at network boundaries.

Figure 13.1 shows an end-to-end service in a sample network using the peer model. The initiator of an end-to-end service in the MPLS network has full visibility of the lower layer GMPLS access and core networks and can route the service across the network making efficient use of resources and choosing a path that provides the required quality of service.

Note that there is a fundamental problem with granularity for end-to-end services in this type of network. The service required by a user is likely to need significantly less bandwidth than would be provided by a single resource allocation in the core network (for example, a user may want 10 Mbps to map their Ethernet connectivity, but an allocation in the lambda switching core uses 10 Gbps and cannot be subdivided). This problem is simply resolved using hierarchical LSPs as described earlier in this book. Once the hierarchical LSP has been established, it can be advertised as a TE link into the traffic engineering domains and can then be used to tunnel the end-to-end service across the core network.

The major benefit of the peer model is that services can be fully tailored to the customer's needs — that is, fully traffic engineered end-to-end across the whole

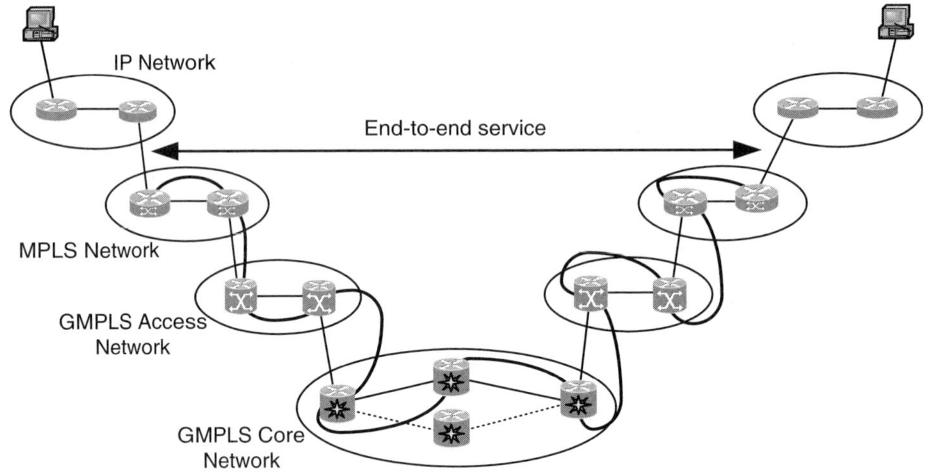

Figure 13.1 The GMPLS peer model.

network under the control of a single path computation engine. Compared with other models in GMPLS and the ITU-T's ASON architecture, which limit the exchange of information at network layer boundaries, this model provides function that is more responsive to the customer and more flexible to the nature of the network because a single view of the entire network is maintained in a central computation entity.

13.2.2 *The Overlay Model*

The *overlay model* (sometimes called the *domain service model*) places a significant service interface between the network layers so that a node in a higher-layer network must request a service across a lower-layer network. Once this service has been established, the higher-layer network may use the service to carry its own traffic across the lower-layer network.

This model has several advantages over the peer model in that it allows the networks to operate independently. This supports different business and administrative models in the different networks, and preserves confidentiality between network operators. It also frees the server network (the lower-layer network) to provide connectivity services in any way it deems suitable as long as they meet the level of service requested.

Figure 13.2 shows the overlay model and highlights that the service across the lower-layer network is requested over a distinct service interface by the higher-layer network. Once the lower-layer service has been established, it can be used as a tunnel or as a stitched LSP to support the requirements of the

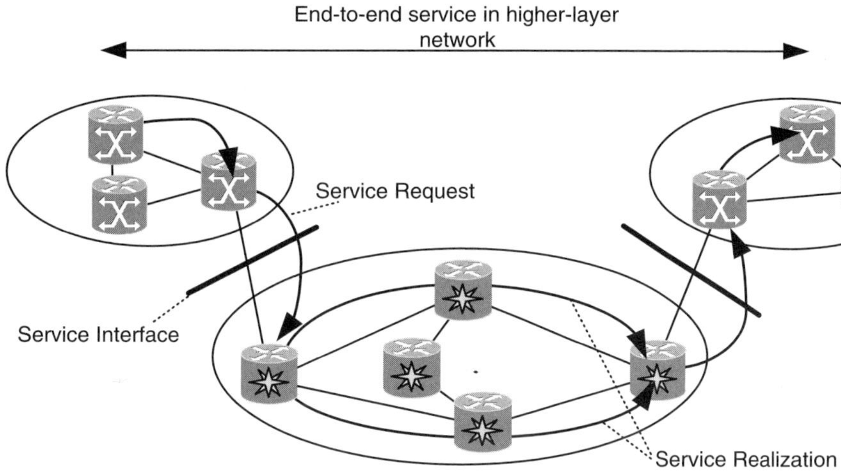

Figure 13.2 The GMPLS overlay model.

higher-layer network. We must be careful with the use of the term "layer" in this context. Although this model is frequently applied where the higher- and lower-layer networks come from different network layers (that is, use different switching technologies or have different switching capabilities) the relationship here is really just a client/server layering. This means that the model is equally applicable within administrative divisions of networks in the same data plane layer. The layering in this model is, therefore, *network service layering*.

This separation of the networks also allows the layers to operate distinct control planes or to utilize different provisioning techniques. For example, the higher-layer network could support MPLS signaling and the lower layer might utilize GMPLS. On the other hand, the higher-layer network might operate GMPLS protocols, but the lower-layer network might not have an intelligent control plane at all, but may require manual configuration.

The service interface in the overlay model can be selected according to the nature of the two networks that meet at the interface. It could use a mediation entity such as an OSS or CNM, or it might use a management protocol such as SNMP. Alternatively, the interface may operate a signaling protocol such as GMPLS RSVP-TE, or one of the User-to-Network protocols described in Section 13.4.

13.2.3 *The Hybrid Model*

The *hybrid model* or *augmented model* acknowledges that the network separation shown in the overlay model provides a valuable split between the administrative domains of different network providers, but also recognizes that a degree of limited trust may be applied between the networks. The full peer model will always remain unpopular among Service Providers because it "leaks" full topology and resource information across network boundaries, allowing an operator too much control of the resources in the neighboring network. But optimal provisioning of services across lower-layer networks can best be achieved with some visibility of the topology and resources of the lower-layer network.

The hybrid model provides for limited and controlled information exchange across network boundaries according to local trust and policy decisions. Each network boundary may share a different amount of information, which varies from the full exchange of the peer model to the complete opacity given by the overlay model. To support this variation, it is necessary to utilize a distinct service request interface as defined in the overlay model, and this interface facilitates the use of distinct protocol sets in the different networks. However, there is no implication that different protocols must be used to achieve this separation, and there are strong arguments in support of the use of GMPLS as both the network protocol and the service request protocol.

This model provides the foundations for support of some of the advanced connectivity services that may be required of an integrated network. Concepts such as bandwidth on demand, integrated traffic engineering, and Layer One VPNs (see Chapter 12) all utilize limited sharing of routing information between the network layers.

Note that the hybrid model parallels how the Global Internet is built for normal IP routing. Individual ASs do not exchange full topology information for reasons of confidentiality and also to prevent information overload. However, a certain amount of reachability information is leaked between ASs to make it possible to route packets end-to-end across the Internet.

13.3. The ITU-T's ASON Architecture

The ITU has developed a Recommendation (G.805) for the generic functional architecture of transport networks. Their aim is to produce an architecture that is independent of technology (data plane and control plane technology) and that can serve as the foundation for a set of Recommendations tailored to specific data plane environments. Thus, the authors of G.805 anticipated subsequent Recommendations describing architectures for ATM, SDH, and PDH networks. The idea was to give a common root and reference point for all such architectures so that they were suitably harmonized.

The ASON was developed as a control plane architecture concept based on a set of requirements laid out in Recommendation G.807. The architecture was based on G.805 foundations and documented in Recommendation G.8080. Although the underlying data plane technology is well known, the architecture retains a high level of abstraction and is expressed in terms of functional components and the interactions between them. This leaves the architecture open for application to a variety of network scenarios and control plane protocols.

In this respect the development process is subtly different from that applied within the IETF. The ITU has taken a very formal, top-down approach by setting out requirements, developing an architecture, and then working on protocol solutions. The IETF's process is more organic, and while it is still requirement-driven, the protocols and architecture have been developed in parallel to allow flexibility and reconsideration of architectural features when the expediency of protocols has dictated.

Note that the G.807 term Automatically Switched Transport Network (ASTN) is sometimes used. There is some confusion between ASON and ASTN, though both apply to transport network types covered by Recommendation G.803. To avoid confusion in this context, we use the more common term ASON, which includes all optical transport networks whether the switching capability is TDM, lambda, or fiber.

13.3.1 *Nodes, Links, and Subnetworks*

There are three basic units within the ASON network. *Nodes* and *links* are quite straightforward and match the physical entities that are familiar in all network architectures. An ASON *subnetwork* is defined as an arbitrary collection of (usually connected) nodes or subnetworks. Thus the most basic subnetwork consists of a single node, and subnetworks can be nested. Each node or subnetwork is not much use without its outward facing (or external) links, so the connection points into/out of the subnetwork are normally part of the definition of the subnetwork. Figure 13.3 shows the progression of building blocks as the ASON network is built up from nodes and subnetworks.

A subnetwork can view the subnetworks that it contains as virtual nodes; that is, each contained subnetwork appears as a single point with external links. This simplification, known as *subnetwork opacity*, makes for significant savings when evaluating the topology of a subnetwork because the connectivity of the embedded subnetworks does not need to be considered. On the other hand, this simplification may mask connectivity issues within the subnetwork, especially when the links within the subnetwork are constrained or sparse. For example, in Figure 13.4, Subnetwork A has four external links and can easily support a service from Source 1 to Destination 1. Examining the properties of Subnetwork A from the perspective of Subnetwork B that contains it, we see that two of the links are in use, but two are still available. This may lead us to assume that we can establish

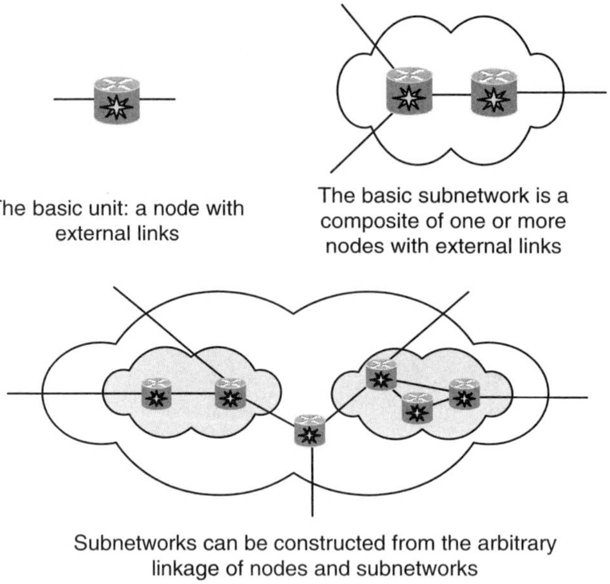

Figure 13.3 The basic building blocks of the ASON architecture are links, nodes, and subnetworks.

a service from Source 2 to Destination 2 through Subnetwork A. However, if we look into the subnetwork we see that the link from Node X to Node Y is already fully used, thus the service cannot be achieved.

Despite the drawbacks of subnetwork opacity illustrated by Figure 13.4, the concept is very powerful. It is very often the case that subnetworks are actually

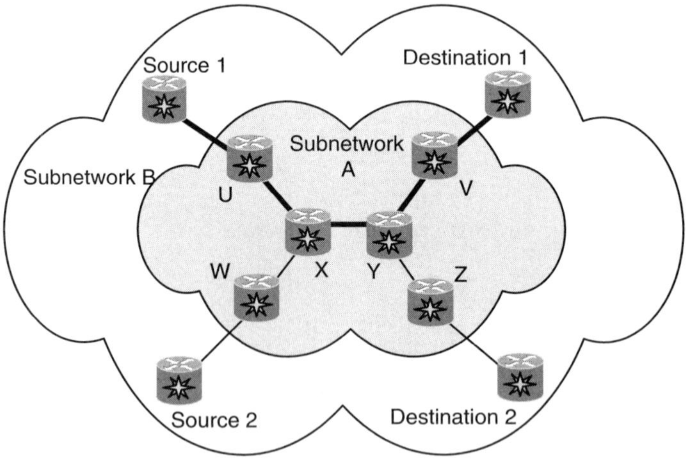

Figure 13.4 Subnetwork opacity represents the Subnetwork as an abstract node with external links.

constructed from well-connected sets of nodes — the most common topology is a ring (for example a SONET/SDH ring), and this sort of topology is much less resource-constrained than the subnetwork in the figure. In practice, this means that the ASON architecture was developed with traditional transport topologies (rings) in mind (although not explicitly stated), and it is less well suited to the requirements of mesh networks where end-to-end protection and full-mesh restoration services will need to be supported across a diverse network topology utilizing traffic engineering. Further, the opaque subnetwork allows for the service to be realized in an arbitrary way as it crosses the subnetwork. For example, the nodes within Subnetwork A in Figure 13.4 may be legacy nodes that are unable to participate in control plane signaling. By representing the subnetwork as an abstract node, the control plane in Subnetwork B may provision a service from Source 1 to Destination 1 without worrying about how the service is achieved within Subnetwork A. This becomes the responsibility of the entry point to the subnetwork (node U) in conjunction with whatever mechanism is used to provision within Subnetwork A. The most common example of this scenario would see the resources within Subnetwork A configured through management control and nodes U and V responsible for "stitching" the configured service to the signaled service. In this type of configuration subnetworks that are under autonomous administrative or management control are referred to as *domains*.

13.3.2 Reference Points

A fundamental concept in the ASON architecture is the *reference point*. A reference point is an abstract functional interface and is useful for partitioning the components of the network and defining the information exchanges between them. The User-to-Network Interface (UNI) exists at the edge of the network and is used to request an end-to-end service from the network. The External Network-to-Network Interface (E-NNI) is placed between subnetworks or network domains and carries the service request between these regions of different administration or technology. The Internal Network-to-Network Interface (I-NNI) exists between network elements within a subnetwork and is responsible for the realization of the service across the subnetwork.

The I-NNI comes closest to an exact match to GMPLS protocols: The signaling and routing exchanges at the I-NNI are concerned only with the provision of services within (or across) the subnetwork. Opinion varies on whether GMPLS can meet the requirements of the ASON UNI and E-NNI without modification, with only minor additions, or through changes that impact the signaling protocols even within the subnetworks. This debate will become clearer in Section 13.6, after we have described some of the additional functions required in the ASON architecture.

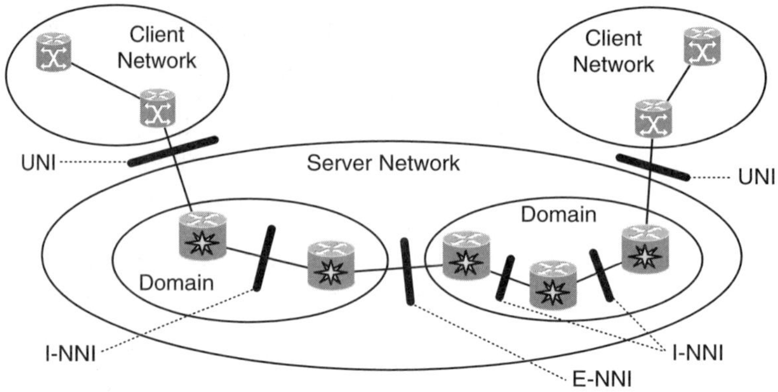

Figure 13.5 The ASON reference points.

Figure 13.5 shows the position of the ASON reference points within an example network. End-to-end connectivity is achieved between the client networks by making use of the server network which is split into two domains. The client node directly connected to the server network takes the role of the service user and is called the UNI Client (UNI-C). The UNI-C makes a request for a service across the server network to a UNI-C in the remote client network — it does this by signaling over the UNI to a UNI Network node (UNI-N), which initiates the service across the server network.

Signaling across a domain or subnetwork using the I-NNI is similar to using GMPLS, but at the domain boundary, the service request is passed across the E-NNI into the next domain. This separation and distinction between reference points helps to preserve the opacity of the subnetworks and the server network. That is, in requesting a service at the UNI, the UNI-C has no knowledge of how the server network will realize that service and only needs to understand the protocols used to achieve the UNI. Similarly, a node in one subnetwork does not need to understand the way in which the service is implemented within another neighboring subnetwork. It simply requests the service using a common protocol at the E-NNI, although it may also have access to limited (perhaps aggregated) topology information advertised between domains across the E-NNI.

Note that the reference points shown in Figure 13.5 are external to network nodes; that is, they are expressed as points over which protocol messages are exchanged to request the end-to-end service. In fact, although this model is a common construct it is not a requirement of the architecture. Another equally valid model places a reference point within a network node and uses internal procedures and mapping functions to translate between the requests. Although this alternate model is unlikely for the I-NNI because the purpose here is actually to convey information between network nodes, it may make a lot of sense at the UNI and, in particular, at the E-NNI. At these two reference points the main function is mapping the service request from one format to another (for example, at the E-NNI the objective is to map between the I-NNI mechanisms and protocols used in two separate domains), and this can be achieved equally well by a single node capable of playing a part in both domains.

13.3.3 *Calls and Connections*

Service provision and realization is achieved by two signaling concepts in the ASON architecture. The *call* is an end-to-end relationship between the UNI clients. It states the level of service required (for example, bandwidth, quality of service, protection) and identifies the calling and called party. The call, therefore, allows for the application of policy and security and ensures that the receiver is happy to be connected to by the caller. But the call does not provision any network resources to carry data for the service. This is achieved by a series of *connections* within the network that are joined together to transport data from one end to the other.

Each connection provides connectivity over one piece of the network. For example, there is a connection between UNI-C and UNI-N, a connection across each subnetwork, a connection over each E-NNI, and a final connection between UNI-N and UNI-C at the destination. Each connection is established from either a UNI-capable node or an E-NNI-capable node to another such node and realizes the service expressed in the call. Looking at the network in Figure 13.6,

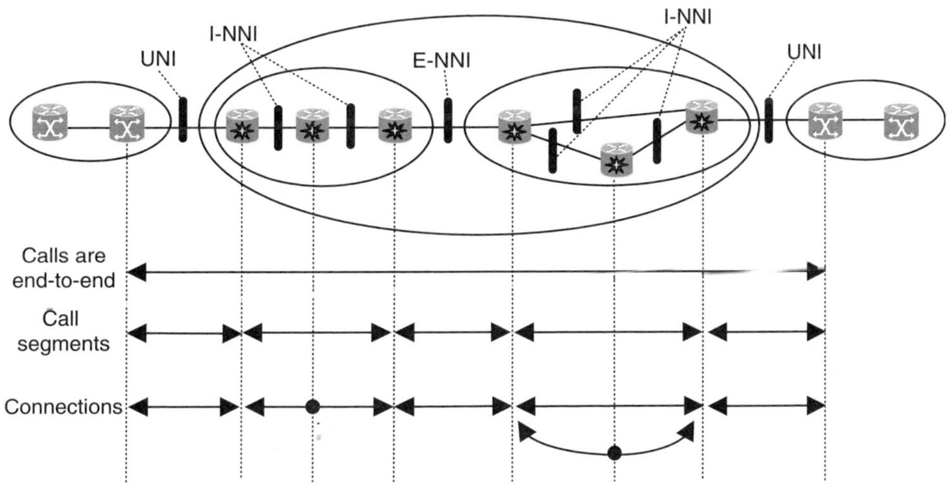

Figure 13.6 Calls, call segments, and connections are the basic units of service provision in the ASON architecture.

we see that the end-to-end call is constructed of a series of *call segments* running between the UNI and E-NNI-capable nodes. This ensures that each such node has sufficient information to apply policy (is this service allowed though this network/subnetwork?) and to establish/terminate the connections necessary to realize the service.

There is a clear relationship between call segments and connections, as can be seen in Figure 13.6. This is because all nodes that initiate or terminate connections must be aware of the service provided. But the relationship between call segments and connections is not one-to-one. First, as can be seen in the left-hand subnetwork in the figure, the call does not touch nodes that are contained between I-NNIs. There is no call processing necessary at these nodes, but they are involved in connection processing because network resources must be provisioned in order that data can flow. Secondly, as can be seen in the right-hand subnetwork in the figure, the service may be realized across a subnetwork using more than one connection — this may be to achieve the required protection or bandwidth.

13.3.4 *Abstract Functional Entities*

The ASON architecture defines abstract functional entities to provide the necessary processing in support of the services in the network. There are three important entities from the control plane perspective: the *call controller*, the *connection controller* (*CC*), the *routing controller* (*RC*) and the *link resource manager* (*LRM*). The link resource manager is responsible for establishing control plane adjacencies between the ends of links, validating the links, exchanging configuration information that pertains to the links, and then informing the routing controller that the link is ready for service.

Call information and requests are exchanged between call controllers, connection information and requests are exchanged between connection controllers, and the routing controllers exchange routing information. There is also some interaction between the different types of controller. For example, a call controller may be responsible for initiating connections to support the next call segment, which it can do by invoking the connection controller. At the same time, the call and connection controllers may need to use routing and topology information gathered and advertised by the routing controllers to select suitable paths.

An important fact about these three controllers is that they do not need to be co-resident with the data plane devices they manage. This is perhaps most obvious with the call controllers, which provide a level of function that is quite close to service management. But connection controllers may also be divorced from the data plane using a management or specialist protocol to program the data plane remotely. (The IETF's Generic Switch Management Protocol, GSMP, is an example of a specialist protocol that fills this niche.) Further, there does not

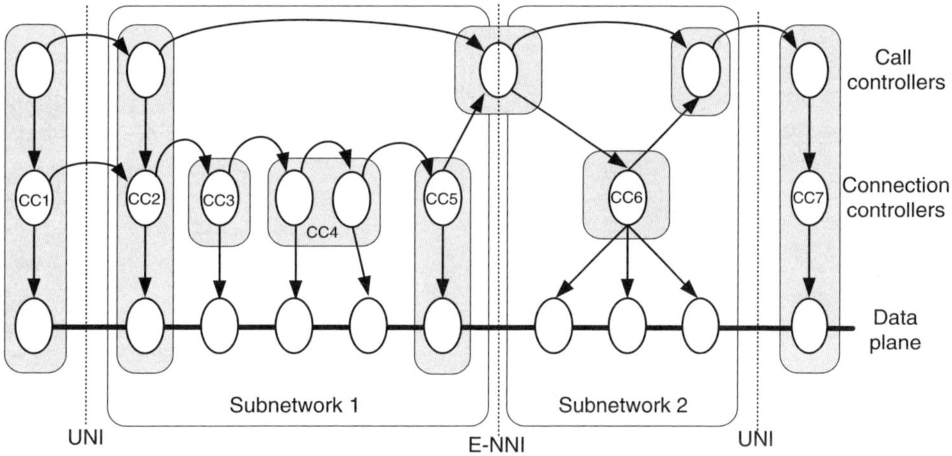

Figure 13.7 Call and connection controllers are not necessarily collocated with the data plane elements that they control.

need to be a strict one-to-one relationship between the connection controllers and the devices they manage. Figure 13.7 shows an example of the interactions between call controllers, connection controllers, and network (data plane) devices in an ASON network. The initiating UNI-C includes call controller, connection controller, and data plane within one device; its call control and connection control components communicate with the call control and connection control entities of the UNI-N, which are also located in a single device. These might be what you would expect from modern, purpose-built, integrated network devices. However, the third connection controller (CC3) is separate from the data plane device that it controls. The fourth connection controller (CC4) actually controls two data plane devices; it may do this by representing itself as one element in the control plane but actually managing the two devices, or (as in the example in the figure) by presenting two logical entities in the control plane.

Call controller five (CC5) is integrated with the data plane components, but uses a remote call controller In fact the call controller for CC5 sits on the boundary between the two subnetworks and works with CC5 and CC6. All of the data plane devices for the second subnetwork are under the control of a single connection controller CC6.

The value of these different modes of operation is the possibility of operating the ASON architecture in environments constructed from a range of different devices with different capabilities. These may range from legacy transport switches that only have management interfaces, to new devices with fully-functional control planes.

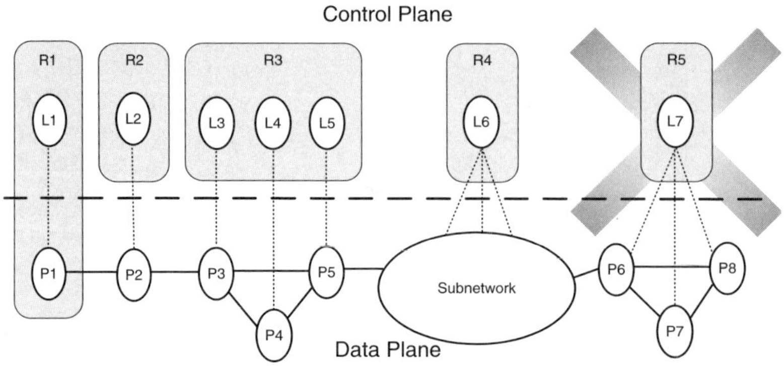

Figure 13.8 Some possible configurations of routing controllers and physical nodes. The configuration on the right of the figure is not supported.

Routing controllers are the functional entities that are responsible for managing and distributing the routing and topology information within a subnetwork or *routing area* in the ASON architecture. There is a subtle difference between a routing area and a subnetwork; a routing area is a subnetwork together with all of its external links. This distinction is important because it makes it possible for a routing controller to connect the subnetwork to the outside world. Because subnetworks are opaque, there is no requirement to distribute topology information from within a subnetwork to another subnetwork, and the routing problem is held at a single level. That is, routing is only performed within a subnetwork where the nodes of the routing graph may be network nodes or other subnetworks. Routing controllers have the same level of abstraction as call and connection controllers within the ASON network. That is, there may be a neat, one-to-one correspondence between routing controllers, connection controllers, and data plane entities as one might see in a GMPLS-enabled transport device running OSPF and RSVP-TE protocols. On the other hand, as in GMPLS, a routing controller may be physically remote from the data plane devices, and may advertise information on behalf of more than one data switch so that legacy nodes can be represented within the control plane. Figure 13.8 shows some of the possible configurations.

In the figure, *Ri* ($i = 1, 2, \ldots$) represents a routing controller — the realization of a functional entity responsible for advertising routing information. *Pi* is a data plane device, such as a transport switch, and *Li* is the logical topological entity that is advertised between routing controllers.

R1 is a conventional, GMPLS-enabled device that collocates the control and data planes within a single unit. R2 shows how the routing controller may be physically separate from the data plane device that it advertises. Routing controllers R3 and R4 demonstrate how the ASON architecture allows a single routing controller to handle the routing and topology advertisements on behalf of multiple data plane devices. R3 contains three logical routing entities (L3, L4, and L5), each of which represents a physical device; R3 is required to advertise as though the three logical entities were distinct routing controllers. The logical routing entities are sometimes known as *virtual routers.* R4, on the other hand, distributes routing information on behalf of an abstract node that is actually a subnetwork. The contents of the subnetwork are opaque, and it may be the case that the elements within the subnetwork do not support routing function, and may not have a control plane at all.

The final routing controller in Figure 13.8 illustrates a configuration that is not within the scope of ASON. A single controller, R5, is attempting to represent three distinct physical elements within the routing topology, but is only using one logical routing entity to achieve this. Either the three data plane devices should be grouped together as a single abstract node (and so represented as a subnetwork) or separate logical entities should be used. If R5 was to attempt to advertise the physical devices, it would have to add a separate piece of information to allow other routing controllers to disambiguate the information that it sends out. This additional piece of information would be functionally equivalent to logical router identities as used by R3.

Note that the control plane connectivity is not relevant to the way that routing controllers are used to represent the physical data plane connectivity. Further, the data plane connectivity shown in the figure is just an example.

13.3.5 *Managing Connectivity Across Subnetworks*

Traffic engineering across the network shown in Figure 13.9 is, on the face of it, quite simple. The traffic engineering database will contain information gathered from advertisements of the links AB, BC, CD, AE, EF, BF, and FD. The information for each link will be accompanied by the usual parameters indicating metric, bandwidth, and so forth. In order to establish a service from A to D, all that

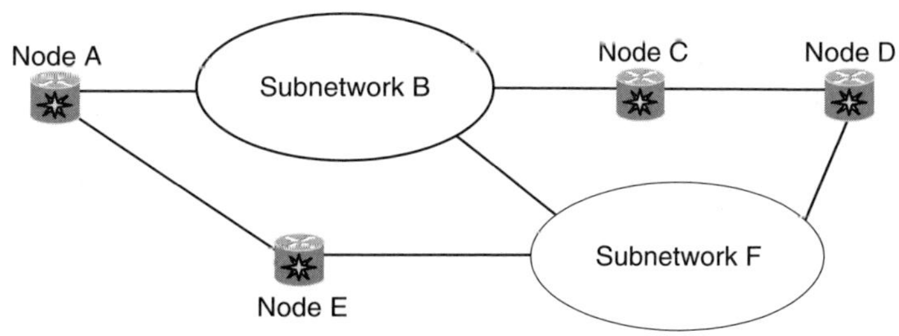

Figure 13.9 Traffic engineering path computation appears simple in the ASON model.

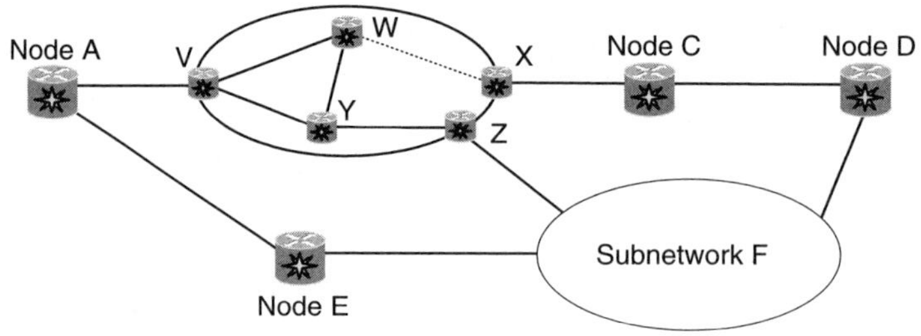

Figure 13.10 Subnetwork abstraction may mask the issues of resource availability within the subnetworks.

a constraint-based path computation engine has to do is evaluate the links with respect to the required service parameters. There is a major advantage in representing subnetworks as abstract nodes, because the complexity of their operation is masked from the path computation process.

The benefits of abstraction mask a difficult problem, because the subnetwork appears as an abstract node and not a collection of abstract links. Consider the network in Figure 13.10. This is the same as in Figure 13.9, but the contents of subnetwork B have been exposed. Without knowledge of the internals of the subnetwork, and representing the subnetwork as a single abstract node, there is no reason to assume that connectivity cannot be achieved along the path ABCD. But the internal link WX is only available at low bandwidth and cannot give us the required service, so ABFD or AEFD would be better paths. Clearly the opacity and abstraction principles of the ASON network need some work to make this type of traffic engineering possible.

It is possible to aggregate the internal subnetwork connectivity information and represent it through the advertised parameters of the external links. In this instance, the link BC would be advertised as only having the same capacity as the internal link WX. This is possible, because (presumably) the routing controller that manages the advertisements for the subnetwork knows about the internal links. However, such aggregation gets increasingly complex as the subnetwork grows. It might require frequent re-advertisements as the internal resources get used for other purposes, and it may become confusing to constrain an external link when it is actually the connectivity between subnetwork edges that is really constrained. To see this, consider a subnetwork with four external connections: A, B, C, and D. Suppose that the subnetwork becomes partitioned so that A and B can be connected, and C and D can be connected, but there is no connectivity between A/B and C/D. How would we now advertise the external links? We do not want an external TE computation to believe that there is connectivity available through AC, so we must advertise the link out of C as having no bandwidth. But now we have lost the ability to use that link along DC.

In fact, it is a huge challenge to come up with a scalable way to achieve (re-) advertisement of abstract/virtual links so that they would be good enough to build a global TE network graph on every controller that could be used to compute end-to-end paths with the necessary constraints. Take, for example, the resource colors link attribute. It is not clear what to advertise for the abstract link: the union of colors of all constituent links or the overlapping colors? In the former case you cannot enforce the use of links of a certain color because an abstract link that advertises a color does not necessarily have every component marked with the specified color. Likewise, you cannot exclude the use of a certain color if the abstract link is advertised with overlap of resource colors of all its components. It gets even worse if you think about optics-related attributes necessary for computing paths for photonic networks. In the face of these challenges, the Path Computation Element architecture described in Chapter 9 is a more attractive choice for a GMPLS network.

13.3.6 *Network Layers and Technology Types*

The ASON architecture states that all nodes within a network (all individual nodes and all nodes within subnetworks in the network) operate at the same level of technology, that is as the same network layer. In GMPLS terms, this means that the nodes all operate at the same switching capability and the entire network is a single layer (see Chapter 8 for a discussion of layers). In order to progress from one layer to another the data must pass through an *adaptation function* to convert it from one encoding to another. Such adaptation may even be required between layers of the same switching type; for example, when an OC-3 data stream is packaged into an OC-48 connection.

Although there is still some work to be done to complete the discussion of adaptation within the ASON architecture, it is a reasonable generalization to state that ASON places the UNI between networks whenever there is an adaptation function. That is, there is a UNI reference point where there is an interaction between network layers. This UNI may be contained within a transport node or exposed as an interaction between external controllers. The client network invokes connectivity across the server network using requests at the UNI and corresponding adaptation in the data plane. This presents strict network layering within the architecture, with the networks at one switching capability appearing at the higher layer of the architecture as subnetworks.

However, the architecture is quite rigid in the way this layer is allowed to operate. No leakage of routing or topology information is allowed between layers across the UNI. There is not even any scope for aggregation, so it is very hard (read, impossible!) for a network at one layer to select from a set of UNI reference points providing access to a server network even though they offer different connectivity services across the server network. Even the most fundamental of connectivity parameters, topological reachability of remote UNI reference points, causes some issues because it is necessary to know of the existence and reachability of remote UNI clients if a call is to be attempted. The ASON network is not a perfectly connected telephone system in which all receivers can be reached from any calling point, so some form of UNI reachability information needs to be made available into the higher-layer network; but this is routing information which, if not specific to the lower, is at least provided by it.

In fact, services such as "bandwidth on demand" are somewhat frowned upon by many of the Service Providers in the ITU-T. To provide for such a service, one needs to have access to routing information from the server layer, but this is not within the architecture. An argument is made that either there is always bandwidth available, in which case services can always be provisioned, or there is simply not enough bandwidth, in which case new hardware must be bought and installed. This claim really only holds up in the simplest of network topologies with server layer networks built from basic rings. When the core of the lower-layer network is a complex mesh, bandwidth on demand becomes a realistic service.

Other similar services such as Layer One VPNs (see Chapter 12) are beginning to gain some attention in the ITU-T, and small modifications are being made to the ASON architecture to attempt to support them because they, too, need help from the routing protocols to manage features such as VPN membership.

13.4 GMPLS and ASON Networks

GMPLS protocols offer a set of well-thought-out building blocks for the control plane of transport networks, thus it makes sense to try to apply them to the ASON architecture. A somewhat scattergun approach has been taken to achieve this end, resulting in too many solutions. From the point of view of the equipment vendor and the network operator, it may be beneficial to have parallel development so that a single, best solution can be derived, but it is not very helpful to have multiple solutions ratified as standards. This means that the vendor must develop and test all possible combinations and the operator must try to make a decision about what to actually deploy. Unfortunately, this is exactly where we stand, with the IETF, ITU-T, and Optical Interworking Forum (OIF) all proposing different ways to utilize GMPLS to meet the requirements of the ASON architecture.

13.4.1 *The OIF UNI Protocol Extensions*

The OIF was the first to start to standardize a protocol solution for the UNI to an optical network. Working with material originally presented in the IETF, they have produced a series of Implementation Agreements that are intended to allow equipment vendors to offer interoperability between UNI-C and UNI-N devices.

The essence of the OIF UNI is a set of additions to the GMPLS signaling protocol. These extensions chiefly deal with addressing/naming issues and the need for additional information to represent calls in what was originally a connection-based protocol. The former additions simply allow non-IP identifiers to be assigned to UNI-C access points in an effort to make them appear more like traditional transport devices. It is not clear if this is a wholly useful operation as all of the access points still need to be assigned IP addresses within the core function of the GMPLS network, but the use of transport names may make operators feel more comfortable with the new technology. The second requirement is more important because call parameters were absent from the initial versions of the GMPLS signaling protocol (see Section 13.6.4). Because the UNI is a single hop, there was a natural tendency to piggyback the call information on the connection signaling messages, and the OIF UNI was developed on this assumption, with the call parameters presented in a new RSVP-TE protocol object. This approach limits the function of the UNI to precisely one connection per call, which means you cannot establish a call without a connection, and you cannot provide a service over the UNI, such as a protected service, which is supported by multiple parallel connections within the same call. Note, however, that the OIF's UNI v2.0 is beginning to examine the issue of multi-homing (allowing a single UNI-C to talk to two UNI-Ns), which addresses a similar, but subtly different, issue.

A major issue with the OIF UNI is how to convey the additional UNI call information to the E-NNI reference points and to the remote UNI. Because the new information is cleanly contained in a protocol object, and because RSVP-TE already has mechanisms for passing objects "transparently" through networks, it has largely been assumed that it is acceptable to continue the piggybacking so that the call information is carried alongside the connection information as the protocol message progresses through the network. This is certainly functional, but it has several operational and architectural failings.

Architecturally, the main concern is that the transit nodes within the GMPLS network (that is, those that only participate at the I-NNI) are required to forward the call information. Although they do not need to actively process the information, it nevertheless forms part of their connection state. Because of the nature of the RSVP protocol, transit nodes are required to store all of the information and react if they detect a change to any of it. This requirement is in direct opposition to the end-to-end architectural principle of the Internet. Within the Internet architecture, this information should be signaled direct between the points that need it (the UNI and E-NNI reference points) and should not cause any additional processing at transit nodes.

Operationally there are two issues. The first is how to handle the connection setup process in the absence of an established call. There is no underlying problem with simply setting up an end-to-end connection (or a series of concatenated connections) in the way that you would in a GMPLS network. The concern comes when the call functionality is added, because it is only when the call is processed by the remote UNI-C and completed back to the initiating UNI-C that we are able to determine what type of connection(s) to establish. In the OIF UNI model, assuming that the call information is piggybacked across the network using the GMPLS connection signaling protocol, the connection setup attempt is made at the same time as the call is requested. Thus there is a significant probability of the connection setup needing to be rejected and tried by another route or with different parameters. Unfortunately, however, there is no way to reject the connection without also rejecting the call, because the two are fundamentally linked by the piggybacking of information on a single message.

The second operational issue concerns diverse routing of connections, just as it does at the UNI. The problem is, however, more complex within the network because the connections needed to support a single service may need to take different routes through a subnetwork and even use different subnetworks as they cross the server network. Should each connection request carry all of the call information or can additional connections be added to an existing call?

There are also some other minor protocol differences specifically introduced in the OIF UNI implementation agreement, and others that have crept in because of new developments in GMPLS. If the core network (and particularly the UNI-N) are sensitive to these differences, then it is possible that the network can be made to operate. But if the UNI-N propagates the OIF UNI behavior into the core GMPLS network there may be interoperability problems.

Finally, there are several versions of the OIF UNI and backward compatibility is not assured; moreover, the current implementation agreement has limited applicability, chiefly to TDM with an out-of-band control plane. All this raises a good number of concerns about the operational complexity and questions as to the actual deployment validity of the OIF UNI within (or at the edge of) GMPLS networks. Nevertheless, there have been some notable successes in interoperability demonstrations, which suggests that there may be sufficient drive to work on solutions to these problems.

13.4.2 *The ITU-T's UNI and E-NNI Protocols*

As might be expected, the ITU-T did not stop at the definition of an abstract architecture, but went on to define specific requirements for the reference points, and then to develop recommendations for protocol solutions for the UNI and E-NNI reference points.

Peculiarly, this process has led to three distinct ASON UNI and E-NNI protocol specifications within the ITU-T. The first of these is based on the Private-Network-Network-Interface (PNNI) protocol used in ATM. It may initially be hard to see why one would go to the trouble of developing a UNI or E-NNI for an ASON network based on PNNI, but there is no requirement that GMPLS should be the core (I-NNI) protocol. In any case, it is perfectly possible to implement a mapping function at the UNI-N or at the E-NNI. In its favor, PNNI was a well-understood and stable signaling protocol that had already been adapted to provide a UNI and an E-NNI in the ATM context.

The second ITU-T ASON UNI and E-NNI specification is based on GMPLS RSVP-TE and is, in fact, very similar to one of the OIF's UNI implementation agreements. It uses the same extensions that do not form part of the core GMPLS definitions. The third UNI and E-NNI protocol solution from the ITU-T is based on CR-LDP. As described in Chapter 4, CR-LDP was initially proposed as an alternative to RSVP-TE as an MPLS TE and GMPLS signaling protocol before it was de-prioritized by the IETF in favor of RSVP-TE. As a side note, it is interesting to observe that the CR-LDP option uses independent call signaling on a separate CR-LDP message, which means that calls and connections can be managed independently and that multiple connections can be added to a call.

All of the ITU-T's UNI/E-NNI proposals have the same issues as those raised in the previous section for the OIF's UNI agreements. Additionally, if GMPLS is to be used as the standard core (I-NNI) signaling protocol, mapping code must be written to convert from the PNNI or CR-LDP alternatives, and this adds complexity to the implementation.

Additionally, one might consider that the definition of three UNI protocols encumbers easy interoperability, because each pair of UNI-C and UNI-N nodes must be selected to utilize the same protocol. The same issue applies at the E-NNI reference point.

13.4.3 *Applying the GMPLS Overlay Model*

As previously described, the original GMPLS protocol specifications were focused entirely on connections and did not make any reference to calls. Further, the connection model employed is very much an end-to-end one, although the stitching together of separately signaled LSPs to form a longer connection is also supported.

This fact does not, however, limit the utility of the GMPLS protocols within the ASON architecture, and an Internet-Draft describes the GMPLS overlay architectural model and its applicability to the UNI and E-NNI reference points. Figure 13.11 shows how an overlay network achieves connectivity using the services of a core network. Simply put, a node in an isolated segment of the overlay network builds an LSP through the core network to a node in another segment of the overlay network. This LSP can be used to carry traffic (IP or MPLS) between components of the overlay network through tunneling or stitching procedures.

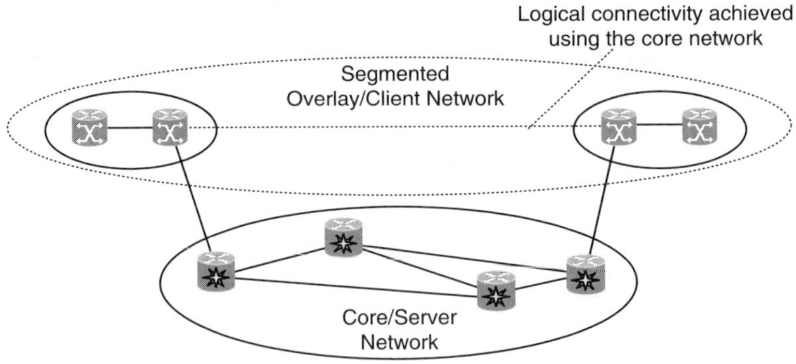

Figure 13.11 The overlay network is a segmented client network that achieves connectivity through the services of a core server network.

The core network is often a different switching technology from the overlay network (for example, the overlay network may be built from packet routers, whereas the core network consists of TDM switches). But note that this architecture is significantly different from the normal use of hierarchical LSPs, partly because the service is directly requested from the client network (in the manner of a UNI), and partly because the service connects elements of the client network where the normal hierarchical technique would build tunnels across only the core network (between the core nodes at the edges of the core network).

It is this similarity to the UNI request-based model that makes the overlay model a suitable way of satisfying some of the requirements of the ASON architecture. As shown in Figure 13.12, the UNI reference point can be placed between the overlay network and the core network, and end-to-end services

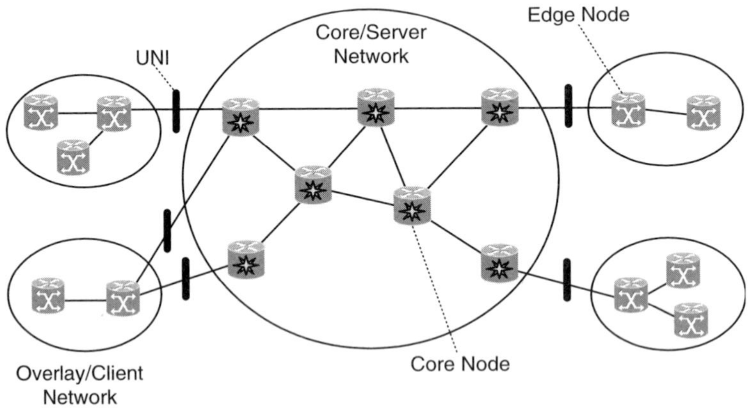

Figure 13.12 The GMPLS overlay network reference model.

(LSP tunnels) can be achieved between edge nodes across the core network. To provide the protection and quality requirements requested by the edge node of the overlay network, the core network is free to apply its own policy and administrative rules, and to utilize any of the GMPLS features described in this book. In this way a core network can support multiple distinct overlay networks and multiple parallel or diverse connections.

Although the E-NNI reference point is less relevant in a GMPLS network because it tends to be more homogenous within the control plane, the E-NNI can still be considered to exist between administrative domains (such as autonomous systems) and between network regions of different switching capabilities. The signaling techniques used in the overlay model are just those of the GMPLS protocols and are suitable for handling these types of subdivision within the network; hence the overlay model extends to the E-NNI reference point without further issues.

13.4.4 Calls and Connections in GMPLS

The GMPLS overlay model is deficient in one significant respect as far as the ASON architecture is concerned: It does not support calls. Although call function is not immediately necessary in the end-to-end model utilized by the overlay network, it is a useful feature for applying additional policy at UNI and E-NNI reference points. There are three approaches currently being worked on within the IETF to fully integrate the ASON call into the GMPLS architecture.

The first technique is quite similar to the proposals to support the ITU-T and OIF UNI call information; that is, it relies on piggybacking call parameters on connection messages. However, various niceties have been proposed to enable calls to be set up without an associated connection (without the reservation of network resources) and for further connections to be added to established calls without being required to carry full call information when they are signaled. Nevertheless, this is not a clean architectural solution and is unlikely to see deployment; rather, it is a stopgap for interoperability testing and serves as a development test bed for the other two techniques.

The second approach is based on the previous idea, but utilizes separate signaling for call establishment. By using the RSVP-TE Notify message that can be targeted to direct specific receivers, it is possible to signal calls between interested reference points (UNIs and E-NNIs) without needing to involve other transit nodes. Once a call has been established and the precise parameters of the service have been agreed, connections (LSPs) can be established from edge node to edge node through the core network, either end-to-end or stitched at administrative boundaries according to the precise policy requirements of the component networks.

The final technique is undoubtedly the correct architectural solution, because it achieves a full and proper separation between call controllers and connection controllers. This model uses a dedicated call signaling protocol to negotiate and establish the call segments and end-to-end calls across the core network. The IETF's call management protocol is the Session Initiation Protocol (SIP) and is specifically designed to operate between call controllers. The GMPLS signaling protocol can then be used to establish connections through the network with only the smallest of changes to support a call identifier. The interactions between call controllers and connection controllers may be internal to implementations, but where the call and connection controllers are not collocated, the Common Open Policy Service (COPS) protocol is used to coordinate calls and connections.

13.4.5 *Contrasting GMPLS and ASON*

Much has been made in the previous sections about the differences and limitations of the various approaches to building optical networks. But in reality, these are relatively minor issues and there is far more in common between GMPLS and ASON than there is different. This should not be a surprise since both architectures are trying to solve the same problem and are being driven by the same Service Providers with real deployment issues.

Both GMPLS and ASON are works in progress. They are continually being refined and updated so that they encompass the reality of transport networks and so that they can satisfy the requirements that network operators need to meet in order to be effective and to derive revenue from the services that they offer to their customers. A few years ago there was a significant gap between the viewpoints of ASON and GMPLS, but this is gradually closing and a recent Internet-Draft that provides a lexicography designed to map the terminology of the two architectures has discovered that the remaining differences are quite small.

13.5 Further Reading

The architecture of the Internet is described in three RFCs available from the IETF:

RFC 1958: Architectural Principles of the Internet
RFC 2775: Internet Transparency
RFC 3724: The Rise of the Middle and the Future of End-to-End: Reflections on the Evolution of the Internet Architecture

The ITU-T recommendations describing the ASON architecture can be obtained from the ITU's web site. Visit http://www.itu.int to see the following documents.

G.803: Architecture of transport networks based on the synchronous digital hierarchy

G.805: Generic functional architecture of transport networks

G.807: Requirements for automatic switched transport networks (ASTN)

G.8080: Architecture for the automatically switched optical network (ASON)

G.7713: Distributed call and connection management (DCM)

G.7713.1: Distributed call and connection management (DCM) based on PNNI

G.7713.2: Distributed Call and Connection Management: Signalling Mechanism Using GMPLS RSVP-TE

G.7713.3: Distributed Call and Connection Management: Signalling mechanism using GMPLS CR-LDP

Internet-Drafts and RFCs describing the requirements on GMPLS to support the ASON architecture and detailing the use of GMPLS protocols in the overlay model are as follows.

draft-ietf-ccamp-gmpls-ason-reqts: Requirements for Generalized MPLS (GMPLS) Signaling Usage and Extensions for Automatically Switched Optical Network (ASON)

draft-ietf-ccamp-gmpls-ason-routing-reqts: Requirements for Generalized MPLS (GMPLS) Routing for Automatically Switched Optical Network (ASON)

RFC 4202: Generalized Multiprotocol Label Switching (GMPLS) User-Network Interface (UNI): Resource ReserVation Protocol-Traffic Engineering (RSVP-TE) Support for the Overlay Model

draft-ietf-ccamp-gmpls-ason-lexicography: A Lexicography for the Interpretation of Generalized Multiprotocol Label Switching (GMPLS) Terminology within The Context of the ITU-T's Automatically Switched Optical Network (ASON) Architecture

CHAPTER 14

Provisioning Systems

This chapter introduces some of the ways transport networks and devices can be managed. GMPLS reduces the management burden in transport networks by offloading functions from the operator and management plane to the control plane. For example, the collection and correlation of information about the status and capabilities of the links are automatically handled and kept up to date by the GMPLS routing protocols. Similarly, the GMPLS signaling protocols make it possible to provision new LSPs and manage existing LSPs with only a small number of management plane interactions. From the perspective of an operator at their console in the Network Operations Center, there may be very little visible difference between the tools used to manage a traditional transport network and a GMPLS-enabled network, but it would be a mistake to assume that the efficiency or mode of operation of the underlying transport plane is unchanged. The GMPLS control plane makes sure that the operator is always working with the most up-to-date information and also makes sure that the services are managed efficiently by the management plane.

Nevertheless, the management plane is an essential component of the GMPLS-enabled network. The first and most important question is the structure that is applied to the management framework for the network: How does the operator coordinate the many devices that make up the network and are physically remote and supplied by different vendors? Next we look at how management networks are physically provided and what network resources are needed so that the network itself can be managed.

The middle of the chapter discusses proprietary management interfaces and describes some of the more common standardized techniques used to manage network devices. The chapter concludes with a brief discussion of alarms and asynchronous events.

14.1 Structure of Management

A transport network is typically constructed from equipment supplied by several different vendors. Despite the long-term goal of complete and free interchangeability of devices from different vendors, operators usually build clusters of devices from the same vendor and manage them as separate administrative domains. There are several benefits to this approach, not the least of which is a reduction in the number of points within the network where genuine interoperability is occurring (a good thing because these are the points where most protocol and hardware problems are likely to be seen).

Devices from different vendors have different management characteristics even though they perform very similar network functions. As we will see later in this chapter, there is a wide variety of proprietary interfaces and standardized protocols that could be used to manage a transport network device. This means that the operator will need to use many different applications or at least remember several different command syntaxes to control the entire network. In this situation it makes good sense to collect the devices with the same management characteristics into separate administrative domains — a different operator can be given control of each domain and they need only be familiar with the management techniques for the devices within their domain. Although interactions between operators will be needed for services that span domains, these interactions can be managed at a more abstract level and will not require a deep understanding of the configuration techniques of the other domains.

Another fact that influences the distribution of vendors' equipment within networks is network mergers. Small networks are typically resourced from one or at most two vendors. This naturally forms clusters of network nodes of a similar type. However, the trend is to increase the size of networks by connecting together the smaller networks within a single company, through corporate acquisitions or through cooperative agreements between Service Providers. The result naturally produces islands or administrative domains of devices from the same vendor.

14.1.1 *Management Tools*

There are four major components to the management system seen in Figure 14.1.

- User interfaces. Most devices have some way for the operator to connect directly so that he can configure and control the local resources. A device may have a dedicated terminal, may support the attachment of a terminal emulator (perhaps through a serial port), and usually also supports remote access through an application such as Telnet. All of these mechanisms give the

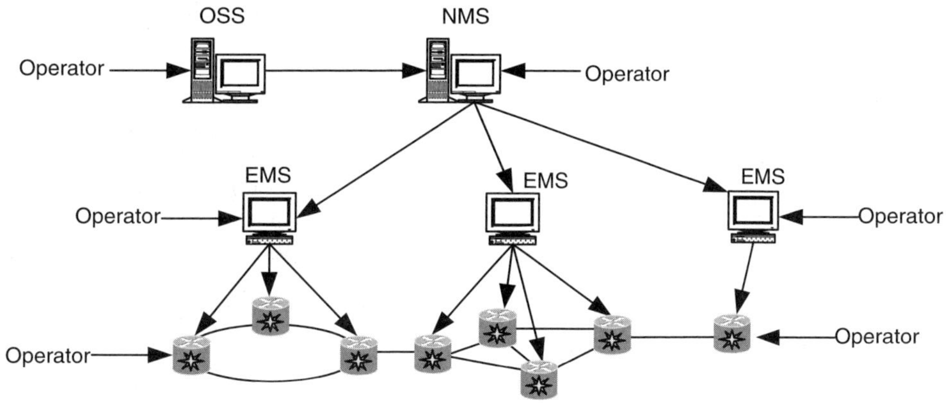

Figure 14.1 The structure of a management network.

operator the ability to connect to individual network nodes as separate entities rather than as part of the whole network.

- The Element Management System (EMS) is an application or workstation dedicated to the management of one or more network elements. Typically, an EMS application is specific to a single vendor's equipment, but can manage multiple nodes of the same type. An EMS workstation may run several EMS applications (for different equipment) and may be where the operator sits to use the remote user interfaces of various network devices. It is important to note that the EMS does not manage the network, but manages individual network nodes.
- The Network Management System (NMS) is a central management station or application that has a view of the whole network and can control and configure all of the devices in the network. The NMS operator does not want to handle multiple applications to control the network, so the NMS provides a single application that presents a common interface to all of the subnetworks, administrative domains, and individual network elements. In practice, the NMS is sometimes bundled with one or more EMSs so that it can talk to network devices directly but more often the NMS speaks a standardized management protocol to a group of EMS workstations that manage the devices.
- The Operations Support System (OSS) is also a central management system, but it has a less hands-on interaction with the network. The OSS is where planning and service installation are managed. The operations at the OSS may be asynchronous and disjointed in time from the day-to-day management of the network. Nevertheless, the OSS needs to issue management requests to provision and control services in the network (or networks) for which it

is responsible. It does this by issuing commands (usually through a standardized protocol) to the NMS.

Additionally, one may consider a fifth component that passively collects information from network devices rather than exerting control over the resources. Management events, such as alarms, are usually fed back up the management tree so that the various components of the management system are fully aware of them. But other operational information, such as statistics and event logs, are normally collected through separate distributed utilities that are responsible for collating and aggregating the information before passing it back to a centralized server. The devices that provide support for statistics gathering and processing may be coincident with the EMS, NMS, and OSS nodes, or may be completely separate workstations.

14.2 Management Networks

Figure 14.1 shows the logical connectivity for control of a network, but it would not be practicable to physically connect the EMSs and network elements in the manner shown — that would require far too many point-to-point connections. In practice, the management plane must achieve the same level of connectivity as the control plane so that the EMSs can send management commands to any network element. Unlike the control plane, the emphasis is not on hop-by-hop connectivity to parallel the data plane; the management plane needs connectivity from the EMSs to networks elements.

This connectivity is usually provided by an IP management network. It may be that each network element is connected directly to the management network, but where there is in-band or in-fiber control plane communication between the network elements, the management messages may be carried that way. This is illustrated in Figure 14.2.

14.3 Proprietary Management Interfaces

As previously described, most network devices are supplied equipped with one or more proprietary interface. The most common format is the Command Line Interface (CLI). Here an operator can issue a series of text commands to manage the device. The CLI may be run through a directly attached terminal or over a remote-access protocol such as Telnet. CLIs are usually the most powerful management tools available for any vendor's equipment: They give access to the

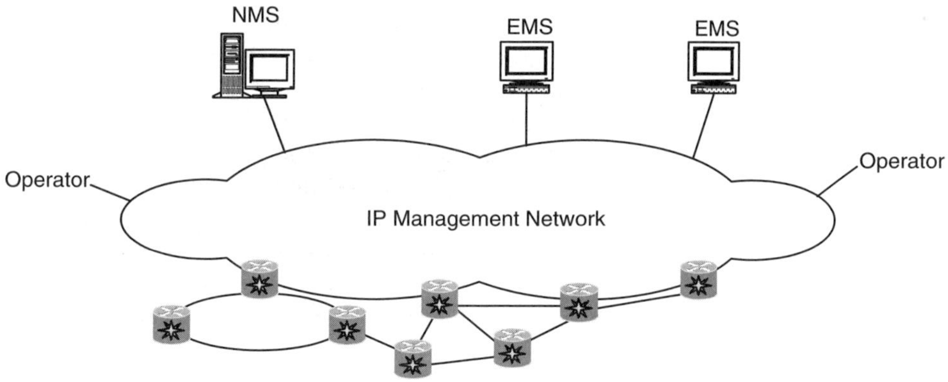

Figure 14.2 The management network may partially coincide with the transport network.

entire function of the device and allow a very fine level of control. For this reason, however, a CLI can also be very hard to use; it has a great number of commands, each with many parameters, and a complex syntax based on keywords, which sometimes have obscure meanings and are hard to remember. The CLI is really a tool for developers, support engineers, or the well-trained operator.

Some vendors also develop their own Graphical User Interfaces (GUIs) to help users manage their devices. There is really no big distinction between a GUI and an EMS in this context, because it is very unusual for a network device to support a GUI through a directly attached terminal; the GUI is usually an application that runs on a separate workstation. A well-organized GUI provides a hierarchical view of the configurable and manageable components of each network device, allows point-and-click navigation, hides complex functions behind an "Advanced" button, and supplies well-thought-out defaults for most parameters. Although there are great similarities between the configurable components and commodities from one network device to another, the GUIs often only bear comparison at the highest level.

14.4 Standardized Management Protocols

Proprietary management interfaces are fine up to a point, but as a Service Provider attempts to add equipment from different vendors to their network it becomes a major problem. Operators are either required to learn the user interfaces, programming languages, and GUI layouts of each new piece of equipment, or some form of homologation is needed to map from the operator's favorite set of commands to the instructions understood by each device. This latter choice makes life considerably easier for the operator, but is only achieved at great expense and effort by the Service Provider.

Many attempts have been made to standardize the way in which management workstations communicate with network devices. The aim in all cases is to produce a single management protocol that will be understood by all equipment in the network and can be spoken by the management station to control the network.

Unfortunately, the standardization process has led not to a single protocol but to a whole set of different solutions. Each has its advantages and disadvantages, and each its proponents and detractors. A few of the more common protocols are described below.

The *Simple Network Management Protocol* (SNMP) is the IETF's management protocol of choice. It has a checkered past, with version one regarded as unscalable and version two insecure. Version three has recently been stabilized and claims to address all issues in previous versions. However, the time that it has taken to evolve, combined with a widespread belief that SNMP is in no way "simple," means that many vendors are reluctant to offer SNMP management of their devices, and where they do, the take-up in live networks (especially core, transport networks) is very poor and the protocol is used for monitoring rather than for control.

Nevertheless, because SNMP is actively promoted by the IETF, it is a significant configuration protocol. In SNMP, data is encoded in Abstract Symbolic Notation One (ASN1). It has two formats, one for carrying data on the wire (within protocol messages) and one for representation in text documents. The total set of data managed in SNMP is known as the Management Information Base (MIB), and each new protocol developed within the IETF is required to have a MIB module defined. The MIB modules for GMPLS are discussed further in the next chapter.

The *Extensible Markup Language* (XML) is a text formatting language that is a subset of the Standard Generalized Markup Language (SGML) specified in the International Standard ISO 8879. XML documents look very much like those written in the Hypertext Markup Language (HTML) used to encode web pages. However, XML includes the ability to characterize data fields giving their data types and encodings as well as their values.

XML is a somewhat verbose way of encoding data. The management data for a device is presented as a document with tags that give meaning and format to each field. The tags are usually descriptive, so several text words may be used to encapsulate a single piece of data. This is a great strength because the format and meaning is encoded in XML in a way that can be simply parsed by the recipient, but it also imposes an overhead compared with a binary encoding of a known structure. XML documents are exchanged using the Simple Object Access Protocol (SOAP), a lightweight, transaction-oriented protocol that utilizes an underlying transport protocol.

The *Common Object Request Broker Architecture* (CORBA) takes an object-oriented approach to management through a distributed management architecture. The CORBA specifications include the definition of the managed objects, the rules for communication between management applications and the managed objects, and the requests, access control, security, and relationships between the objects.

In CORBA, data is encoded using Interface Definition Language (IDL), which extends a subset of the C++ programming language by adding constructs to support the type of object management that is needed in the context of network management. Data sets are constructed as objects and are exchanged using the General Inter-ORB Protocol (GIOP), a message-based transaction protocol. When GIOP is adapted to use TCP/IP as its transport, it is known as the Internet Inter-ORB Protocol (IIOP).

Transaction Language 1 (TL1) is a standardized, transaction-based ASCII scripting language that is very popular in management systems. It grew out of the Man Machine Language (MML) specified by Bellcore as a standard language for controlling network elements within the Regional Bell Operating Companies (RBOCs).

TL1 is certainly the most common management protocol in transport networks. It owes this position partly to the fact that it is a man-machine language — a language that is understood both by users and by the devices it controls. However, its success must also be attributed to the fact that around 80% of the devices in telecommunication networks in the United States utilize OSS software from Telcordia: Telcordia compatibility certification (through OSMINE) is therefore a crucial (if expensive) requirement for vendors in this market, and because Telcordia uses TL1, most vendors support TL1 either directly to their network devices or as a management interface to their EMSs.

The *Lightweight Directory Access Protocol* (LDAP) is a set of protocols for sharing and accessing information in distributed directories. When you look at the requirements for controlling and managing the equipment within a network, you discover that it is not far removed from a distributed directory with some portions of the data held on the network devices, and a central directory held on the EMS or NMS.

LDAP has grown out of the X.500 set of directory standards, and the data is encoded in ASN.1. But unlike X.500, LDAP operates over TCP/IP, making it available within the Internet and across an IP management network. Although not currently very popular as a management tool, LDAP is increasingly used as an automated inventory mechanism. In this mode, network elements can report the components and cards that they have installed (and the status of those components) to the EMS.

As can be seen from the descriptions above, the common standardized management protocol solutions do not just use different message exchanges, they also have entirely different ways of representing and encoding the configuration

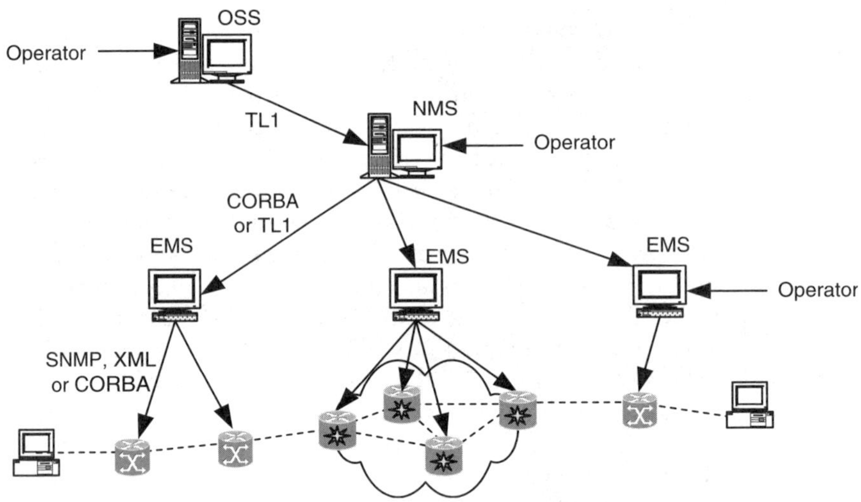

Figure 14.3 Common network management usage is assigning specific roles to the different network management protocols within the management network.

data for the managed devices. Far from making things easier, the array of choices tends to reduce the take-up of interoperable solutions by vendors who, unable to decide which standard solution to offer, simply stick with their own proprietary solution.

Some multi-vendor interoperability consortia under pressure from Service Providers are now beginning to develop and agree upon common approaches (for example, the TeleManagement Forum and the Multiservice Switching Forum). These are tending to converge on CORBA and TL1, with XML still making a strong showing, resulting in the model shown in Figure 14.3.

14.5 Web Management

There is nothing very special about web management of network devices, although it is hyped somewhat by equipment vendors. The chief advantage for operators is that they are able to use a GUI to control and configure their network without actually having to run a specific application (such as an EMS) on their own workstation. All that an operator needs is a web browser and connectivity (usually across the IP management network) to the server that runs the management application. The management application generates control panels as forms that the operator can complete.

The most common implementation of web management simply provides a remote GUI to a vendor-specific EMS. The facilities of HTML mean that this sort of management tool can be made to look very sexy and can perform all sorts of clever point-and-click operations.

In some extreme cases, network devices may be capable of running web servers to allow browsers to connect to them direct and send configuration commands. This, however, is very rare because the primary purpose of a network device is not to host HTTP sessions, and it is unusual for there to be space to put this kind of software support on a switch or router.

14.6 Alarms and Events

The collection, correlation, and servicing of alarms or events raised by network elements is an important feature of network management systems. Although some alarms may be handled by the network elements, possibly in conjunction with the control plane, to minimize the impact on services, it is crucial that the alarms are passed on to the management system so that the operator (or some automatic trouble-ticketing system) can take remedial actions to protect existing services and to repair the fault.

To ensure that the operator or his applications are fully informed of their status, the network elements report (*raise*) alarms and other key events to their EMS. The EMS passes the fault notifications on to the NMS, and the NMS may even tell the OSS, so that planning and procurement actions can be taken. Although any layer in this model may take remedial action, the notifications are still sent so that the higher layers can make their own judgments.

Note, however, that a network device may raise many alarms in response to a single fault. For example, if a fiber is cut, the associated line card may raise a Loss of Light alarm, but other components of the device such as the cross-connect and the downstream transmitter may also suffer from the error and raise corresponding Loss of Signal alarms. These alarms can be correlated vertically; that is, the alarms can be seen to all correspond to the same event and are in some sense a chain reaction. In other circumstances a single failure, such as of a whole line card, may cause multiple parallel alarms to be raised; for example, an Interface Down alarm for each port on the line card. These alarms can be correlated horizontally.

If each device passed all alarms to its EMS, and each EMS passed all alarms to the NMS, the NMS could be seriously overloaded. To prevent this from happening, two features are configurable within the network. The first assigns priorities or severities to each alarm or event and allows control of which faults are reported and which are silently ignored or just logged. The second feature allows levels within the management network to correlate alarms and only report the issue to which all other alarms can be traced (and from which all other alarms can be deduced).

Alarm and event reporting mechanisms typically utilize the same protocols that are used for management control. Thus SNMP has the concept of a Trap or Notification that allows a device to pass unsolicited information to its management station. Similarly CORBA and TL1 all allow a lower management level to report an event to a higher level.

Other asynchronous event protocols such as Syslog can also be used to collect alarm and event notifications from network elements, but these are typically used for historic archival and are examined by operators and field engineers who want to understand what has been happening in the network.

14.7 Further Reading

A discussion of some of the different options for network management and of the key network management protocols can be found in Chapter 13 of *The Internet and Its Protocols: A Comparative Approach*, by Adrian Farrel (2004), Morgan Kaufmann.

More details of the specific management protocols can be found in the following texts:

Essential SNMP, by Douglas R. Mauro and Kevin J. Schmidt (2001). O'Reilly.
XML in a Nutshell, by Elliotte Rusty Harold and W. Scott Means (2002). O'Reilly.
CORBA/IIOP Clearly Explained, by Michael Hittersdorf (2000). AP Professional.

CHAPTER 15

GMPLS MIB Modules

The Simple Network Management Protocol (SNMP) is *the* management protocol of choice within the IETF. This does not mean that GMPLS-conformant devices are restricted to SNMP or are forced to implement SNMP. Indeed, most GMPLS-capable network elements have a variety of management interfaces as described in the previous chapter.

However, it is an IETF requirement that all IETF protocols have Management Interface Base (MIB) modules defined to allow implementations to be modeled and managed. The MIB is the global distributed database for management and control of SNMP-capable devices, and a MIB module is a collection of individual objects and tables of objects, each of which contains a value that describes the configuration or status of a manageable entity or logical entity of the same type.

This chapter briefly describes the MIB modules that exist for MPLS traffic engineering and then describes how those modules are extended for GMPLS.

15.1 MPLS TE MIB Management

Three MIB modules are of particular relevance to the management of devices in an MPLS traffic engineered network: the MPLS Textual Conventions MIB module, the MPLS LSR MIB module, and the MPLS traffic engineering MIB module.

The MPLS Textual Conventions MIB module (MPLS-TC-STD-MIB) contains an assortment of general definitions for use in other MIB modules. In a sense it is a little like a header file that defines types and structures for use in other files. It includes definitions of things like bit rates, but more important, it defines textual conventions (that is, types) for use when representing tunnel IDs, extended tunnel IDs, LSP IDs, and MPLS labels.

The MPLS LSR MIB module (MPLS-LSR-STD-MIB) is used to model and control an individual MPLS LSR. This MIB module concerns itself with the core function of an LSR (that is, forwarding of labeled packets), so it is as applicable to LDP as it is to RSVP-TE. In fact, the LSR MIB module could be used in the absence of any signaling protocol to manually configure LSPs through the LSR.

There are four basic units to the LSR MIB module. There is a table of MPLS-capable interfaces on which labeled packets can be sent and received. There is a table of "in-segments" corresponding to labels received on interfaces or upstream legs of LSPs; there is a table of "out-segments" modeling downstream legs of LSPs identified with a stack of one or more labels to be pushed onto a packet and indicating the interface out of which to send the packet. The fourth unit is a table of "cross-connects" that shows the relationships (which may be more complex than one-to-one) between in- and out-segments.

A third MIB module, the MPLS traffic engineering MIB module (MPLS-TE-STD-MIB), is used to model and control MPLS TE LSPs. The primary purpose of the module is to allow an operator to configure and activate a TE LSP at an ingress LSR, but the module is equally valid for examining the LSP at any LSR along its path.

The MPLS TE MIB module contains tables to configure multiple instances of an LSP tunnel for simultaneous activation (such as for load-sharing or protection) or for sequential activation (such as for recovery). Thus a tunnel, which is an end-to-end traffic trunk or service, has a common root in the mplsTunnelTable and may be supported by one or more LSPs either at the same time or at different times. Each LSP is represented in the mplsTunnelTable as an "instance" of the tunnel.

Other tables allow the configuration and inspection of resource usage for the LSP, and the requested, computed, and actual routes of the LSP.

The dependencies between the MPLS TE MIB modules can be seen in Figure 15.1. The arrows indicate the relationship, "depends on."

15.2 GMPLS MIB Modules

GMPLS MIB management is built upon MPLS TE management. Nearly every aspect of the MPLS TE MIB modules is reused, but a fair amount of new objects are needed to handle the extra complexity and function of a GMPLS system.

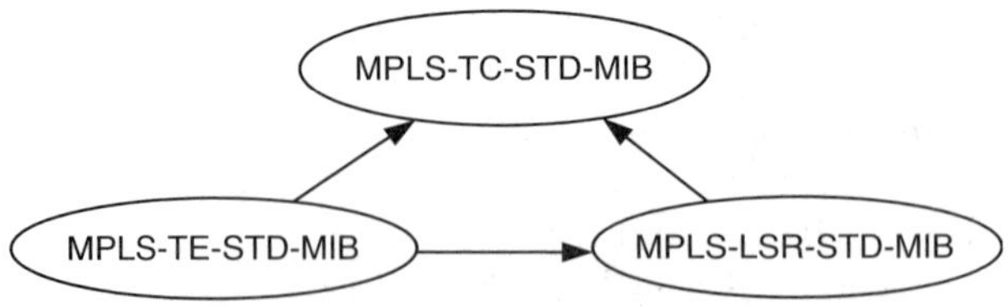

Figure 15.1 The relationship between the MPLS TE MIB modules.

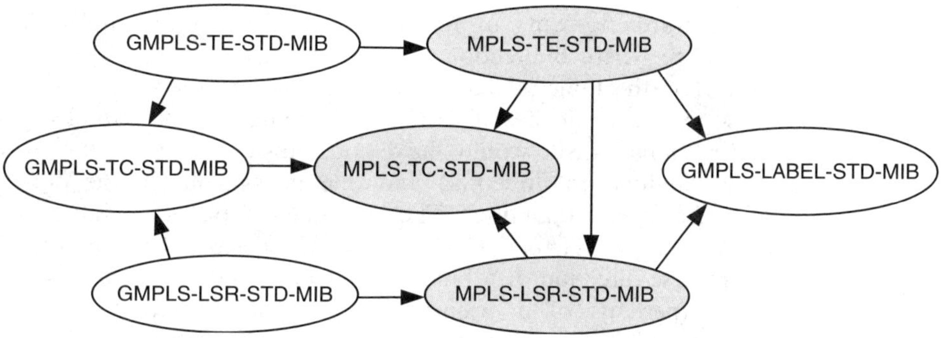

Figure 15.2 The relationship between the GMPLS MIB modules.

Figure 15.2 shows the new MIB modules (in white) and their relationship to the MPLS TE MIB modules (in gray). As can be seen, there are four new modules for GMPLS. The GMPLS-TC-STD-MIB provides some additional textual conventions specific to GMPLS. The GMPLS-LSR-STD-MIB and the GMPLS-TE-STD-MIB are mainly used to "extend" tables in the MPLS TE MIB modules; that is, they effectively provide additional objects for inclusion in the tables defined in the MPLS TE MIB modules.

The GMPLS Label Management MIB module (GMPLS-LABEL-STD-MIB) is a new module designed to handle the fact that GMPLS labels may be considerably more complex than the 20-bit numbers used as labels in MPLS. It contains a table of labels that have simple indexes, but may have complex forms, and that may be referenced from the other MIB modules.

15.3 GMPLS LSR Management

The GMPLS LSR is managed using all of the tables in the MPLS LSR MIB with extensions to handle the additional function for GMPLS.

The table of MPLS-capable interfaces (mplsInterfaceTable) is extended by the gmplsInterfaceTable. An entry in the former means that the interface uses RSVP-TE for MPLS unless there is also an entry in the GMPLS table. In this case there is an object in the gmplsInterfaceTable that defines the GMPLS signaling protocol in use, and another that defines the signaling Hello period to use on the interface.

The performance of label switching on the interface is recorded in the mplsInterfacePerfTable, and no extensions are made for GMPLS. In fact, two of the counters are specific to packet processing and are consequently only valid when GMPLS is used in a packet-capable environment.

Inward segments in MPLS are tracked in the mplsInSegmentTable. For GMPLS, where bidirectional LSPs are permitted, this might appear confusing; however, the table is well named and the entries refer to the direction of data flow and have no bearing on the signaling used to establish the LSP. Thus, a bidirectional LSP would have one in-segment on the upstream interface (for the forward direction) and one in-segment on the downstream interface (for the reverse direction). The in-segment table is extended for GMPLS by the gmplsInSegmentTable, which tells us whether the segment is used on the forward or reverse direction of a bidirectional LSP, and provides a pointer to an external table (perhaps of a proprietary MIB module) that can contain additional parameters to support technology-specific transports (for example, SONET resource usage). The mplsInSegmentTable may contain a pointer into the gmplsLabelTable to handle the encoding of complex labels.

The performance of in-segments is tracked in the mplsInSegmentPerfTable. Most of the objects in this table are specific to bytes and packets and would only be used when GMPLS is running in a packet-capable environment.

The mplsInSegmentMapTable allows an operator to make a reverse lookup from {interface, label} to find the relevant in-segment in the mplsInSegmentTable. This useful function is preserved for GMPLS, but is slightly complicated by the fact that the label may be found by an indirection to the gmplsLabelTable.

Similar extensions are made for the mplsOutSegmentTable that contains the details of LSP legs that carry data out of the device. The top label to impose on the outgoing traffic may now be found, through indirection, in the gmplsLabelTable. The gmplsOutSegmentTable extends the MPLS table to say whether the segment is in use on the forward or reverse path of the LSP. There is also a pointer to an external table to encode additional parameters if appropriate. Finally, the gmplsOutSegmentTable contains an object to specify by how much to decrement the TTL of any payload packets forwarded on the segment if per-hop decrementing is done; this is clearly also only relevant in packet switching environments.

The performance of out-segments is tracked in the mplsOutSegmentPerfTable. In the same way as for in-segments, most of the objects in this table are specific to bytes and packets and would only be used when GMPLS is running in a packet-capable environment.

The mplsLabelStackTable is preserved for GMPLS, but also only applies in packet environments because this is the only time that label stacking is relevant. This table lists the additional label stack to be applied to outgoing packets beneath the topmost label. These labels may also be found through indirection to the gmplsLabelTable (although this particular usage is unlikely because the stack will be made up from simple 23-bit labels).

Both the in- and out-segment tables may contain pointers to an external table that contains parameters that describe the traffic on this LSP. The pointer may indicate an entry in the mplsTunnelResourceTable in the MPLS TE MIB module, or it may point to an entry in a proprietary MIB module.

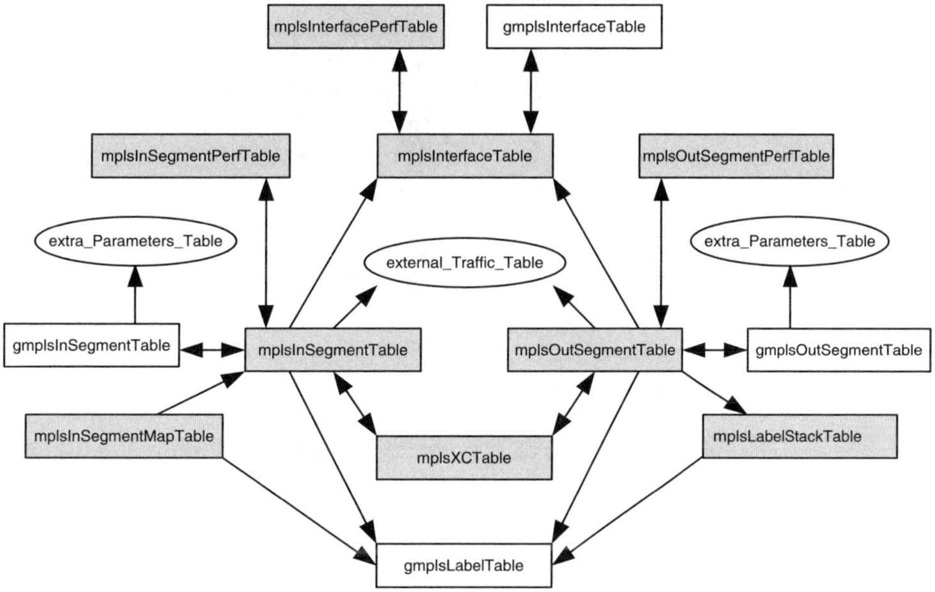

Figure 15.3 The relationship between MIB tables in GMPLS LSR management.

This leaves just the mplsXCTable which is unchanged in usage from MPLS. That is, it ties together in- and out-segments to provide LSPs through the device.

Figure 15.3 shows all of the MIB tables used for managing a GMPLS LSR with their relationships indicated by arrows. Gray boxes denote tables in the MPLS LSR MIB module, hashed boxes are tables in external MIB modules, and white boxes are tables in the GMPLS LSR MIB module.

15.4 GMPLS Traffic Engineering LSP Management

Management of individual TE LSPs is slightly simpler and requires fewer tables than the management of the LSR described above. The basis of the management is the mplsTunnelTable, which contains active and configured LSP tunnels that start, end, or transit the device. Entries in the tunnel table are not indexed by the five-tuple that defines the LSP, as might seem natural, but by a slightly different set of parameters. That is, the normal group of identifiers of the LSP {source, destination, tunnel ID, extended tunnel ID, LSP ID} is replaced in this MIB table by {tunnel index, tunnel instance, ingress LSR ID, egress LSR ID}. The tunnel index maps to the tunnel ID that is signaled, while the tunnel instance disambiguates distinct LSPs that support the tunnel (either simultaneously or over time) and thus may be safely mapped to the LSP ID that is signaled. The MIB module assumes that the source and destination of the LSP will be expressed as LSR IDs (which might not be the case) and makes the false assumption that the extended tunnel ID will always be set equal to the ingress LSR ID and thus does not need to be configured. Having said this, the indexing scheme is actually quite acceptable for non-packet systems and, because it is now used for MPLS packet systems, it is clearly extensible for GMPLS packet LSPs.

The purpose of the GMPLS TE MIB module is both to allow LSPs to be configured and managed at their ingresses and to allow the LSPs to be inspected at any point within the network. To configure an LSP it must be possible to select parameters for any constraint or option that can be signaled. The core set of objects for this are found in the mplsTunnelTable, and this is extended by the gmplsTunnelTable to support the following additional features:

- Presentation of this tunnel within the LSR as an unnumbered interface
- Selection of label recording
- The encoding type requested for the LSP
- The switching type requested for the LSP
- The link protection requested for the LSP
- The payload (G-PID) carried by the LSP
- Whether the LSP is a secondary (that is, backup) LSP
- Whether the LSP is unidirectional or bidirectional
- The control of alarms and other LSP attributes
- What manner of path computation the ingress LSR is required to perform

Some of these attributes are useful in MPLS as well as GMPLS and can be used by picking up the gmplsTunnelTable and setting the encoding type to zero to indicate an MPLS LSP. All of the objects listed above are also used when an LSP is examined at a transit or egress LSR. Additionally, it is possible to see the Notify recipients for forward and backward notification and the Admin Status flags. A pointer from the gmplsTunnelTable can be used to reference an additional external table (perhaps of a proprietary MIB module) that can contain additional parameters to support technology-specific transports (for example, SONET resource usage).

The MPLS TE MIB module contains the mplsTunnelPerfTable to record the performance of the LSP. However, because the MPLS tunnels are unidirectional, the GMPLS TE MIB module introduces the gmplsTunnelReversePerfTable to record the performance in the opposite direction. Both performance tables are primarily concerned with packets and bytes and may be largely inappropriate in non-packet environments.

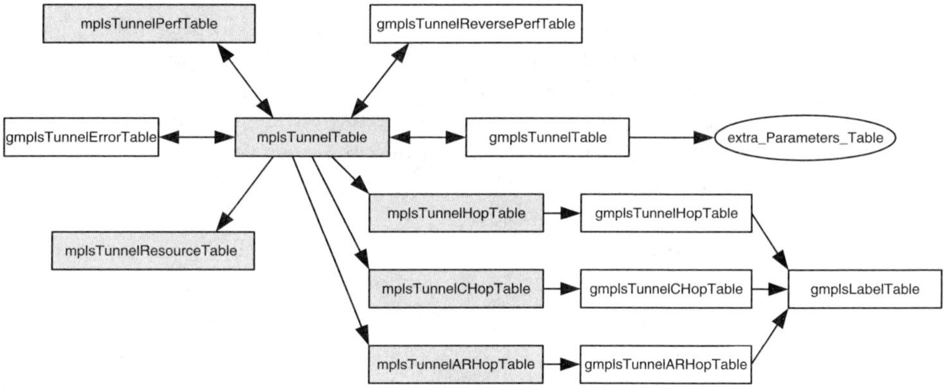

Figure 15.4 The relationship between MIB tables in GMPLS TE management.

The resource requirements/usage of each LSP are recorded in the mplsTunnelResourceTable. No changes are needed to this table for GMPLS.

A significant part of TE LSP management relates to the specification, computation, and recording of the path taken by the LSP. The MPLS TE MIB module provides three tables for this function: the mplsTunnelHopTable, the mplsTunnelCHopTable, and the mplsTunnelARHopTable, respectively. GMPLS increases the level of control that may be specified in a configured and signaled route (for example, by adding explicit control of labels) and also allows for this information to be recorded. Thus it is necessary to extend all three of the tables within the GMPLS TE MIB module. Further, because labels are now involved, the new tables include pointers into the gmplsLabelTable.

The final extension in the GMPLS TE MIB is the gmplsTunnelErrorTable. This table is not really specific to GMPLS because it records errors that occur when trying to establish an LSP or when the LSP fails at some later stage. Because it extends the mplsTunnelTable it may be used equally in MPLS and GMPLS systems.

Figure 15.4 shows all of the MIB tables used for managing GMPLS TE LSPs with their relationships indicated by arrows. Gray boxes denote tables in the MPLS TE MIB module, hashed boxes are tables in external MIB modules, and white boxes are tables in the GMPLS TE MIB module.

15.5 The TE Link MIB Module

The Traffic Engineering (TE) Link MIB module is equally applicable to MPLS and GMPLS systems. It allows TE links to be configured and managed to helping an operator to set up and use link bundles. Configuring a bundled link involves defining the bundled link and the TE links, assigning SRLGs to the TE link, configuring the component links to their bandwidth parameters, associating the component links with the appropriate TE link, and associating the TE links with the appropriate bundled link.

To this end, the TE Link MIB module includes seven tables.

- Entries in the teLinkTable represent the TE links, including bundled links, and their generic traffic engineering parameters.
- The teLinkDescriptorTable contains the TE link interface switching capabilities.
- The teLinkSrlgTable lists the shared risk link groups (SRLGs) that may be associated with the TE links.
- Priority-based bandwidth traffic engineering parameters for association with the TE links are placed in the teLinkBandwidthTable.
- Entries in the componentLinkTable represent the component links and show their generic traffic engineering parameters.
- The componentLinkDescriptorTable holds the switching capability descriptors for each component link.
- Priority-based bandwidth traffic engineering parameters for association with each component link are placed in the componentLinkBandwidthTable.

This MIB module contains the basic necessities for managing TE links but is somewhat short of configurable constraints for links in optical networks. Further developments and extensions to this MIB are likely as traffic engineering becomes more established in photonic networks.

15.6 The LMP MIB Module

The TE Link MIB module allows an operator to configure and manage data links so that they can be bundled and advertised as TE links. But what is also needed is a way to manage the use of LMP on links between GMPLS devices. This can be found in the LMP MIB module (LMP-STD-MIB).

The first requirement to run LMP is to configure the neighbors with which an LSR will exchange LMP messages. LMP does not have a neighbor discovery mechanism, so each would-be peer must be configured in the lmpNbrTable. The operator must configure the node ID of each partner and can also provide values for the retransmission interval and limit for each message that is sent.

Once we know about neighbors, we need control channels to be configured. Although control channel activation involves a degree of negotiation, it is nevertheless underpinned by configuration, and the lmpControlChannelTable is used to enable LMP exchanges on a per-interface basis. The addresses to use for the control channel messages, and the options including the Hello and Dead Interval timers, can be configured.

The behavior of the control channel can be monitored through the lmpControlChannelPerfTable. Unlike the management of the signaling protocols where the performance tables show the characteristics of data traffic, this table strictly monitors the LMP traffic, indicating the number of bytes sent and received, recording the number of errors, and counting the number of each message type used on the control channel.

At this point, the protocol can be run and monitored, and the remainder of the MIB module is concerned with the TE links that will be reported and monitored by LMP. The lmpTeLinkTable is used to specify those TE links for which LMP exchanges information, and contains some basic LMP parameters. The information that can be configured includes the LMP neighbor to which the link connects, and whether the optional procedures (link verification, fault management, and LMP-WDM) are supported.

If link verification is used, the verification parameters are configured through the lmpLinkVerificationTable for each TE link. As well as configuring the timer values for the verification process, the MIB table includes an object to select the transport verification mechanism(s) to use on the associated data links.

The results of the LMP discovery procedures are recorded in the lmpDataLinkTable. An entry is created in this table for each data link, and the relevant local information (interface address and encoding type) is configured. As LMP discovers the remote configuration information, it updates the table with the remote interface address and interface index. This information can then be utilized by GMPLS signaling to ensure that adjacent nodes have the same understanding of which data link is being referred to.

The performance of LMP in relation to a given TE link is recorded in the lmpTeLinkPerfTable. The objects count the same events that are found in the lmpControlChannelPerfTable (protocol messages), but in this case only the messages specifically related to the TE link are recorded. In the case where there is only one control channel between a pair of LMP peers, the numbers in this table are a subset of those in the lmpControlChannelPerfTable, but where more than one control channel is used the relationship is not so simple.

The performance of the data link is still related to the exchange of protocol messages, but because the only messages sent on the data link are Test messages (and even those might not be sent on the data link), lmpDataLinkPerfTable records the performance of the link verification process for each data link.

15.7 The Interfaces MIB Module

The Interfaces MIB module defines generic managed objects for managing interfaces. An interface in this context is the end of a logical connection through which an application can send or receive data. This concept used to be limited to physical connections but has been extended to include logical connections (such as LSPs) that are carried by physical connections. In the context of GMPLS, this meaning of interface is synonymous with the term "data link end" as defined in Chapter 8. The GMPLS and MPLS MIB modules make references to interfaces so that it can be clearly determined where the procedures managed by the MIB modules should be performed and, specifically, to manage those interfaces.

Additionally, modules utilize *interface stacking* when there is a hierarchical relationship between interfaces on a device. Such interface stacking is primarily used for logical interfaces, although the bottom element in any stack is a physical interface. Note that this hierarchical relationship is not the hierarchy of LSPs (see Chapter 8), but a familiar concept from the Interfaces MIB that allows a subdivision of a physical interface (a *logical interface*) to be presented to an application for its use as though it was a dedicated physical interface.

The TE MIB modules based on MPLS-TE-STD-MIB allow TE LSPs to be managed as logical interfaces. The Interfaces MIB module contains a table (the interfaces table — ifTable) that includes information on each interface, and is constructed so that each sub-layer below the internetwork layer of a network interface is considered an interface in its own right. Thus, a TE LSP managed as an interface is represented as an entry in the ifTable.

The interrelation of entries in the ifTable is defined as interface stacking. When TE LSPs are managed as interfaces, the interface stack might appear as in Figure 15.5. In the figure, the "underlying layer" refers to the ifIndex of any interface type for which (G)MPLS internetworking has been defined.

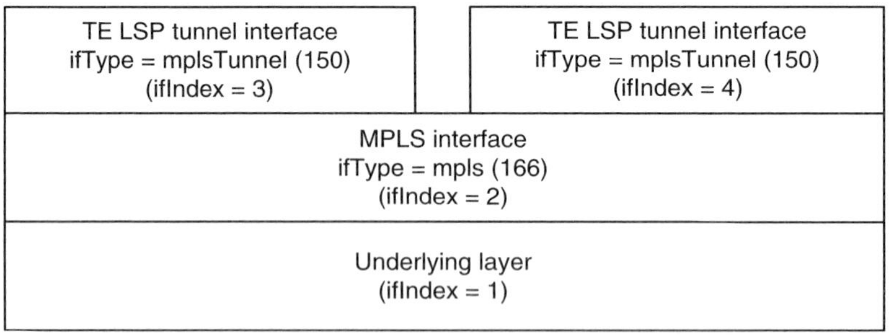

Figure 15.5 Two TE LSPs managed as interfaces over a single MPLS-capable interface.

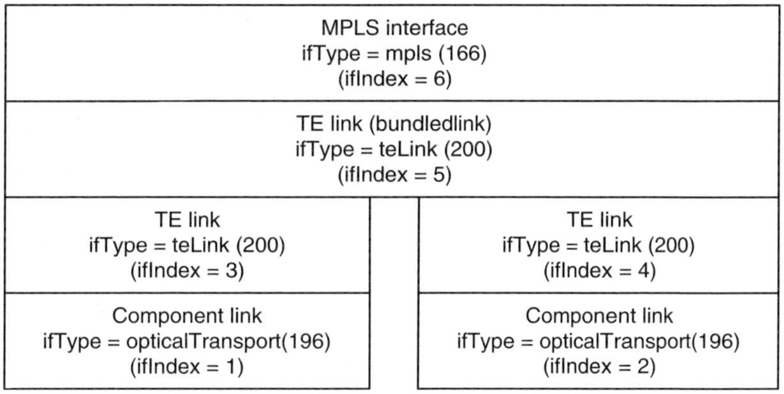

Figure 15.6 Two physical component links managed as separate TE links and then bundled.

Thus, two distinct TE LSPs may be presented as separate interfaces to their applications, but may actually be carried over a single, (G)MPLS-enabled physical interface. GMPLS inherits the terminology of the MPLS usage so that interfaces that are realized through TE LSPs are known as *TE LSP tunnel interfaces*, and physical interfaces that are MPLS- or GMPLS-enabled are called *MPLS interfaces*.

Interface stacking is also used in the TE Link MIB module to manage TE links as logical interfaces. The TE Link interface is represented as an entry in the ifTable and stacking may be carried out as before. When using TE Link interfaces, the interface stack table might appear as in Figure 15.6. In the figure, "opticalTransport" is an example of an underlying physical interface. Both TE link management and link bundling can be seen in the figure. Two TE links are defined, each managing an optical transport link; these two TE links are combined into a single bundle that is managed as a single TE link interface that supports MPLS and is presented as an MPLS interface.

15.8 Further Reading

Understanding SNMP MIBs by David Perkins and Evan McGinnis (1996), Prentice Hall. This book covers how MIB modules are put together and how they work.

MPLS Network Management: MIBs Tools, and Techniques by Thomas Nadeau (2003), Morgan Kaufmann. This book gives a very detailed account of the MIB modules used in MPLS traffic engineering.

The various MIB modules are described in a series of Internet Drafts that are in the process of becoming RFCs.

draft-ietf-mpls-mgmt-overview	MPLS Management Overview
RFC 3811	Definitions of Textual Conventions for MPLS Management
RFC 3812	MPLS Traffic Engineering Management Information Base
RFC 3813	MPLS Label Switching Router (LSR) Management Information Base
draft-ietf-mpls-telink-mib	Traffic Engineering Link Management Information Base
draft-ietf-ccamp-gmpls-tc-mib	Definitions of Textual Conventions for GMPLS Management
draft-ietf-ccamp-gmpls-lsr-mib	GMPLS Label Switching Router (LSR) Management Information Base
draft-ietf-ccamp-gmpls-te-mib	GMPLS Traffic Engineering Management Information Base
draft-ietf-ccamp-lmp-mib	Link Management Protocol Management Information Base
RFC 2863	The Interfaces Group MIB

Glossary

Adaptation capability — A property of a link interface that connects a particular data link to a transport node. Within GMPLS, this property characterizes the interface's ability to perform a nesting function; that is, to use a locally terminated LSP that belongs to one network layer as a data link for some other network layer(s).

All-pairs shortest path problem — The computational problem of finding the shortest paths between every pair of vertices in the TE network graph.

Alternative LSP — See *Recovery LSP*.

Availability — The availability of a network or a network element is the probability that the network or network element can deliver some specified Quality of Service (QoS) at some point in time.

Backup Designated Router (*BDR*) — A routing controller elected among neighbors in a multi-access network. The BDR is expected to assume the functions of the DR when it detects that the DR is non-functional. The BDR establishes routing adjacencies with each of the neighbors in the network. See *Designated Router (DR)*.

Best disjoint paths — Two or more paths that have the smallest number of TE links, transport nodes, and SRLGs in common.

Command Line Interface (*CLI*) — The basic management interface at which an operator can issue a series of text commands to control the managed device. The CLI may be run through a directly attached terminal, or over a remote access protocol such as Telnet.

Common Object Request Broker Architecture (*CORBA*) — A network management technology that takes an object-oriented approach to management through distributed management architecture. The CORBA specifications include the definition of the managed objects, the rules for communication between management applications and the managed objects, and the requests, access control, security, and other relationships between the objects.

Component link — A logical grouping of network resources that is not advertised as an individual TE link.

Connection — See *GMPLS Label Switched Path*.

Constraint — See *Path computation constraint*.

Constraint-based path computation — Path computation that is performed under conditions of one or more constraints.

Control channel — An abstraction that characterizes the network resources necessary to deliver control plane messages between adjacent controllers.

Control interface — An abstraction that connects a controller to the local side of a control channel.

Controller — An entity realizing control plane intelligence (for example, routing and signaling protocols, path computer, traffic engineering applications). See also *Signaling controller* and *Routing controller*.

Control plane failure — A fault in a controller or a control channel.

Control plane network — An IP network used for delivery of control plane (protocol) messages exchanged by controllers.

Control plane partitioned LSP — An LSP with at least one of the controllers involved in its provisioning (temporarily) out of service.

Customer device (C device) — A Customer network node that has links only to other Customer network nodes.

Customer Edge device (CE device) — A Customer network node that has at least one link connecting the node to the Provider network. In other words, a CE has one or more links connecting it to one or more Provider Edge devices.

Customer network — Two or more isolated Customer sites interconnected via the Provider network.

Customer of layer one services (Customer) — An organization that uses services provided by the Provider.

Customer site — A segment of the Customer network built from Customer devices and Customer Edge devices whose interconnection within the site is realized by means not related to the services provided by the Provider, but whose connection to the rest of the Customer network depends on the Provider.

Data link (link) — An abstraction representing network resources that could be used for the transfer of user data traffic between two transport nodes adjacent in a particular network layer. A data link is a topological construct of a particular network layer; that is, it defines the network flexibility in that network layer.

Deciding entity (*Master node*) — A control plane entity (usually a PLR, but could be an MN) supervising the service recovery operation after a fault. See *Point of local repair (PLR)*.

Designated Router (*DR*) — A routing controller elected among neighbors in a multi-access network. The DR is responsible for advertising the network into the routing area. The DR establishes routing adjacencies with each of the neighbors in the network.

Detour — A backup tunnel protecting a single LSP that traverses the protected resource in the context of FRR. See *Fast Re-route (FRR)*.

Diverse path computation — The process of determining two or more links, nodes, SRLGs, or best disjoint paths.

DLCI — Frame Relay packet identifiers.

Element Management System (*EMS*) — An application or workstation dedicated to the management of one or more network devices/elements.

End-to-end recovery — A scope of recovery covering the entire protected LSP. In the case of end-to-end recovery, an alternative LSP starts and ends on the same pair of nodes as the protected LSP and provides recovery from a failure of any link or node on the protected LSP.

Equal Cost Multi-Path (*ECMP*) *forwarding* — A technique of using multiple parallel paths for the purpose of traffic load balancing.

ERO sub-object — A part of an ERO that contains information about one path constituent (TE link ID, transport node ID, abstract node ID, and so forth).

Explicit Route Object (*ERO*) — An RSVP-TE object that contains instructions on the path through the network to be taken by an LSP in terms of TE links, and/or transport nodes, and/or abstract nodes.

Extensible Markup Language (*XML*) — A text formatting language that is a subset of the Standard Generalized Markup Language (SGML) specified in the International Standard ISO 8879. XML includes the ability to characterize data fields giving their data types and encodings as well as their values.

Extra traffic service — A service mapped onto one or more idle protecting LSPs provisioned to protect other service(s).

Facility bypass tunnel — A backup tunnel protecting all LSPs that traverse the protected resource in the context of FRR. See *Fast Re-route (FRR)*.

Failure — The failure of a network or a network element is the moment when the network or network element stops delivering the specified Quality of Service. See also *Repair*.

Fast Re-route (*FRR*) — A method of local recovery in which each resource of a protected LSP, link, or node is separately protected by an individual backup tunnel.

Fault (*outage*) — The fault or outage is the period of time when a network or network element is not functional; that is, the period of time between a failure and subsequent repair.

Fault correlation — The stage in fault management at which locally detected faults are correlated for the purpose of optimizing the number and size of fault notification messages.

Fault detection — The stage in fault management at which a fault is detected by the data plane, and a fault notification is sent to the control plane.

Fault hold-off — The stage in fault management that follows immediately after fault detection; at this stage no action is taken by the control plane on the assumption that the necessary recovery procedures may be carried out in a lower layer.

Fault Indication Signal (*FIS*) — One of two types of fault notification message originated by a fault reporting node. See also *Fault Restoration Signal.*

Fault localization — The stage in fault management that follows immediately after fault hold-off; at this stage the faulted network element is identified, and the scope of the service recovery is determined.

Fault management — The process of detecting, localizing, and recovering from a fault.

Fault notification message — A message sent to the deciding entity by the fault reporting node or by the fault restoration reporting node.

Fault Restoration Signal (*FRS*) — One of two types of fault notification message; originated by a fault restoration reporting node. See also *Fault Indication Signal.*

Flooding — A process of reliable distribution of routing and TE advertisements among routing controllers within a particular routing area.

Forwarding Adjacency (*FA*) — A TE link that does not require a direct routing adjacency (peering) between routing controllers managing either of its ends to guarantee control plane connectivity (control channel) between the controllers.

Full mesh restoration — A form of effective distribution of network resources between multiple services where a relatively small amount of resources, allocated for protection purposes, covers (protects against faults) a relatively large amount of resources carrying normal traffic.

Full re-routing — A form of service restoration where neither pre-computation nor pre-provisioning of the recovery LSP happens before a fault has been detected on the protected LSP.

Full TE visibility — A situation where a routing controller receives all TE advertisements from every other routing controller in a particular set of routing controllers, and where those advertisements are not modified, aggregated, filtered, or summarized.

Generalized Label Object — A GMPLS RSVP-TE signaling object that is used to identify the label allocated by an LSR to be used by its immediate upstream neighbor. See also *Upstream Label Object*.

Generalized Label Request Object — GMPLS RSVP-TE signaling object that defines the context of the LSP.

Generalized Multiprotocol Label Switching (*GMPLS*) — The expansion and extension of MPLS for use in both packet switched and non-packet switched (circuit switched) environments.

Generalized PID (*G-PID*) — An attribute of the Generalized Label Request object identifying the use to which the LSP will be put; that is, the LSP payload. In general, the G-PID is of use only to the egress node of the LSP, and allows it to know whether it can successfully terminate the LSP — in other words, whether it will be able to process the signal that it receives.

GMPLS Label Switched Path (*LSP*, *connection*) — A single resource or a set of cross-connected resources of a particular layer that can deliver user traffic in this layer between one or more sources (ingresses) and one or more destinations (egresses).

GMPLS overlays — A GMPLS solution for the Layer One VPN application that does not require the use of BGP.

(G)MPLS tunnel — A transport service dynamically provisioned via the MPLS or GMPLS control plane and identified by a combination of RSVP-TE Session and Sender-Template signaling objects.

GVPNs — A Generalized VPN is a GMPLS solution for the Layer One VPN application that extends the BGP-VPN framework that is used for Layer Three and Layer Two VPNs.

Hierarchical LSP (*H-LSP, hierarchy*) — An LSP created in some network layer for the purpose of providing data links (extra network flexibility) in higher network layers.

Hierarchical P2MP Tunnel — A P2MP tunnel that is decomposed in such a way that one or more egresses of one or more P2MP LSPs originate a P2MP LSP of their own for the same P2MP tunnel.

Horizontal network integration — A set of collaborative mechanisms within a single instance of the control plane driving multiple (at least two) TE domains, or between different instances of the control plane.

In-band control channel — A control channel that utilizes the same data links that are used for delivery of user traffic.

In-fiber out-of-band control channel — A data link resource (data channel) specifically dedicated to the delivery of control plane traffic.

In-place modify — A provisioning procedure that modifies an LSP by means of direct re-provisioning. In-place modification is accomplished by an LSP Modify message originated by the LSP ingress and processed by all LSRs along the LSP. Sometimes, the process may also be achieved by an LSP AcceptModify message originated by the LSP egress.

Intermediate System to Intermediate System (*IS-IS*) — A popular link state IP routing protocol.

ISIS-TE — A traffic engineering advertisement protocol used in GMPLS.

Label Forwarding Information Base (*LFIB*) — A data structure maintained by an LSR that is used for determining the next hop for labeled data. The LFIB contains a mapping of {incoming interface, incoming label} to {outgoing interface, outgoing label}.

Label stack — A stack of shim headers located between network (Layer Two) and IP (Layer Three) headers. Used to apply a stack of more than one label to a data packet.

Label Switching Router (*LSR*) — A transport node capable of MPLS label switching.

Layer One service — A full set of services that could be provided by the Layer One Provider network. This includes services in both the Layer One data plane and the control plane.

Layer One VPN (*L1VPN*) — A Layer One service that interconnects three or more Customer sites. The service features the control of which CEs may be involved in the service, the publishing of membership information to all CEs involved in the service, and the implementation of policies that are applied by the Customer on a per-service basis for each component of the service.

Layer One VPN connection (*L1VPN connection*) — A connection between CEs located in different Customer sites of a Layer One VPN.

Lightweight Directory Access Protocol (*LDAP*) — A set of protocols for sharing and accessing information in distributed directories. LDAP nicely meets those requirements for controlling and managing network equipment that envision some portions of the management information held on the network devices, whereas other portions are held in a central repository on the EMS or NMS.

Limited branching capability problem — The case where a branch node is capable of replicating data onto no more than a given number of outgoing links because of a hardware or data plane technology limitation, because of an unacceptable delay introduced by multiple replications, or because of some configuration limitation.

Limited TE visibility — A situation where a routing controller receives summarized TE information, or does not receive full TE advertisement from some of the routing controllers in the network.

Link (span) — An abstraction associated with network resources that are necessary to deliver user traffic between a pair of nodes that are adjacent in a particular network layer.

Link (arc or edge) disjoint paths — Two or more paths that have no TE links in common.

Link interface — An abstraction that connects a transport node to the local end of a data link and represents data plane intelligence such as switching, termination, and adaptation.

Link Management Protocol (LMP) — A protocol introduced as part of GMPLS. It allows for a controller managing a particular data link to discover the link's existence and connectivity; to learn the identity of the neighboring transport node; the link's remote end identifier, capabilities, and attributes; and to verify the status and health of the link's constituent resources. LMP also helps routing controllers that manage data switches that are adjacent in a particular layer to discover and agree upon the components of a TE bundle they advertise. LMP can be used to localize data plane faults detected by multiple transport nodes. LMP may also be used to identify protecting and protected spans in certain link protection schemes.

Link (span) recovery — A service recovery level at which all protected LSPs traversing a particular link/span are recovered from any failure detected on the span.

Link State Advertisement (LSA) — A link state advertisement in the context of OSPF.

Link State Database (LSDB) — A data structure within any given link state routing protocol speaker. The LSDB is a repository of all link state advertisements in a particular routing area.

Link State Protocol Data Unit (LSP) — A link state advertisement in the context of IS-IS.

Link-type constraint — A constraint applicable to individual TE links. Examples of link-type constraints are available bandwidth and link protection capabilities.

Local recovery — A scope of recovery covering some segment of the protected LSP. There are two methods of local recovery: Fast Re-Route (FRR) and path segment recovery.

Loose ERO — An ERO that contains at least one loose ERO sub-object.

Loose ERO sub-objects — See *Strict, loose ERO sub-objects*.

LSDB synchronization — The process of merging LSDBs of two neighboring link state routing protocol speakers for the purpose of achieving identical LSDBs on both speakers containing the most recent link state advertisements.

LSP — See *GMPLS Label Switched Path*.

LSP Accept message — An abstract signaling message that is sent from node to node along the LSP path in the upstream direction confirming the LSP setup. In the context of RSVP-TE, the LSP Accept message is a Resv message.

LSP AcceptModify message — An abstract signaling message that is sent from node to node along the LSP path in the upstream direction confirming some modification to an already provisioned LSP. In the context of RSVP-TE, the LSP AcceptModify message is a Resv message.

LSP Confirm message — An abstract signaling message that is sent by the LSP ingress to the LSP egress confirming the receipt of the LSP Accept message. In the context of RSVP-TE, the LSP Confirm message is a ResvConf message.

LSP DownstreamError message — An abstract signaling message that is sent from node to node along the LSP path in the downstream direction, which indicates some error condition detected during LSP setup or after the LSP has been established. In the context of RSVP-TE, the LSP DownstreamError message is a ResvErr message.

LSP DownstreamRelease message — An abstract signaling message that is sent from node to node along the LSP path in the downstream direction requesting teardown of the LSP. In the context of RSVP-TE, the LSP DownstreamRelease message is a PathTear message.

LSP Encoding Type — An attribute of the Generalized Label Request object indicating the way that data will be packaged within the traffic flow carried by the LSP.

LSP Modify message — An abstract signaling message that is sent from node to node along the LSP path in the downstream direction requesting some modification to an already provisioned LSP. In the context of RSVP-TE, the LSP Modify message is a Path message.

LSP Notify message — An abstract signaling message that is sent to the address specified in a previous NotifyRequest object. The message is sent either direct to the specified address or from node to node along the LSP path in the upstream or downstream direction, and carries a notification of some important event such as a data plane fault. In the context of GMPLS RSVP-TE, the LSP Notify message is an RSVP-TE Notify message.

LSP Setup message — An abstract signaling message that is sent from node to node along the LSP path in the downstream direction requesting the establishment of an LSP. In the context of RSVP-TE, the LSP Setup message is a Path message.

LSP UpstreamError message — An abstract signaling message that is sent from node to node along the LSP path in the upstream direction which indicates some error condition detected during LSP setup or after the LSP has been established. In the context of RSVP-TE, the LSP UpstreamError message is a PathErr message.

LSP UpstreamRelease message — An abstract signaling message that is sent from node to node along the LSP path in the upstream direction requesting teardown of the LSP. In the context of RSVP-TE, the LSP UpstreamRelease message is a PathErr message.

Make-before-break modify — A provisioning procedure that modifies an LSP by first creating a new instance of the LSP that shares resources with the old instance on common links, and, after that, tearing down the old instance of the LSP.

Management-based service model — A Layer One VPN service model in which Customer and Provider networks communicate only via the management plane.

Management Information Base (MIB) — The set of data comprising configuration and statistical information for the managed network. MIBs are usually accessed using SNMP.

Master node — See *Deciding entity*.

MEMS — Micro-electro-mechanical systems.

Merge Node (MN) — A control plane entity that terminates an alternative LSP.

Micro-Electro-Mechanical Systems (MEMS) — A miniaturized mechanical device or machine such as the electrostatically controlled mirrors in an optical switch.

Misconnection — The situation where traffic is sent to an unintended receiver.

MPLS Label Switched Path (LSP) — The path that labeled data follows across the network. See also GMPLS LSP.

Multiprotocol Label Switching (MPLS) — A data forwarding technology developed by the IETF for use in packet networks. It relies on labeling each packet with a short, unique identifier (or label) that each router can use to determine the next hop for the data packet. Often also applied to the routing and signaling protocols used within the control plane of an MPLS network.

Multiprotocol Lambda Switching (MPλS) — An early attempt at applying MPLS control plane techniques to optical networks.

Network layer (layer) — A complete set of network resources of the same type that could be used for establishing a connection (LSP) or used for connectionless data delivery.

Network Management System (NMS) — A central management station or application that has a view of the whole network, and can control and configure all of the devices in the network.

Network resource (resource) — A basic data plane construct representing a particular class of physical network equipment. A resource is identified by a combination of a switching type, a data encoding type and a switching/terminating bandwidth granularity. It is meaningful in the context of a particular network layer, and is atomic in the network layer where it is defined.

NHOP tunnel — A backup tunnel protecting against the failure of a particular link on the protected LSP in the context of FRR.

NNHOP tunnel — A backup tunnel protecting against the failure of a particular node on the protected LSP in the context of FRR.

Node — An association of a transport node and the controller that manages the transport node.

Node- (vertex-) disjoint paths — Two or more paths that have no transport nodes in common. Node-disjoint paths are also link-disjoint paths by definition.

Non-packet-based resource — A channel of a particular bandwidth that can be allocated in a non-packet network data plane of a particular technology for the purpose of user traffic delivery. See also *Network resource.*

Non-root P2MP tunnel decomposition — The situation where a P2MP intermediate node originates one or more additional P2MP LSPs for the same P2MP tunnel. See also *P2MP tunnel decomposition.*

NotifyRequest Object — GMPLS RSVP-TE signaling object that is used to signal the address at which the signaling node wishes to receive LSP Notify messages.

Off-line path computation — Path computation performed in advance of LSP provisioning.

On-line path computation — Path computation performed on a controller that manages one or more transport nodes or on a stand-alone path computation element at the time of LSP provisioning.

Opaque LSA — An OSPF LSA whose content is not understood by OSPF.

Opaque LSA service — A service provided by OSPF to other protocols or applications (for example, OSPF-TE) so that they can distribute advertisements of their own between immediate neighbors (link-scope), within the OSPF routing area (area-scope), or within the entire routing domain (domain-scope) using OSPF internal distribution mechanisms (flooding, LSDB synchronization, and so forth).

Open Short Path First (*OSPF*) — A popular link state IP routing protocol.

Operations Support System (*OSS*) — A central management system where planning and service installation is managed by issuing management requests (usually through a standardized protocol) to one or more Network Management Systems.

OSPF-TE — A traffic engineering advertisement protocol used in GMPLS.

Outage — See *Fault*.

Out-of-band control channel — A control channel that utilizes network resources specifically dedicated for control plane traffic.

Out-of-fiber out-of-band control channel — A control channel that is fully disjoint from any data link used for delivery of user traffic.

P2MP branch — A part of a P2MP sub-tree that describes how a particular branch node that belongs to the sub-tree is connected to a subset of leaves.

P2MP branch node — A node that performs data replication for a P2MP tunnel.

P2MP bud node — A node that performs the functions of a branch node and a leaf for the same P2MP tunnel.

P2MP grafting — The procedure of connecting one or more additional leaves to an operational P2MP tunnel on the initiative of the root or an intermediate node.

P2MP *leaf-initiated drop* (*LID*) — The procedure by which a leaf disconnects itself from the P2MP tunnel.

P2MP leaf-initiated join (*LIJ*) — The procedure of connecting a new leaf to a P2MP tunnel on the initiative of the leaf.

P2MP LSP — An LSP that is provisioned for the purpose of data delivery from the LSP ingress (one of the P2MP tunnel nodes that is usually, but not necessarily, the root) to all LSP egresses (a subset of the P2MP tunnel nodes that are usually, but not necessarily, leaves).

P2MP pruning (*pruning*) — The procedure by which the tunnel root or an intermediate node disconnects one or more leaves from the P2MP tunnel.

P2MP sub-tree — A part of a P2MP tree that describes how the root or an intermediate node is connected to a particular subset of leaves.

P2MP tree — A graphical representation of all the TE links that are committed for a particular P2MP tunnel. That is, a representation of the P2MP tunnel on the network TE graph.

P2MP tunnel decomposition — The mapping of a P2MP tunnel onto more than one P2MP LSP.

P2MP tunnel leaf — The destination of a P2MP tunnel.

P2MP tunnel root — The source of a P2MP tunnel.

Packet-based resource — An abstraction hiding the means of traffic delivery with particular Quality of Service (QoS) over packet-switching media that is associated with particular parameters (most importantly, bandwidth). See also *Network resource*.

Path computation — The process of selecting or determining a path (of an LSP) in terms of TE links and/or transport nodes that could realize a particular service.

Path computation constraint — A condition that disallows or enforces the selection of certain TE links, transport nodes, and/or path segments during the path computation process. Such a constraint may be explicit (by naming the TE link, and so forth) or qualitative (expressing a quality of the TE links, and so forth, to be included in the path). See also *Link-type constraint* and *Path-type constraint*.

Path recovery — A service recovery level at which each protected LSP is recovered from a failure independently.

Path recovery domain — See *Recovery domain*.

Path segment recovery — A method of local recovery in which a particular recovery scheme covers one segment of the protected LSP.

Path-type constraint — A constraint applicable to path segments and/or entire paths. Examples of path-type constraints are end-to-end delay, wavelength continuity, and overall path length.

Per-VPN Peer service model — A sub-class of the Signaling and Routing service model in the context of Layer One VPNs in which Customer network devices view the Provider network as a set of PE and P devices interconnected by TE links. The necessary TE information is leaked by PE devices into Customer sites on a per-VPN basis.

Plain Old Telephone Service (POTS) — The legacy telephone network and associated equipment and procedures. In reality, POTS is neither plain nor simple.

Point of local repair (PLR) — A control plane entity that originates an alternative LSP.

Point-to-Multipoint (P2MP) tunnel — A service that delivers data traffic with specified characteristics from a single source to one or more destinations with an agreed Quality of Service (QoS), blocking probability, and resilience against network failures.

Pre-planned re-routing — A form of service restoration where resources on the alternative LSP are not bound into cross-connects until after a failure on the protected LSP has been detected.

Primary LSP — A fully provisioned LSP; that is, an LSP whose resources are allocated and bound into cross-connects at the time of LSP provisioning.

Protected LSP — An LSP subject to protection against faults.

Protecting LSP — A fully pre-provisioned recovery LSP; that is, a recovery LSP that does not require additional provisioning signaling after the fault has been detected.

Protection switchback — See *Reversion.*

Protection switchover — The process of switching user traffic from a protected to a protecting LSP.

Protection switchover signaling — The signaling between the PLR and MN for the purpose of protection switchover synchronization.

Provider device (P device) — A Provider network node that has TE links only to other Provider network nodes.

Provider Edge device (PE device) — A Provider network node that has at least one TE link connecting the node to a Customer site.

Provider network — A network that provides a service to another network. For example, a Layer One network that supports a Layer One VPN.

Provider of Layer One services (Provider) — An organization that has administrative control over a Layer One network.

Recovery domain — A combination of a segment of the protected LSP and all alternative LSPs protecting against any faults on the segment. In end-to-end path protection, the recovery domain covers the entire protected LSP. In path segment protection, the recovery domain covers one segment of the protected LSP so that protection against any faults on the protected LSP is achieved via a concatenation, and/or overlap, and/or nesting of multiple recovery domains.

Recovery LSP — An LSP onto which user traffic is switched during the recovery operation.

Re-merge problem — The re-merging onto the same link of P2MP LSPs that support the same P2MP tunnel but that carry data to non-matching sets of leaves.

Repair — The repair of a network or a network element is the moment when the network or network element regains its ability to deliver the specified Quality of Service (QoS). See also *Failure*.

Resource — See *Network resource*.

Restoration LSP — A recovery LSP that requires some provisioning signaling after the fault has been detected.

Reversion (protection switchback) — The process of switching user traffic from the protecting to the protected path.

Reversion signaling — Signaling between the PLR and MN for the purpose of reversion synchronization.

Root P2MP tunnel decomposition — The situation where a P2MP root originates more than one P2MP LSP for the same P2MP tunnel. See also *P2MP tunnel decomposition*.

Router Address — A network-unique identifier of a transport node permanently routable in the control plane network.

Routing adjacency (peering) — A relationship (routing protocol conversation) between a pair of neighboring routing controllers that governs the exchange of link state information.

Routing area — A part of a network whose topology is hidden from the rest of the network. The routing area is the scope of the distribution for unmodified native IGP (OSPF, ISIS) link state advertisements.

Routing controller — An entity (software modules and/or physical device) realizing the routing elements of the control plane and responsible for the advertisement of the capabilities and resources of one or more transport nodes. See also *Controller*.

Routing protocol speaker — A routing controller that supports a particular routing protocol.

RSVP session — A grouping of traffic flows to a particular destination. The RSVP-TE session is identified by an IP address (IPv4 or IPv6) of the destination, a Tunnel Identifier, and an Extended Tunnel Identifier.

RSVP-TE — A signaling protocol developed as part of MPLS and expanded for use in GMPLS for the purpose of dynamic provisioning of LSPs.

Secondary LSP — A partially provisioned LSP; that is, an LSP whose resources are not bound into cross-connects at the time of LSP provisioning. Secondary LSPs require additional provisioning signaling before they can be activated.

Sender Template Object — RSVP-TE signaling object that identifies the signaled LSP source and LSP instance.

Sender TSpec Object — RSVP-TE signaling object that identifies the signaled LSP bandwidth and some other data plane technology specific requirements.

Service protection — A class of service recovery that does not require any provisioning signaling for the alternative LSP after the failure indication.

Service recovery — A stage in fault management during which a service is recovered from one or multiple faults.

Service recovery operation — A set of actions in the control and data planes performed during the service recovery stage of fault management. There are two classes of service recovery operations: service protection and service restoration.

Service recovery time — The time interval between the moment of fault occurrence and full traffic recovery.

Service restoration — A class of service recovery that requires some provisioning signaling for the alternative LSP after the failure indication.

Session Object — RSVP-TE signaling object that identifies the RSVP session of the signaled LSP.

Shared Risk Link Group (SRLG) — A network-unique number that identifies a physical device, set of devices, or physical location that the operational status of multiple links depends upon. A single fault within an SRLG may simultaneously affect all links associated with the SRLG.

Shim header — A piece of information used for labeling data packets in an MPLS network that is inserted between the network (Layer Two) headers and the IP (Layer Three) header.

Shortest path — A path between a pair of vertices on the TE network graph that has minimal sum cost of the constituent arc.

Shortest Path Tree (SPT) — A graph $G'(V', E')$, where V' is a subset of vertices reachable from the source vertex s, and E' is a subset of arcs that interconnect vertex s with every reachable vertex v via the shortest path between vertex s and vertex v.

Signaling adjacency (peering) – A relationship between two signaling controllers that directly exchange signaling messages with each other. The two controllers need not be physically adjacent.

Signaling and Routing service model — A Layer One VPN service model in which the CE-PE control plane communication includes signaling and routing message exchanges.

Signaling controller — An entity (software modules and/or physical device) realizing the signaling elements of the control plane that is responsible for the control of one or more transport nodes. See also *Controller*.

Signaling Only service model — A Layer One VPN service model in which the scope of the CE-PE control plane communication is limited to the exchange of signaling messages.

Signaling protocol — The collection of signaling messages and their processing rules. In GMPLS, signaling protocols are used to establish and maintain LSPs. The GMPLS signaling protocol of choice is RSVP-TE.

Simple Network Management Protocol (SNMP) — The IETF's management and configuration protocol of choice. In SNMP, data is encoded in Abstract Symbolic Notation One (ASN.1) which has two formats, one for carrying data on the wire (that is, within protocol messages) and one for representation in text documents.

Single-destination shortest path problem — The computational problem of finding the shortest paths to a given vertex from each of the other vertices in the TE network graph.

Single-pair shortest path problem — The computational problem of finding the shortest path between two given vertices in the TE network graph.

Single-source shortest path problem — The computational problem of finding the shortest paths from a given vertex to each of the other vertices in the TE network graph.

Slave node — A control plane entity that plays the subordinate role in protection/reversion operations.

Span — See *Link*.

Span flapping — The situation when the span failure indication/restoration sequence happens many times in quick succession.

SRLG-disjoint paths — Two or more paths that have no common SRLGs associated with the constituent TE links of the paths.

Strict ERO — An ERO that contains only strict ERO sub-objects.

Strict, loose ERO sub-objects — An ERO sub-object is strict with relation to the sub-object previously specified in the ERO if no additional hops are allowed on the LSP's path between the path constituents identified by the two sub-objects. Otherwise, the ERO sub-object is loose. Note that any path expansion within an abstract node (for example, an AS) identified by a particular ERO sub-object is allowed even if the next sub-object in the ERO is specified as strict.

Stitching — A method of dynamic LSP provisioning that assumes the use of stitching segments.

Stitching segment — An LSP created in some network layer for the purpose of providing data links (extra network flexibility) in the same layer.

Switching capability — A property of a link interface that connects a data link to a transport node. This property characterizes the interface's ability to cooperate with other link interfaces connecting data links within the same network layer to the same transport node for the purpose of binding resources in cross-connects.

Switching Type — An attribute of the Generalized Label Request object that governs the type of label that is allocated. The attribute indicates the type of switching to be performed on the LSP when the data is received by the downstream LSR.

Synchronized TE link — A TE link for which consistent advertisements are received from routing controllers managing both sides of the TE link. Only synchronized TE links are made available for path computation.

TE bundle — An association of several parallel (that is, connecting the same pair of transport nodes) component links whose attributes are identical or whose differences are sufficiently negligible that the TE domain can view the entire association as a single TE link.

TE database (TED) — A memory structure within a speaker of a TE routing protocol (for example, a routing controller, a PCE, and so forth) that contains all TE advertisements generated by the protocol speaker and received from the network.

TE domain — A set of routing controllers, each of which has full TE visibility within the set.

TE link — A logical grouping of network resources for the purposes of TE advertisement and path selection.

TE link attribute — A parameter or property belonging to the set of network resources associated with a TE link, and that is significant in the context of path computation.

TE network graph — A connected, weighted graph $G(V, A)$, where $V = \{v0, v1, \ldots, vN\}$ are vertices representing transport nodes and $A = \{a0, a1, \ldots, aM\}$ are arcs representing TE links. Each arc has a *cost*, positive, zero, or negative, representing the relative preference of using the arc (and hence the associated TE link) with respect to the other arcs (TE links).

TE region — A set of one or more network layers that are associated with the same type of data plane technology. Regions are significant for the signaling sub-system of the control plane because LSPs are signaled substantially differently in different regions. Furthermore, TE advertisement and path computation could be performed differently in different regions. Also called an LSP region.

Termination capability — A property of a link interface that connects a particular data link to a transport node. This property characterizes the interface's ability to terminate connections within the network layer to which the data link belongs.

Traffic Engineering (TE) — A technology that is concerned with performance optimization of operational networks. In general, this is a set of applications, mechanisms, tools, and scientific principles that allows for measuring, modeling, characterization, and control of user data traffic in order to achieve specific performance objectives.

Traffic recovery — The final stage in fault management during which user traffic settles down on the alternative LSP.

Transaction Language 1 (TL1) — A standardized transaction-based ASCII scripting language popular in management systems.

Transport node — A logical network device that is capable of originating and/or terminating a data flow, and/or of switching the data flow on the route to its destination.

Transport service — A service that delivers user traffic with specified characteristics between two or more user sites interconnected via the Service Provider network with an agreed Quality of Service (QoS), blocking probability, and resilience against network failures.

Tunnel — See *(G)MPLS tunnel.*

Upstream Label Object — GMPLS RSVP-TE signaling object that is used to identify the label allocated by an LSR to be used by its immediate downstream neighbor. The object has the same format as the *Generalized Label Object*.

Vertical network integration — A set of collaborative mechanisms within a single node driving multiple (at least two) network layers, and the adaptation between those layers.

Virtual Link service model — A sub-class of the Signaling and Routing service model in the context of Layer One VPNs in which Customer network devices view the Provider network as a set of PE devices interconnected by TE links advertised by the PE devices into the Customer sites on a per-VPN basis.

Virtual network topology (VNT) — A set of hierarchical LSPs that are or could be created in a particular network layer to provide network flexibility in other higher layers.

Virtual Node service model — A sub-class of the Signaling and Routing service model in the context of Layer One VPNs in which Customer network devices view the entire Provider network as a single transport node that can be entered and exited by LSPs that use the CE-PE links associated with the particular VPN.

VPI/VCI — ATM cell identifiers.

Wait-to-Restore Time (WRT) — The period of time between the moment of receiving a fault restoration indication and the moment of initiating the reversion process.

Wavelength continuity — A constraint for path selection in an optical layer network that requires each link of the selected path to have at least one lambda channel of the same frequency available for reservation.

Index

H

I

J

K

L

M

N